COLLECTING
MICHAEL
JORDAN

THE ULTIMATE IDENTIFICATION & VALUE GUIDE

MEMORABILIA

Happy 15th TC ~
love you ~
Mom, Dad &
MJ — haha!

OSCAR GRACIA

Published by

 krause
publications

700 East State Street, Iola, WI 54990-0001

Please call or write for our free catalog. Our toll-free number to place an order or obtain a free catalog is 800-258-0929 or please use our regular business telephone 715-445-2214 for editorial comment and further information.

Library of Congress Catalog Number: 98-84442
ISBN: 0-87341-666-X
Printed in the United States of America

Neither Krause Publications nor the author are associated with Michael Jordan, NBA properties, or any other product mentioned in this book.

Table of Contents

Greetings

Greetings fellow Michael Jordan fans and collectors of Michael Jordan cards and memorabilia! I am anxious and excited to share with you all the experience and knowledge I have acquired in my numerous years of collecting. I hope you enjoy yourself as much as I do and that this book will help you experience the fun and satisfaction that comes with collecting. I know you will find this book helpful in identifying and pricing items that you have or hope to find.

I would like to be sure and mention that this collection strictly consists of Michael Jordan cards and memorabilia. I also feel it necessary to mention the state of sports card collecting today. In recent years, the market has been flooded with Michael Jordan cards. This has made it impossible for ordinary collectors to keep up with the production and sale of these cards. Since this entire book could be entirely consumed by card listings, we've narrowed our card section to a sampling of what's out there, and listed many of the most interesting and valuable cards. We do believe our collection is a good one and can serve as a perfect starting point.

I would like to dedicate this book to all the Michael Jordan collectors around the world: collectors of all ages—both men and women. Many people don't realize the amount of work involved in assembling a well-balanced and interesting collection. There are numerous obstacles to overcome—from a lack of time and money to a lack of space to house your collection. I urge you to continue collecting and I wish you continued success in your efforts.

How I Became a Die-Hard Collector

I was a closet collector for ten years. Only my friends and family knew I had such an extensive collection of Michael Jordan memorabilia. But, as is true of many collectors, I came to the point where I was interested in showing off my collection and sharing it with others.

I first became interested in the hobby after I began taking my two boys, Rich and Vinson, to collection shows on Sunday afternoons at various locations in the Chicago area. I would usually give them a few bucks to spend while I waited in the lobby outside the show watching a football game on TV. Eventually, I decided to go inside and see what all the fuss was about. I began by collecting baseball cards of some of

my childhood heroes from the Chicago Cubs. I bought a few cards and it didn't take long before I wanted to collect the whole 1969 Cubs team. Then, I continued by collecting cards from the three years prior to and the three years after the 1969 team.

When basketball season started I collected Michael Jordan cards. I have always taken special interest in Michael Jordan because of his unparalleled athletic skill. I couldn't get over how fast he was, how high he could jump and how hard he played. In my opinion there is no other player with that kind of all-around game. It didn't take long before I had all of his cards. Then I began collecting anything and everything with his name or likeness. I have collected everything—both items of little value and great value including Broader cards, which are generally inexpensive, but I find interesting. This includes background cards—other players' cards that show Michael Jordan only in the background of the picture. These cards are fun to find and inexpensive to collect. Once I discovered Michael Jordan, I stopped collecting everything else. Therefore, my collection is limited to Michael Jordan cards and memorabilia. From the beginning it has been an adventure for me and I continue to enjoy it to this very day.

Many different people have encouraged me to put

together this first-ever compilation of Jordan collectibles. From friends of mine in the hobby business who wanted a valuable pricing tool for their own use to general dealers and collectors who, wherever I went, asked me to price items for them. I also received many requests for particular items, which I did my best to include, and have helped Beckett Publications with their pricing guide for several years. My name has been mentioned in the *Beckett Basketball Card Price Guide* and Krause Publications' *Sports Collectors Digest*. But my main reason for putting this book together is because I enjoy the hobby so immensely.

Tips on Collecting

I would like to share with you a few tips I have learned in my years of collecting. I hope you find them helpful, too.

The most important advice I can give you has to do with attending shows and talking to dealers of cards and memorabilia. Plan to take your time. Spend two or three hours looking at various items and be sure to walk around the show at least two or three times. This may seem time-consuming and unnecessary, but it's possible you could miss something the first time around and making the trip a second time will give you another chance to see it. Also, while you are looking and perhaps buying, so are the dealers. They rotate the stock on their tables because they might purchase something that day that they want to sell, or their tables were full and after they sell some merchandise they have more room to put out new items.

The second tip has helped me control the expense of collecting. If you notice that a dealer has multiples of an item, you may want to consider purchasing all of them. For one, you will get each of them at a lesser cost. You can then resell the extra ones you don't want and make some of the money that you spent back. You may also be able to trade those items for others that you don't have.

Tip three has to do with selling items that you don't want. You can try doing so at a show but I've found the most success by placing an ad for an item or group of items in a collector's guide. You will be amazed at the volume of responses you receive. This will be helpful to you in more than one way. First, you will sell more than you ever imagined, and second, you will meet other collectors like yourself. Making connections will bring you into contact with all sorts of knowledgeable and helpful people who will lead you to items you want or those you didn't even know existed. These people will also be more willing to trade—another great way to keep cost to a minimum.

Finally, attend as many shows as you can. There are local and national shows where you can find anything if you look hard enough. The most difficult

part of collecting I have found is that it can drive your family crazy. When you are gone often, are broke most of the time, and your house is overflowing with your prized collection, it can be a source of contention. Get them involved and enjoy it as much as possible.

I urge you to become a well-rounded collector. Collect anything and everything.

Pricing

There are several methods I use to determine pricing. These methods involve both personal contact with dealers and collectors and research on current pricing available through catalogs. I acquire items in a variety of ways including trade as well as purchase. There are many additional costs related to collecting, such as phone calls, faxes, shipping, and the hours of time I spend at it, but my main goal is to build my collection virtually cost-free. This involves a lot of research and time, and to achieve this goal I have made several contacts who help me find what I need as I help them.

To begin, I base the prices in this book on what I paid for an item. Several factors influence what I might pay. Oftentimes I pay less for an item because I purchase them in quantity. Other times I receive an item free because I trade with other collectors. I have also consulted other dealers and collectors regarding prices they have paid for particular items.

Secondly, I go to shows to keep up on current prices. Because I only look at Michael Jordan items, it is not too difficult. I usually ask a dealer if they have anything with Michael Jordan and if not, I just move on. In that respect, I am able to save time. If a dealer does have Michael Jordan cards or memorabilia, that is the only merchandise I look at. Even if they appear to be a dealer in football or hockey cards, I still make it a point to ask if they have anything with Michael Jordan. It is rare, but occasionally they do have something on the side that is not on their table. I have made several unique purchases that way.

Lastly, my prices are partly determined by the current market price. One way I research these is by looking through sports collecting magazines and digests for advertisements to see the price of a particular item. These are the generally the "high" prices that I indicate in my book. The "low" price indicated in my book is usually determined by the price I would pay a close associate or friends in the hobby business. Because we're so involved in the hobby, we often give each other better deals than is ordinarily afforded the average collector and is probably the lowest price one could expect to pay for a similar item.

Also, please keep in mind that certain items, such as autographed items, are extremely hard to price given the volatility of the market. What I have provided are approximations based on my experience, but the actual value can fluctuate from day to day, based on numerous factors.

Thank You

I would like to give a big thank you to all the people who helped me put this book together. Some helped a lot, some a little, but all were important to me and instrumental in producing a successful reference. Because I did not have my own equipment, I relied on friends and colleagues to do scanning and photography for me. Others input data and gave me continual encouragement. In addition to doing a great job, they taught me a lot. Thanks for sticking with me through all the delays and problems. I would like to especially thank Bill Watts, Al Leyva, Vinson Gracia, William Stephens, and Roy Obregon.

One person who especially helped me learn the collecting trade is Sally Grace, a well-known dealer. She taught me a great deal about collecting by allowing me to hang out with her at shows. She is now a collector of Beanie Babies. Good luck, Sally, and thanks for the ride.

Some of the other dealers that I have worked with and would like to thank are Bob Lewis of Graf Baseball Cards, Brad Ross of Spanky's, Steve Taff of Steve Taff Enterprises, Jess Guffey of Ball Park Cards, Manny's of Legend Sports Cards, Bill of Past-Time Hobbies, Jimmy of Boston's All Sports, William Huffman of Player's Hand, Mike Mosier of Columbia City Collectibles, and Sally Grace of Sally's Cards.

Thank you to Krause Publications for encouraging this project and for being patient with me as I learned the process. I look forward to a Book Two and am already preparing for it. And to all those people who lent me equipment, I would just like to say that I have purchased all that I need to do future books on my own. Thanks for being there for this one.

The Next Edition

Most of the items in this book are items that I own, except for a few, and I have organized them in an easy-to-use alphabetical format. For items that are not my own, I have given the market price instead of the high/low prices I assigned the remainder of the items. These additions, I feel, are important to the book and to collectors. Obviously, with the vast variety and number of Michael Jordan collectibles out there, there was no way to fit them all into one volume. I do hope, though, that this book will heighten the already intense interest in Michael Jordan collectibles, and that in turn, will facilitate the need for additional books on the subject. I am constantly updating and adding to my own collection and hope to someday share more of it with you. In the mean time, I hope you enjoy this guide. I know I've had fun assembling it.

— Oscar Gracia

Michael Jordan is the single most recognizable athlete in the world today. His popularity stretches across oceans, nationalities and generations. He has appeared in movies, on cereal boxes and endorsed every product from sports drinks to sunglasses.

The following is a timeline of his life, starting out in New York, through his playing days with the Chicago Bulls. A tribute of sorts, to arguably the greatest basketball player of all time.

With his future hanging in the balance, what better time to take a look back at the life of Jordan and chronicle his playing days as it unfolded in front of the public.

Childhood

Michael Jeffrey Jordan was born to James and Deloris Jordan in Brooklyn, N.Y., on Feb. 17, 1963. At the age of 7, the family settled in Wilmington, N.C., where his legendary status is celebrated to this day. Interestingly enough, Jordan's first love was baseball, rather than the sport he was to become world famous for.

He attended Emsley A. Laney High School in Wilmington, N.C., where, ironically, he was cut from the high school varsity basketball team as a sophomore. He also played football in high school, but gave it up when he decided to concentrate on basketball. In 1980, Jordan signed a letter of intent to play at the University of North Carolina. Jordan wanted to attend Virginia and play with Ralph Sampson, but the school didn't offer him a scholarship.

During his senior year of high school, Jordan led the team to the Division II Championship, and his basketball legacy started to grow.

North Carolina

He enrolled the following year at North Carolina, which paid immediate dividends for coach Dean Smith.

During his freshman year, Jordan played an integral part in the 1982 NCAA Championships, helping North Carolina win the title with the game-winning shot — the first of many in his career.

His collegiate career took off from there, and he won the NCAA Player of the Year award his sophomore and junior years. Upon completion of his junior year, Jordan opted for the NBA, forgoing his final year of eligibility at North Carolina.

However, his collegiate playing days are still special to him, evidenced by the fact he still wears his North Carolina shorts under his Bulls uniform for good luck.

That summer, in 1984, he played for the gold medal-winning USA basketball team in the Olympics held in Los Angeles. Jordan was the co-captain of the team and led the squad in scoring with a 17.1 scoring average.

On June 19, Jordan was the third overall pick in the NBA Draft, selected by the Chicago Bulls. Drafted ahead of Jordan were Hakeem Olajuwon (Houston) and Sam Bowie (Portland).

NBA Journey Begins

Jordan excelled everywhere else, and the NBA was no different. He made an immediate impact, sending Chicago fans in a frenzy with his high-flyin' aerial act. He went on to win the Rookie of the Year award, scoring 28.2 points a game.

The nickname "Air" was born, and his play was taking the league by storm. In 1985, Jordan was temporarily grounded, however, when he suffered the only serious injury of his career on Oct. 6, 1985. Jordan missed 64 games with a broken foot, finishing the year with the lowest scoring average of his career at 22.7 points a game.

The injury gave the league a slight reprieve from his domination, but in the next seven years, Jordan would erase any doubt who was the best player in the NBA.

Scoring Titles Mount

In 1986, Jordan became the only player at the time besides Wilt Chamberlain to score more than 3,000 points (3,041) in a season. It was also the year he won his first scoring title.

During the playoffs, on April 20, Jordan poured in a playoff record 63 points in a 135-131 double overtime loss to the Boston Celtics.

Now emerging as a bona fide star, Jordan raised his game to another level in the 1987-88 season. He simply dominated. Jordan won the first of his five league MVP awards, adding a Defensive Player of the Year award along the way. Jordan also won his second consecutive scoring title.

During the season, on March 16, Jordan scored 23 consecutive points against the Atlanta Hawks, an NBA record. The following season, he won his third scoring title, as the Bulls crept closer to being a championship-caliber team.

Again Jordan made magic in the playoffs. On May 7, 1989, Jordan hit the game-winning jumper against Cleveland to win the series. The image of him leaping through the air and pumping his fist after the shot is still seen today.

In the 1989-90 season, Jordan wrote another chapter in his record book. Jordan scored a career-high 69 points in a 117-113 overtime victory over Cleveland. Jordan had many nights with high scoring outputs that season, and again led the league in scoring for the fourth consecutive year.

Championship Run Part 1

The 1990-91 season is one neither Jordan nor the Chicago Bulls will ever forget. It marked the first of six world championships the Bulls would win in the 1990s.

Jordan finally got his elusive title, and the image of him clutching the trophy and crying will not soon be forgotten.

It was another big year for Jordan individually as well. He won his fifth scoring title, his second league MVP award and his first NBA Finals MVP award.

The Bulls weren't done winning yet. The next year Chicago won their second straight NBA Championship, with Jordan again named the Finals MVP. Jordan also won his second consecutive league MVP award and his sixth scoring title during the regular season.

The summer of 1992, Jordan and the rest of the "Dream Team" dominated at the Olympics in Barcelona. Jordan joined Patrick Ewing and Chris Mullin as the only American basketball players to win two Olympic gold medals.

Even with a summer of basketball instead of rest,

Jordan continued his outstanding play throughout the 1992-93 season as the Bulls won their third straight NBA title.

Jordan was once again named the Finals MVP, and he led the league in scoring for the seventh time.

Tragedy and Retirement

On Aug. 13, 1993, Jordan suffered a deep personal loss. His father, James, was murdered along a roadside in North Carolina. On Oct. 6, Jordan announced his retirement from the game, shocking the NBA. However, the competitive juices were still flowing in Jordan, and in the spring of 1994 he tried his hand at baseball.

Play Ball

He played for the Chicago White Sox minor league affiliate, the Birmingham Barons, as an outfielder. Jordan's game was definitely basketball; he hit a meager .202 with three home runs in 127 games with the Barons.

On Nov. 11, 1994, Jordan's #23 jersey was retired at the United Center in Chicago.

Jordan then quit baseball in March of 1995, after playing for one season to go back to the game he loved.

The dust barely settled on his retired jersey when he came back to basketball late in the 1994-95 season

wearing jersey #45. His play was rusty in the 17 games he saw action in, and the Bulls failed to advance to the NBA Finals.

He's Back

Now that Jordan was back concentrating on hoops again, the Bulls returned with renewed strength for the 1995-96 season. The Bulls won their fourth title in the 1990s. In game five of the Finals, Jordan scored 38 points in a Bulls' win, despite suffering from dehydration and nausea.

During the regular season the Bulls won an NBA record 72 games, with what many argue was the best team ever.

The Pizza

The illness that struck Jordan during the '96 Finals was due to a now-famous pizza. Jordan described the incident in the December 1997 issue of *Fantasy Sports*.

"We were staying up in Park City, Utah, and we didn't have room service at our hotel," Jordan said. "So we ordered some pizzas, and I ordered a sausage with cheese. What came was a pepperoni with cheese.

"About 3:30 in the morning, I woke up, and my stomach was killing me. I couldn't go back to sleep. Around 9 o'clock, I called our trainer and asked him to help me out because I couldn't stand still, my stomach was hurting so bad. He gave me some sleeping pills so that I could sleep during the afternoon and get my energy back. But I couldn't sleep. Then, an hour before the game starts, I start getting sleepy. So then I started drinking coffee to try and get some energy to go out and play."

Jordan said he would never play again feeling that way, but no one will forget the courageous effort it took to do so.

More Awards

The season was capped off as Jordan won his eighth scoring title, his fourth MVP trophy and his fourth Finals MVP award. He was definitely back.

After the season, Jordan reflected on how his career had changed with age.

"I've learned how to apply my skills in different situations," Jordan said. "Earlier in my career, I was more athletic in certain ways. But now I think I show more savvy out there and utilize my energy to my benefit."

Justice

During the season, in March of 1996, Daniel Green was convicted of murdering James Jordan. Green received a life sentence in prison.

Championship Run Part 2

The next season was a repeat performance for Jordan and the Bulls. The team repeated as world champions, Jordan won his ninth scoring title, and was named the Finals MVP for the fifth time.

Then came the 1997-98 season, a season that many believe will be the last of the running of the Bulls with Jordan holding court.

Tim Iannone
Anthony Jinwright
Doug Johnson
Jody Jones
Linda Jones
Neil Jones
Mike Jordan

Sophomore class photo 1978-79

Baseball team photo 1980-81, Jordan second row, fifth from the left, listed as "Mike Jordan"

Sophomore, 1978-79

Sophomore , 1978-79

xi

The Last Run?

If the 1997-98 season was his last, there is no better way to end a remarkable career. He led the Bulls to their third straight NBA championship by hitting the game-winning shot in game six against the Jazz. After the game, Jordan spoke about the shot.

"When I saw a moment of opportunity to take advantage of the Jazz defense, I took advantage of that moment. And I never doubted myself," Jordan said.

He also once again led the league in scoring. Jordan earned his sixth NBA Finals MVP trophy and grabbed his fifth regular season MVP trophy as well.

His Legacy

He became only the third player in NBA history to record five or more MVP awards. Jordan was the oldest player ever, at 35, to win the regular season award. Bill Russell and Kareem Abdul-Jabbar are the other two players to win at least five MVP awards. Abdul-Jabbar won it six times, Russell five.

Former Bulls' coach Phil Jackson felt someday the MVP trophy's name will be changed due to Jordan's play.

"I think that's one of the reasons why the MVP trophy is, probably when he retires, going to be called the Michael Jordan Trophy."

Jordan, however, believes just like he won the MVP award five times, so too will someone else.

"I'm pretty sure when Bill and Kareem won, they were probably thinking there wouldn't be someone else to win it five times," Jordan said in a Chicago Sun Times article. "If that can happen somewhere down the road, I may come back to present it to that individual."

Jordan's play transcends to those not associated with the NBA as well. In the June '98 issue of *Hoops* magazine, Anita De Frantz, vice president of the International Olympic Committee, said Jordan is not like

Career Highlights

Michael Jordan's career reads like a wish list for any player's career in the NBA. Here's a look at many of his achievements.
- College Player of the Year- '83, '84
- Scoring champion- '87, '88, '89, '90, '91, '92, '93, '96, '97, '98
- League MVP- '88, '91, '92, '96, '98
- Finals MVP- '91, '92, '93, '96, '97, '98
- All-Star Game MVP- '88, '96, '98
- NBA leader in steals- '88, '90, '93
- Defensive Player of the Year- '88
- World Championships- '91, '92, '93, '96, '97, '98

any other human being.

"As I often say, Mr. Jordan is from another planet. He is not a mere mortal. He is so far removed from day-to-day life. Even the 'bad stuff' he does is so removed from the commonplace citizen it doesn't relate to me."

Jordan's life reads like a super-hero comic book – he can do no wrong.

Along with his regular season and post-season heroics, the Bulls have won six World Championships in eight years. Their run in the 1990s ranks as one of the best ever.

Jordan put the Bulls on his back for majority of his career, bringing a sellout crowd to every arena he played in. His status in the league is second-to-none, and when Jordan retires, the league will have a void that will be nearly impossible to fill.

Jordan's life is full of remarkable achievements, sprinkled with success at every level. That is the purpose of this book — to showcase his immense popularity and give the avid Jordan fan the ultimate guide to his or her collectibles.

JV football team photo 1978-79 year book, Jordan back row, eighth from left, listed as "Mike Jordan"

A

Year	Aklaim Electronic Computer Games Location		Low	High
96	Game, "Space Jam The Video Game," Play Station, Sega Saturn., DOS		15.00	25.00

Year	All-Star Game Items	Location	Low	High
2/6/88	Program, NBA All-Star Game, night screen, skyline (1.1)	inside	25.00	45.00
2/5/88	Guide, NBA All-Star Game Weekend in Chicago Stadium (1.2)	inside	20.00	35.00
2/6/88	Program, Chicago Theatre, Salute to the NBA All-Stars, MJ name inside (1.3)		15.00	25.00
97	Program, 2/7-8, Cleveland (1.4)		10.00	15.00
97	Newspaper, 2/7/97, "The Plain Dealer"	front	5.00	10.00
97	Poster, NBA Inside Stuff #3, 3/97, large size	front	15.00	20.00
97	Ad, Direct TV, League Pass (1.5)	front	1.00	2.00

Year	Atlanta Journal & Constitution	Location	Low	High
92	Ad Sheet, There's Something in the Air... Jordan The Slam & Dunk of It		15.00	20.00

Year	Atlantic Coast Conference	Amount	Low	High
3/82	Program, ACC Tournament, MJ's freshman year		100.00	120.00
83	Program, ACC Tournament, MJ's last year		65.00	90.00
92	ACC BB Tournament Champions Set	40 cards	15.00	25.00
	---'82 UNC Tar Heels Team Card/MJ	29	8.00	12.00
	---ACC Certificate of Authenticity, # of 10,000	5259		
92	ACC BB Tournament Champions Set, gold, one gold card inserted in each box	40 cards	125.00	175.00
	---'82 UNC Tar Heels Team Card/MJ	29	100.00	125.00

Year	Automotive Racing Cards	Card #	Low	High
94	Upper Deck, Championship Pit Crew, silver side stripe front and back (1.6)	133	5.00	8.00
94	Upper Deck, Championship Pit Crew-silver signature, silver side stripe front and back (1.7)	133	12.00	15.00
94	Upper Deck, Championship Pit Crew-gold signature, gold side stripe front and back, gold front logo (1.8)	133	68.00	90.00
95	SP, 1995 Comebacks, Irvin & MJ , die cut (1.9)	CB-1	75.00	100.00

Year	Avon	Card #		
96	Cards, UD Metal Collector, MJ close-up and jump shot on box, white 23 (1.10)	5 cards	20.00	25.00
	---close-up, red warm-up jacket, #23 bottom left front (1.11)		4.00	5.00
	---right hand layup, red 23, #23 bottom right front (1.12)		4.00	5.00
	---right hand dunk, white 23, #23 bottom left front (1.13)		4.00	5.00
	---right hand out front, white 23, #23 bottom right front (1.14)		4.00	5.00
	---right hand 4 fingers, white 23, #23 bottom right front (1.15)		4.00	5.00
96	Mug, UD Commemorative Tankard, white background, 5 MJ pictures, gold signature (1.16)	18 oz	20.00	30.00
96	Watch, Wilson, black band with 2-#23 on each side, MJ dribbling on face, numbers on bezel, silver bezel, white #23, Wilson & signature on red & black basketball case, Wilson on watch glass (1.16)	NNO	30.00	45.00
96	Product Book, MJ items inside (1.17)	cover	1.00	2.00
6/97	Ad Sheet, MJ Watch/holder (1.18)	883719	1.00	2.00

1.5

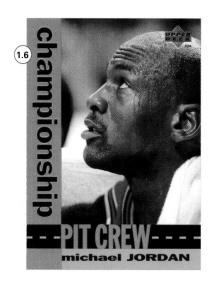

1.6

1.7

1.8

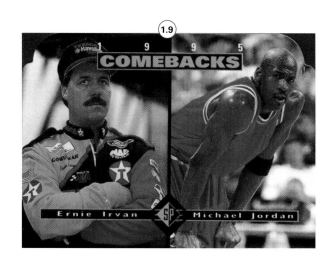

1.9

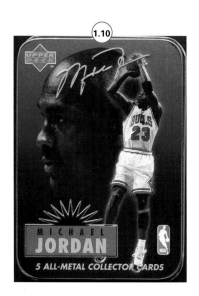

1.10

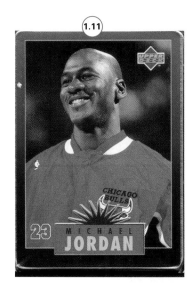

1.11

1.12

1.13

1.14

1.16

1.15

1.17

1.18

Year	BACKGROUND CARDS (MJ appears in background)	Card #	Low	High
	Background-NBA Cards			
86-87	Fleer			
	-Checklist	132 of 132	1.50	2.50
87-88	Fleer			
	-Checklist	132 of 132	1.00	2.00
88-89	Fleer			
	-Horace Grant/MJ front	16 of 132	2.00	3.00
	-Checklist	132of 132	.50	1.00
89-90	Fleer			
	-Checklist	168	.25	.75
90-91	Fleer			
	-Stacy King/MJ front	27	.75	1.00
	-Rony E. Seikaly/MJ front	102	.75	1.00
	-Checklist	197	.25	.50
90-91	Hoops			
	-Sam Vincent/MJ front	223	1.50	2.50
	-Bulls Team Checklist/MJ front	358	.75	1.00
	-Checklist	332	.25	.50
	-Checklist	439	.25	.50
90-91	Skybox			
	-Checklist	295	.25	.50
91-92	Fleer			
	-Joe Dumars/MJ front	59	.75	1.00
	-All-Star Game/MJ front	233	.75	1.00
	-All-Star Game/MJ front	236	.75	1.00
	-All-Star Game/MJ front	237	.75	1.00
	-All-Star Game/MJ front	238	.75	1.00
	-Checklist	239	.25	.50
	-Checklist	240	.25	.50
	-Checklist	400	.25	.50
91-92	Hoops			
	-Chris Ford/MJ back, Team Picture, 91 East Conference All-Star	260	.75	1.00
	-1991 NBA Champions Bulls/MJ front (1.18a)	277	.25	.50
	-Checklist #1	328	.25	.50
	-Checklist #2	330	.25	.50
	-Checklist #3	329	.25	.50
	-Checklist #5	590	.25	.50
91-92	Sky Box			
	-Darrel Walker card, MJ's top rebounding statistics on back	304	.25	.50
	-Vlade Divac/MJ front	335	.75	1.00
	-Bulls Starting Team/MJ front, Great Moments/NBA	337	.75	1.00
	-Checklist	345	.25	.50
	-Checklist	350	.25	.50
	-Chicago Bulls Game Frame/MJ front	408	.75	1.00
	-Team Barcelona '92/MJ on back	544	1.00	2.00
	-Team Barcelona '92/MJ front & back	545	2.00	4.00
	-Team Barcelona '92/MJ on back	546	1.00	2.00
	-Checklist	657	.25	.540
	-Checklist	658	.25	.50
91-92	Upper Deck			
	-Stay in School/MJ on back	22	.75	1.00
	-All-Star Checklist/MJ front, Charlotte 2/8-10/91	48	.75	1.00
	-David Robinson AS West/MJ front, Charlotte 2/8-10/91	58	.75	1.00
	-Charles Barkley AS East/MJ front, Charlotte 2/8-10/91	70	1.50	2.50
	-Bulls Checklist/MJ front	75	.75	1.00
	-Checklist	100	.25	.50

Year	BACKGROUND CARDS	Card #	Low	High
	-B.J. Armstrong/MJ back	184	1.00	2.00
	-Patrick Ewing/MJ on back	343	1.00	2.00
	-Charles Barkley/MJ front	345	.75	1.00
	-Kenny Walker/MJ on back	347	1.00	2.50
	-Checklist	500	.25	.50
92-93	Fleer			
	-Checklist	262	.25	.50
	-Checklist	264	.25	.50
	-Slam Dunk Checklist/MJ back, NBA Jam Session	NNO	1.0	2.00
92-93	Hoops			
	-Bull Team Card/MJ front	269	.75	1.00
	-USA BB Team, BB Tournament of the Americas, flag background/MJ front, white, team picture front and back	NNO	4.00	8.00
	-USA BB Team, BB Tournament of the Americas, flag background, David Robinson Autograph/MJ front, white, team picture front and back, factory send in card	#50 of 200	100.00	150.00
	-Tribune NBA Championship Series, Drexler/MJ front	TR-1	1.00	2.00
	-92 Summer Olympics Barcelona, Spain, Team Picture/MJ on back, shooting arrow, stadium view, black card	NNO	30.00	40.00
92-93	Skybox			
	--Checklist	99	.25	.50
	-East in Action Orlando AS/MJ back	312	1.00	1.50
	-'92 NBA Finals Blazers/MJ front & back	315	.75	1.00
	-'92 NBA Finals Bulls/MJ on back (1.18b)	318	1.00	2.50
	-Scottie Pippen/MJ on back	586	1.50	2.50
	-Chris Mullins/MJ on back	USA-2	1.00	2.00
	-Larry Bird/MJ on back	USA-6	2.00	3.00
	-Charles Barkley/MJ on back	USA-7	1.00	2.00
	-Christian Laettner/MJ on back	USA-9	1.00	2.50
	-David Robinson/MJ on back	USA-10	1.00	2.00
	-Magic Johnson/MJ on back (1.18c)	USA-12	1.00	2.00
	-USA Basketball Team Card/MJ front, blue, MJ front & back	NNO	30.00	40.00
	-Barcelona '92 Team Card/MJ front, white, double-sided	NNO	30.00	40.00
	---Certificate of Authenticity			
92-93	Stadium Club			
	-Ledell Eackles/MJ front	37	.25	.50
	-L Eackles Members Only/MJ front, Members Only Logo	37	.50	1.00
	-Stacy King/MJ front	86	1.00	2.00
	-Stacy King Members Only/MJ front, Members Only Logo	86	2.00	3.00
	-Greg Grant/MJ front	225	.75	1.00
	-Greg Grant Members Only/MJ front, Members Only Logo	225	2.00	3.00
	-Joe Dumars/MJ front	386	.75	1.00
	-Joe Dumars Members Only/MJ, Members Only Logo	386	2.00	3.00
	-Checklist 201-300	399	.50	1.00
	-Checklist 201-300, Members Only Logo	399	1.00	2.00
92-93	Topps			
	-Bill Cartwright/MJ front	165	.75	1.00
	-Bill Cartwright gold/MJ front	165	1.00	1.50
(93)	-Bill Cartwright Card/MJ front, from Rust-Oleum Sheet Card	CB-2	2.00	3.00
	-Brian Shaw Card/MJ front	185	.75	1.00
	-Brian Shaw Card gold/MJ front	185	1.00	1.50
	-Checklist	197	.25	.50
	-Checklist	198	.25	.50
	-Checklist, Series #2	395	.25	.50
92-93	Ultra			
	-Grant Long/MJ front	100	1.00	2.00
	-Checklist	199	.25	.50
	-Harold Miner/MJ front (1.18d)	293	.75	1.00
92-93	Upper Deck			
	-NBA All-Star Collector Set, Utah, 2/19-21/93	40 cards		
	---NBA All-Star, Malone/MJ front	16	2.00	4.00
	-NBA All-Star Collector Set, gold, Utah, 2/19-21/93	40 cards		

Year	BACKGROUND CARDS	Card #	Low	High
	---NBA All-Star-K. Malone/MJ front	16	4.00	8.00
	-Tony Campbell/MJ front	182	.75	1.00
	-Brian Shaw/MJ front	189	.75	1.00
	-Bill Laimbeer/MJ front	223	.75	1.00
	-Joe Dumars/MJ front	268	.75	1.00
	-Danny Manning/MJ front	271	.75	1.00
	-Randy Breuer/MJ front	276	1.50	2.50
	-Larry Nance/MJ front	281	.75	1.00
	-John Starks/MJ	282	.75	1.00
	-Stacy King/MJ back	285	1.00	2.00
	-Checklist 1-90/MJ front & back	90	1.00	2.00
	-Checklist 91-200/MJ front & back	200	1.00	2.00
	-Checklist 201-310/MJ front & back	310	1.00	2.00
	-Checklist 311-420/MJ front & back	419	1.00	2.00
	-Checklist 421-510/MJ front & back	420	1.00	2.00
	-Shaquille O'Neal AS/MJ front, Utah, 2/19-21/93	424	.75	1.00
	-Patrick Ewing AS/MJ back,	429	1.00	2.00
	-Clyde Drexler/MJ front	438	.75	1.00
	-Dan Majerle/MJ front (1.18e)	442	.75	1.00
	-T. Day, NBA Top Prospects/MJ front	470	1.00	2.00
	-Larry Nance 15,000/MJ front	PC-18	1.00	2.00
	-Checklist Team MVP/MJ front	TM-1	15.00	20.00
	-Patrick Ewing Team MVP/MJ	TM-19	1.00	2.00
93-94	Fleer			
	-Bill Cartwright/MJ front	26	.75	1.00
	-Nick Anderson/MJ front	147	.75	1.00
93-94	Hoops			
	-Horace Grant/MJ front	27	.75	1.00
	-Horace Grant gold/MJ front	27	1.00	1.50
	-LaBradford Smith/MJ front	228	.75	1.00
	-LaBradford Smith gold/MJ front	228	1.00	1.50
	-Clyde Drexler/MJ front	270	.75	1.00
	-Clyde Drexler gold/MJ front	270	1.00	1.50
	-East NBA All-Star Team/MJ front	281	.75	1.00
	-East NBA All-Star Team gold/MJ front	281	1.00	1.50
	-Tribute Suns Win 3-OT/MJ front	294	.75	1.00
	-Tribute Suns Win 3-OT/MJ front, gold	294	1.00	1.50
	-Checklist, Series #2	490	.50	1.00
93-94	Sky Box			
	-Kevin Johnson NBA on NBC/MJ front	20	.75	1.25
	-Shaq Talk Set	10 cards		
	---Scoring/MJ back	6	3.00	5.00
	---Legends/MJ back (1.18f)	10	3.00	5.00
93-94	Stadium Club			
	-J. Paxson/MJ front	92	.75	1.00
	-J. Paxson, 1st Day Issue/MJ front, 1st Day Issue Logo	92	2.00	4.00
	-J. Paxson, Members Only/MJ front, Members Only Logo	92	2.00	4.00
	-J. Starks/MJ front	116	.75	1.00
	-J. Starks, 1st Day Issue/MJ front, 1st Day Issue Logo	116	2.00	4.00
	-J. Starks, Members Only/MJ front, Members Only Logo	116	2.00	4.00
	-J. Starks, Division Winners/MJ front	116	2.00	4.00
	-G. Wilkins/MJ front	145	.75	1.00
	-G. Wilkins, 1st Day Issue/MJ front, 1st Day Issue Logo	145	2.00	4.00
	-G. Wilkins, Members Only/MJ front, Members Only Logo	145	2.00	4.00
	-P. Ewing/MJ front	200	.75	1.00
	-P. Ewing, 1st Day Issue/MJ front, 1st Day Issue Logo	200	2.00	4.00
	-P. Ewing, Members Only/MJ front, Members Only Logo	200	2.00	4.00
	-P. Ewing, Division Winners/MJ front	200	2.00	4.00
	-D. Majerle Frequent Flyers/MJ front	353	.75	1.00
	-D. Majerle Frequent Flyers, 1st Day Issue/MJ, front, 1st Day Issue Logo (1.18g)	353	2.00	4.00
	-Dan Majerle Frequent Flyers, Members Only/MJ, front, Members Only Logo	353	2.00	4.00
	-Dan Majerle Frequent Flyers, Upgrades/MJ front, front, Members Only Logo	353	2.00	4.00

Year	BACKGROUND CARDS	Card #	Low	High
	-1994 NBA Western Finals Set	360cards		
	---John Paxson/MJ front, NBA Finals Logo	92	2.00	4.00
	---John Starks/MJ front, NBA Finals Logo	116	2.00	4.00
	---Gerald Wilkins/MJ front, NBA Finals Logo	145	2.00	4.00
	---Patrick Ewing/MJ front	200	3.00	6.00
	---D. Majerle Frequent Flyer/MJ front	353	2.00	4.00
	---Master Photo Eastern Conference Set, sealed,			
	New York Knicks, 5x7	10 cards		
	---P. Ewing/MJ front, 5x7	4 of 10	6.00	12.00
	---J. Starks/MJ front, 5x7	10 of 10	6.00	12.00
	---Chicago Bulls Super Team Card, orange back with NBA			
	Super Team Card Rules	4 of 27	1.00	2.00
	---Chicago Bulls Super Team Card, Members Only, back Bulls Logo			
	on 92/93 Win Loss Record-57/25, purple back (1.18h)	4 of 27	2.00	4.00
93-94	Topps			
	-Charles Oakley Card/MJ front	25	.75	1.00
	-Charles Oakley, gold/MJ front	25	1.00	2.00
	-Checklist	395	.50	1.00
	-Checklist	396	.50	1.00
93-94	Ultra			
	-T. Gugliotta, All Rookie Team/MJfront (1.18i)	2 of 5	1.00	2.00
	-Larry Nance/MJ front	39	.75	1.00
	-John Starks/MJ front	132	.75	1.00
	-Checklist	199	.25	.50
	-Checklist	200	.25	.50
93-94	Upper Deck			
	-Bill Cartwright Card/MJ back	155	1.50	2.50
	-93 NBA Playoffs Highlights: First Round: Bulls 3, Hawks 0/MJ			
	front & on back	180	.75	1.00
	-93 NBA Playoffs Highlights: East Semifinals: Bulls 4, Cavaliers			
	0/MJ front & back	187	.75	1.00
	-93 NBA Finals Highlights Game 1: Bulls Feisty.../MJ front & back	198	1.00	2.00
	-93 NBA Finals Highlights Game 6: Bulls Join NBA's Elite.../MJ front	203	1.00	2.00
	-93 NBA Finals Highlights: Bulls Stampede to Third NBA.../MJ front	208	.75	1.00
	-93/94 Bulls Schedule/MJ front	213	.75	1.00
	-Hit the Books, M. Williams/MJ front, Stay in School	481	1.00	2.00
	-Patrick Ewing, 2nd Team/MJ front, All NBA	AN-8	.75	1.00
	-All NBA Teams Checklist/MJ front	AN-15	2.00	3.00
	-Behind the Glass Set	15 cards		
	---K. Willis/MJ front	G-9	2.00	3.00
	-C.Barkley Team MVP/MJ front	TM-21	.75	1.00
	-Pro View Checklist 1-55/MJ front, MJ waist up view	109	2.00	4.00
	-Pro View Checklist 56-110/MJ front, MJ waist down view	110	2.00	4.00
	-Holojam Checklist	NNO	2.00	3.00
	-MJ Flight Team Regular Set	20 cards	60.00	90.00
	---S. Augmon/MJ back	FT-1	3.00	4.50
	---C. Barkley/MJ back	FT-2	3.00	4.50
	---D. Benoit/MJ back	FT-3	3.00	4.50
	---D. Brown/MJ back	FT-4	3.00	4.50
	---C. Ceballos/MJ back	FT-5	3.00	4.50
	---D. Coleman/MJ back	FT-6	3.00	4.50
	---C. Drexler/MJ back	FT-7	3.00	4.50
	---S. Elliott/MJ back	FT-8	3.00	4.50
	---L. P. Ellis/MJ back	FT-9	3.00	4.50
	---K. Gill/MJ back	FT-10	3.00	4.50
	---L. Johnson/MJ back	FT-11	3.00	4.50
	---S. Kemp/MJ back	FT-12	3.00	4.50
	---K. Malone/MJ back	FT-13	3.00	4.50
	---H. Miner/MJ back	FT-14	3.00	4.50
	---A. Mourning/MJ back (1.18j)	FT-15	3.00	4.50
	---S. O'Neal/MJ back	FT-16	3.00	4.50
	---S. Pippen/MJ back	FT-17	3.00	4.50
	---C. Weatherspoon/MJ back	FT-18	3.00	4.50
	---S. Webb/MJ back	FT-19	3.00	4.50
	---D. Wilkins/MJ back	FT-20	3.00	4.50

Year	BACKGROUND CARDS	Card #	Low	High
94-95	Collectors Choice			
	-Will Purdue/MJ front	149	.75	1.00
	-Will Purdue silver/MJ front	149	1.00	2.00
	-Will Purdue gold/MJ front	149	2.00	4.00
	-Checklist, Tim Hardaway, MJ's name on back	207	.25	.50
	-Checklist, BJ Armstrong, MJ's name on back	210	.25	.50
	-MJ, Checklist	420	1.00	2.00
	-MJ, Checklist, silver signature	420	2.00	4.00
	-MJ, Checklist, gold signature	420	20.00	30.00
94-95	Skybox			
	-Dell Curry/MJ	12	.75	1.00
94-95	Upper Deck			
	-USA Basketball Set, The Jordan Report	90 cards		
	---Derrick Coleman/MJ back	5	.50	1.00
	---Joe Dumars/MJ back	11	.50	1.00
	---Tim Hardaway/MJ back	17	.50	1.00
	---Larry Johnson/MJ back	23	.50	1.00
	---Shawn Kemp/MJ back	29	.50	1.00
	---Dan Majerle/MJ back	35	.50	1.00
	---Reggie Miller/MJ back	41	.50	1.00
	---Alonzo Mourning/MJ back	47	.50	1.00
	---Shaquille O'Neal ROY/MJ front	50	.50	1.00
	---Shaquille O'Neal/MJ back	53	.50	1.00
	---Mark Price/MJ back	59	.50	1.00
	---Steve Smith/MJ back	65	.50	1.00
	---Isiah Thomas/MJ back	71	.50	1.00
	---Dominique Wilkins/MJ back	77	.50	1.00
	-USA Basketball Gold Metal Set, The Jordan Report	90 cards		
	---Derrick Coleman/MJ back	5	1.00	2.00
	---Joe Dumars/MJ back	11	1.00	2.00
	---Tim Hardaway/MJ back	17	1.00	2.00
	---Larry Johnson/MJ back	23	1.00	2.00
	---Shawn Kemp/MJ back	29	1.00	2.00
	---Dan Majerle/MJ back	35	1.00	2.00
	---Reggie Miller/MJ back	41	1.00	2.00
	---Alonzo Mourning/MJ back	47	1.00	2.00
	---Shaquille O'Neal ROY/MJ front	50	1.00	2.00
	---Shaquille O'Neal/MJ back	53	1.00	2.00
	---Mark Price/MJ back	59	1.00	2.00
	---Steve Smith/MJ back	65	1.00	2.00
	---Isiah Thomas/MJ back	71	1.00	2.00
	---Dominique Wilkins/MJ back	77	1.00	2.00
95-96	Collector's Choice			
	-Fun Club G. Hill/MJ front (1.18k)	173	.75	1.00
	-Fun Club Players Club G. Hill/MJ	173	10.00	15.00
	-Fun Club Players Club G. Hill/MJ, Platinum	173	15.00	25.00
	-Checklist	210	.25	50.00
	-Checklist Players Club	210	2.00	4.00
	-Checklist Players Club Platinum	210	6.00	12.00
	-Playoff Time Bulls & Hornets/MJ/Wingate front	353	.75	1.00
	-Playoff Time Bulls & Hornets Players Club/MJ/ Wingate front	353	10.00	15.00
	-Playoff Time Bulls & Hornets Players Club Platinum/MJ/Wingate front	353	15.00	25.00
	-Checklist	410	25.00	.50
	-Checklist Players Club	410	2.00	4.00
	-Checklist Players Club Platinum	410	6.00	12.00
	-Crash the Game Debut Trade Set, Upper Deck Redemption	30 cards		
	---Magic Johnson/MJ front	T-1	2.00	4.00
	-Crash the Game Players Club Debut, UD Redemption-Trade Set	30 cards		
	---Magic Johnson/MJ front	T-1	4.00	8.00
	-Crash the Game Platinum Players, UD Redemption-Club Debut Set	30 cards		
	---Magic Johnson/MJ front	T-1	8.00	15.00
95-96	Flair			
	-George Zidak Card/MJ back	228	2.00	4.00

260 1991 EASTERN CONFERENCE ALL-STARS

Front Row (l-r): Dominique Wilkins, Brad Daugherty, Robert Parish, Head Coach Chris Ford, Kevin McHale, Patrick Ewing, Charles Barkley. Back Row (l-r): Trainer Terry Kofler, Assistant Coach Jon Jennings, Michael Jordan, Joe Dumars, Hersey Hawkins, Alvin Robertson, Bernard King, Ricky Pierce, Assistant Coach Don Casey.

Copr. ©1991 NBA Properties, Inc. The Official NBA Basketball Card

1.18a

318

CHICAGO BULLS

NBA CHAMPIONS

The third team in a row to win back-to-back NBA titles. Chicago has established itself as one of the best NBA teams of all time. After losing just 15 games in the regular season and posting a re... (67-15) 10 games better than any... else, the Bulls answered every Pla... challenge en route to title No. 2.

Copr. © 1992 NBA Properties, Inc.
© 1992 SKYBOX INTERNATIONAL

1.18b

USA12

GOLD MEDAL CEREMONY

For the members of the greatest men's basketball team of all time, it was a dream realized to stand before the world and accept the Olympic gold medal for the USA. The team averaged 117.3 points per game and scored at least 100 points in every Olympic basketball game, both Olympic Games records. When it was over, the sport's best players had provided a basketball benchmark, defining by their performance a new level of excellence for future generations of basketball players to strive for.

SkyBox Copr. © 1992 NBA Properties, Inc.
© 1992 SKYBOX INTERNATIONAL 36 USC 380 USA BASKETBALL

1.18c

'92-93 FLEER **ULTRA** ROOKIE

HAROLD MINER

1.18d

1.18e

LEGENDS

"When I retire, I hope to be mentioned with the greats
Russell, Chamberlain, Kareem, Dr. J, Bird, Magic, Robinson, a...
Jordan. Each of these guys left a mark on the NBA that fore...
changed the way people played basketball. These legends have insp...
me to excite fans and win championships for many years to come."
—Shaquille O'Neal

SkyBox © 1994 SkyBox International. Copr. © 1994 NBA Properties, Inc.
Printed in U.S.A.

1.18f

TOPPS STADIUM CLUB

Frequent FLYERS UPGRADE

1.18g

TOPPS STADIUM CLUB

1.18h

'93-94 FLEER **ULTRA**

NBA ALL-ROOKIE TEAM

TOM GUGLIOTTA

1.18i

FT15

MICHAEL JORDAN'S FLIGHT TEAM

This guy doesn't have too far to go to the basket with his height and his long arms, but he skies when he has to. His jumping ability is more evident on defense, when he's matched against Patrick, Hakeem, David and the others. 'Zo not only goes strong to the hoop, but he defends the basket with authority.
—Michael Jordan

ALONZO MOURNING

CHARLOTTE HORNETS

1.18j

COLLECTOR'S CHOICE

PISTONS

Grant Hill

FUN

UPPER DECK

pistons

1.18k

9

Year	BACKGROUND CARDS	Card #	Low	High
95-96	Fleer -Stackhouse Scrapbook/MJ front	S-7	4.00	6.00
95-96	Hoops -Charles Oakley/MJ front	110	.75	1.00
95-96	SP -Magic Johnson/MJ front	66	1.00	2.00
95-96	SP Championship -Hakeem Olajuwon Card/MJ front	41	1.00	2.00
95-96	Stadium Club -Karl Malone Card/MJ front	76	1.00	2.00
	-Karl Malone Card/MJ front, upgrade	76	2.00	4.00
	-Members Only "Break the Rules Set," Topps NBA at 50, Topps Stars Set, Members Only Club, # of 750 produced	225 cards		
	---Karl Malone Card/MJ front, Topps Stars Logo	41	4.00	8.00
95-96	Upper Deck -Bill Cartwright Card/MJ	SE-11	.75	1.00
	-Bill Cartwright Card/MJ, gold	SE-11	4.00	8.00
	-Dennis Scot/MJ front	SE-62	.75	1.00
	-Dennis Scot/MJ front, gold	SE-62	4.00	8.00
	-Special Edition Rodman/MJ front	SE-102	.75	1.00
	-Special Edition Rodman/MJ front, gold	SE-102	6.00	10.00
	Background-NBA UD Foreign Issue Cards			
91-92	Upper Deck Italian -Orlando AS Weekend, Team Picture, checklist	1	2.00	4.00
	-Charles Barkley East AS/MJ	6	.50	1.00
91-92	Upper Deck Spanish -Orlando AS Weekend, Team Picture, checklist	1	2.00	4.00
	-Charles Barkley East AS/MJ	6	.50	1.00
92-93	Upper Deck French -Shaqulle O'Neal Utah AS/MJ	4	1.00	2.00
	-Patrick Ewing Utah AS/MJ	9	1.00	2.00
	-Clyde Drexler Utah AS/MJ	18	1.00	2.00
	-Dan Majerle Utah AS/MJ	22	1.00	2.00
	-Stacy King/MJ	119	1.00	2.00
	-Larry Nance/MJ	127	1.00	2.00
	-Joe Dumars/MJ	148	1.00	2.00
	-Bill Laimbeer/MJ	150	1.00	2.00
	-Danny Manning/MJ	182	1.00	2.00
	-Brian Shaw/MJ	202	1.00	2.00
	-Todd Day/MJ	204	1.00	2.00
	-John Starks/MJ	218	1.00	2.00
	-Checklist	254	4.00	8.00
	-Checklist	255	4.00	8.00
92-93	Upper Deck Italian -Shaqulle O'Neal Utah AS/MJ	4	1.00	2.00
	-Patrick Ewing Utah AS/MJ	9	1.00	2.00
	-Clyde Drexler Utah AS/MJ	18	1.00	2.00
	-Dan Majerle Utah AS/MJ	22	1.00	2.00
	-Stacy King/MJ	119	1.00	2.00
	-Larry Nance/MJ	127	1.00	2.00
	-Joe Dumars/MJ	148	1.00	2.00
	-Bill Laimbeer/MJ	150	1.00	2.00
	-Danny Manning/MJ	182	1.00	2.00
	-Brian Shaw/MJ	202	1.00	2.00
	-Todd Day/MJ	204	1.00	2.00
	-John Starks/MJ	218	1.00	2.00
	-Checklist	254	4.00	8.00
	-Checklist	255	4.00	8.00

Year	BACKGROUND CARDS	Card #	Low	High
92-93	Upper Deck Spanish			
	-Shaquille O'Neal/MJ-Utah AS	4	1.00	2.00
	-Patrick Ewing/MJ-Utah AS	9	1.00	2.00
	-Clyde Drexler/MJ-Utah AS	18	1.00	2.00
	-Dan Majerle/MJ-Utah AS	22	1.00	2.00
	-Stacy King/MJ	119	1.00	2.00
	-Larry Nance/MJ	127	1.00	2.00
	-Joe Dumars/MJ	148	1.00	2.00
	-Bill Laimbeer/MJ	150	1.00	2.00
	-Danny Manning/MJ	182	1.00	2.00
	-Brian Shaw/MJ	202	1.00	2.00
	-Todd Day/MJ	204	1.00	2.00
	-John Starks/MJ	218	1.00	2.00
	-Checklist	254	3.00	6.00
	-Checklist	255	3.00	6.00
93-94	Upper Deck-French			
	-Bill Cartwright/MJ	135	1.00	2.00
93-94	Upper Deck-German			
	-Bill Cartwright/MJ	135	1.00	2.00
93-94	Upper Deck Italian			
	-Bill Cartwright/MJ	135	1.00	2.00
93-94	Upper Deck Spanish			
	-Bill Cartwright/MJ	135	1.00	2.00
94-95	UD Collectors Choice-French			
	-Will Purdue/MJ	149	1.00	2.00
	-Heroes, Checklist	219	8.00	15.00
	-Checklist	420	3.00	5.00
94-95	UD Collectors Choice-German			
	-Will Purdue/MJ	149	1.00	2.00
	-Heroes, Checklist	219	8.00	15.00
	-Checklist	420	3.00	5.00
94-95	UD Collectors Choice-Italian			
	-Will Purdue/MJ	149	1.00	2.00
	-Heroes, Checklist	219	4.00	8.00
	-Checklist	420	1.00	2.00
94-95	UD Collectors Choice-Japanese			
	-Will Purdue/MJ	149	1.00	2.00
	-Heroes, Checklist	219	10.00	15.00
	-Checklist	420	6.00	10.00
94-95	UD Collectors Choice-Spanish			
	-Will Purdue/MJ	149	1.00	2.00
	-Heroes, Checklist	219	4.00	8.00
	-Checklist	201	1.00	2.00
95-96	UD Collector's Choice-England			
	-Grant Hill Fun Club/MJ	173	1.00	2.00
	-MJ Checklist	210	4.00	8.00
95-96	Collector's Choice Stickers-England			
	-Will Purdue/MJ front	125	1.00	2.00
95-96	UD Collectors Choice-French			
	-Playoff Time, Eastern Conference/MJ/Wingate, Bulls vs. Hornets	143	1.00	2.00
	-Grant Hill Fun Club/MJ	173	1.00	2.00
	-MJ Checklist Card	210	4.00	8.00
	-Checklist, Series II	200	4.00	8.00
95-96	UD Collectors Choice-German			
	-Playoff Time, Eastern Conference/MJ/Wingate, Bulls vs. Hornets	143	1.00	2.00
	-Grant Hill Fun Club/MJ	173	1.00	2.00
	-MJ Checklist Card	210	4.00	8.00
	-Checklist, Series II	200	4.00	8.00

Year	BACKGROUND CARDS	Card #	Low	High
95-96	UD Collectors Choice-Italian			
	-Playoff Time, Eastern Conference/MJ/Wingate, Bulls vs. Hornets	143	1.00	2.00
	-Grant Hill Fun Club/MJ	173	1.00	2.00
	-MJ Checklist Card	210	4.00	8.00
	-Checklist, Series II	200	4.00	8.00
95-96	UD Collectors Choice-Japanese			
	-Playoff Time, Eastern Conference/MJ/Wingate, Bulls vs. Hornets	353	1.00	2.00
	-Grant Hill Fun Club/MJ	173	1.00	2.00
	-MJ Checklist Card	210	5.00	10.00
95-96	UD Collectors Choice-Portuguese			
	-Checklist	200	5.00	10.00
95-96	UD Collectors Choice-Spanish			
	-Playoff Time, Eastern Conference/MJ/Wingate, Bulls vs Hornets	143	1.00	2.00
	-Grant Hill Fun Club/MJ	173	1.00	2.00
	-MJ Checklist Card	210	4.00	8.00
	-Checklist, Series II	200	4.00	8.00
Year	**Background-Star Company Cards**			
85	Crunch 'n Munch AS Checklist, MJ listed on back		5.00	10.00
85	Gatorade Slam Dunk Checklist, MJ listed on back		5.00	10.00
85	Lite Beer All-Stars Checklist, MJ listed on back		5.00	10.00
85	Slam Dunk Supers Set	10 cds		
	---Team Card/MJ front, 5x7		35.00	45.00
90	Isiah Thomas/MJ front	12 of 14	2.00	3.00
Year	**Ball Corporation**			
96	Can, Soda, MJ & SP in black 23/33, sealed white can (1.19)		25.00	40.00

Year	Ball Park Franks	item # # of items	Low	High
2/93	Ad Sheet, "Ball Park Franks. The Hot dogs Hot Dogs Love." Actmedia Inc., MJ + package (1.20)	8339	12.00	15.00
93	Ad Sheet, Fun Franks, "Honey, I Shrunk the Ball Park.", voided $.35 coupon on sheet (1.21)	30692	3.00	5.00
93	Ad Sheet, Lunch Bag & Clik Cooler, with "Official Order Form"	8.5 x 11	3.00	5.00
93	Bag/Cooler, MJ black Lunch Bag and yellow hard plastic Clik! Cooler, bag with MJ picture, cooler with autograph, mail in offer (1.22)		75.00	100.00
93	Order Card, Lunch Bag/Clik Cooler	3 x 5	6.00	10.00
95	Cards, UD Set, red, white & blue borders, flag like background, MJ name on bottom front	5 cds	35.00	50.00

Year	Ball Park Franks	item #	# of items	Low	High
	---dribbling, white & blue uniform (1.23)	BP-1		7.00	10.00
	---jumpshot, black & red uniform (1.24)	BP-2		7.00	10.00
	---jumping, white & red uniform (1.25)	BP-3		7.00	10.00
	---dribbling, red & white uniform (1.26)	BP-4		7.00	10.00
	---defending, black & red uniform (1.27)	BP-5		7.00	10.00
95	Cards, UD Gold Set, sealed set, 5 cards in one bag (1.28)	5 cds		60.00	
	---	BP-1			
	---	BP-2			
	---	BP-3			
	---	BP-4			
	---	BP-5			

Year	Ball Park Franks	item #	# of items	Low	High
95	Coupon, $.40 Off Fat Free Classic Franks, "The Perfect Marriage of Taste & Greatness." MJ & Juanita, Look for Juanita Jordan's Healthy Recipes & Coupons (1.29)	603268		2.00	5.00
95	Coupon, $.40 Off Fat Free Classic Franks, "The Taste of Greatness," Introducing BP Fat Free Classics (1.30)	602930		2.00	5.00
95	Coupon, $.40 Off Fat Free Classic Franks, "Only BP Can Make Fat Free Taste This Good, Great BP Taste, None of the Fat, white signature (1.31)	602518		2.00	5.00
96	Coupons-2, $.40 Off Any Fat Free Product, $.50 Off Any 2 BP Products, "Michael's Family Values Enjoy BP Franks, Fat Free Classics, and Kid size Fun Franks..." (1.32)	604100 604043		2.00	5.00
96	Coupon, $.50 Off Any 2 Packages of Fat Free or Lite Franks (or any BP Product), "Jordan's Trademark Move Off the Court," white signature (1.33)	610164		2.00	5.00
96	Coupon, $.25 Off Any BP Product, Jordan's Trademark Move Off the Court., "Here's the best part: it's a move anyone can do. BP Franks..." (1.34)	610214		2.00	5.00

Year	Ball Park Franks	item #	# of items	Low	High
96	Coupon, $.50 Off Any 2 Ball Park Fat Free Products, Coupon for Go For The Gold! card set, BP Franks & Michael's Trading Cards Both Worth Shooting For! (1.35)	610586		2.00	5.00
96	Coupons-2, $.50 Off Any 2 BP Fat Fee Product, $.50 Off Any 2 BP Product, different pages, "How Michael Looks Cool All Summer," Micro Magic coupons above (1.36)	610867			
		610875		2.00	5.00
96	Coupons-2, $.50 Off Any 2 BP Fat Fee Product, $.50 Off Any 2 BP Product, different pages, "How Michael Looks Cool All Summer," Nabisco Granola Bars coupons above (1.37)	610867			
		610875		2.00	5.00
96	Cards, UD Set, each card sealed, yellow & red borders		5 cds	20.00	35.00
	---dunk shot, black red & white uniform (1.38)		1 of 5	4.00	7.00
	---jump shot, black & red uniform (1.39)		2 of 5	4.00	7.00
	---close-up side, red & white uniform (1.40)		3 of 5	4.00	7.00
	---close-up front, red & white uniform (1.41)		4 of 5	4.00	7.00
	---dribbling, red & white uniform (1.42)		5 of 5	4.00	7.00

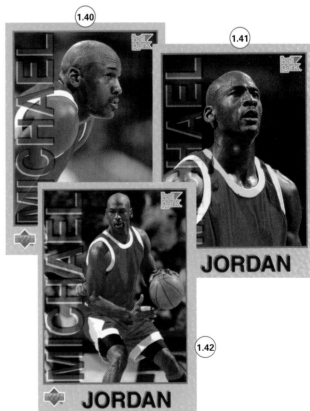

Year	Ball Park Franks	item #	# of items	Low	High
96	Cards, UD Card Set, sealed set, gold border on front (1.43)	5 cds		15.00	20.00
	---dunk shot, black red & white uniform	1 of 5		3.00	4.00
	---jump shot, black & red uniform	2 of 5		3.00	4.00
	---close-up side, red & white uniform	3 of 5		3.00	4.00
	---close-up front, red & white uniform	4 of 5		3.00	4.00
	---dribbling, red & white uniform	5 of 5		3.00	4.00
8/96	Boxes, Fun Franks, Michael's Magic Mania, 6 Microwaveable Fun Franks, 12 different magic tricks on box bottoms (1.44)	12 oz / 340 g			
	---Magically Make a Playing Card, Rise Out of a Cup! (1.45)	Trick1		3.00	6.00
	---Make a Penny Mysteriously, Disappear From a Cup! (1.46)	Trick2		3.00	6.00
	---Baffle Your Audience as You Magically Levitate a Piece Rope (1.47)	Trick3		3.00	6.00
	---Make a Random Card Appear as the Last Card in the Deck (1.48)	Trick4		3.00	6.00
	---	Trick5		5.00	10.00
	---	Trick6		5.00	10.00
	---	Trick7		5.00	10.00
	---	Trick8		5.00	10.00
	---	Trick9		5.00	10.00

1.43

1.46

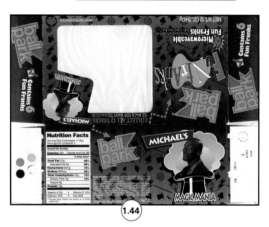

1.44

1.47

1.45

1.48

Year	Ball Park Franks	item #	# of items	Low	High
	---	Trick10		5.00	10.00
	---	Trick11		5.00	10.00
96	---	Trick12		5.00	10.00
96	Booklet, "Commemorative Stickers" from Atlanta Olympic Games, "Izzy & Michael Stick Together" (1.49)			35.00	45.00
96	Sticker Sheets, "Fun Franks" for Atlanta Olympic Games, white background, each sheet sealed		6 sheets	180.00	240.00
	---MJ holding hot dog in left hand in red suit & standing next to blue cartoon character in red suit coat and black pants (1.50)		7 stickers	30.00	40.00
	---MJ holding sunglasses on head with left hand, hot dog right hand & with cartoon character with hands overhead & basketball (1.51)		8 stickers	30.00	40.00
	---MJ holding hot dog in right hand red #23 & standing in suit with hot dog in left hand next to blue cartoon character (1.52)		7 stickers	30.00	40.00
	---MJ in blue sweater gray shirt holding hot dog in right hand & standing in red suit jacket holding ball (1.53)		7 stickers	30.00	40.00
	---MJ in blue sweater gray shirt with blue cartoon character & standing with hands on hips in red #23 uniform (1.54)		7 stickers	30.00	40.00
	---MJ in blue sweater gray shirt sitting on ball with blue cartoon character (1.55)		8 stickers	30.00	40.00
5/97	Coupon, $.50 Off Any Two BP Products, "It's not really summer 'til you have your BP" (1.56)	611949		2.00	4.00

1.49

1.50

1.51

1.52

1.53

1.54

1.55

1.56

Year	Ball Park Franks	item #	# of items	Low	High
8/97	Coupons-2, $.50 Off Any Two BP Products, $.40 off Any BP Fat Free Product, "We Grilled Michael on His Favorite Part of Summer" (1.57)	612145			
		612285		2.00	4.00
10/97	Coupons-3, $1.00 off Bag of Halloween Candy, $.40 off Any Package of BP Fat Free or Lite Franks, $1.00 of Any Two Packages of BP Fun Franks or Corn Dogs "Treat Yourself to the Monster, Taste of Ball Park." (1.58)	612582			
		612624			
		612608		2.00	4.00
97	Coupons-2, $1.00 Off a Bag of Halloween Candy, $.40 Off Any Package of BP Fat Free or Lite Franks Treat Yourself to the Monster, Taste of Ball Park (1.60)	612574			
		612616		2.00	4.00
97	Coupon, $.40 Off Any BP Product, "Monster Space Jam Video $5.00 Rebate!," (1.61)	611667		2.00	4.00
97	Coupon, UFO $5.00 Rebate/Space Jam (1.62)			1.00	2.00
98	Coupons-2, $.40 Off Any BP Product, $1.00 Off Any 2 BP Fun Franks or Corn Dogs, all sheets, MJ holding dog/bun RH, Betty Crocker Au Gratin above (1.63)	612913			

1.57

1.58

1.60

1.61

1.62

1.63

			612947	3.00	5.00
-	Box, Fun Franks, red 23, holding hot dog in right hand, Free Funtoos inside box, MJ, Corn Doggie & Fun Frank cutouts on bottom (1.64)		12 oz	6.00	10.00
-	Disc, "Jordan Buys A Ball Park," MJ in red shirt, hot dog in right hand (1.65)		5"	5.00	10.00

Year	Banners, Pennants				
80's	MJ, black signature, dunking, folded			12.00	20.00
92	Back to Back			10.00	15.00
-	MJ Banner/Flag, cartoon like MJ picture, large size, 13 basketballs			5.00	10.00
11/94	Banner with MJ photo, top says, "Michael Jordan Day, the People of Chicago Salute You," bottom says, "City of Chicago, Richard M. Daley, Mayor" (1.65a)			450.00	1500.00
98	Banner, 1998 Chicago Bulls 6 Time NBA Champions (1.65b)		28 x 42	25.00	50.00
98	Pennants, 1998 Chicago Bulls 6 Time Standard Pennants (1.65c)			4.00	6.00

Year	Basketballs				
96	Mini, Best Team Ever 72-10, Mini Litho, clear case SCCA Produced, Sportacular Art,			45.00	70.00
96	Mini, Best Team Ever 72-10, cardboard case, TSC Members Only Club-SCCA Produced			35.00	60.00

Year	Birmingham Barons				
94	Souvenir Program, 93 Baseball Southern League Championship Ring, black cover			15.00	20.00
94	Book Collectors Edition (1.66)		cover	7.00	10.00
95	Merchandise Brochure-8 sided foldout, MJ full front cover, hats back cover (1.67)			8.00	12.00
95	Group Planner, schedule, ticket brochure		cover	15.00	20.00

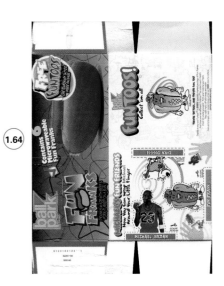

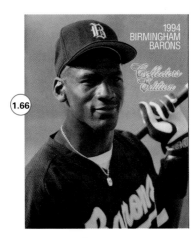
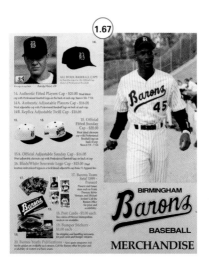

1.84

1.65b

1.83

1.65a

MICHAEL JORDAN DAY
November 1, 1994

The People of Chicago Salute You!

City of Chicago
Richard M. Daley, Mayor

1.68a

THE CHICAGO AREA
SCOUTER

"Join Our Team"
Roundup Kick Off

1.65c

Year	Boy Scouts of America			
84	Card, Bulls, BSA, Interlake, blank back, original issue, dull finish, 5 x 7 (1.68)	NNO	100.00	150.00
84	Card, Bulls, BSA, Interlake, blank backs, re-issued high glossy finish, 2nd series issue, 5 x 7,	NNO	12.00	15.00
9/85	Newspaper, Chicago Area Scouter, "Join Our Team" (1.68a)	V13 N8	100.00	150.00
-	Frisbee, Join Scouting Today, Chicago Area Council, Chicago Tribune Proud To Be Partner in Scouting (1.69)		30.00	50.00

Year	Bradford Exchange Plates			
95-96	-MJ Collection-12 flat plates, Artist-Chuck Gillies, 95 non consecutive firing days			
	--1st Championship-84-B10-244.1	1	35.00	45.00
	--The Comeback-84-B10-244.2	2	35.00	45.00
	--'92 Champions-84-B10-244.3	3	35.00	45.00
	--'82 NCAA Championship-84-B10-244.4	4	35.00	45.00
	--'93 Champions-84-B10-244.5	5	35.00	45.00
	--'88 Slam Dunk Champion-84-B10-244.6	6	35.00	45.00
	--'86 Playoffs-84-B10-244.7	7	35.00	45.00
	--Rookie Year-84-B10-244.8	8	35.00	45.00
		9	35.00	45.00
		10	35.00	45.00
		11	35.00	45.00
		12	35.00	45.00
	--Returns to Greatness-12 flat plates, Artist-Glen Greast, 95 non consecutive firing days			
	--Record 72 Wins-84-B10-700.1	1	40.00	50.00
	--MVP-84-B10-700.1	2	40.00	50.00
	--The 4th Title-84-B10-700.1	3	40.00	50.00
	--The Sweep-84-B10-700.1	4	40.00	50.00
	--Return to Greatness	5	40.00	50.00
	--New York Knockout-84-B10-700.1	6	40.00	50.00
		7	40.00	50.00
		8	40.00	50.00
		9	40.00	50.00
		10	40.00	50.00
		11	40.00	50.00
		12	40.00	50.00
	--Legend for All Time-4 plates, 3-D Plates			
	--Soaring Star, 84-B10-268.1, 7,200 produced	5103A	60.00	80.00
	--Rim Rockers, 84-B10-268.2	2	75.00	100.00
		3		
		4		
	--Soaring Above the Rest-5 plates			
	--Taking It Higher	1	40.00	50.00
		2	40.00	50.00
		3	40.00	50.00
		4	40.00	50.00
		5	40.00	50.00

(1.68)

CHICAGO BULLS

MICHAEL JORDAN
6'6" Guard

(1.69)

JOIN SCOUTING TODAY

MICHAEL JORDAN SAYS... "DON'T FOUL OUT, STAY IN SCHOOL."

PROUD TO BE A PARTNER IN SCOUTING · BOY SCOUTS OF AMERICA · CHICAGO AREA COUNCIL

312/559-0990

6/97	97 NBA Championship Finals Commemorative Set, SLU-like figures and boxes, Contemporary Artists & Classic Artists are copyrights of B's Toys & J.P. Garland	6 pieces		
	---S. Pippen, bb background front, "Chicago Bulls" left side, "Game 1" top between Jazz logo on left and Bulls logo on right, "NBA" & logo center, 1/2 of "NBA Finals 1997" in background, back SP in white 33 holding ball both hand looking up, bb and "5" in background, game score by quarters	game 1	50.00	100.00
	---M. Jordan, bb background front, "Chicago Bulls" right side, "Game 2" top between Bulls logo and score-97 on left and Jazz logo and score-85 on right, "NBA Finals 1997" & trophy center, back MJ dribbling with right hand, white 23, bb and Bulls logo in background, game score by quarters	game 2	125.00	200.00
	---J. Stockton, bb background front, 1/2 of Utah logo on right side, "Game 3" top between Bulls logo and score-93 on left and Jazz logo and score-104 on right, "NBA Finals 1997" & trophy center, back JS dribbling with right hand, white 12, bb in background, game score by quarters, "Roll" top right	game 3	50.00	100.00
	---K. Malone, bb background front, 1/2 of Utah logo left side, "Game 4" top between Bulls logo and score-73 on left and Jazz logo and score-78 on right, "NBA Finals 1997" & trophy center, back KM side view, white uniform, bb in background, game scores by quarters, "Pick" bottom left	game 4	60.00	120.00
	---M. Jordan, bb in background front, "Game 5" top right between "Chicago Bulls," bb with black and white "23" top left, back MJ standing looking, red 23, bb background, game scores by quarters, story "Jordan The Miracle Man" bottom	game 5	125.00	200.00
	---S. Kerr, gray bb background, "Game 6" top between Bulls logo, trophy and score-90 on left and Jazz logo and score-86 on right, "5" & NBA Finals 1997" in middle, "1997 NBA Champions" left side back SK jump shot, white 25, game scores by quarters, 5 trophies top right, "High Five" right side, gray bb background, 1/2 of Bulls logo left horn goes with game 6 MJ & SP below	game 6	30.00	60.00
	97 NBA Championship Finals Commemorative Sub Set, SLU-like figures and cases	4 pieces		
	---M. Jordan, bb in background front, "Game 1" top with Bulls logo on left and Jazz logo on right, "Game Winning Shot" on left," trophy & 1/2 of "NBA Finals 1997" center background, back MJ shooting overhead two hands, white 23, basketball background, "5" on left side, "game 1" & game scores by quarters in top of "5"	game 1	125.00	200.00
	---M. Jordan, gray bb in background front, "Game 6" top between Bulls logo, trophy and score-90 on left and Jazz logo and score-86 on right, "5" in middle with "NBA Finals 1997" in top of "5," "1997 NBA Champions" on left side, "MVP" on top right, back side view of MJ with five finger held up, white uniform, game scores by quarters, 5 NBA trophies with "Chicago Bulls Dynasty" below, MVP trophies with "Michael Jordan 1997 Finals MVP" below, center section of Bulls logo and gray basketball background	game 6	125.00	200.00
	---S. Pippen, gray bb in background front, "Game 6" top between Bulls logo, trophy and score-90 on left and Jazz logo and score-86 on right, "5" in middle with "NBA Finals 1997" in top of "5," "1997 NBA Champions" on left side, back SP standing, white 33, game scores by quarters, gray bb background, .5 of Bull's logo right horn, NBA trophies	game 6	50.00	100.00

---M. Jordan, Grant Park background front, "Grant Park 1997 Championship Rally" top, yellow insert in lid "MJ Dressed in rally day attire Includes official locker room cap, Bonus 1997 NBA Championship Trophy" on right side, MJ figure has black hat and shirt, white pants, black & white shoes, holding trophy overhead looking up at it, back pictures of all boxes of 6 piece set and 4 piece sub set, starting lineup with name and numbers SP, DR, LL, RH, MJ, BW, TK, SK, JC, JB, RB on bottom left, "Chicago Bulls" bottom center, Proof of Purchase Seal has Jeff P. Garland and MJ's name (1.70)   Rally Day   125.00   200.00

Year	Budweiser				
3/86	Bud Bulletin (1.71)		inside	45.00	75.00
	---MJ inside		page 6		
	---MJ inside		page 8		
	---MJ inside		page 12		
5/90	Bud Bulletin (1.73)		inside	15.00	20.00
	---MJ inside (1.74)		page 8		
	---MJ inside		page 13		
	---MJ inside		page 14		

Year	Bulls Official Calendars	item #		
84-94	Ten Year Anniversary, Day Dream 1994	4 1502	25.00	35.00
86-87	Chicago Bulls Official Team Calendar		30.00	40.00
87-88	Bulls Official, MJ, Oakley, Paxson & Collins on cover		20.00	30.00
88-89	Players huddled in warm-ups, back Merle Harmon's FanFair		20.00	30.00
89	Calendar & Pull Out Calendar Poster, Silverberg/Jordan Partnership		18.00	25.00
90-91	Bulls 25th Anniversary		15.00	20.00
92-93	Back 2 Back World Champions CB		12.00	18.00
93-94	Three-Time World Champion Chicago Bulls, vs. Suns, hands in air, red and black front, Coca Cola Ad on back		20.00	30.00
94-95	Bulls Official, United Center from above, Pippen Feat		10.00	15.00
95-96	Chicago Bulls Calendar	Nov.	8.00	12.00
95-96	Bulls Official, 30th Anniversary MJ's comeback		8.00	12.00

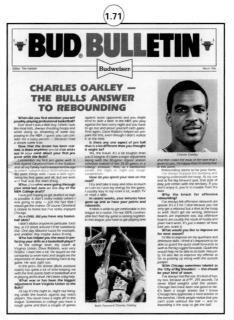

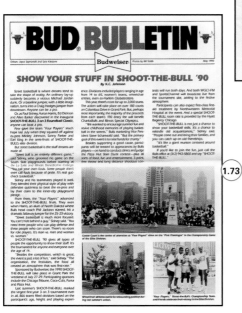

---Sheet, "Most Wins in NBA History" (1.75)	white	7.00	10.00
---Official Scorers Report-1st half, MJ name listed (1.76)	yellow	7.00	10.00
---Official Scorers Report-1st quarter, MJ name listed (1.77)	white	7.00	10.00
---Official Scorers Report-2nd quarter, MJ name listed (1.78)	white	7.00	10.00
---Official Play-By-Play Report 1st quarter, MJ name listed (1.79)	white	7.00	10.00
---Official Play-By-Play Report 2nd quarter, MJ name listed (1.80)	white	7.00	10.00
---Season Subscriber Ticket (1.81)		8.00	12.00
---Gate Ticket (1.82)		8.00	12.00
---Program, MJ cover, & 4/16/96 sticker, white/green cover, white/purple sticker (1.83)	cover	20.00	25.00
Program, MJ cover, & 4/16/97, black cover		15.00	20.00
Program, Vin Baker cover, & 4/16/96 sticker, white/red cover, white/purple sticker (1.84)	inside	20.00	25.00
Program, 4/16/96, Vin Baker & G. Robinson cover		15.00	20.00
Program Sticker		5.00	8.00

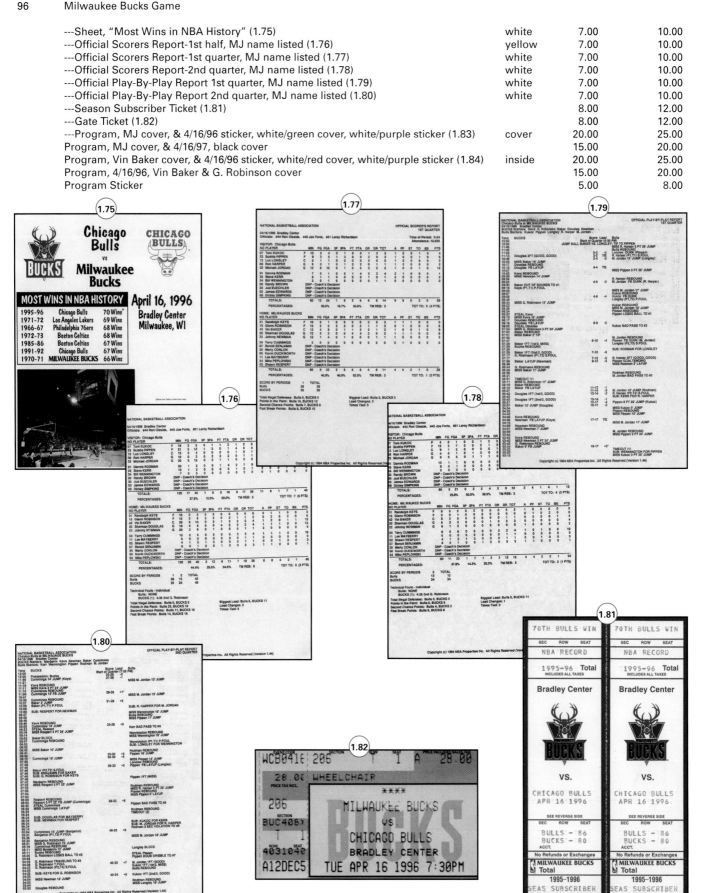

Year	Cachets	cachet#		
4/16/87	Gateway Stamp Company, MJ 3000 points in a season, C of Am MJ Autograph, 1000 issued in 96 (2.1)		125.00	140.00
1/11/91	Wild Horse, Heir Jordan, 100th Anniversary of Basketball, 150 produced (2.2)	57	25.00	35.00
1/25/91	Wild Horse, R. Seikaly & MJ, Chicago vs. 55 produced Miami (2.3)	10	25.00	35.00
6/2/91	Wild Horse, Magic & MJ, Best of Best, 125 produced (2.4)	31	25.00	35.00
8/28/91	Colorado "Silk" Cachet, 1000 produced (2.5)		10.00	15.00
7 & 8/92	Triumph, Barcelona Olympic Basketball Team Picture & Flag, #10 envelope (2.6)		10.00	15.00
7 & 8/92	Triumph, Barcelona Olympics Michael Jordan, dunking, white #9, #10 envelope (2.7)		10.00	15.00
10/6/93	Wild Horse, MJ No Peat (2.8)	143	54.00	75.00

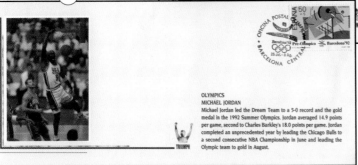

1993	Wild Horse, Playoff Finals Set, 4 different		121.00	150.00
	—6/9, MJ & Barkley, 85 produced (2.9)	61		
	—6/11, S. Pippen, No MJ, 85 produced (2.10)	61		
	—6/18, Final Seconds, No MJ, 85 produced (2.11)	61		
	—6/20, 3 Peat, MJ, 85 produced (2.12)	61		
4/7/94	SA Sports Covers, Windy City Classic, MJ First Appearance at Wrigley Field, C of A, 50 produced, White Sox 4, Cubs 4, hand painted (2.13)	20	30.00	40.00
4/8/94	LS Baseball Monuments, Jordan - Barons, MJ baseball cap, hand drawn with story, 600 produced (2.14)	12	10.00	15.00
6/10/94	SA Sports Covers, 94 MJ RMCC Celebrity Golf Classic, /Barkley, 50 produced, hand painted, C of A (2.15)	11	30.00	40.00
9/3/94	SA Sports Covers, MJ Premiere Season Birmingham Barons, C of A, 50 produced, 94 statistics, hand painted (2.16)	19	30.00	40.00

9/9/94	SA Sports Covers, SP AS Classic at Chicago Stadium, MJ kissing floor, C of A, 50 signed by artist, 1929-1994 (2.17)	14	30.00	40.00
3/24/95	Bevil, MJ is Back, 275 produced (2.18)	188	70.00	90.00
3/19/95	Colorado Silk, The Return of MJ (2.19)		7.00	10.00
3/19/95	Gateway Stamp Company, MJ Returns to NBA MJ Autograph, 500 issued in 96 (2.20)		125.00	150.00
2/11/96	SA Sports Covers, 1996 MVP All-Star Game, C of A, 50 signed, East 129, West 118 (2.21)	17	30.00	40.00
4/16/96	Bevil, Bulls 70 Game Win, MJ, SP & Rodman, hand painted, C of A, #10 envelope, 550 signed by artist (2.22)	144	40.00	60.00
4/16/96	Bulls Win No 70!, MJ & SP photo, 200 produced (2.23)	69	7.00	10.00

Year	Canon Sheets-stadium handouts			
84	Canon Camera Night Sheet Nov. 13, 1984, 1 MJ front, black dirt on borders, tan front, Gretzky & Canon T70 back (2.24)	fold out	50.00	75.00
85-86	Canon Camera Autograph Night, MJ front & inside, no date, T-70 back, negative like pictures + Stan Albeck front (2.25)	fold out	45.00	50.00
87	Canon Camera Night March 3, 1987, MJ front & inside, tan front, vs. Celtics, Canon T90 back (2.26)	fold out	35.00	45.00

| 88 | Canon Camera Night Sheet Feb. 27, 1988, 1 MJ front, gray front, Canon EOS back (2.27) | fold out | 25.00 | 35.00 |
| 89 | Canon Camera Night Feb. 16, 1989, MJ front & inside, light blue front, Canon EOS 750/850 back (2.28) | fold out | 20.00 | 25.00 |

Year	CDs and Cassette Tapes		
97	CD, Bullistic, MJ picture on Chicago Sun Times ad flyer insert (2.29)		10.00
95	CD, Rom Classics, MJ in Flight, tan back, black front, dunking		10.00
91	Cassette tape, Teknoe, "I Wanna Be Like Mike" (2.30)		12.00

2.27

2.28

2.29

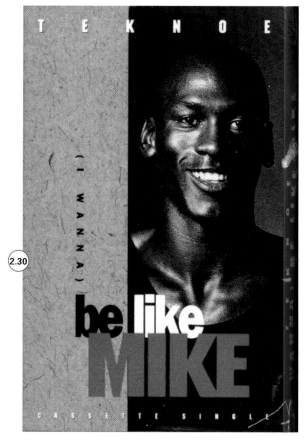

2.30

Michael Jordan Cereal Boxes

The backs of many boxes have the same information and photos. These will be noted as: Common backs. Prices for factory flat are 25 percent more than full box price. For viewing of actual inserts and send-in items offered, check poster section for posters, games, basketball cards, etc. There are three Canada (ProStar) and five German (Kellogg) issued cereal boxes noted. All others are by Wheaties.

Year	Series	Size Oz.	Item Information Front	Back	Price Full	Empty
1988	53	12	1st edition Basketball offering (2.31)	Photo and Story	100.00	80.00
1988	53	18	Same as 12oz		100.00	80.00
1989	56	8	Jumpshot (2.32)	Photo and Story #2	45.00	35.00
1989	56	12	Same as 8oz.		45.00	35.00
1989	56	18	Same as 12oz.		45.00	35.00
1989	56	24	Same as 18oz.		100.00	75.00
1989	57	18	Same as series 56, except… (2.33)	Different photo and story	55.00	45.00
1989	43	18	Same as series 56, 57 except…	Large bowl of Wheaties with all blue background.	75.00	55.00
1989	43,56,57	18	Some boxes came with "Free Poster Included" and "Collect all 4" (2.34)		+5	+5
1989	70	12	Holding spoon and bowl. "Now 25% less sodium. Made with 100% whole grain" (2.35)	Is common	55.00	45.00
1989	70	18	Same as 12oz.		55.00	45.00
1989	73	12	Holding spoon and bowl. "Made with 100% whole grain" (2.36)	Is common	55.00	45.00
1989	73	18	Same as 12oz.		55.00	45.00
1989	73Z	12	Same as series 73		50.00	40.00

Year	Series	Size Oz.	Item Information Front	Back	Price Full	Empty
1989	73Z	18	Free blue color poster included on the front of this box. States it is a special bonus poster Part A. MJ is breaking out of box. (2.37)	Is common	55.00	45.00
1989	73Z	18	Free green color poster included on the front of this box. States it is a special bonus poster Part B. MJ is breaking out of box. (2.38)	Is common	55.00	45.00
1989	73Z	18	Free purple color poster included on the front of this box. States it is a special bonus poster Part C. MJ is breaking out of box. (2.39)	Is common	55.00	45.00
1989	73Z	18	"Box without" Free poster on the front of box. Same as series 73, 73Z 12oz. (2.40)		50.00	40.00
1989	73Z	24	MJ holding spoon and bowl. Same 73 and 73Z without poster on it		100.00	75.00

1989	82	18	Air Jordan Flight Club calendar (2.41)	MJ "Quotes"	45.00	30.00
1989	82Z	18	Same as series 82		45.00	30.00
1989	83	18	Same as series 82, 82Z (2.42)		45.00	30.00
1989	82, 82Z, 83	18	Box without free calendar on the front		40.00	25.00
1990	2	18	Pouring Wheaties into bowl (2.43)	Photo and story #3	75.00	60.00
1990	8	18	Four poses of MJ "Shoot Hoops" (2.44)	Pull down Action Game flap	60.00	40.00
1990	9	18	Four poses of MJ "Shoot Hoops"	Pull down Action Game flap	60.00	40.00
1990	10	12	Pouring Wheaties into bowl (2.45)	Common	55.00	40.00
1990	10	18	Pouring Wheaties into bowl	Common	45.00	35.00
1990	10	24	Pouring Wheaties into bowl	Common	100.00	75.00
1990	11	12	Pouring Wheaties into bowl	Common	45.00	35.00
1990	11	18	Pouring Wheaties into bowl	Common	55.00	40.00
1990	37	24	Pouring Wheaties into bowl (2.46)	Common	100.00	75.00
1990	46	12	Pouring Wheaties into bowl	Common	50.00	40.00
1990	47	12	Pouring Wheaties into bowl	Common	50.00	40.00
1990	6912		Holding spoon and bowl. "Now made with 25% less sodium" (2.47)	Common	75.00	60.00

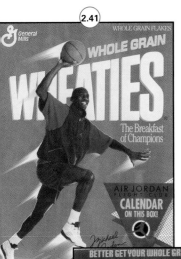

1990	78Z	12	Holding spoon and bowl. (2.48)	Common	50.00	35.00
1990	78Z	18	Same as 12oz.		40.00	25.00
1990	86	18	Pouring Cereal	Common	50.00	35.00
1990	86Z	12	Pouring Cereal (2.49)	Common	50.00	35.00
1990	86Z	18	Pouring Cereal	Common	45.00	35.00
1990	87	18	Pouring Cereal (2.50)	Common	35.00	25.00
1990	26	1	Holding spoon and bowl in hands; with hair (2.51)	Back same as front	10.00	8.00
1991	1	1	Holding spoon and bowl, carrying bag (2.52)	Back same as front	10.00	6.00
1991	1	1	Holding spoon and bowl. "Sample not for resale" on white background (2.53)	Back same as front	15.00	10.00
1991	1	1	Holding spoon and bowl; with hair	Back same as front	15.00	10.00
1991	27	3/4	Holding spoon and bowl; with hair (2.54)	Back same as front	10.00	6.00
1991	28	1	Holding spoon and bowl. "Sample not for resale" Not on white background (2.55)	Back same as front	15.00	10.00
1991	29	3/4	1991 NBA World Champion (2.56)	Team Photo	15.00	10.00

2.48

2.49

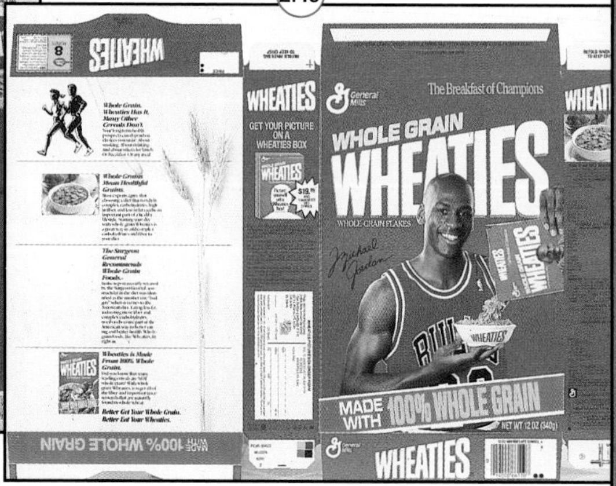

2.50

2.51

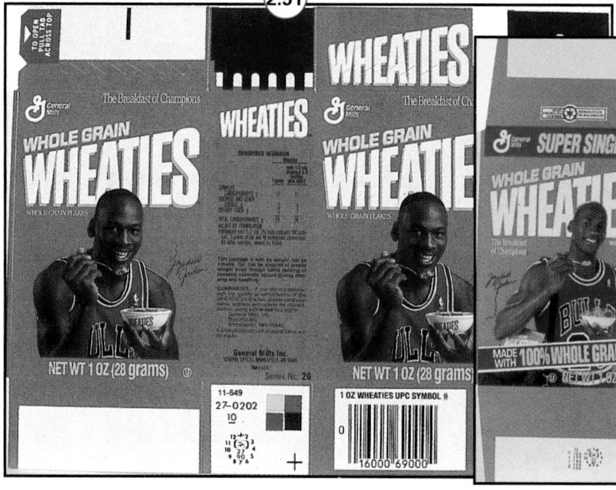

2.52

2.53

2.55

2.54

2.56

1991	32	18	1991 NBA World Champion (2.57)	Team Photo	45.00	30.00
1991	30	3/4	Holding spoon and bowl, carrying bag (2.58)	Save $.50 coupon	15.00	10.00
1991	34	12	Holding spoon and bowl, carrying bag (2.59)	Common	60.00	40.00
1991	34	18	Holding spoon and bowl, carrying bag	Common	60.00	40.00
1991	35	12	Holding spoon and bowl, carrying bag (2.60)	Common	50.00	35.00
1991	14	12	Pouring cereal. $5.00 refund offer (2.61)	Save $5.00	45.00	30.00
1991	15	12	Pouring cereal. $5.00 refund offer	Save $5.00 and three MJ pictures	50.00	35.00
1991	48A	18	Holding spoon and bowl, carrying bag. "Fleer NBA basketball card collecting sheet on Back Panel" (Collect all 8 card sheet) (2.62)	Fleer NBA basketball card collector cutout sheet # 1 of 8, Nine different cards	40.00	25.00
1991	48B	18	Same as 48A	2 of 8	40.00	25.00
1991	48C	18	Same as 48A (2.63)	3 of 8	40.00	25.00
1991	48D	18	Same as 48A (2.64)	4 of 8	40.00	25.00

1991	48E	18	Same as 48A (2.65)		5 of 8	40.00	25.00
1991	48F	18	Same as 48A (2.66)		6 of 8 with MJ Card	55.00	40.00
1991	48G	18	Same as 48A (2.67)		7 of 8 with Larry Bird card	45.00	30.00
1991	48H	18	Same as 48A (2.68)		8 of 8	40.00	25.00
1991	49A -						
	49H	18	Front and back same as 48A through 48H, but a different series number. Prices are also the same by series number.				
1991	20	525g	Canada Pro-Star with free poster inside (2.69)	Photo of four different posters. Two MJ's.		40.00	25.00
1992	21	400g	Canada Pro-Star with free cards inside (2.70)	Photo of nine different cards. One MJ, two background with MJ		60.00	45.00
1992	47k	18	Holding spoon and bowl, carrying bag (2.71).	"What will you find in a bowl of Wheaties"?		30.00	20.00
1992	50	12	Holding spoon and bowl, carrying bag (2.72)	Common		50.00	35.00
1992	50	18	Holding spoon and bowl, carrying bag	Common		50.00	35.00
1992	63K	18	91-92 NBA World Champ, Back to Back (2.73)			40.00	30.00

1993	No #	1	91-92 NBA World Champ, Back to Back (2.74)		30.00	20.00
1993	75	18	MJ golfing (2.75)	Golf course picture	50.00	35.00
1993	1C	500g	Canadian version - Silver Collection Edition (2.76)	Three MJ photos	45.00	35.00
1993	91	18	Silver Collection Edition (2.77)	Three MJ photos	30.00	20.00
1993	83	18	91-92-93 World Champion (2.78)	Team Picture	35.00	20.00
1993	16	14.75	Honey Gold - Meet MJ Offer (2.79)	Meet MJ Offer	40.00	30.00
1993	16	21.25	Honey Gold - Meet MJ Offer	Meet MJ Offer	60.00	40.00
1994	11	18	No MJ (2.80)	MJ Picture	45.00	35.00
1995	22	18	Jordan's Back (2.81)	Newspaper Edition - Limited Edition	30.00	20.00
1996	43	13	Golden Grahams (2.82)	Free Space Jam hoop and ball	40.00	25.00

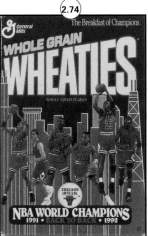

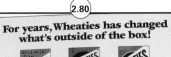

1996	43	18	Same as 13oz. (2.83)		40.00	25.00
1996	62	18	1996 Champions (2.84)	"Better Than Ever; Unstop-a-Bull"	25.00	20.00
1996	71	18	Orange Box, Space Jam jersey offer (2.85)	Space Jam jersey coupon	25.00	20.00
1996	14	14.75	Blue Box, Honey Frosted Space Jam offer (2.86)	Same as series 71	25.00	20.00
1996	13	18	Purple Box, Crispy Raisin. Space Jam offer (2.87)	Same as series 71	25.00	20.00
1996	4879	375g	German Kelloggs Green Box, Chocos with Bear and Space Jam Movie 3D card offer (2.88)	Photo of seven movie cards. 2 MJ's	15.00	12.00
1996	4881	375g	German Kelloggs Yellow Box, Corn Pops with Flying Space Jam movie. Three card offer (2.89)	Same as series 4879	15.00	12.00
1996	4933	500g	German Kelloggs Gold Box, Crunchy Nut with "Cup of Coffee and Space Jam #D" movie offer (2.90)	Same as series 4879	15.00	12.00
1996	4887	375g	German Kelloggs Blue Box, Frosties with Tony the Tiger and Space Jam 3D movie offer (2.91)	Same as series 4879	15.00	12.00

1996	4883	375	German Kelloggs Gold Box, Honey Nut Loops with Bee and Space Jam 3D movie offer (2.92)	Same as series 4879	15.00	12.00
1997	91	18	Orange Box, Win an autographed MJ basketball. (2.93)	Two ways to get your own MJ basketball	25.00	20.00
1997	21	14.75	Blue Box, Jump shot different than series 91-20. Win an autographed MJ basketball. (2.94)	Two ways to get your own MJ basketball	25.00	20.00
1997	20	18	Purple Box, Jump shot different than series 91-21. Win an autographed MJ basketball. (2.95)	Two ways to get your own MJ basketball	25.00	20.00

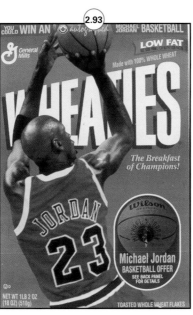

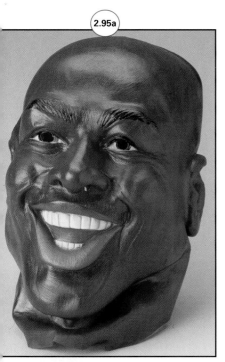

Year	Cesar	Low Price	High Price
95	Rubber Mask, head covering, rubber (2.95a)	60.00	120.00

Year	Chevrolet & General Motors			
84-85	Garbage Bag, "When I drive, I drive a Chevy.," MJ dribbling right hand, USA uniform, white bag; blue writing, signature, & pictures		60.00	90.00
87	Chart, Growth Chart Chicagoland & NW Indiana Chevy.Dealers.		25.00	40.00
93	Mask, Chevy & Restaurant, & Bulls Logo on back (2.96)	7 x 10	12.00	20.00
2/98	Sticker, "The Greatest," MJ & Ali, Chicago Auto Show Handout (2.97)		3.00	5.00
90's	Sticker, Chevrolet/Geo, MJ head in a basketball, "Drives A Blazer Just Like You Do" (2.98)	4 x 4	3.00	6.00

Year	Chicago Cubs			
4/7/94	Scorecard, Cubs vs. White Sox, MJ player for Sox, MJ's name listed, 6 sided fold out (2.99)		15.00	25.00

Year	Chicago Public High School			
97-98	Student Advisory Planner, Plan To Aim High (2.100)	cover	10.00	15.00

Year	Chicago Stadium			
-	Handout, MJ dunking RH, white 23, vs. Pacers (2.101)		8.00	
-	Ad sheet, "When he finally did touch down, this is where he landed," Chicago Stadium floor and seats (2.102)	fold out	2.00	

Chicago Sun Times Newspaper

Year	Description			
85-87	Newsstand Ad Sheet, "Your Hometown Sports Authority, Catch it Today, Just $.35," 2 slots on bottom to insert on box edge, MJ going for layup, "CST It's a Smart Move to Make"	display board	75.00	100.00
87-88	Newsstand Ad Sheet, Chicago's MVP-Complete Playoff Coverage, MJ picture		15.00	20.00
88	Newsstand Ad Sheet, Don't Miss the Best Bulls Coverage in Town, MJ picture		15.00	20.00
2/8/88	Newspaper, MJ MVP		18.00	25.00
90-91	Newsstand Ad Sheet, Chicago's Air Force, Chicago Bulls, Eastern Conference Champions 1990/91, Team picture with MJ		30.00	40.00
6/13/91	Newspaper, Bulls Win It	cover	15.00	20.00
6/14/91	Newpaper, NBA Champs, Souvenir Edition	cover	15.00	20.00
10/27/91	11/2/91-Newpaper Insert, TV Prevue Ready to Repeat	cover	15.00	20.00
10/30/91	Having Second Thoughts	cover	15.00	20.00
91	Book, The Bulls, A Season to Remember	cover	12.00	15.00
6/8/92	Newspaper, Bulls Regain Edge on the Road	cover	10.00	15.00
6/15/92	Ad Sheet, Front Page Reprint	cover	8.00	15.00
6/15/92	Newspaper, Champs!	cover	10.00	15.00
6/16/92	Newspaper, Back To Back	cover	10.00	15.00
6/16/92	Newspaper, Championship Edition	cover	10.00	15.00
6/9/93	Newspaper, Let's Get It On	cover	8.00	15.00
6/10/93	Newspaper, Talk of the Town, Bulls vs. Suns 1	cover	8.00	15.00
6/12/93	Newspaper, The Broom, Bulls vs. Suns 2	cover	8.00	15.00
6/22/93	Newspaper, 3 Cheers, Championship Edition	cover	8.00	15.00
10/6/93	Newspaper, Say it Ain't So Mike	cover	8.00	15.00
10/7/93	Newspaper, Thanks, Sports Final	cover	8.00	15.00
11/4/93	Newspaper, NBA 93-94, Some Big Shoes to Fill	inside	8.00	15.00
10/4/94	Ad Sheet, home delivery, Two Chicago Sports Legend	cover	6.00	12.00
3/19/95	Newspaper, The Comeback, Sports Final	cover	6.00	12.00
3/20/95	Newspaper, The Comeback, Sports Final	cover	6.00	12.00
4/17/96	Newspaper, Bulls Reach 70!, Souvenir Edition	cover	5.00	10.00
6/17/96	Newspaper, Worth Its Wait!, Souvenir Edition	cover	8.00	10.00
6/18/96	Newspaper, Hail to the Champs		5.00	10.00
11/10/96	Newspaper, Showcase Section, "Pump Up the Jam"	cover	5.00	10.00
96	Newsstand Ad Sheet, Back To Back Starters at Game Time		5.00	10.00
96	Newsstand Ad Sheet, Dynamic Duel Complete Coverage in Chicago Sun Times, Bulls vs. Magic/MJ and Shaq pictured		15.00	20.00
96	Newsstand Ad Sheet, We Got It 4 Chicago Bulls, Chicago Sun-Times, No MJ, trophy, Bulls head		5.00	10.00
96	Newsstand Ad Sheet, 1996 Champs Chicago Sun-Times, Bulls Logo + pictures of: MJ, SP, DR, LL, RH, TK		5.00	10.00
96	Newsstand Ad Sheet, Unstop-A-Bull, side view of MJ, SP & DR		5.00	10.00
6/12/97	Newspaper, Miracle Cure	front	3.00	8.00
6/13/97	Newspaper, City Girds for Victor	front	3.00	8.00
6/14/97	Newspaper, Gimme 5!	front	3.00	8.00
6/15/97	Newspaper, Party of 5	front	3.00	8.00
6/16/97	Newspaper, Party On	front	3.00	8.00
-	Ad Sheet, Showdown!, MJ & Ewing		6.00	10.00

Chicago Tribune Newspaper

Year	Description			
5/28/91	Sports Section, Bulls end Pistons' reign of terror	cover	10.00	15.00
5/29/91	Sports Section, Bulls not relaxing just yet	cover	10.00	15.00
5/30/91	Sports Section, Pippen get apology, Bulls get antsy	back	10.00	15.00
5/31/91	Sports Section, It's Lakers vs. Bulls after all	inside	10.00	15.00
6/1/91	Sports Section, Dream one a nightmare	cover	10.00	15.00
6/2/91	Newspaper, Michael: City's most valuable imagemaker	cover	10.00	15.00
6/3/91	Newspaper, Lakers gore Bulls, 93-91	cover	10.00	15.00
6/4/91	Newspaper, Bull's good old days were mostly just old	cover	10.00	15.00
6/5/91	Newspaper, Jordan keeps a vow, We're going to hit it	cover	10.00	15.00
6/6/91	Newspaper, Blowout! Bulls roar right back in it	cover	10.00	15.00
6/7/91	Newspaper, Jackson turned Bulls in potential champions	cover	10.00	15.00
6/8/91	Newspaper, Bulls win in OT	cover	10.00	15.00
6/9/91	Newspaper, Bulls get up off the floor, KO Lakers	cover	10.00	15.00
6/10/91	Newspaper, Bulls storm to the brink of title	cover	10.00	15.00
6/11/91	Newspaper, Feeling Bullish	inside	10.00	15.00
6/12/91	Newpaper, 911? I'm dying! But wait until half time	cover	10.00	15.00
6/13/91	Front Page Printing Plate, Five High! Bulls are Champs	front	300.00	450.00
6/13/91	Newspaper, Five High! Bulls Are Champs!	cover	10.00	15.00
6/13/91	Paper Weight, High Five! Bulls are Champs	front	10.00	15.00
6/13/91	Plaque, High Five! Bulls Are Champs		10.00	15.00
6/14/91	Newspaper, A champion city opens up its arms	cover	10.00	15.00
6/15/91	Newspaper, Hundreds of thousands reach out touch bulls	cover	10.00	15.00
6/16/91	Newspaper, Bulls bring out the champion in everyone	cover	10.00	15.00
6/17/91	Section 7, Champions	cover	10.00	15.00
91	Book, Stampede, soft cover	book	15.00	20.00
92	Book, DaBull, soft cover	book	10.00	15.00

Date	Description	Type	Low	High
92	Book, DaBull, hard cover	book	20.00	25.00
6/15/92	Front Page Printing Plate, Two for Two: Bulls Still Champs!	front	250.00	350.00
6/15/92	Newspaper, Two for Two: Bulls Still Champs!	cover	8.00	12.00
6/15/92	Newspaper, Sports Section, Twice as Nice	cover	8.00	12.00
6/15/92	Paper Weight, Two For Two, Still Champs		8.00	12.00
6/15/92	Plaque, Two for Two, Still Champs		8.00	12.00
93	Book, Three Peat, soft cover	book	10.00	15.00
6/21/93	Front Page Printing Plate, Three-Mendous!	cover	200.00	300.00
6/21/93	Newspaper, Three-Mendous!	cover	8.00	15.00
6/21/93	Paper Weight, Three Mendous		8.00	15.00
6/21/93	Plaque, Three Mendous		8.00	15.00
6/24/93	Commemorative Section		8.00	15.00
10/6/93	Newspaper, Jordan Retires from Basketball	cover	8.00	15.00
10/7/93	Newspaper, So Long Michael It's Been Great	cover	8.00	15.00
3/19/95	Newspaper, The Jordan Comeback	cover	6.00	12.00
3/20/96	Newspaper, Relaunched		5.00	10.00
4/17/96	Newspaper, 70 Bookit		5.00	10.00
6/17/96	Front Page Printing Plate, Ringmasters	front	150.00	250.00
6/17/96	Newspaper, Ringmasters		5.00	10.00
6/17/96	Paper Weight, Ring Masters		5.00	10.00
6/17/96	Plaque, Ring Masters		5.00	10.00
6/18/96	Newspaper, Commemorating Championship Year		5.00	10.00
10/27/96	TV Week, Bulls' Eyes, Megaviews of Jordan & Co.	cover	5.00	10.00
96	Newsstand Ad Sheet, 1996 NBA Champions, No MJ, only 4 rings and Bull head		5.00	10.00
97	Ad Insert, 150 Years of Headlines	inside	4.00	8.00
4/24/97	Front page proof sheet, A Day in the Life of the World Champions (2.103)	cover	300.00	400.00
4/24/97	Newspaper, A Day in the Life of the World Champions (2.103)	cover	15.00	20.00
6/12/97	Newspaper, Heart of a Champion	front	4.00	8.00
6/13/97	Newspaper	front	4.00	8.00
6/14/97	Front Page proof sheet, 5 Enough Said (2.103)	front	200.00	300.00
6/14/97	Front Page Printing Plate, 5 Enough Said	front	100.00	200.00
6/14/97	Newspaper, Enough Said (2.103)	front	4.00	8.00
6/15/97	Newspaper, Champs Add 5th	front	4.00	8.00
6/15/97	Newspaper, Champs Add 5th, Northwest Ed.	front	4.00	8.00
6/15/97	Newspaper, Champs Add 5th, Northwest Final Edition, different photos	front	4.00	8.00
6/16/97	Newspaper, The Fifth Element	front	4.00	8.00
8/10/97	Newspaper, 150 Anniversary, Sports Section only	cover	4.00	8.00
9/10/97	Newspaper, Business , Section only	cover	4.00	8.00
10/22/97	Newspaper, Business, Section only	cover	4.00	8.00
10/31/97	Front Page Printing Plate	cover	75.00	150.00
10/31/97	Newspaper	cover	3.00	6.00
11/24/97	Front page Printing Plate	cover	75.00	150.00
11/24/97	Newspaper	cover	3.00	6.00
1/11/98	Front Page Printing Plate	cover	75.00	150.00
1/11/98	Newspaper	cover	3.00	6.00
4/6/98	Front Page Proof Sheet	cover	100.00	125.00
4/6/98	Newspaper	cover	3.00	6.00
4/8/98	Front Page Proof Sheet	cover	100.00	125.00
4/8/98	Newspaper	cover	3.00	6.00
4/15/98	Front Page Proof Sheet	cover	100.00	125.00
4/15/98	Newspaper	cover	3.00	6.00
4/19/98	Front Page Proof Sheet	cover	150.00	200.00
4/19/98	Newspaper	cover	3.00	6.00
4/98	Ad Insert, "2+3=5" on red shirt & bb, blue background		3.00	6.00
5/14/98	Front Page Proof Sheet	cover	150.00	200.00
5/14/98	Newspaper	cover	3.00	6.00
5/98	Insert, front page collectibles, "Two for Two: Bulls still champs!, from 6/15/92 newspaper, attached to 5/10-5/15/98 newspapers		3.00	6.00
5/98	Insert, front page collectibles, "Three-mendous!," from 6/21/93 newspaper, attached to 5/10-5/15/98 newspapers		3.00	6.00

2.103

6/4/98	Newspaper, Breathless in Utah	front	3.00	6.00
6/6/98	Newspaper, May we cut in?	front	3.00	6.00
6/8/98	Newspaper, Utah sits on out	front	3.00	6.00
6/11/98	Newspaper, The fat lady warms up	front	3.00	6.00
6/12/98	Newspaper, O, we of little faith	front	3.00	6.00
6/13/98	Newspaper, Ouch!	front	3.00	6.00
6/14/98	Newspaper, The band takes a break	front	3.00	6.00
6/14/98	Newspaper, Relax, take a deep breath, Final Edition	front	3.00	6.00
6/15/98	Front Page Printing Plate, Bulls Repeat the 3 Peat!, Sports Section front plate (2.103)	front	75.00	150.00
6/15/98	Front Page Printing Plate, The Joy of Six	front	75.00	150.00
6/15/98	Newspaper, the Joy of Six	front	3.00	6.00
6/16/98	Newspaper, And then there were 6	front	3.00	6.00
6/16/98	Front Page Proof Sheet	front	100.00	150.00
6/17/98	Newspaper, Bulls leave them Cheering	front	3.00	6.00

Year	Chicle NBA, Consigue Las Insignials Metalicas De La NBA	card #	Low Price	High Price
93	Card, pink, green, yellow, blue vertical stripes on front, silver finish, front red #23 MJ dribbling vs. #20 with Stars, NBA logo, "Michael Jordan (Bulls)" on bottom (2.104)	NNO	300.00	450.00
93	Card, pink, green, yellow, blue dots on front. Silver finish, Buc Williams Card/MJ front, front red #23, MJ shooting with right hand vs. #52 with Nets, NBA logo, "Buck Williams (Nets)," blank back (2.105)	NNO	35.00	70.00
93	Card, "Michael Jordan (Bulls)" on bottom, silver background, closeup, hair, smiling, white t-shirt, yellow/gold jagged halo around head going from shoulder to shoulder (2.106)	NNO	400.00	600.00
93	Wrapper, blue background, "NBA" white letters with red background, red & dark blue stars, NBA Logo, blank back (2.107)		5.00	10.00

Year	Chris Martin Enterprises Magnets			
94-95	Pro Magnets, Rodman/MJ, Chris Martin Enterprises on front (2.108)	NNO	5.00	10.00

Year	Christmas			
85-86	Card, Chicago Bulls 20th Anniversary Christmas Card, for season ticket holders		60.00	90.00
94	Oranament, Christmas Tree, Birmingham Barons, "94 Jordan Rookie Year," holding bat, gray background, black figue, box		25.00	45.00
96	Oranament, Christmas Tree, Sports Collectors Series, white, Team members signatures & 4 trophies		5.00	10.00

Year	Classic Sports Sheet & Card	sheet#		
92	MJ 3 poses, painting like poster, 5,000 produced	1137	25.00	35.00
92	Card for the Sheet, 3 poses of MJ		20.00	30.00

Year	Coca Cola	size		
89-90	Sticker, Chevy Blazer, Hot Tops (2.109)	5 x 7	20.00	30.00

Year	Description			
89-90	Sticker, Chevy Blazer, Hot Tops	5 x 12	30.00	40.00

Year	**Coins-miscellaneous**	**coin #**		
87-88	Chicago Bulls, MJ picture name, 86-87 Scoring Champ, 3,041 Season Point, & stars on front, silver, 1987 & 1988, NBA, Don't Foul Out on back (2.110)	NNO	30.00	45.00
91	MVP top, 1992 middle, NBA bottom on back, silver, MJ name, picture & No. 23 on front (2.110)	1,117	30.00	45.00
92	USA Basketball on back, silver, MJ name, picture & No. 9 on front (2.110)	2,889	30.00	45.00
92	MVP top, 1992 middle, NBA bottom on back, silver, MJ name, picture & No. 23 on front (2.110)	13,918	30.00	45.00

Year	**Collegiate Collection/NCAA/UNC-Items**	**card #**		
82	Ticket, NCAA Final 4, LA Super Dome, MJ last minute jump shot		125.00	200.00
82	Pennant, UNC Final 4, NCAA Champs, white print over teal field		25.00	50.00
82	Can, UNC/NCAA Champions, listed as Mike Jordan on side (2.111)		125.00	175.00
83	Yearbook UNC Annual		75.00	125.00
84	Yearbook, UNC Annual, 15 pictures		65.00	115.00
89	Sheet	100cds	60.00	100.00
	—MJ	65		
	—82 NCAA Champions Team/MJ front	200		
89	Sheet	100cds	60.00	100.00
	—MJ	13		
	—MJ	14		
	—MJ	15		
	—MJ	16		
	—MJ	17		
	—MJ	18		
89	Gold Sheet-I	25 cds	125.00	175.00
	—MJ	13		
	—MJ	15		
	—MJ	16		
89	Gold Sheet-II, III, IV	25 cds /each	375.00	525.00
	—MJ	14		
	—MJ	17		
	—MJ	18		
	—MJ	65		
	—MJ	200		
89-90	Cards, Collegiate Collection NC, Finest & Coca Cola Set	200cds	15.00	25.00
	—MJ (2.112)	13	1.50	2.50
	—MJ	14	1.50	2.50
	—MJ	15	1.50	2.50
	—MJ	16	1.50	2.50
	—MJ	17	1.50	2.50
	—MJ	18	1.50	2.50
	—1980/1981 Team Picture/MJ front, MJ may have been in HS	50	1.50	2.50
	—Matt Doherty/MJ front left	62	1.50	2.50
	—MJ	65	1.50	2.50
	—Jimmy Black/MJ front	93	.50	1.00

Year		# cds		
	—-Matt Doherty/MJ front	128	.50	1.00
	—-82 NCAA Champions Team/MJ front	200	1.00	2.00
89-90	Cards, Collegiate Collection, gold set, NC Finest/Coca Cola	200cds	125.00	175.00
	—-MJ	13	12.00	15.00
	—-MJ	14	12.00	15.00
	—-MJ	15	12.00	15.00
	—-MJ	16	12.00	15.00
	—-MJ	17	12.00	15.00
	—-MJ	18	12.00	15.00
	—-1980/1981 Team Picture/MJ front, MJ may have been in HS	50	12.00	15.00
	—-Matt Doherty/MJ front left	62	4.00	8.00
	—-MJ	65	12.00	15.00
	—-Jimmy Black/MJ front	93	4.00	8.00
	—-Matt Doherty/MJ front	128	4.00	8.00
	—-82 NCAA Champions Team/MJ front	200	8.00	12.00
89-90	Display box back, Coca Cola, Limited First Edition, North Carolina vs. North Carolina State, Uncut Press Sheets at $49.00 each, by Collegiate Collection	11x28	20.00	30.00
90	Cards, Collegiate Collection NC	10 cds	4.00	8.00
	—-MJ (2.113)	NC-1		
	—-Ethan Horton	NC-2		
	—-Steve Hale	NC-3		
	—-Mark Maye	NC-4		
	—-Matt Doherty	NC-5		
	—-Tyrone Anthony	NC-6		
	—-Sam Perkins	NC-7		
	—-Kelvin Bryant	NC-8		
	—-Kenny Smith	NC-9		
	—-Kenan Stadium	NC-10		
90	Cards, Collegiate Collection UNC 200 Set, 2nd Edition	200cds	15.00	25.00
	—-MJ	3	2.00	4.00
	—-MJ	44	2.00	4.00
	—-Sam Perkins/MJ front	39	2.00	4.00
	—-MJ	61	2.00	4.00
	—-Matt Doherty/MJ front	65	2.00	4.00
	—-MJ	89	2.00	4.00
	—-MJ	93	2.00	4.00
92	Card, Collegiate Collection MJ & Magic 12th National (2.114)	NNO	12.00	20.00

Year	Cologne	size		
96	Demo Cards		2.00	4.00
96	Spray	3.4 oz	35.00	45.00
96	Box, Spray	1.7 oz	23.00	30.00
96	Travel Size Spray	.5 oz	12.00	15.00
96	Travel Kit		25.00	35.00
	—-shower gel	1.7 oz		
	—-spray	.5 oz		
	—-body oil spray	1.7 oz		
96	Water Bottle		6.00	12.00

MAGIC AND MICHAEL

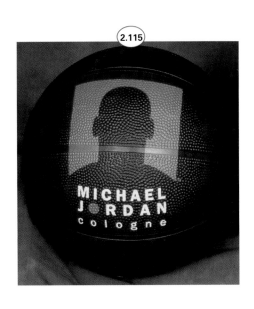

96	Sticker		2.00	4.00
97	Coupon, Free MJ Basketball Magazine		1.00	2.00
97	Pin		20.00	30.00
97	Splash, Royal Selections No.33, "Our Alternative to Michael Jordan for Men," black box with MJ dunking, clear bottle with red "Michael Jordan" writing	3.3 oz	15.00	20.00
97	Ad sheet, Macy's, Collector's Icon, Pin Offer		1.00	2.00
98	Basketball, Wilson, black with MJ silhouette, free with and $35.00 purchase (2.115)		35.00	45.00
-	Spray, M Jam, Cologne for Men, #01310	2.7 oz	20.00	25.00
-	Spray, Slam, MJ Deodorant Body Spray	3 oz	8.00	15.00

Year	**Costascos**			
90	Post Card, "Space the Final Frontier," red 23, reverse dunk, sunset at skyline in background (2.116)			15.00
90	Post Card, Standing, 23 white, 3 x 9 (2.117)			10.00
90	Post Card, dunk, red 23, 3.5x 10 (2.118)			10.00
90	Post Card, "Space The Final Frontier on top, Michael Jordan on bottom," reverse layup world in RH, red 23, back "MJ-Guard, CB, Space the Final Frontier," CB & Logo middle, Costascos Brothers on bottom	4 x 6	10.00	20.00
		28		
95	Poster Sample Card, A. Mourning/MJ background	3 x 5	8.00	15.00
-	Ad Card, Dunk over #44, Bucks, 3 x 9 (2.119)		8.00	15.00
-	Ad Card, Space, flying above Chicago skyline		8.00	15.00
-	Ad Card, Space 2, floating in sky, door size		8.00	15.00
-	Ad Card, Out of This World, floating in outer		8.00	15.00
-	Ad Card, Second Coming, coming down from heavens		8.00	15.00
-	Ad Card, MJ Jam Session, confident quote		8.00	15.00
-	Ad Card, Aerial Assault		8.00	15.00
-	Ad Card, The Great Chicago Flyer		8.00	15.00
-	Ad Card, 5,4,3,2,1; Jordan rocket		8.00	15.00
-	Ad Card, Class for All Seasons; MJ, Payton, Dawson		8.00	15.00

Year	**D.B. Kaplan's Delicatessen in the Watertower Place**	**mag #**		
-	Napkin, D. B. Kaplan's, MJ picture (2.120)	front		15.00

2.116

2.117

2.118

Year	Daily Herald Newspaper			
6/13/91	A glorious Bull run to NBA title	inside	20.00	25.00
6/15/92	What a sweet repeat!	cover	1.00	20.00
6/17/92	Bold Bulls call in No.3 in '93	cover	15.00	20.00
6/21/93	The Triple Crown!	cover	10.00	15.00
10/7/93	Goodbye Michael	cover	10.00	15.00
11/7/93	The Final Ovation	cover	10.00	15.00
3/19/95	I'm Back	cover	8.00	12.00
3/20/05	Up, Up & Away	cover	6.00	12.00
4/17/96	Sports, Bull's Eye	cover	6.00	12.00
6/12/96	The Un4GettaBulls	cover	6.00	12.00
6/17/96	Souvenir Section, Chicago Bulls 1996 NBA Champions	cover	6.00	10.00
6/12/97	Winning cures all	cover	5.00	10.00
6/14/97	5 Golden Rings!	cover	5.00	10.00
6/15/97	The Party Continues	cover	5.00	10.00
6/17/96	Souvenir section, Chicago Bulls 1997 NBA Champions	cover	6.00	12.00
6/8/98	Bulls Rewrite History Book	cover	4.00	8.00
6/15/98	Sweet Six Team!	cover	4.00	8.00
6/16/98	Sports, What we do know	cover	4.00	8.00
6/17/98	Sweet Sorrow	cover	4.00	8.00

Year	Duncan Yo-Yo			
95	Red, "Stack 1 Way" one side, MJ pog other side two hand shot over head, white #23		35.00	50.00
	—-1992 Duncan mini "Yo-Yo Trick Book" inserted (2.121)	417054		
95	Red, "Kap V" one side, MJ pog other side, stand with clenched fist, red #45		35.00	50.00
	—-1992 Duncan mini "Yo-Yo Trick Book" inserted (2.121)	417054		
95	Red, "Queen" woman's face on one side, MJ pog other side shooting two hands, red #23		35.00	50.00
	—-1992 Duncan mini "Yo-Yo Trick Book" inserted (2.121)	417054		
95	Red, "TNT" one side, MJ pog other side, reaching up for the ball white #45		35.00	50.00
	—-1992 Duncan mini "Yo-Yo Trick Book" inserted (2.121)	417054		
95	Red, "Rent A Cop" one side, MJ pog other side, walking with back view to us, red #23		35.00	50.00
	—-1992 Duncan mini "Yo-Yo Trick Book" inserted			

2.119

2.120

2.121

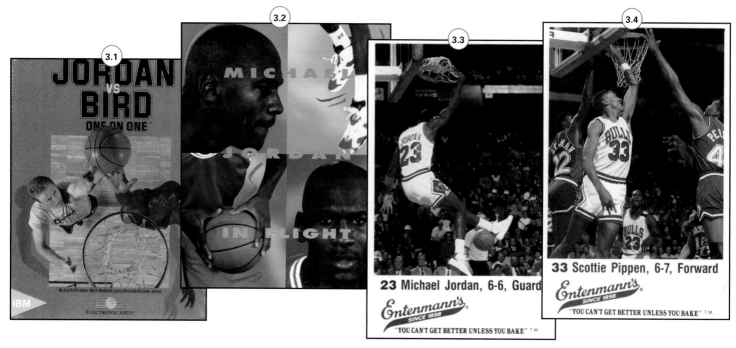

Year	Electronic Arts Computer Games			
88	IBM, Jordan vs. Bird One on One Game, computer game Bird & MJ under basket reaching for BB on rim, ISBN #1-55543-240-9 (3.1)		14633 01436	60.00
92	IBM, MJ In Flight Game, 3.5" disc, MJ in multi-colored uniform, dunking, back has 4 MJ pictures, ISBN #1-55543-605-6 (3.2)		14633 441701	35.00

Year	Entenmanns Bakery Card Sets	card # # cards		
87-88	Bulls Set, 2-5/8" x 4"	12 cards	150.00	225.00
	——MJ (3.3)	23	100.00	125.00
	——Scottie Pippen/MJ front (3.4)	33	20.00	25.00
88-89	Bulls Set, 2-5/8" x 4"	12 cards	100.00	150.00
	——MJ (3.5)	23	75.00	100.00
	——Charles Davis/MJ front (3.6)	22	10.00	15.00
	——Scottie Pippen/MJ front (3.7)	33	20.00	25.00

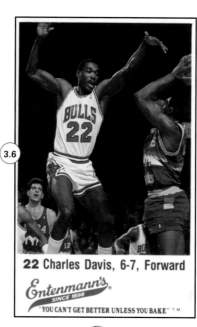

Year	Environment	coin # # coins		
94	Medallion Set (3.8)	2 coins	35.00	50.00
	—MJ name, picture in baseball cap, No. 45 & Birmingham Barons on front, silver, MJ in BB uniform & batting helmet, mintage 25,000	252		
	—Birmingham Barons Baseball on front, silver, "B" on back, mintage 5,000	252		
94	Medallion, MJ name, picture in baseball cap, No. 45 & Birmingham Barons on front, silver, MJ in BB uniform & batting helmet, mintage 25,000 (3.8)	4,956	35.00	50.00
95-96	Card & Medallion Set, 500 sets produced (3.8)		225.00	300.00
	—Silver Coin with gold trim	334		
	—#45 He's Back Metal Card, nickel/silver etched, 24kt gold trim	334		
95-96	Ad Sheet, Card & Medallion Set		1.00	2.00
95-96	Ad Sheet, Commemorative Proof Set		1.00	2.00
95-96	Medallions 95-96 Commemorative Proof Set, black case, 500 sets produced (3.8)		160.00	225.00
	—24kt Gold Select Medallion, MJ dunking, #23	163		
	—Silver Medallion, Chicago Bulls, logo, & stats	163		
	—Bronze Medallion, MJ on back	163		
95-96	Medallion, Most Wins in an NBA Season, 72-10, Chicago Bulls, Logo, front, silver, 1966 Chicago Bulls 1996, 30 Years and Running, XXX, 15,000 sets produced (3.8)	6,181	35.00	50.00
96	Ad Sheet, #45 He's Back Medallion & Card		1.00	2.00
96	MVP Scoring Champion, silver, 10,000 mintage	coin	market	price
96	MVP Scoring Champion, 24kt select, 1,996 mintage	coin	market	price
96	MVP Scoring Champion 3 piece set, 500 mintage	3 coins	market	price
96	MVP Scoring Champion, gold, 96 mintage	coin	market	price
96	Coin/Card, Scoring Champion & MVP, silver, 500 mintage		market	price
96	Coin/Card, Scoring Champion & MVP, 24kt select, 23 mintage		market	price
96	Bulls Team Set, silver, 1,000 mintage	6 coins	market	price
96	Bulls Team Set, 24kt select, 196 mintage	6 coins	market	price
96	Chicago Bulls "Best Record in NBA, History" silver, 500 mintage	5 coins	market	price
96	8 Time Scoring Champion, silver, 10,000 mintage	coin	market	price
96	Scoring & MVP silver, 2,500 mintage	card	market	price
96	Scoring & MVP, 24kt select, 1,996 mintage	coin	market	price

Year	Equal Card Sets	card # # cards		
89-90	Bulls Team Set, 3"x 4.25"	12 cards	20.00	35.00
	—MJ (3.9)	23	12.00	15.00
	—Ed Nealy/MJ front (3.9a)	45	3.00	5.00

Year		size or #of item		
90-91	Bulls Team Set, The Silver Season, 25th Anniversary, The Star Company	16 cards	15.00	25.00
	—MJ (3.10)	23	10.00	15.00
90-91	Bulls Glossy Team Set, The Silver Season, 25th Anniversary, The Star Company	16 cards	125.00	200.00
	—MJ (same as 3.10, except glossy)	23		

Year   Farley Fruit Company

There are 12 different boxes with 3 sets of 4 cartons. Two sets are the same except they are 10 oz. and 40 oz. boxes. The third set has a special Michael Jordan Digital Watch offer. The third set is 10 oz. Each set of boxes has 3 different Michael Jordan photos on the side panel. Each box has four Michael Jordan trivia questions for a total of 16 questions. All boxes were inserted with 4 different fruit snack bags. Each bag has 4 different photos and 4 different answers to the trivia questions on the outside of the box. There were 10 packs of fruit snack bags in the 10 oz. box and 40 bags in the 40 oz box. The digital watch boxes are the most difficult to find. (3.12)

Year		size or #of item		
91	Full Sealed Box Set	10 oz	60.00	75.00
91	Box, poses on side; towel on head, golfing, rebounding white 23, Box A on bottom end flap	10 oz	15.00	25.00
91	Box, poses on side; holding ball white 23, layup blue shorts, behind the back dunk red 23. Box B on bottom end flap, 10 pouches	10 oz	15.00	25.00
91	Box, poses on side; shooting ball, arms on ball, dribbling red 23, Box C on bottom end flap	10 oz	15.00	25.00
91	Box, poses on side; shooting pool, closeup with tongue out, white 23 towel on shoulders hands on hips, Box D on bottom end flap	10 oz	15.00	25.00
91	Full Sealed Box Set, Digital Watch Offer	10 oz	75.00	120.00
91	Box, poses on side; towel on head, golfing, rebounding white 23, Special MJ Digital Watch Offer on front/back	10 oz	25.00	40.00
91	Box, poses on side; holding ball white 23, layup blue shorts, behind the back dunk red 23, Special MJ Digital Watch Offer on front/back	10 oz	25.00	40.00
91	Box, poses on side; shooting ball, arms on ball, dribbling red 23, Special MJ Digital Watch Offer on front/back	10 oz	25.00	40.00
91	Box, poses on side; shooting pool, close up with tongue out, white 23 towel on shoulders hands on hips, Special MJ Digital Watch Offer on front/back	10 oz	25.00	40.00
91	Full Sealed Box Set	40 oz	150.00	225.00
91	Box, poses on side; towel on head, golfing, rebounding white 23	40 oz	50.00	75.00
91	Box, poses on side; holding ball white 23, layup blue shorts, behind the back dunk red 23.	40 oz	50.00	75.00
91	Box, poses on side; shooting ball, arms on ball, dribbling red 23	40 oz	50.00	75.00
91	Box, poses on side; shooting pool, closeup with tongue out, white 23 towel on shoulders hands on hips	40 oz	50.00	75.00
91	Bag, full, holding ball	1 bag	4.00	6.00
91	Bag, full, dribbling right hand	1 bag	4.00	6.00
91	Bag, full, shooting overhead	1 bag	4.00	6.00
91	Bag, full, closeup	1 bag	4.00	6.00
91	Pogs, MJ dribbling, holding ball, shooting	3 pogs		
	—MJ dribbling		1.00	2.00
	—MJ ready to shoot		1.00	2.00
	—MJ tossing basketball		1.00	2.00
91	Watch, Wilson Action, black band loop & buckle, red "23" on loop, red "W" on buckle end, MJ with bb in right hand & basket on hole end, Mail in Offer, square black face no bezel, red "Wilson" & "Michael Jordan," square digital opening, sealed plastic holder	LMJ003 49353 05963	75.00	100.00

Year	Fasson Items, Canadian Product			
90	Sticker, "Chicago Times," "Crack n Peel Plus," 4 x 6 (3.13)		35.00	50.00
90	Sticker, dunking, "Crack n Peel Plus," 3 x 8.25 (3.14)		35.00	50.00
90	Sticker, closeup & towel, "Crack n Peel Plus," 3.25 x 3.5 (3.15)		35.00	50.00
90	Sticker, closeup & towel, "Crack n Peel Plus," 3.25 x 4.75 (3.16)		35.00	50.00

Year	Fax Pax World of Sports Cards	card # #cards		
93	Set, sealed box	40 cards	8.00	15.00
	—MJ Card (3.17)	7	4.00	8.00
-	Ad Sheet, Fax Pax and 5 European Sets, Fournier Estrellas NBA also (3.18)		15.00	20.00

Year	Finish Line		
98	Ad Mailer, dribbling, closeup head, view on back, AJFC logo (3.19)		2.00

Year	Flair Sheets			
95-96	Flair Hardwood Leader Sheet, non perforated	27 cards	25.00	35.00
	—MJ Card	4 of 27		

Year	Fleer Sheets			
92-93	Fleer/Shell Back 2 Back Sheets, perforated sheet	12 cards	5.00	15.00
	—S. King			
	—R. McCray			
	—S. Pippen			

3.13 3.14 3.15 3.16 3.17 3.18 3.19

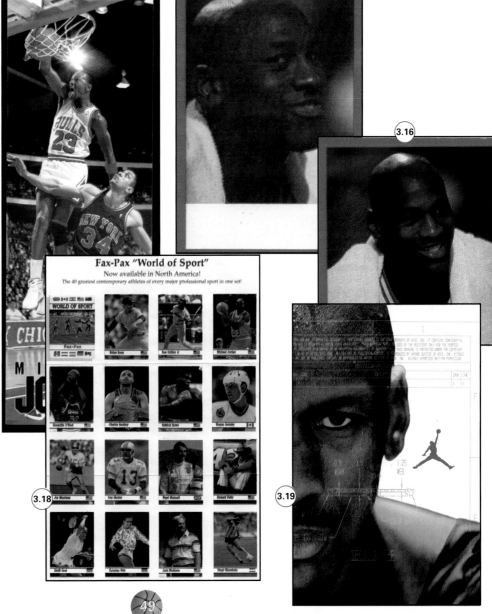

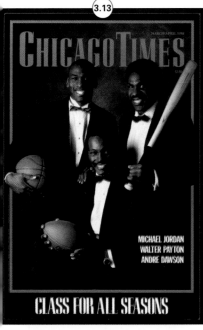

- —W. Perdue
- —S. Williams
- —B. Cartwright
- —B.J. Armstrong
- —H. Grant
- —M. Jordan Card
- —C. Williams
- —T. Tucher
- —J. Paxson

Year	Flip Flex Puzzle			
92	The Hidden Picture Challenge, Western Pub. Sealed (3.20)		40.00	65.00

- —MJ
- —E. Campbell
- —D. Wilkins
- —D. Robinson
- —P. Ewing
- —Slam Dunk Logo
- —Hidden Picture

Year	Formal Affair Tux	item #		
91	Disc, MJ 23 Night Celebrity Tuxedoes (3.21)		15.00	20.00
-	Book, Geno's All-Star Collection, hands out to side (3.22)	cover	12.00	15.00
	—"The Jam MJ Collection," "23 Night for MJ" logo on bottom right, picture inside, hands out to side		8.00	12.00
-	Sheet, Jam Full Dress Ad, MJ in Tux, hands behind back, "23 Night for MJ" logo on bottom white border (3.23)	405	3.00	62.00
-	Postcard, Street's Formal Shoppe," "23 Night for MJ" logo on bottom right, white & brown color, back "10% Discount on Prom or Banquet Order," address, hours and map, Thurston Moore Country, Ltd. Madison TN 37115 (3.24)		15.00	20.00

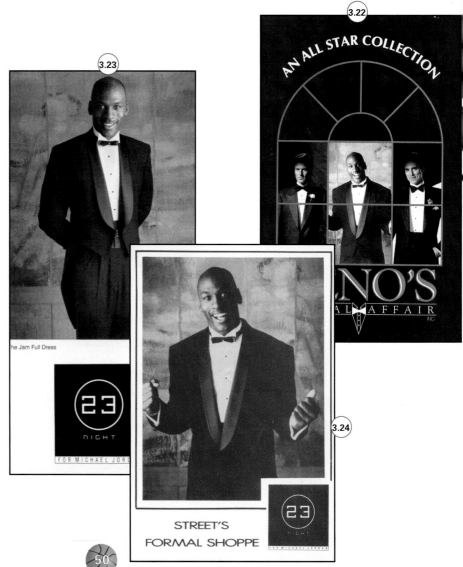

Year	Foto Products			
86	Window Decal, facsimile autograph under basket, holding ball, jumping	2.75 x 3.25	45.00	75.00
86	Window Decal, licensed by NBA Players Assoc. not NBA Properties, under basket, holding ball, jumping, production halted due to licensing problems	4 x 6	60.00	90.00

Year	Fournier NBA Estrelles	card# # cards		
88	Set	33 cards	20.00	35.00
	—-MJ on Box (3.25)		2.00	5.00
	—-MJ Card, Header (3.26)	NNO	8.00	10.00
	—-MJ Card (3.27)	22	8.00	10.00
88	Sticker (3.28)	5	12.00	15.00

Year	French	item #		
3/94	Sports Action Basketball, "Super Teams"	cover	20.00	30.00
93-94	Phone card, World Com, WS swinging bat, "Batman Mike"	5616	35.00	50.00
93-94	Phone card, World Com, red 23, ball in hands, jumping, "Flying Mike"	5317	35.00	50.00
97	Flip book, Animagic MVP BB 3D, not assembled, 2 closeups yelling	4 sheets	30.00	40.00
	—-Page 1 (3.29)			
	—-Page 2 (3.30)			
	—-Page 3 (3.31)			
	—-page 4 (3.32)			
97	Flip Book, Animagic MVP BB 3D, 2 closeups yelling, cover	small	45.00	75.00

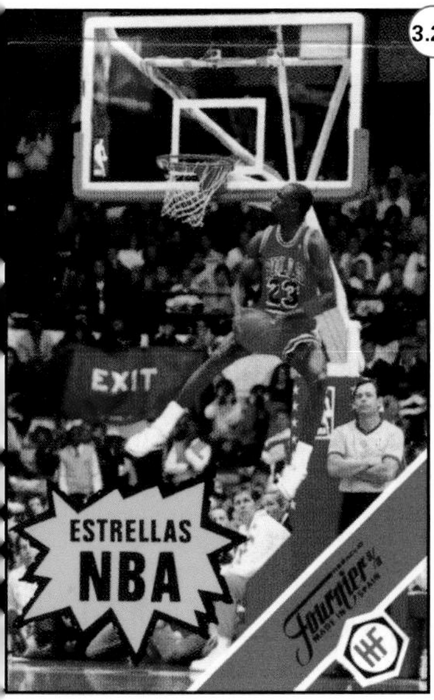

EXIT
ESTRELLAS NBA
3.25

EXIT
ESTRELLAS NBA
3.26

22
MICHAEL JORDAN
(Chicago Bulls)
Edad 25 Puntos 32,7
Altura 1,99 Rebotes 5,5
Puesto Base Asistencias 5,2
3.27

SIGUE TUS MEJORES CANASTAS CON
Fournier
VITORIA - SPAIN
Gran promoción «NBA»
SIGUE TUS MEJORES CANASTAS CON
Fournier
VITORIA - SPAIN
Gran promoción «NBA»
3.28

1
2
3
4
5
6
Michael Jordan
3.29

7
8
9
10
11
12
3.30

13
14
15
16
17
18
3.31

19
20
21
22
23
24
3.32

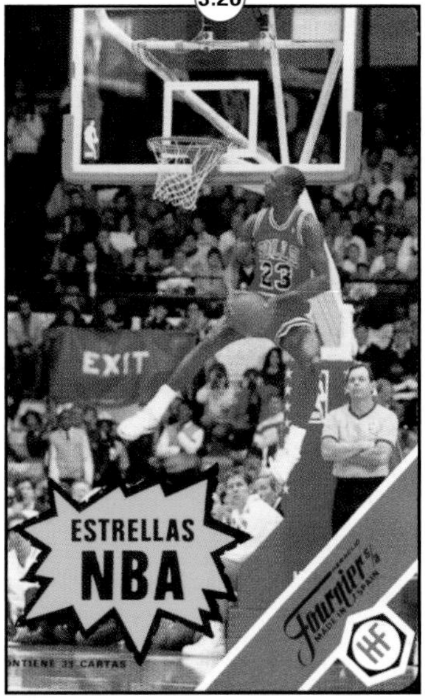

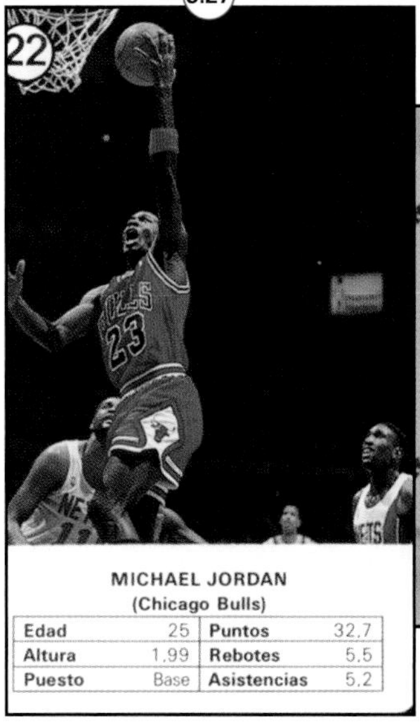

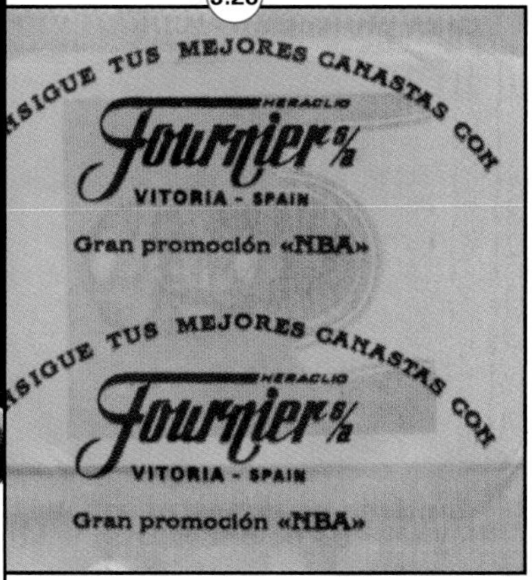

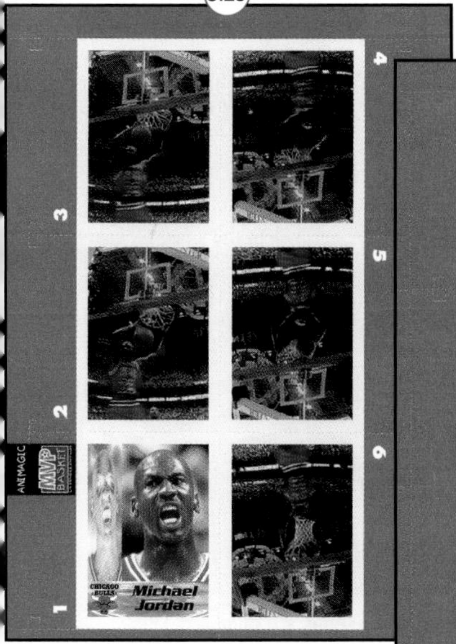

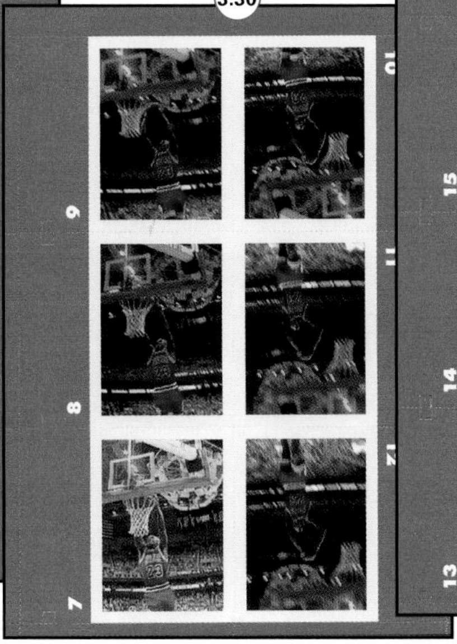

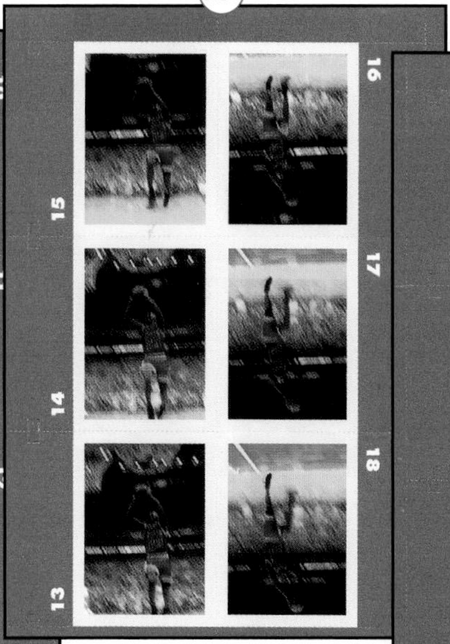

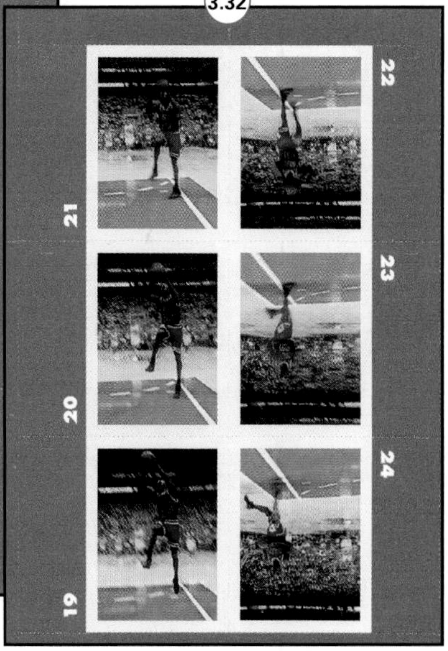

2/97	Magazine, Basket, MJ inside (3.33)	poster	15.00	25.00
97	Sheet, Best of Basketball, clear, red 23, closeup of teeth & towel		20.00	35.00
97	Sheet, Best of Basketball, clear, red 23, dribbling, tongue out		4.00	8.00
-	Cut out, "Basket," white 23, ball overhead shooting (3.34)		60.00	75.00
-	Iron-ons, Transferts: Conseils Et Precati, red/black initals, MJ jumping		25.00	35.00
-	Sheet, "Basket" stamps, "The Face 2 Face Chicago Bulls"		25.00	35.00
-	Sheet, "Basket" stickers, white 23, "Dunk Machine"		25.00	35.00
-	Tattoos, "Air Michael," jumping with ball over head, black 23		25.00	50.00

Year	Fugi	item #		
-	Pog Disc, BB like Pog Holder, Kukoc, MJ, Rodman, Longley, Pippen & Harper pictures front side, black signatures & Bulls logo back side (3.35)	6 pogs inserts	20.00	45.00

G

Year	Games-miscellaneous	item #		
87	Interactive VCR Games, The VCR Basketball Game, MJ on VCR tape	76625 80010	60.00	90.00
88	Cadaco, NBA Real Basketball in Miniature Game, MJ on cover and backboards, NBA Bas-Ket court, balls, net and levers to shoot balls (3.36)	267	45.00	75.00
91	Sports World Game Company, Hornet Mania, MJ listed on team sheet, dice, game board, team sheets, 2 chips		45.00	75.00
91-92	Sports Adventure Lets The Games Begin, box, book, 5-5" floppies, MS Dos Version		40.00	65.00
93	Wall Ball UD Sticker Sheet, 4 players		4.00	8.00
96	Display board, "NBA Pick-Up Game, Pick Three and Win Big," send in coupons, MJ on board		2.00	4.00
96-97	Cameo Container Corporation movable puzzle, "The World Champion Chicago Bulls, 96-97 Basketball Season," Bulls schedule calendar 11/97-4/97 on left side, top Bulls Logo and 4 trophies, front right side players SP, DR, SK, MJ, LL, JB, TK, RH; background front & back is wood grain, back "Un-Stop-A-Bulls" (player with a bulls head), "Taking The Fifth" (3.36a)	2.5' x 2.5'	75.00	125.00

Year	Gatorade	size		
89	Calendar, Slam Dunk Championship, Day Dreams Manufacturer	50895	20.00	30.00
90	Pin, "It's All You're Thirsting For"		30.00	40.00
91	Sticker, "It's All You're Thirsting For," crack and peel, black MJ signature, "$" sign on front, 8.25 x 7.5 (3.37)	453-92 IP/JT		15.00

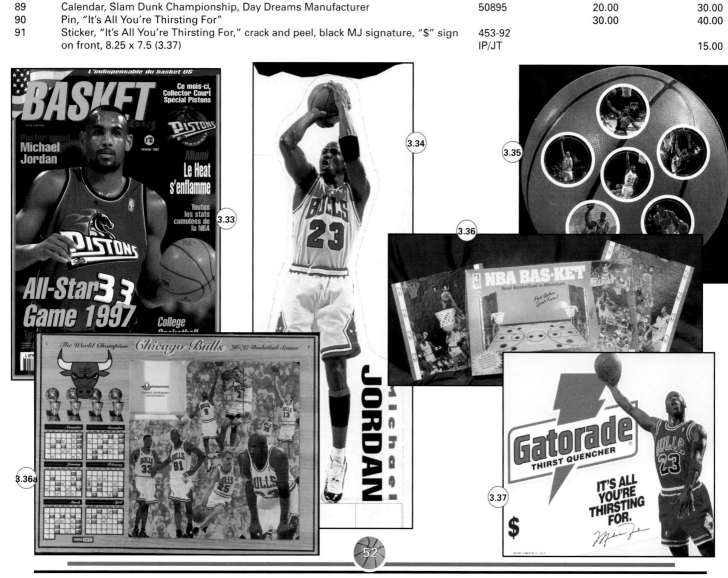

91	Ad Display, Jam Header Card and Figure for carton inserts, "It's All You're Thirsting For.," white signature, red 23, ball in right hand reaching over head, addition MJ figure to insert over MJ on the Ad Display to produce a 3D or die-cut effect (3.38)	45-4-92 19 x 32"	30.00	40.00
92	Can, Thirst Quencher, 14 quarts, Lemon Lime (3.39)	30.6oz	40.00	60.00
92	Figure, Life Size Cardboard, "Its All You're Thirsting For," white 23, dribbling with right hand, black signature, Gatorade logo and words in basketball	R6891 R92192	75.00	125.00
92	Juice Box, MJ Poster Offer, green, Lemon Lime Flavor (3.39a)	8.45oz	45.00	70.00
92	Juice Box, MJ Poster Offer, red, Fruit Punch Flavor (3.39a)	8.45oz	45.00	70.00
92	Juice Box, MJ Poster Offer, orange, Orange Flavor (3.39a)	8.45oz	45.00	70.00
92	Label, aqua, MJ dribbling right hand, looking right, red 23, 1988 Defensive Player of the Year, Tropical Fruit Flavor, red arm band left forearm, blue signature (3.40)	32 oz	15.00	
92	Label, black, MJ dribbling right hand, looking front, red 23, Mike's #1 Flavor top front, Citrus Cooler Flavor, white signature (3.41)	32 oz	15.00	
92	Label, black, MJ dribbling right hand, looking front, red 23, Mike's Favorite Flavor top front, Citrus Cooler Flavor, white signature (3.42)	32 oz	15.00	
92	Label, blue, MJ jump shot, red 23, Hold NBA playoff record points scored-Citrus Cooler Flavor, blue signature, red arm band left forearm 63 against Boston in 1986 (3.43)	32 oz	15.00	
92	Label, blue, glass bottle, MJ jump shot, red 23, Hold NBA playoff record points scored 63 against Boston in 1986, Citrus Cooler Flavor, blue signature, red arm band left forearm	32 oz	15.00	
92	Label, green, glass bottle, MJ dribbling right hand, looking left, red 23, Lemon Lime Flavor	32 oz	15.00	

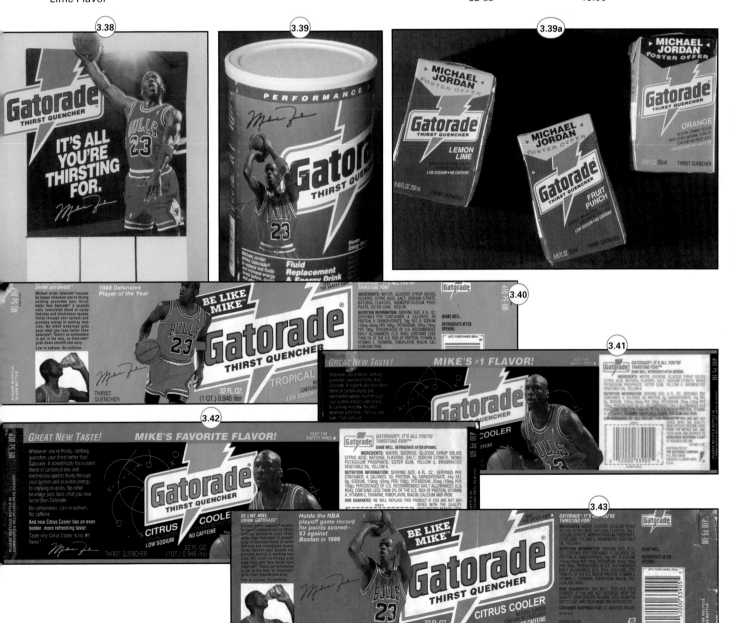

Year	Description	Size	Price	Price2
92	Label, green, MJ dribbling right hand, looking left, red 23, Led NBA in scoring 87, 88, 89, 90, 91, Lemon Lime Flavor, black signature, red arm band left forearm (3.44)	32 oz	15.00	
92	Label, green with aqua boarder, MJ hand print, "The Big Grip," Tropical Burst Flavor, MJ Air Plan	1 gallon	15.00	
92	Label, orange, MJ holding ball in USA #9, Member 92 Dream Team, Orange Flavor (3.45)	32 oz	15.00	
92	Label, red, MJ dribbling right hand, looking left, white 23, Named 91 NBA Finals MVP, Fruit Punch Flavor, black signature, black arm band left elbow (3.46)	32 oz	15.00	
92	Label, red, glass bottle, MJ dribbling right hand, looking left, white 23, Named 91 NBA Finals MVP, Fruit Punch Flavor, black signature, black arm band left elbow	32 oz	15.00	
92	Label, yellow, glass bottle, MJ right hand dunk, red 23, Lemonade Flavor	32 oz	15.00	
92	Label, yellow, MJ right hand dunk, red 23, 87 & 88 Gatorade Slam Dunk Champ, 88 All Lemonade Flavor, black signature Star MVP (3.47)	32 oz	15.00	
92	Magazine Sheet, "Gatorade Slam, Dunk Winology" (3.48)	2 sheets	3.00	
92	Window Ad, "Be Like Mike, Drink Gatorade," sticky clear background, red 23, ball in RH, layup, black signature	R91292 R92492	45.00	60.00
93	Ad, "Nothing Beats Gatorade, Works 30% Faster Than Water," cardboard, MJ holding plastic bottle, white/red shirt	28" x 20"	25.00	40.00
93	Label, black, MJ dribbling right hand, looking front, red 23, Citrus Cooler Flavor, Mike's Favorite Flavor top front (3.49)	64 oz	15.00	
93	Label, black, plastic jug, red 23, MJ dribbling right hand, looking front, Citrus Cooler Flavor, Mike's Favorite Flavor top front	64 oz	15.00	
93	Magazine Sheet, "Gatorade Quenchology" (3.50)		3.00	

93	Ad, #23, red undershirt, 6.5 x 7.5 (3.51)	R9-19-93	25.00	
94	Sticker, "Quench It," 3D, towel on shoulders, 6.5 x 7 (3.52)	KB-39-94	25.00	
95	Book Cover, "Drive+Skills+Guts+Passion+Life" (3.53)		5.00	10.00
95	Book Cover, "Life is Sport, Drink it Up, What's on Your Mind," MJ walking on his own head (3.53)		6.00	12.00
95	Label, green with light green border, plastic jug, "The Big Grip," MJ hand print, Lemon Lime, blue & white signature	1 gallon	5.00	10.00
95	Label, green with blue border, plastic jug, "The Big Grip," MJ hand print, Tropical Burst, blue & white signature	1 gallon	5.00	10.00
95	Label, green with orange border, plastic jug, "The Big Grip," MJ hand print, Orange, blue & white signature	1 gallon	5.00	10.00
95	Label, green with yellow border, plastic jug, "The Big Grip," MJ hand print, Lemon Ice, blue & white signature	1 gallon	5.00	10.00
95	Label, blue with black border, plastic jug, "The Big Grip," MJ hand print, Cool Blue Raspberry, blue & white signature	1 gallon	5.00	10.00
95	Mask, "Life is Sport, Drink it Up, What's on Your Mind," MJ walking on his own head		6.00	12.00
95	Shelf Insert, "Life is Sport, Drink It Up," blue t-shirt, holding bottle right hand, t-handle top, MJ picture bottom (3.54)	GGC0128C96	3.00	
96	Magazine Sheet, "Life is Sport," closeup head view (3.55)		2.00	
96	Magazine Sheet, "Life is Sport," back "Buzz Beamer" (3.56)		2.00	
96	Magazine Sheet, "Life is Sport," back "Sports Shorts"			
97	UD/Gatorade Send In Card, "MJ Four Time NBA Champions 1991, 1992, 1993, 1996," envelope, backing, MJ holding ball on front with Harper in background, MJ pointing on back, 3 x 5 (3.57)	MJ-1	3.00	
97	Window Ad, acetate sticker, dribbling ball RH, white 23, "Life is a Sport Drink it UP" in upper left, 7 Eleven logo in bottom left, Lemon Lime 32 oz and Fruit Punch 20 oz in lower right	14 inches x 3 feet	35.00	60.00
-	Can, MJs Favorite, from Korea, Citrus Cooler, full (3.58)	340 ml 12 oz	50.00	100.00

Year	Golden Jigsaw Puzzles	item #		
1992	USA Basketball Barcelona '92, 300 pieces, 2 x 3 feet, team picture with 10 players, sealed box (3.59)	5159	75.00	90.00
	——Insert Card			
1992	USA Basketball Barcelona '92, 200 pieces, Skybox group picture with 5 players	5471A	30.00	50.00
1992	USA Basketball Barcelona '92, 200 pieces, 5 Skybox single cards on puzzle	5471D	30.00	50.00
	——NBA Sky Box Insert Card			
1992	NBA Inside Stuff Slam Dunk, Sky Jams, MJ, Shawn Kemp, Tom Champers, 200 piece puzzle with Magazine Coupon Offer	5474C	75.00	125.00
1993	Slam Dunk Champions, 1985-92, 300 pieces, Wilkens, Walker, Ceballos, Brown, Jordan, Nance, Webb on cover	5226	70.00	100.00

Year	Grolier Story of America Cards	card #		
96-97	-Life in America Series			
	——-Chicago Bulls, 97 NBA Champs	118 9	50.00	100.00
	——-MJ, The Bulls Win NBA Championship (3.59a)	E-16	50.00	100.00
	——-Magic Johnson/MJ front	49-10	50.00	100.00

H

Year	Hanes Underwear	size	
93	Display Board, Briefs Rebate Coupon, Fathers Day, 2 MJ views holding underwear/Air Time Video	9" x 12"	15.00
93	Display Board, MJ Air Time Video, Rebate Offer, $5.00	17" x 12"	15.00
93	Magnet, red signature, brown coat, closeup, smiling, white t-shirt (3.60)	#1	15.00
93	Magnet, red signature, brown coat, closeup mouth open with ball, white t-shirt (3.61)	#2	15.00
93	Magnet, black signature, brown coat, waist up view with ball, white t-shirt (3.62)	#3	15.00
95	Phone Card (3.63)	10 min	30.00
	——folder		
	——coupon, prepaid MJ phone card		
95	Phone Card (3.64)	15 min	35.00
	——folder		
95	Phone Card (3.65)	20 min	40.00
	——folder		
	——coupon, prepaid MJ phone card	#RN15763	
	——post card, Holiday Phone Card, Promotion		
	——mailing envelope		

3.59

3.59a

3.60

3.61

3.62

3.63

3.64

3.65

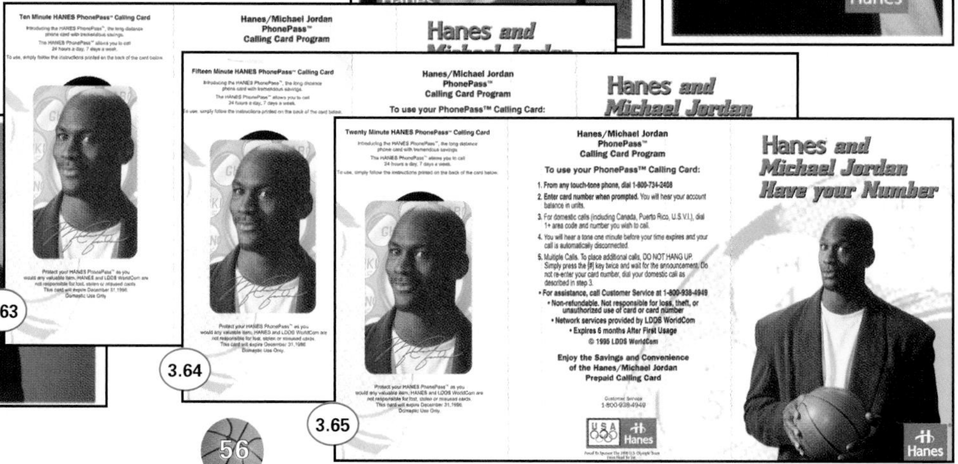

95	Coupon, Prepaid MJ Phone Card (3.66)	RN15763	2.00	
97	Box, underwear, empty, MJ front, red & black (3.67)	medium	2.00	
	——Insert, MJ front (3.68)	5 x 8	5.00	
97	Package, Knit Boxers, large, no boxers (3.69)	90231	15.00	
97	Package, Knit Boxers, x small, no boxers (3.70)	90228	15.00	
-	Ad Sheet, MJ holding basketball in street clothes, folded sheet, white signature, MJ for Hanes, Hanes red logo	11 x 17	1.00	2.00

Year	Hang Time Gum			
92	Ad Sheet, Free Life Size Poster		5.00	10.00
92	Order form, Life Size Michael Jordan Poster (3.71)		2.00	3.00
94	Pack, grape flavor, pink, under small photo on back: Named NBA MVP, 1991 (3.72)		10.00	15.00

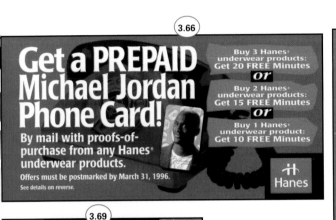

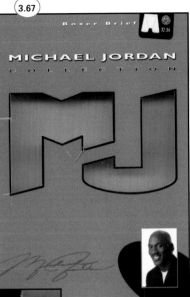

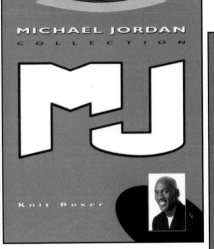

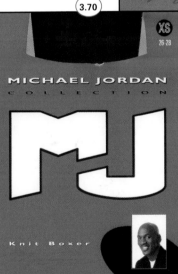

94	Pack, grape flavor, purple, under small photo on back: Selected NBA Rookie-of-the-Year, 1984-85 (3.73)		10.00	15.00
94	Pack, original flavor, red, under small photo on back: Pro Team: Chicago Bulls (3.74)		10.00	15.00
94	Pack, original flavor, red, small print for "weight" front bottom, under small photo on back: Pro Team: 1991 NBA World Champion Chicago Bulls (3.75)		10.00	15.00
94	Pack, strawberry flavor, pink, under small photo on back: Became only the second player ever in the NBA to score over 3,000 points in a season (3.76)		10.00	15.00

| 94 | Pack, strawberry flavor, pink, under small photo on back: NBA Finals Most Valuable Player, 1991 (3.77) | 10.00 | 15.00 |

Year	High School & Junior High School		
75-76	Yearbook, "1975-1976 M.C.S. Noble Yearbook," bird carrying banner "Happy Birthday America 1776-1976," 7th grade, blue cover white lettering and bird, no page numbers in book (3.78) cover	1000.00	1700.00
	—MJ in 7th grade class picture, striped t-shirt with white collar, edge, listed as "Mike Jordan" (3.79)	pg. 15	

76-77   Yearbook, "TheYear1977 Emma B. Trask" in white letters, white bear in white square
with three lines on red front cover, "Emma B. Trask 7th & 8th Center" on insides title
page, MJ in 8th grade (3.80)   cover   900.00   1,600.00
—MJ's class picture with Mrs. Moore's Eighth Grade, MJ in print shirt, open
collar, shoulder to head photograph, listed "Michael Jordan" (3.81)   pg. 12
—MJ's basketball team picture, MJ in front with #42 (3.82)   pg. 38

77-78	Yearbook, D.C. Virgo Junior High School, "Horizons 78" bottom right front, color front cover with water falls, trees, rocks & rainbow, back cover tan, 9th Grade (3.83)	cover	800.00	1500.00
	—-maybe MJ	pg. 3		
	—-maybe MJ	pg. 4		
	—-MJ	pg. 5		
	—-MJ sitting, waist up view, print shirt, collar open, white t-shirt underneath, arms on legs, listed as "Mike Jordan" (3.84)	pg. 27		
	—-MJ class picture, dark sweater with white collar underneath, listed as "Mike Jordan" (3.85)	pg. 34		
	—-MJ in "Paw Print" staff picture, striped sweater with white collar underneath, in third row standing against paneled wall, listed as "Mike Jordan" (3.86)	pg. 59		
	—-MJ in "Physical Conditioning Club" picture, in warmups sitting first row, listed as "Michael Jordan" (3.87)	pg. 65		
	—-MJ in "Football" team picture, third row, listed as "Mike Jordan" (3.88)	pg. 72		
	—-MJ in "Boy's Basketball" team picture, kneeling, white #12 first row, listed as "Mike Jordan" (3.89)	pg. 74		
	—- maybe MJ	pg. 85		
1/78	Newspaper, Paw Print, D.C. Virgo Junior High School, MJ listed on Paw Print Sports Staff (3.90)	V3 N3	50.00	200.00
	—-"Mike Jordan" listed as Paw Print Staff under "Sports" (3.91)	page 2		

—-"Mike Jordan" listed as member of "Cougars 77-78 Basketball Team," article on top left of page (3.92)   page 6

—-"Mike Jordan" listed as leading scorer with 26 points, win over Jacksonville on 12/15, article on top right (3.92)   page 6

—-"Mike Jordan" listed as leading scorer with 37 points with win over Clear Run, article on bottom left (3.92)   page 6

| 78-79 | Yearbook, "The Spinnaker 1978-1979," traffic light on cover, Emsley A. Laney High School, blue cover with yellow letters and traffic light, MJ's Sophomore year (3.93) | cover | 700.00 | 1400.00 |

—-MJ pictured with the Junior Varsity Football Team, pictured in top row, listed as "Mike Jordan"   pg.73

—-MJ pictured with the Junior Varsity Basketball Team, pictured in bottom row, listed as "Mike Jordan"   pg. 84

—-MJ jumping for tip-off   pg. 84

—-MJ batting for rebound, #45 jersey   pg. 85

—-MJ class picture, listed as "Mike Jordan"   pg. 150

| 79-80 | Yearbook, "Nineteen Eighty Spinnaker '80," gold pirate on blue front cover, Emsley A Laney High School, MJ's junior year (3.94) | Vol. 4 cover | 600.00 | 1000.00 |

—-MJ color picture with group that served refreshments at the Junior Senior Prom, MJ in 4th row back right (3.95)   pg. 9

—-MJ's Junior class picture, in plaid shirt, listed as "Mike Jordan" (3.96)   pg. 110

—-MJ playing defense against #64, MJ reaching for ball with right hand, #23 white (3.97)   pg. 166

Twenty-two Sophomores served refreshments at the Junior Senior Prom: **1st row:** Richard Ellison, Steve Latham, Alan Moore. **2nd row:** Todd Parker, Robert Diemel, Roderick Gaymon, John Chisolm. **3rd row:** Suzanne Talley, Kelley Reaves, Carol Blanton, Kim Rawley, Laura Lawrence, Diana Babson, Yolanda Butcher. **4th row:** Mary Jeffries, Leroy Smith, Lynelle Williams, Vickie McKee, Anita Brown, Mike Jordan, Belinda Wilson.

Defensive moves are just as important as offensive moves. Kelvin Wells blocks a shot against Holy Cross.

Lynol Jones
Robert Jones
Mike Jonkheer
Darnette Jordan
Christie Jordan
Mike Jordan

—-MJ jumping and holding ball in right hand, white #23, crowd in background on bleachers (3.98) · pg. 166

—-MJ slam dunking with right hand, "Welcome" in background on gym wall (3.99) · · · pg. 167

—-MJ near bench-timer table waiting to enter the game · · · · · · · · · · · · · · · pg. 168

—-MJ pictured in Fellowship of Christian Athletes Club, group picture, MJ in fifth row center, golf shirt and white t-shirt, listed as "Mike Jordan" (3.101) · · · · · · · · pg. 187

—-MJ pictured in Spanish Club, group picture, MJ in third row center, dark sweater, white shirt, listed as "Mike Jordan" (3.102) · pg. 220

80-81   Yearbook, "Buccaneers 1981" bottom right, Emsley A. Laney High School, Buccaneer repeated 13 times in green, blue, purple, orange, red, yellow and black letters on white insert over blue background, Senior year (3.103)   Vol. V cover   1000.00   2000.00

—-MJ in suit with vest, waist up view, listed as "Michael J. Jordan," member of baseball team 10, 11, 12; basketball team 10, 11, 12; homeroom rep 10; Spanish Club 11; FCA 10, 11, 12; Track 11; New Hanover Hearing Board 12; Boys State 11; Football 10; Pep Club 10 (3.104)   Pg. 127

3.98

3.99

3.103

3.102

3.101

3.104

3.105

BUCCANEERS
BUCCANEERS
BUCCANEERS
BUCCANEERS
BUCCANEERS
BUCCANEERS
BUCCANEERS
BUCCANEERS
BUCCANEERS
BUCCANEERS
BUCCANEERS
BUCCANEERS

BUCCANEERS 1981

—-MJ pictured with basketball team, #23 white shirt with striped pants, back row, listed as "Mike Jordan" (3.105)

—-MJ slam dunking from side of basket (3.106)   pg. 200

—-MJ eating cereal, plaid shirt #23 (3.107)   pg. 200

—-MJ shooting a foul shot (3.108)   pg. 202

—-MJ with Coach Herring posing for "Star News," press release (3.109)   pg. 202

—-MJ's family picture for donating money   pg. 202

—-MJ pictured with baseball team in second row, listed as "Mike Jordan"   pg. 218

    pg. 219

—-MJ sitting on front end of Pontiac Grand Prix, license plate "Mike," warm ups, holding BB in right arm, holding books in left arm (3.110)   pg. 2

—-MJ hand written note to Mary, listed only in "Mary" yearbook only (3.111)   inside cover

81   Pamphlet, Laney HS Graduation Information   75.00   125.00

Year	Highland Mint Cards & Medallions	coin # # coins		
95	Card, bronze, baseball (3.112)	18	75.00	100.00
	Card, silver, baseball (3.112)	18	275.00	300.00
	Card, gold, baseball (3.112)	18	700.00	900.00

Year				
95-96	Coin, bronze, MJ picture, name, 23, & signature, on front, Hardcourt Heroes, dates, back, 25,000 produced (3.8)	18,003	10.00	20.00
95-96	Coin, silver, MJ picture, name, 23, & signature, on front, Hardcourt Heroes, dates, back, 7,500 produced (3.8)	6,724	25.00	50.00
95-96	Coin, gold, MJ picture, name, 23, & signature, on front, Hardcourt Heroes, dates, back, 100 produced (3.8)	80	1,100.00	1,500.00
95-96	Coin, silver, First 70 Win Season, Chicago Bulls, Logo, 1995-1996, 1966 Chicago Bulls 1996, XXX, logo, 30 Years and Running, 2,500 produced (3.8)	991	35.00	60.00
95-96	Coin, silver with gold picture & signature on front, Signature Series, gold Hardcourt Heroes, MJ & number on back, 1,000 produced (3.8)	770	100.00	150.00
95-96	MJ & Bird Set, 7,500 issued (3.8)		60.00	100.00
	—Coin, MJ, pictures, names, team numbers & signatures on front	101		
	—Coin, Bird, Hardcourt Legends, names, & dates on back	101		
96	Card, bronze, basketball (3.112)	190	55.00	75.00
96	Card, silver, basketball (3.112)	190	275.00	350.00
96	Card, gold, basketball (3.112)	190	600.00	750.00
96	Highland Mint Magnum Discs		market	price
	—bronze			
	—silver			
	—gold			
96	Highland Mint Mini Mint Cards			
	—bronze, 5,000 mintage		75.00	250.00
	—silver, 1,000 mintage		185.00	260.00
	—gold, 500 mintage		330.00	450.00

Year	Hoops	item #		
1/87	Magazine			
3/21/87	Magazine, Mike Slam Dunk Cover, Bulls vs. Kings		45.00	65.00
2/1/88	Magazine, MJ Layup Shot with press notes, Bulls vs. Kings		40.00	60.00
89	Magazine, dunking, white #23 & signature, vs. NY #33 (3.114)	cover	35.00	55.00

Hoops NBA All-Star Sheets

Hoops issued perforated sheets of six cards that they produced for the NBA's All-Star programs sold at the Miami game in 1989 and the Charlotte game in 1990. It took 4 different programs to complete the 24-card set for the Miami game. For the Charlotte game there were 5 different sheets to complete the 30-card set. They are of standard card size but without numbers. Special Note: There is one panel that has not been previously listed with the following players: Larry Bird, Clyde Drexler and John Stockton.

| 89-90 | Sheet, NBA All-Star Game, Houston 2/10/89, Issued at 2/9/90 Miami Game, 15,000 produced, perforated sheet, 5.5 x 10.5 (3.115) | 4 of4 6 cards | | 8.00 |

3.8

3.114

3.115

	M. Eaton	174	
	M. Jordan	21	
	J. Worthy	219	
	P. Ewing	159	
	C. Drexler	69	
	C. Barkley	96	
90	Magazine, Alvin Robertson vs. MJ & Pippen		
90	Photo, NBA Official, dribbling, red 23, vs. Jazz, NBA stamp on front and back (3.116) 8 x 10		15.00
90	Photo, NBA Official, layup, red 23, vs. Mavericks, NBA stamp on front and back (3.117) 8 x 10		15.00
90	Photo, NBA Official, closeup, red 23, hands on hips, NBA stamp on front and back (3.118) 8 x 10		15.00
90	Photo, NBA Official, layup, white 23, vs. New York, NBA stamp on front and back (3.119) 8 x 10		15.00
90	Photo, NBA Official, jump shot, red 23, vs. Dumars, NBA stamp on front/back (3.120) 8 x 10		15.00

Hoops NBA Action Photo
There are 4 different borderless glossy color action photos (8 x 10) with career
statistics on the back. Two were released in Feburary 1990 and two more were
released in January 1991. Each have there own code # located on the bottom
corner next to the Bulls Logo on the front of each photo. The January 1991 releases
are presently difficult to find.

2/90	Photo, Action, Team Sets, layup, sealed pack, white 23, vs. New York (3.121)	90N1	
	—-cardboard backing, brown (3.122)	8 x 10	8.00

	—-Hoops insert ad brochure, tan (3.123)			
2/90	Photo, Action, Team Sets, jump shot, red 23, vs. Dumars (3.124)	90T32A		
	—-cardboard backing, brown	8 x 10		8.00
	—-Hoops insert ad brochure, tan			
90-91	Sheet, Hoops Kodak/Osco Drug Team Nite, Bulls 25th Anniversary, perforated sheet	11 cards		
	—-S. Pippen	10 x 10	10.00	20.00
	—-J. Paxson			
	—-M. Jordan Card			
	—-C. Levingston			
	—-B.J. Armstrong			
	—-S. King			
	—-D. Hopson			
	—-H. Grant			
	—-B. Cartwright			
	—-S. Pippen & H. Grant			
	—-W. Perdue			
90-91	Sheet, NBA All-Star Game, Miami 2/9/90, Issued at Charlotte 2/8-10/91, perforated sheet, 5.5 x 10.75 (3.125)	1 of 1 6 cards		7.00
	—-M. Jordan Card			
	—-J. Worthy			
	—-I. Thomas			
	—-A.C. Green			
	—-R. Miller			
	—-A. Olajuwon			
90-91	Sheet, NBA All-Star Game, Miami 2/9/90, Issued at Charlotte 2/8-10/91, perforated sheet, 5.5 x 10.75 (3.126)	2 of 2 6 cards		7.00
	—-K. Malone			
	—-E. Johnson			
	—-P. Ewing			
	—-D. Robinson			
	—-M. Jordan Card			
	—-C. Barkley			
7/91	Sheet, Commemorative Press Proof, 12th NSCC, Anaheim, CA; blank back (3.127)	8x10		25.00
91	Magazine, In Air Ready to Slam		15.00	25.00
1/91	Photo, Action, dunking, red 23, mouth open, 8 x 10 (3.128)	91N1		10.00

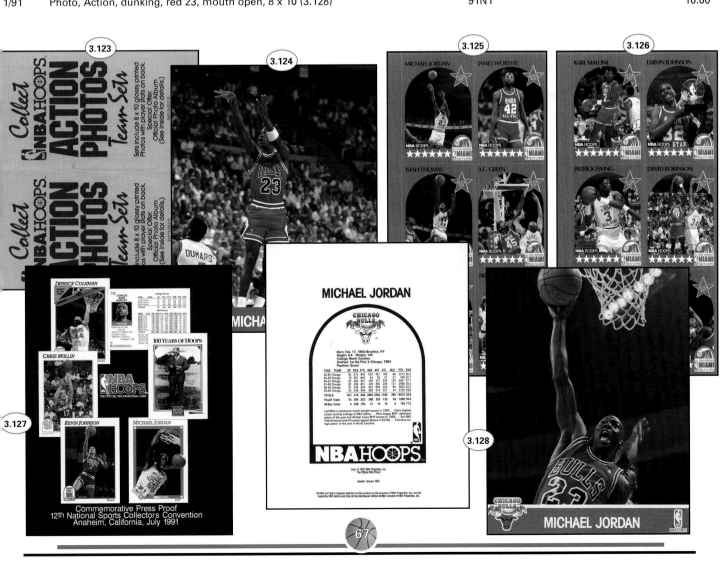

	—cardboard backing, white (3.129)			
	—Hoops insert ad brochure, blue (3.130)			
1/91	Photo, Action, holding ball, vs. Heat, red #23, 8 x 10 (3.131)	91T32B		10.00
	—cardboard backing, white			
	—Hoops insert ad brochure, blue			
91-92	Magazine Sheet, "Rise Above the Rest with UD," dunking, red 23, back "We're Jammin'," NBA Hoops Cards		2.00	3.00
91-92	Sheet, Team Nite		5.00	10.00
	-Kodak, Osco, Sports Channel, perforated sheet	12 cards		
	—J. Paxson	10 x 10		
	—C. Levingston			
	—B.J. Armstrong			
	—S. Pippen			
	—S. King			
	—M. Jordan MVP Card			
	—W. Perdue			
	—C. Hodges			
	—B. Cartwright			
	—M. Randall			
	—B. Hansen			
	—H. Grant			
95/96	Magazine, Mother's Cookies, 8.5 x 11 cards in game programs	4	25.00	50.00
95-96	Sheet, Jewel & Nabisco, perforated sheet (3.132)	9 cards		20.00
	—P. Jackson	7.5 x 10		
	—J. Caffey			
	—M. Jordan Card			
	—T. Kukoc			
	—L. Longley			
	—S. Pippen			
	—D. Rodman			
	—D. Simpkins			
	—Jewel & Nabisco Card			
6/96	Magazine, Playoff Hopefuls		15.00	20.00
96-97	Sheet, Jewel & Nabisco, perforated sheet (3.133)	9 cards		20.00
	—R. Harper	7.5 x 10		
	—M. Jordan Card			
	—S. Kerr			
	—T. Kukoc			
	—L. Longley			
	—S. Pippen			
	—D. Rodman			
	—P. Jackson			
	—Nabisco & Jewel Card			

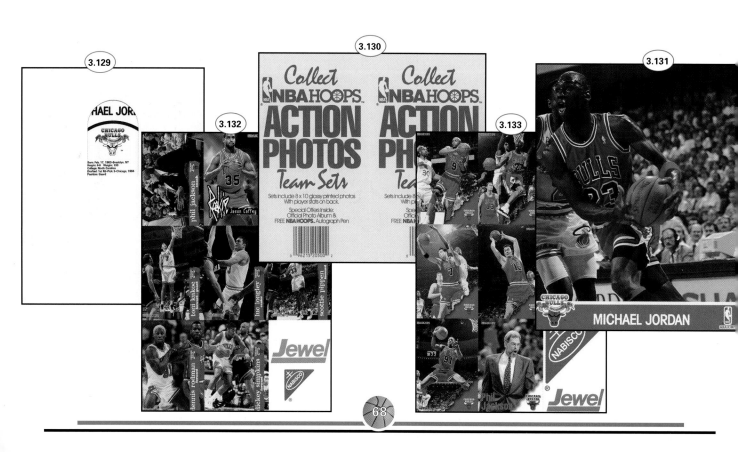

Year	Illinois			
91	Coupon, Flip Book, mail in with 15 Little Lotto bonus points (3.134)	cover		5.00
91	Flip Book, Lottery (3.135)	cover		10.00
96	Brochure, Special Olympics Raffle, "MJ wants to give you the keys to his Blazer, All you have to give is $23.00," 2 MJ pictures on front, inside "How to Win," "Special Olympics Training for Life," back Dealers, Official Rules Regulations	cover	25.00	35.00

Year	Impel USA Cards	card # # cards		
91	Set	12 cards		
	—MJ (3.136)	12	5.00	7.00
	—Team Picture/MJ front (3.137)	18	3.00	5.00

Year	Israel Stickers	card #		
92-93	MJ holding ball with both hands, white USA #9 (3.138)	1	250.00	350.00
	MJ going for layup under basket, ball in right hand, red #23 (3.139)	2	250.00	350.00

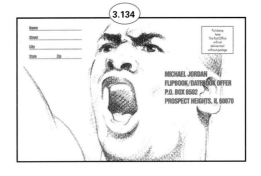

3.134

3.136

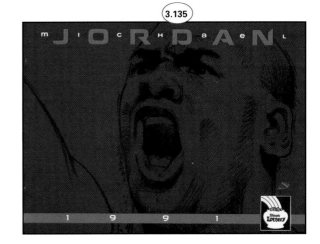

3.135

3.137

3.138

3.139

MJ shooting ball, right hand, mouth open, red #23 (3.140)	64	250.00	350.00
MJ background card, grouped in huddle around Phil Jackson, MJ, Pippen, Paxson, Grant, & Cartwright, "Chicago" bottom left (3.141)	66	150.00	250.00
MJ shooting vs. 21 New York, red #23 (3.142)	72	250.00	350.00
MJ going for layup, right hand, red #23 (3.143)	73	250.00	350.00
MJ kissing trophy, with hat, red uniform (3.144)	74	250.00	350.00
Ten pack holder, blue background, "Bulls Logo" center, red stripe top area, "NBA & NBA, Logo" on bottom front, back is blue with four packs lined up vertically, green, red, yellow and green packs, No MJ (3.145)	184272	5.00	10.00

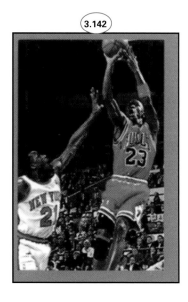

J-L

Year			
	Japanese McDonald's Card Set		
8/94	Cards, Japanese, McDonald's, NBA, "Be the Best! NBA McDonalds's"	3 cards	
	——MJ shooting, dunk right hand, red 23, Bullets & map on back, white stars on blue and red background on top back (4.1)	100.00	125.00
	——MJ pointing with right hand, white 23, Seattle Supersonics & map on back, white stars on blue and red background on top back (4.2)	100.00	125.00
	——MJ dribbling with right hand, looking left, red 23, Detroit Pistons & map on back, white stars on blue and red background on top back (4.3)	100.00	125.00
Year	**Japanese Playing Card Set**		
90	Soccer player on cover card, sealed card deck 52 cards	45.00	75.00
	——MJ CardQueen of Spades		
Year	**Jell-O Products, 6 container cartons**	# cards	
96	Carton, Space Jam Pudding Snacks, Chocolate/Vanilla Swirls, , Green Stripe (4.4)	3 cards	12.00
	——Daffy Duck		
	——MJ Card		
	——Pound		
96	Carton, Space Jam Pudding Snacks, Chocolate, Brown Stripe (4.5)	3 cards	12.00
	——Bugs Bunny		
	——MJ Card		
	——Lola bunny		
96	Carton, Space Jam Gelatin Snacks, Tropical Fruit Punch/Orange/ Strawberry/Banana, Red Stripe (4.6)	3 cards	12.00
	——Road Runner		
	——MJ Card		
	——Blanko		
96	Carton, Space Jam Gelatin Snacks, Strawberry, Red Stripe (4.7)	3 cards	12.00
	——Sylvester		
	——MJ Card		
	——Bang		
96	Carton, Space Jam Gelatin Snacks, Strawberry & Raspberry, Red Stripe (4.8)	3 cards	12.00
	——Porky Pig		

―MJ Card
―Bang

96	Carton, Space Jam Gelatin Snacks, Wild Watermelon & Rhymin' Lymon, Green to Pink Stripe (4.9)	3 cards	12.00	
	―Foghorn Leghorn			
	―MJ Card			
	―Bupkus			
96	Coupons-2, Save $.30 on Jell-O Gelatin Snacks, Save $.30 on Jell-O Pudding Snacks, Jell-O Snacks Instant Win Game (4.10)	10113 10116	2.00	

Jerseys: For information on Jerseys, please see Appendix I, located near the end of the book.

Year	Jewel Products			
85	Prism Sticker- "Michael Jordan" red with black outline, 1985 NBPA on right side, lime green shiny background, silver & rainbow like border with a black line, main picture right side of card red 23 waist-up shot, smaller picture left side jumping to hoop ball in right hand white 23, 2-cartoon like picture of MJ, bottom left corner signature, 2-11/16" x 4," blank back	NNO	400.00	900.00
91-92	Oreo Team Nite Sheet, 8.75 x 13.75 (4.11)	12 pictures	15.00	20.00
	―MJ Picture			
	―Number 3 Oreo Stacking Coupon Contest Winner			
	―Save $1.00 Coupon at Jewel for package of Oreos			

Year	John Wooden Award			
91	Cards & Book, Wooden Award Set, # of 28,000	22 cards	10.00	20.00
	―MJ (4.11a)	13		

Year	Jump, Gibson & Cleo	item #/# items		
89	Button pin, Gibson, ball in right hand, red 23, white signature	8-0010/3"	10.00	
89	Button pin, Gibson, dribbling right hand, white #23, black signature (4.12)	8-0011/3"	10.00	
89	Button pin, Gibson, looking, red 23, black signature	5-0011/3"	10.00	
89	Magnet Button, Gibson, dribbling, tongue out, black signature (4.13)	70010	15.00	
89	Magnet Button, Gibson, closeup, gold signature	70011	10.00	
89	Magnet Button, Gibson, closeup, black signature (4.14)	40011/2.5"	12.00	
90	Greeting Card, Gibson, red front, dribbling, white signature, It's impossible to keep up with you! What's New? (4.15)	52729	8.00	

4.9

4.10

4.11

4.11a

MICHAEL JORDAN

4.12

4.13

4.14

4.15

Year	Description	Code	Price 1	Price 2
90	Magnet, Jump Inc., 2 pictures on one magnet (4.16) ——closeup, waist up, red 23, looking ——closeup, holding basketball, red #23	NNO	10.00	
90	Wrapping Paper, Gibson, 2 sheets, #289wh131-1787, and #004-00175-9 (4.17) ——Insert MJ gift card	8.3 ft sq 3 x 4	60.00 45.00	75.00 60.00
9/91-12/92	Calendar, Gibson, "MJ Takes It to the Hoop In This Locker," dunking, white 23, #899Z80365	CA 316	15.00	20.00
91	MJ Indoor Sleeping Bag & Comforter in bag with Ad sheet, red & black bag with "Michael 23 Jordan" black portrait and dunking RH red 23, 40 Winks Industries Inc., Gibson/Jump, bag with MJ & #23 on top and bottom, label with "MVP World Champion All Star" and gold stars	30" x 67"	60.00	100.00
91	Ad sheet, MJ Indoor Slumber Bag & Comforter, purple top strip, little boy with bag, two pictures on bag on sheet, ERO Industries, Mt. Prospect, Ill.	ERO# 71533	15.00	20.00
91	MJ Indoor Slumber Bag & Comforter, BB in right hand, white 23, black, gray, blue, purple, orange background on front, purple inside, zipper on two sides, white back, 5 MJ front pictures, Jump Inc., 30" x 57"		60.00	100.00
91	MJ Mini Sleeping Bag, BB in right hand, white 23, black, gray, blue, purple, orange background on front, purple inside, zipper on two sides, white back, 5 MJ front pictures, Jump Inc., 9" x 18" (4.18)		50.00	75.00
91	Sticker, Jump Inc., black signature, one sticker, MJ front view jump shot, tongue out, 4.75" x 6" (4.19)	ST008	15.00	
91	Sticker, Jump Inc., black signature, one sticker, MJ side view jump shot, tongue out, 4.75" x 6" (4.20)	ST010	15.00	
91	Sticker, Jump Inc., 2 side by side pictures one sticker, hands on hips, red #23, jumping with ball mouth open white #23, 4.75" x 6" (4.21)	1 sticker	15.00	
91	Stickers, Cleo, Self Adhesive Valentine Basketball 4 sheets, #314-0086, 9 different pictures, red border (4.22)	36 stickers	15.00	
91	Stickers, Cleo, Self Adhesive Basketball, 4 sheets#314 0115, orange BBs on border, 9 MJ pictures (4.23)	36 stickers	15.00	

92	Calendar, Cleo, MJ + Giant MJ Action Photo, red 23, Slam Dunk Contest photo, #7050890011		
92	Calendar, Cleo, Dream Team, 92 USA Basketball Team, #260-7040	695 Cleo92	25.00
92-93	Calendar, Michael Jordan	999 Cleo93	25.00
		899 Cleo93	25.00
92	Greeting Card, MJ in black tux, red signature, white background, inside "You're Simply the Best" (4.24)	175QA995-0010	7.00
92	Greeting Card, MJ shooting ball right hand, back view, red 23, "You're 16," tan background, red stripes top and bottom, inside "...and you're simply the best! Happy Birthday" (4.25)	200BS341-0011	10.00
92	Greeting Card, MJ shooting ball, white 23, gold background, 6 black BBs, black stripes, white signature, "When it comes to being a Great Son...," inside "You never miss! Happy Birthday" (4.26)	200BN715-1005	10.00
92	Puzzle, Greeting Card Valentine, Cleo, one handed jump shot, slam dunk contest, "Have a High Flying Valentine's Day," 5-7/8 x 7-3/8 (4.28)	325-1011	9.00
92	Tags, Cleo, Self Stick, 6 tags of MJ dribbling in top & bottom, sections, #60-0219 (4.29)	6 tags	12.00
92	Tags, Cleo, Self Stick, 3 tags of MJ dribbling in bottom section, #60-0219, 3 tags MJ's name in top section (4.30)	6 tags	12.00
92	Tags, Cleo, Self Stick, 3 tags of MJ dribbling in top section, #60-0219, 3 tags MJ's name in bottom section (4.31)	6 tags	12.00
93	Calendar, The Best On Earth, The Best on Mars, Nike Calendar, MJ & Spike, black and gray background, #70508 90056	899 Cleo93	20.00

93	Calendar, Cleo, Michael Jordan, A 1993 Bonus 16 Month Calendar, highway background, dribbling left hand, red 23 front, #70508 90038	899 Cleo93	20.00
9/93-12/94	Calendar, Gibson, It's Michael, holding ball in RH, red 23, 16 month calendar, #899Z80727	CA 430	10.00
93	Shopping Bag, Cleo, MJ vs. Wilkins Slam Dunk Contest, 7 3/4" x 9 3/8" (4.32)	233 6004	8.00
93	Shopping Bag, Cleo, 2 poses of MJ front & back, yellow signature, 9.5" x 8.25" (4.33)	233-6045	8.00
93	Shopping Bag, Gibson, red, 3 MJ poses, 9 x 13 (4.34)	GB145	8.00
93	Valentines, Cleo, "Michael Jordan," sealed wall pack, #60 0232 (4.35)	15 cards 15 env.	12.00
93	Wrapping Paper, Gibson, MJ shooting, red background, 8.33 sq. ft., 2 sheets, sealed package (4.36)	035-073299	15.00
96	Greeting Card, Space Jam, front "MJ" and drawing like color picture, green inside, blue "MJ" and "What's Up Doc," yellow envelope (4.37)	50616	4.00
96	Greeting Card, Space Jam, front MJ dribbling and cartoon characters, "C'mon make a fast bweak!" green inside, "We got some celebwating to do! Happy Biwthday" (4.38)	50617	4.00
96	Greeting Card, Space Jam, MJ holding ball in left hand, Bugs & Monstars, "It Ain't Easy Being this Goodlooking & Talented," green dots on purple background inside, "However do we do it!" (4.39)	50621	4.00

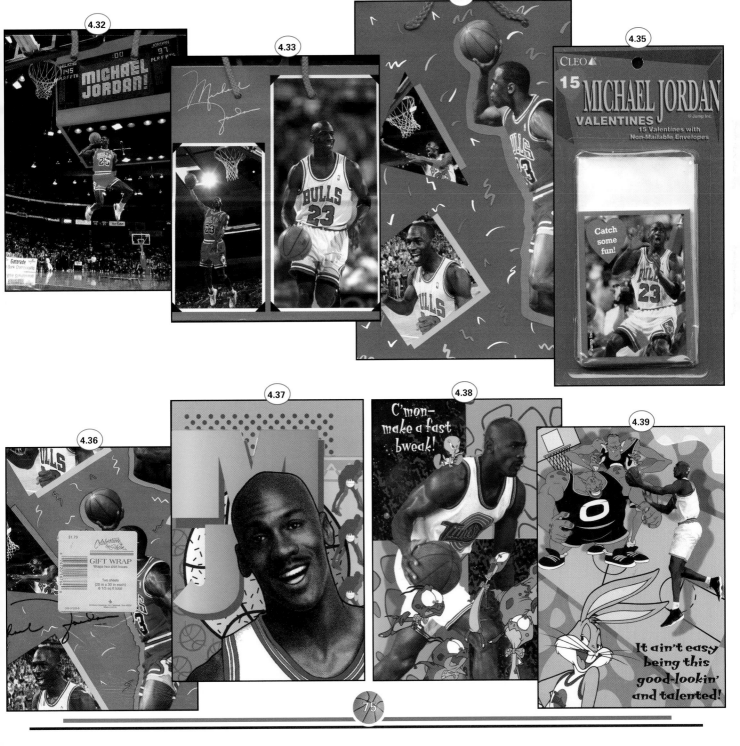

96	Shopping Bag, Cleo, Space Jam, purple, characters, 7.5" x 9.5" (4.40)	233-1282	5.00	
96	Wrapping Paper Roll, Space Jam, colored paper	35 sq. ft.	45.00	65.00
96	Wrapping Paper Roll, Space Jam, colored paper	10 sq. ft.	4.00	8.00
96	Wrapping Paper Roll, Space Jam, white & gray background with color figures	10 sq. ft.	4.00	8.00
96	Wrapping Paper Roll, Space Jam, white & gray background with color figures	35 sq. ft.	4.00	8.00
97	Greeting Card, Space Jam, MJ with blue colored monster "O," green dots on purple background inside, "Ever Have Just One Of Those Days" (4.41)	50622	4.00	
97	Greeting Card Rack Divider, Space Jam, black middle, colored ends, blank back (4.42)	028086279	1.00	
-	Cup, 4 MJ pictures, 5 black signatures	99PR610-0010	15.00	20.00
-	Pencil, MJ signatures, BB on top, red color		5.00	8.00
-	Wrapping Paper, Cleo, roll, red & white stripes with basketballs on it	50 ft	20.00	25.00
-	Wrapping Paper, MJ pictures, blue background, red letters, 2 sheets, sealed package	304-0300	3.00	6.00
-	Wrapping Paper, MJ shooting, blue background, white stripe with BB and signature, 2 sheets, sealed package	304-6296	3.00	6.00
-	Wrapping Paper, MJ shooting, red background, white stripe with BB and signature, 2 sheets, sealed package	304-0235	3.00	6.00

Jump, Gibson and Cleo Valentine Boxes and Cards
Early 1990s

Cleo and Gibson are subsidiaries of the Jump Company. There are 8 boxes, to our knowledge, with different Michael Jordan photos on the box fronts. The boxes have a count of 32 or 38 valentines, all of the same style.

There are also 6 different cut-out valentines from the back of the boxes. The cut-outs are identical to the insert valentines except they are on cardboard stock and have blank backs.

Listed below are the different paper stock valentines numbered 1 through 26 and the cardboard stock valentines numbered 27 through 32 (numbers were assigned by the author). The cardboard valentines are listed with the number of their corresponding match—insert valentines 1 through 27. For example, "27/4" refers to cardboard stock valentine number 27, which is identical to paper stock valentine number 4.

Note: #2, 13, have the same photo but 13 has extra comments printed, "Teacher, You're The Best!"

Note: #21, 22, have the same photo, but have different border colors, #21 is Red, #22 is Pink.

Note: #4, 20, have the same photo, but have different color borders and comments, "Teacher" is added.

Note: The two pairs, #8 & 10, and #11 & 23, have the same comments but all have different photos.

Note: Boxes with code numbers 7030, 7528, 3040 and 7508 are scarce in the present market.

	Low	High
Complete set of (8) full boxes	40.00	80.00
Common full box	5.00	10.00
Common empty box	2.00	4.00
Common cards (1-26)	.15	.30
Common cards (27-32)	.50	1.00

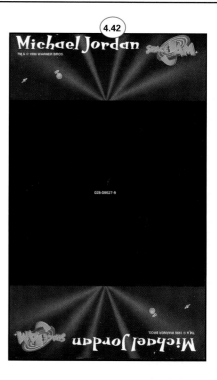

Under the company names below are the last four code numbers listed on the back of each box and the number of valentines in each box.
(All box codes' numbers are preceded by #350)

Valentine Box Names, Numbers and Counts	Gibson #7030 32 count	Cleo #6020 #3047 38 count	Gibson #7528 32 count	Cleo #7521 32 count	Cleo #3040 38 count	Cleo #2047 32 count	Cleo #7508 38 count	Cleo #2040 32 count
	A	B	C	D	E	F	G	H
Valentine Card Numbers and Descriptions								
1 Hi! Have a high flying day! (4.43)	●	●						
2 Hope your day is a Winner (4.44)	●	●						
3 Valentine, you're looking fine (4.45)	●	●						
4 You're a winner Teacher! (4.46)	●	●						●
5 Valentine, you're right up there Cool! (4.47)	●	●					●	
6 Hey, Champ! Have a great day (4.48)	●	●					●	
7 Slam dunk, a super day! (4.49)	●	●					●	
8 You're cool! (uniform) (4.50)	●	●					●	
9 Time out for fun! (4.51)	●	●			●	●	●	●
10 You're cool! (sweater) (4.52)	●	●			●	●	●	●
11 Have a high flying day! (photo from waist up) (4.53)			●	●			●	
12 You're 'in'! (4.54)			●	●			●	
13 Teacher, You're The Best! (4.55)			●	●			●	
14 You're The Coolest! (4.56)			●	●			●	
15 I'm on your team! (4.57)			●	●			●	
16 You're Lookin' Fine! (4.58)			●	●			●	
17 Catch Some Fun! (4.59)			●	●			●	
18 You Give Me A Lift! (4.60)					●	●		●
19 Happy Valentines Day! Champ! (4.61)					●	●		●
20 You're A Winner! (4.62)					●	●		●
21 No One Could Fill Your Shoes! (red background)					●	●		●
22 No One Could Fill Your Shoes! (pink background) (4.63)					●	●		●
23 Have A High-Flying Day! (photo of whole body) (4.64)					●	●		●
24 Lookin' Fine! (4.65)					●	●		●
25 Have A Jammin' Day! (4.66)					●	●		●
26 I Like Your Style! (4.67)					●	●		●
27/4 You're A Winner Teacher! (4.46)	●	●			●	●		●
28/9 Time Out For Fun! (4.51)	●	●			●	●		●
29/10 You're Cool (4.52)	●	●			●	●		●
30/7 Slamdunk, A Super Day! (4.49)			●	●			●	
31/13 Teacher, You're The Best! (4.55)			●	●			●	
32/15 I'm On Your Team (4.57)			●	●			●	

4.43

Hi!

Have a high-flying day!

Jump Inc.

4.44

BULLS 23

Hope your day's a WINNER

Jump Inc.

4.45

BULLS 23

Valentine, you're lookin' fine

Jump Inc.

4.46

You're A Winner, Teacher!

4.47

Valentine you're right up there!

BULLS 23

Cool!

© Jump Inc.

4.48

Hey, Champ! Have a great day!

BULLS 23

© Jump Inc.

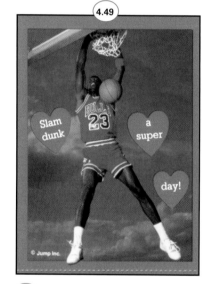
4.49

BULLS 23

Slam dunk

a super

day!

© Jump Inc.

4.50

© Jump Inc.

BULLS

You're

cool

!!!

4.51

Time out for fun!

BULLS

© Jump

4.52

You're cool!

© Jump Inc. © NBA Properties In

4.53

Have a high-flying day!

© Jump Inc.

4.54

You're "IN"!

BULLS 23

© Jump Inc.

4.55

TEACHER CARD

Teacher, you're the best!

BULLS 23

Hope your day's a WINNER

© Jump Inc.

LARGER CARDS REQUIRE FOLDING BEFORE PLACEMENT IN ENVELOPES.

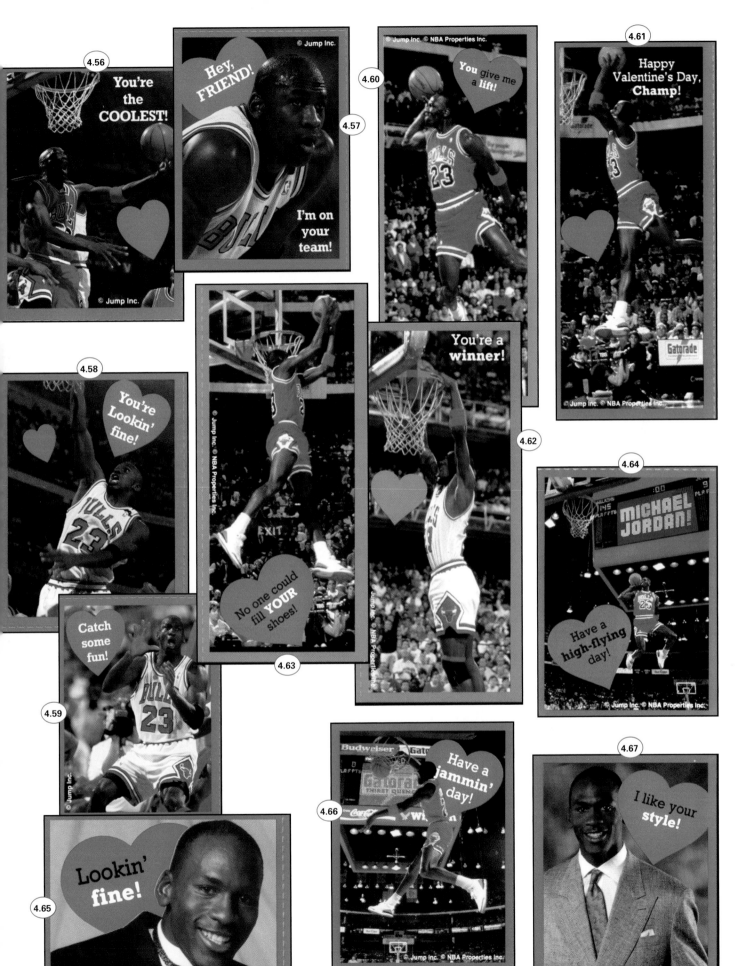

4.56 You're the COOLEST!

© Jump Inc.

4.57 Hey, FRIEND! I'm on your team!

© Jump Inc.

4.60 You give me a lift!

© Jump Inc. © NBA Properties Inc.

4.61 Happy Valentine's Day, Champ!

© Jump Inc. © NBA Properties Inc.

4.58 You're Lookin' fine!

4.63 No one could fill YOUR shoes!

© Jump Inc. © NBA Properties Inc.

4.62 You're a winner!

© Jump Inc. © NBA Properties Inc.

4.64 MICHAEL JORDAN! Have a high-flying day!

© Jump Inc. © NBA Properties Inc.

4.59 Catch some fun!

© Jump Inc.

4.66 Have a jammin' day!

© Jump Inc. © NBA Properties Inc.

4.67 I like your style!

© Jump Inc. © NBA Properties Inc.

4.65 Lookin' fine!

© Jump Inc. © NBA Properties Inc.

79

Jump, Gibson & Cleo Valentine Boxes and Cards. Space Jam 1996-1997

There are 5 different boxes, to our knowledge, with different Michael Jordan photos on the box fronts. The boxes have 32 or 40 valentines. The valentines have 7 different Michael Jordan photos. The table below details the differences in the 15 valentines listed. Valentine numbers were assigned by the author.

Note: #1, 2, 3, 4/2, 5, 6, 7, have the same front photo of Michael Jordan
Note: #4/2 is a cardboard stock cut-out valentine from the back of the box. The "/2" refers to the paper stock valentine that is numbered "2." The back of this valentine is blank.
Note: #5, 6, 7, have added MJ photo on back.
Note: #8, 9, 10, 11, 12, only have MJ photo on back
Note: #13, are stickers on a sheet
Note: #14, 15, have different MJ photos from the rest
Note: Boxes with code numbers 21179 and 411790 are scarce in the present market.

	Low	High
Complete set of (5) full boxes	35.00	60.00
Common full box	6.00	12.00
Common empty box	1.00	2.00
Common cards (1, 2, 3, 5, 6, 7, 8, 9, 10, 11, 12)	.15	.25
Common cards (4/2, 13, 14, 15)	.75	1.00

Listed under the company names below are the box code numbers listed on the box backs and the number of valentines in each box.

Valentine Box Names, Years, Numbers and Counts	Cleo—1996 8480-211790 32 count	Gibson—1996 249v59073 32 count	Cleo—1996 8480-411790 40 count	Cleo—1997 8480-1118km 40 count	Cleo—1997 8480-211890 32 count
	I	J	K	L	M
	•	•	•		
#1 (4.74) Tic-tac-toe back	•	•	•		
#2 (4.75) Cupid maze back	•	•	•		
#3 (4.76) Crossword puzzle back	•	•	•		
#4/2 Same as #2 (4.75) but blank back					
#5 Same as #1 (4.74) but postcard on back too				•	•
#6 Same as #2 (4.75) but postcard on back too				•	•
#7 Same as #3 (4.76) but postcard on back too				•	•
#8 (4.81) Bugs & Lola front				•	•
#9 (4.82) Bugs dancing front				•	•
#10 (4.83) 5 Nerdlucks front				•	•
#11 (4.84) Purple blanko front				•	•
#12 (4.85) Lola front				•	•
#13 (4.86) Sticker sheet				•	•
#14 (4.87) Hearts and postcard back					•
#15 (4.88) Valentine tote box					•

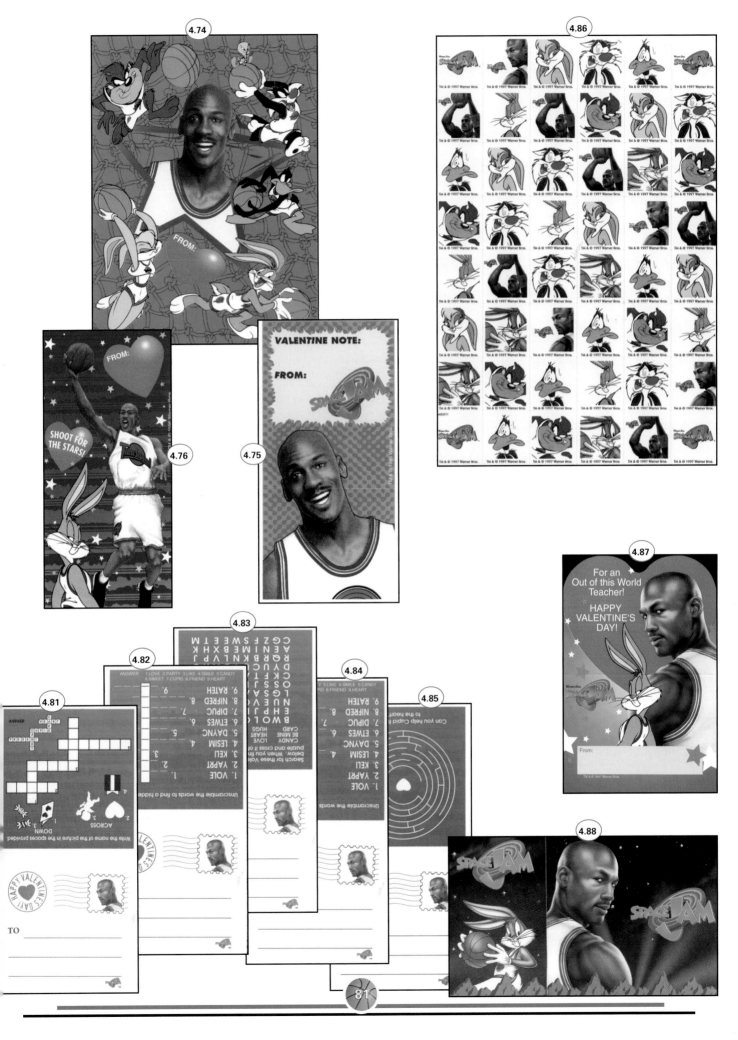

Space Jam Valentine Descriptions—-1996

#1   MJ head view in a "star." Taz, Tweety, Sylvester, Daffy, Bugs and Lola around the star, green background and one heart. Back has tic-tac-toe game, heart with ring around it and "To," and number 8480211-711.

#2   MJ close-up from shoulders, head tilted to right, white SJ shirt, gold background, "Valentine Note: From:" Back has game of Cupid finding his way to the heart, heart with ring around it and "To."

#3   MJ jumping with BB in RH overhead, Bugs looking over right shoulder, 2 hearts, one with "From" the second with "Shoot for the Stars!" Purple, green and blue stripes in background. Back has crossword puzzle game, heart with ring around it and "To."

#4/2   MJ close-up from shoulders, head tilted to right, white SJ shirt, gold background, "Valentine Note: From:" Blank back. Cardboard box cutout.

Space Jam Valentine Descriptions—-1997   (no cutouts on box backs, only pictures of valentines)

#5   MJ head view in a "star." Taz, Tweety, Sylvester, Daffy, Bugs and Lola around the star, green background and one heart. Back has tic-tac-toe game on 1/2 and MJ in stamp on postcard-like 2nd half, number 8480211-801.

#6   MJ close-up from shoulders, head tilted to right, white SJ shirt, gold background, "Valentine Note: From:" Back has game of Cupid finding his way to the heart on 1/2 and MJ in stamp on postcard-like 2nd half.

#7   MJ jumping with BB in RH overhead, Bugs looking over right shoulder, 2 hearts, one with "From" the second with "Shoot for the Stars!" Purple, green and blue stripes in background. Back has crossword puzzle game on 1/2 and MJ in stamp on postcard-like 2nd half.

#8   Bugs and Lola, 2 hearts the first with "From" and the second with "Will you be my Valentine," green and blue stripe in background. Back has crossword puzzle game on 1/2 and MJ in stamp on postcard-like 2nd half.

#9   Bugs dancing with hand in air, 2 hearts the first with "From" and the second with "You make my heart spin!" green and blue background with figures and stars. Back has word scramble puzzle on 1/2 and MJ in stamp on postcard-like 2nd half.

#10   Five Nurdlucks monsters with guns, 2 hearts, the first with "From" and the second with "You will be my valentine!" green and blue background. Back has word search puzzle on 1/2 and MJ in stamp on postcard-like 2nd half.

#11   Purple Blanko monster holding basketball, white square with "Valentine Note:" and "From." Back has word scramble puzzle on 1/2 and MJ in stamp on postcard-like 2nd half.

#12   Lola sitting on a yellow circle, one heart with "Happy Valentine's Day," red and pink background. Back has game of Cupid finding his way to the heart on 1/2 and MJ in stamp on postcard-like 2nd half.

#13   Sticker sheet, 4 stickers of MJ looking over left shoulder, 6 stickers of MJ shooting two hands overhead

#14   MJ giant bonus valentine, MJ looking over left shoulder with Bugs, big heart with "For an Out of this World Teacher! Happy Valentine's Day!" Back has red hearts on 1/2 and post-card like on second 1/2.

#15   Valentine Tote Box, MJ looking over right shoulder on front of tote.

K

Year	Kelloggs Cereal Box Cards-Germany			
96	Space Jam Movie Card Set, Germany, 3-D type of cards	7 cards	125.00	175.00
	——Bugs Bunny with hand to face	No. 1	5.00	8.00
	——Swackhammer eating and talking	No. 2	5.00	8.00
	——MJ & Tweety (4.89)	No. 3	45.00	60.00
	——Daffy & Lola	No. 4	5.00	8.00
	——MJ with right fist in air (4.90)	No. 5	65.00	75.00
	——Sylvester & Tweety	No. 6	5.00	8.00
	——Nerdlucks, two of them	No. 7	5.00	8.00

Year	Knowledge Adventure Computer Game			
92	"Sports Adventure Let the Game Begin," MJ front and back of box (4.90a)	5-5.25 discs	40.00	
	——Knowledge Adventure Brochure, foldout			
	——User Guide, MJ on cover same on box front			
	——Sports Adventure Entry Form, MJ on front & back (4.91)			
	——Free Bonus Disc offer form			

Year	Korea Cards			
93	Set	6 cards	300.00	375.00
	-MJ dribbling, red #23 uniform, back-power meter 15 (4.92)		45.00	60.00
	-MJ hook shot vs. Lakers, red #23, back-power meter 10statistics (4.93)		45.00	60.00
	-MJ dunk shot vs. Lakers, red #23, back-power meter 10statistics (4.94)		45.00	60.00
	-MJ jump shot/#41 Nuggets, red #23, back-power meter 5,statistics (4.95)		45.00	60.00
	-MJ closeup sneer, red #23 uniform, back-power meter 20,dribbling (4.96)		45.00	60.00
	-MJ closeup waist shot, red #23, back-power meter 5, dribbling (4.97)		45.00	60.00
	-S Pippen dunk vs. #37 Lakers card, with MJ in background, back-power meter 15, no picture (4.98)		10.00	15.00

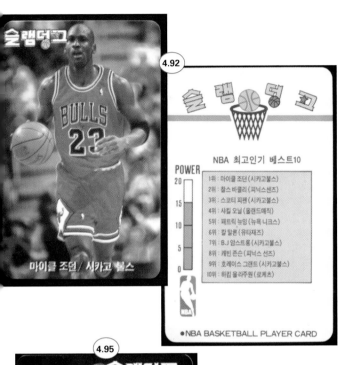

Year	Kraft Products		size	
96	Boxes, Macaroni & Cheese, poster offer on box		2 boxes	
	—MJ Space Jam Edition (4.99)		5.5 oz	4.00
	—The Cheesiest, MJ & Jam Characters (4.100)		7.25oz	4.00
96	Stickers, Name Tag Shrink, Space Jam Uniform, Australian Product, oven heated, personal data spaces on back 3 stickers			
	—front angle, dribbling right (4.101)			25.00
	—closeup head view (4.102)			25.00
	—waist up view, head tilt to MJ's right (4.103)			25.00

L

Year	LDDS & World Com Phone Cards	card #	
95	50 min, looking over shoulder, red "Jordan," t-shirt with white stripes, 4.5 x 6.75 (4.104)	2000	100.00
	—folder, "World Class," MJ name inside		
96	10 min, looking over shoulder, red "Jordan" t-shirt with white stripes, 2 x 3.5 (4.105)	2001	20.00
96	10 min, looking over shoulder, red "Jordan," t-shirt with white stripes, 2 x 3.5	2005	20.00
96	10 min, 3 pictures of MJ, shooting, 2 dribbling, red #23, 2 x 3.5	3996	20.00
96	10 min, 3 pictures of MJ, shooting, 2 dribbling, red #23, 2 x 3.5 (4.106)	1647	20.00
96	10 min, holding ball, black #23 with red stripes, 2 x 3.5	2075-706686	20.00
96	10 min, holding ball, black #23 with red stripes, big plastic sealed case (4.107)	30010	20.00
	—Ad card insert, MJ		

96	10 min, holding ball, black #23, with red stripes, sealed plastic case (4.108)	40010	15.00
96	20 min, holding ball, black #23, with red stripes sealed plastic case (4.109)	40020	15.00
96	30 min, holding ball, black #23, with red stripes sealed plastic case (4.110)	40030	20.00
96	50 min, holding ball to right side, 2 background pictures, red #23, white signature, 1630 of 2500 produced, 4.5 x 6.67 (4.111)	22476054870507	40.00
	—folder, "Introduction," BB, & white MJ signature on gray cover, inside MJ picture & "The MJ Jumbo Card" (4.112)		
96	60 min, holding ball, black #23 with red stripes, sealed plastic case (4.113)	40060	35.00
96	100 min, holding ball, black #23 with red stripes sealed plastic case (4.114)	40100	55.00
96	50 units, Space Jam, holding ring of characters, # of 3000 produced, 4.5 x 6.75 (4.115)	58749596964143	40.00
	—folder, "LDDS & World Com is pleased to introduce our new interstellar cosmic collectible!		
97	30 min., Space Jam, MJ holding ring of characters (4.116)	1570904024	15.00
	—package with MJ shooting, sealed, 2 x 3.25		

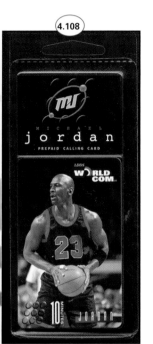
(4.108)

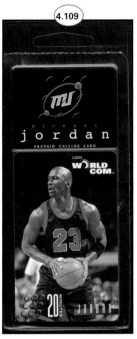
(4.109)

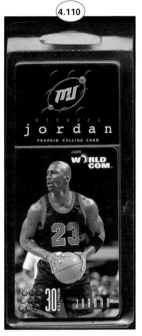
(4.110)

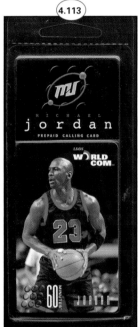
(4.113)

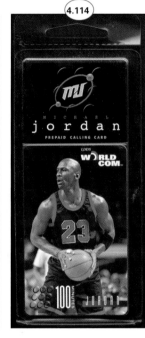
(4.114)

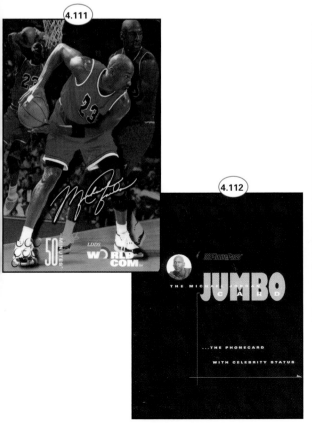
(4.111)

(4.112)

(4.115)

(4.116)

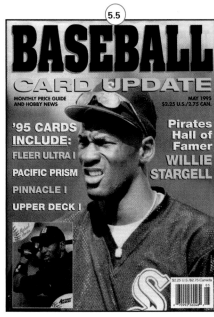

MAGAZINES AND BOOKS SECTION

Year	Baseball America Magazines			
11/10/91	If MJ Can Play in the Olympics		20.00	35.00
3/6/94	Scouting Report: MJ		10.00	20.00

Year	Baseball Cards Magazine	mag #		
12/90	Meet Your Favorite:, Sandberg & MJ Issue 64, Vol. 10, No. 12, Card(s), MJ on Skybox card (5.3)	cover	15.00	20.00
1/21/91	News Price Guide, MJ cover	V10 N2	10.00	20.00
5/94	"Sports Cards," formerly Baseball Cards, "Can Jordan Do It" (5.4)	V14 N5		
		#105	10.00	15.00
5/95	"Update," monthly price guide (5.5)	cover	16.00	20.00

Year	Basketball Annual Magazine	mag #		
91-92	Guide, Roster, Schedules, Statistics (5.6)	cover	3.00	6.00
91-92	Special NBA Preview, NBA Champion Chicago Bulls (5.7)	V 32	6.00	10.00
92-93	NCAA Hoop Fever, The Road to the Final Four (5.8)	V 33	6.00	10.00
92-93	Guide, MJ Eyes a Third Title (5.9)	cover	3.00	6.00

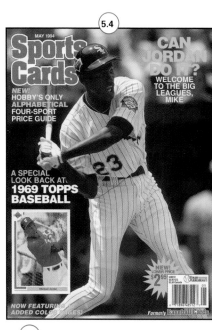

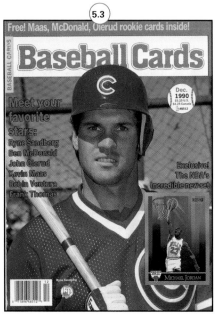

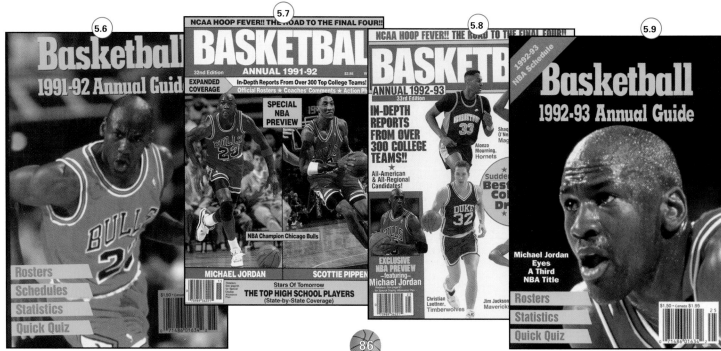

Year	Basketball Digest Magazine	mag #		
7/85	MJ Rookie of the Year (5.10)	V12 N8	20.00	25.00
86-87	NBA BB Yearbook, Teams to Beat		18.00	25.00
1/87	MJ Chicago's Raging Bull Challenges the NBA (5.11)	V14 N3	15.00	20.00
4/88	The New and Improved MJ (5.12)	V15 N6	12.00	18.00
6/89	MJ Player of the Year	V16 N8	12.00	18.00
88/89	NBA BB Yearbook, Teams to Beat, MJ, Bird, Thomas, Magic	cover	12.00	18.00
1/90	The NBA Zone Trap (5.14)	V17 N3	10.00	15.00
6/91	No 1! MJ is our Player of the Year (5.15)	V18 N8	7.00	12.00
92	Annual, MJ Cover with inserts of Malone, Mullin, & Ewing		7.00	12.00
6/92	Barcelona Bound, 92 Player of the Year, MJ (5.16)	V19 N8	7.00	10.00
92-93	NBA Preview-Can Anyone Knock Off Chicago? (5.17)		5.00	8.00

Year	Basketball Forecast Magazine	mag #		
88-89	Cover Story, CB Incomparable Sky Walker, NBA Scoring Champ & MVP	V 12	2.00	5.00
91-92	Superstar, Special Featuring MJ poster (5.19)	V 15	5.00	10.00
92-93	Dream Team Coverage, cover & poster		5.00	13.00
93-94	Superstar, Countdown to Immortality, 2 MJ posters/cover (5.20)	V 17	12.00	15.00

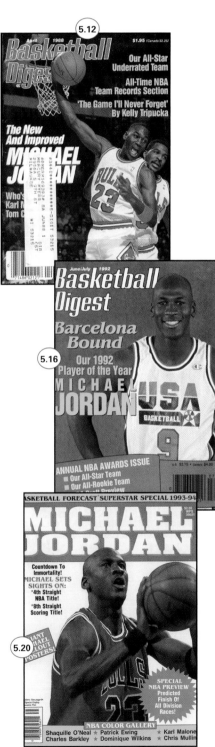

Year	Basketball Legends Book Set, Chelsea House, two book set		10.00	15.00
94	——MJ Book, by S. Dolan (5.21)	cover		
	——Babe Ruth Book, by N.L. Macht (5.22)			

				Year
	Basketball (Magazines/Books)			
87-88	Scene, 9th Big Year, Roundup of all NBA Teams (5.23)	cover	20.00	25.00
88-89	Dick Vitale's, Mega Talents Light Up NBA's Toughest Division	cover	18.00	24.00
89-90	Dick Vitale's, To 'Air' is Not Human!	cover	16.00	22.00
90-91	Dick Vitale's, Looking for A Title!	cover	16.00	22.00
90	Super Stars, B. Allison, dribbling left hand, paperback book (5.24)	cover	10.00	15.00
91	Awesome Guards by BJ Arneson, paperback book (5.25)	cover	2.00	5.00
91-92	Dick Vitale's, Bravo!, MJ & Bulls 2nd Title	cover	15.00	20.00
92-93	Action, Mike Warren's, Incredi-Bull	cover	15.00	20.00
92-93	Dick Vitale's, Colossal Collegians (5.26)	cover	15.00	20.00
93	Greats, by M. Teitelbaum, book (5.27)	cover	13.00	18.00
93-94	Hubie Brown's, Premiere Issue	cover	12.00	18.00

Year	Basketball Times Magazine			
3/15/84	Jordan & Perkins, BB's Best 1-2 Punch (5.28)	cover	150.00	200.00

Year	Beckett Magazines		mag #		
3/90	Basketball Card-MJ on cover (5.29)		1	9.00	15.00
91	Basketball Guide Premiere Edition (5.30)		1	5.00	10.00
5/91	Basketball-MJ on cover (5.31)		10	5.00	10.00
9/91	Basketball-MJ on cover (5.32)		14	5.00	10.00
7/92	Basketball-Olympics, MJ on back cover (5.33)		24	4.00	8.00
8/92	Basketball-MJ on cover (5.34)		25	4.00	8.00
2/93	Basketball-MJ on cover (5.35)		31	3.00	6.00
9/93	Basketball-MJ on cover (5.36)		38	3.00	6.00

12/93	Basketball-MJ on cover (5.37)	41	3.00	6.00
93	Dr. James Beckett Official Price Guide, Basketball Cards 1993, MJ front cover (5.38)	2nd ed	4.00	8.00
94	Tribute-Michael Jordan, cover, NC on back cover (5.39)	3	5.00	10.00
4/94	Baseball-MJ on cover (5.40)	109	3.00	6.00
1/95	Basketball-MJ on back cover (5.41)	54	3.00	6.00
5/95	Basketball-MJ on cover, MJ red 45 uniform (5.42)	58	5.00	8.00
5/95	Baseball-MJ on back cover	123	2.00	3.00
95	Sports Heroes-Michael Jordan (5.44)	1	9.00	15.00
95	Great Sport Heroes-Michael Jordan, hard cover (5.45)	1	15.00	20.00
2/96	Basketball-MJ on cover (5.46)	67	3.00	5.00

Date	Description	Qty		
3/96	Future Stars-MJ on cover, NC 23 (5.47)	59	4.00	7.00
4/96	Basketball-MJ on cover (5.48)	69	3.00	6.00
5/96	Bulls Tribute 72 Wins-MJ on cover (5.49)	16	5.00	10.00
6/96	Championship Commemorative-cover, 17th NSCC-Fantastic Four (5.50)	165	5.00	10.00
6/96	Basketball Card Price Guide-cover, 1st large size (5.51)	5	18.00	25.00
9/96	Basketball-MJ on cover (5.52)	74	4.00	8.00
96-97	Pro Basketball-MJ on cover (5.53)	4	5.00	10.00
97	Basketball Alphabetical Checklist (5.54)	1	14.00	14.00
8/97	Five High	85	4.00	6.00
97	Tribute: Chicago Bulls, V Championship, Commemorative Issue		7.00	10.00
12/97	Beckett, Chinese Edition, Premier Edition, cover (5.55)	1	20.00	25.00
97-98	Basketball Card Price Guide, MJ front	6	20.00	30.00

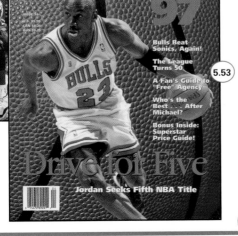

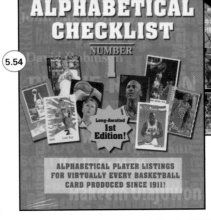

Year	Boon Extra Magazine			
91	Japanese, Jordan Premium, MJ merchandise, MJ in Hanes ad on back cover (5.56)	V-3	25.00	40.00
95	Boon Extra	cover	20.00	30.00

Year	Bull Pen Game Program	mag #		
90-91	25 Anniversary Issue, walking to team huddle, drawing like picture (5.57)	cover	7.00	10.00
90-91	25 Anniversary Issue, flying in air, basketball in right hand (5.58)	cover	7.00	10.00
94-95	He's Back, #45 (5.59)	E1 V3	20.00	25.00
94-95	A Drive for 4, Edition-1 (5.60)	Playoff	5.00	10.00
96-97	Who's Got Next?, Edition-1, Who's Got Next?		5.00	10.00
96-97	Dye Hard With A Vengeance (5.61)	E3 V2	5.00	10.00
96-97	Gimme Five. (5.62)	E4 V2	5.00	10.00
97-98	Six Shooter, The Bulls Top Gun	E7 V3	5.00	10.00
97-98	NBA Playoffs 98, closeup of face	cover	5.00	10.00

Year	Bulls BasketBull Magazine	mag #		
93	MJ, SP & B. Cartwright cover, post finals pub covers playoff, parade	cover	45.00	65.00
96	Four has a Nice Ring to It, MJ inside (5.63)	V7 N1	5.00	10.00

96	NBA at 50, MJ inside (5.64)	V7 N2	5.00	10.00
97	The Fifth Title Was A Work of Art, MJ inside (5.65)	V7 N9	20.00	
97	We'll Always Have Paris, Bulls Tower over Europe's Best, 97 McDonald's Championship, MJ cover with team	V8 N1	20.00	

Year	Bulls Game Programs	mag #		
86-87		cover	75.00	9.00
90-91	12/7/90, MJ jamming over Lambeer	cover	25.00	35.00
90-91	12/14/90, MJ flying in air	cover	25.00	35.00
91-92	12/10/91	cover	20.00	30.00

Year	Bulls Magazines & Books			
97	The Authorized Chicago Bulls Pictorial		40.00	50.00
98	Chicago Bulls Hoop, Year of Worm, MJ's Record Pace article	inside	20.00	25.00

Year	Bulls Media Guides			
87/88	All-Star Game, 2/7/88, Chicago, 38th Annual (5.67)	cover	35.00	40.00
88/89	West Side Story, Directed by Doug Collins (5.68)	cover	30.00	35.00
89/90	The Adventures of Chicago Bulls (5.69)	cover	25.00	30.00
90/91	Chicago Bulls (5.70)	cover	20.00	25.00
91/92			20.00	25.00
92/93	Chicago Bulls Back 2 Back (5.71)	cover	20.00	25.00

5.64

5.65

5.67

5.69

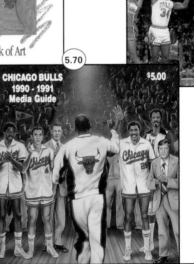

5.70

5.68

5.71

93/94	CB NBA World Champions 91-92-93, 3 Trophy Cover (5.72)		15.00	20.00
94-95	Chicago Bulls-United Center cover (5.73)		5.00	10.00
95-96	30th Anniversary Bulls Logo Cover		10.00	15.00
96-97	NBA 50th (5.74)	cover	20.00	30.00

Year	Bulls Playoff Guides & Magazine			
94-95	NBA Eastern Finals, Bulls vs. Magic, "MJ He's Back #45"	cover	20.00	25.00
95	Official Playoff Guide, MJ, SP, Jackson, TK, BJA	cover	20.00	25.00
95-96	NBA Finals, Bulls vs. Seattle	cover	20.00	25.00
96	Official Playoff Guide, shot from above center court		15.00	20.00
96	Official Playoff Program, MJ, SP, DR on cover	cover	15.00	20.00
96	Official NBA Finals Guide, Bulls Team Art		15.00	20.00
97	Official Playoff Guide, MJ Action Art cover		10.00	15.00
97	Official NBA Finals Guide, Bulls Team glossy	cover	10.00	15.00

Year	Bulls Tip Off Magazine			
94	HOOP, MJ in SP Ameritech Uniform, tongue out, Michael's Back, No. 23, Send CS..., holding ball (5.75)	cover	8.00	15.00
95	HOOP, MJ dribbling RH, red 45, P. Jackson Still Playing His Role...(article) (5.76)	cover	7.00	15.00
96	no HOOP, MJ holding trophy, P. Jackson Strangely Successful (article) (5.77)	cover	7.00	12.00
96	HOOP, MJ in 3 pictures, P. Jackson Strangely Successful (article) (5.78)	cover	7.00	12.00
97	HOOP, S. Pippen dunking on cover, MJ name on cover & inside (5.79)	inside	5.00	10.00

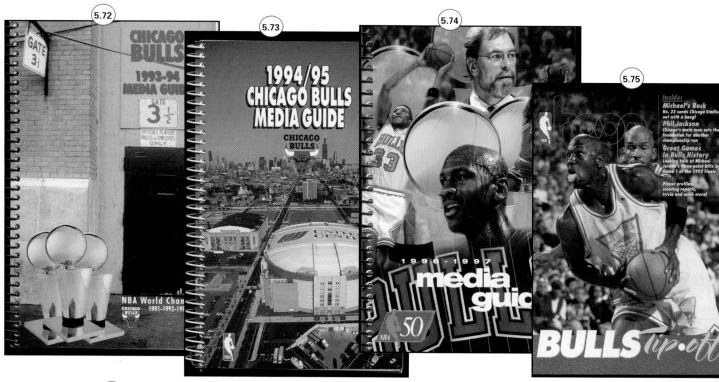

Year	Bulls Yearbooks			
84/85	MJ and Woolridge (5.80)	cover	40.00	50.00
88-89	Players huddled in warmups, CB & logo upper left side (5.81)	cover	30.00	40.00
89-90	MJ layup, white 23, drawing like cover (5.82)	cover	25.00	30.00
90-91	25th Anniversary		20.00	25.00
91-92	MJ holding trophy, cheering crowd (5.83)	cover	20.00	25.00
92-93	MJ holding ball with hat, 6 picture (5.84)	cover	15.00	20.00
93-94	World Champions Chicago Bulls		15.00	20.00
95-96	MJ & SP shooting (5.85)	cover	10.00	15.00
96-97	MJ shooting in crowd (5.86)	cover	10.00	12.00

Year	Cable Guide Magazine			
5/91	MJ holding ball, red 23 (5.87)	cover	15.00	20.00
11/96	MJ, Russel, Bird, Robertson, Johnson, Auerbach (5.88)	cover	10.00	15.00

Year	Chicago Life Magazine			
5&6/88	Michael Jordan, N-IV, closeup of side of head (5.89)	V-IV	20.00	25.00

Year	Chicago Sports Profiles Magazine			
89	The Stadium Rocks This Season, Winter Issue 1989 (5.90)	cover	25.00	30.00
11/90				
90	The Bulls, Supplement to CSP, red 23 holding ball (5.91)	cover	15.00	20.00
8/91	Bulls Scrapbook Inside, NBA Champs, Thanks for a Great.. (5.92)	cover	10.00	15.00
91	Expanded Bulls Coverage (5.93)	cover	7.00	12.00
91	The Bulls, Special Supplement (5.94)	cover	7.00	12.00
4/92	The Luvabulls, Acolades, Holland (5.95)	cover	5.00	10.00
8/92	Thanks for A Sensational Season! (5.96)	cover	5.00	10.00
4/93	Chicago's Best Defense (5.97)	cover	4.00	8.00
6/95	MJ art like cover	cover	6.00	10.00
2/96			4.00	8.00
6/96	One Un-Forget A Bull Season	cover	4.00	8.00

Year	Chicago White Sox Media Guide		
94	Chicago White Sox, MJ listed & pictured on page #119 (5.98)	inside	10.00

Year	Collecting Figures Magazine	mag #	
5/95	MJ Salvino Baseball Figure Cover (5.99)	V1-N5	5.00
4/96	MJ Space Jam Talking MJ Cover	V2-N4	5.00

Year	Collectors Sportslook Magazine		
8/94	MJ Eyes on the Majors, baseball, sealed (5.101)	cover	8.00
12/94	25 Most Popular Athletes, sealed (5.102)	cover	8.00
5/95	Michael is Back!, MJ Rocks the Sports Card Market (5.103)	V2 N6	10.00
6/95	Cal Ripkin Cover, MJ on cover, no MJ card (5.104)		7.00

Year	Comic Books	mag #/card #	
10/90	Parachute Comics, The Best, by Michael Teitelbaum		
6/91	Personality Comics, 2 views, white #23 bb in RH, suit BB in LH, Bill Shaftner on back (5.105)	6	20.00

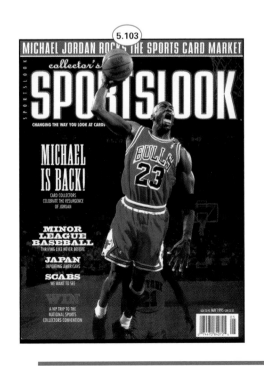

3/92	Personality Comics Presents, Slam Dunk Kings #1 Featuring MJ, blue front cover with 2 MJs, Joe DiMaggio back cover (5.106)	1	15.00
4/92	Revolutionary Comics Sports Superstars Comics, 3 views, red #23, white #23, closeup, blue and blue cover (5.107)	1	15.00
94	Ad Sheet, Revolutionary Comics MJ Tribute Cover for 4/94 issue, 4523 produced, dated & autograph by Wayne McDonald (5.108)	501	25.00
4/94	Revolutionary Comics MJ Tribute Special (5.109)	1	8.00
93	Shaquille O'Neal vs. Michael Jordan in red letters, Shaq on front cover, MJ on back cover, red shirt, illustrations by Deborah Max, Script by John DiMeola (5.110)	Part 1	15.00
93	Shaquille O'Neal vs. Michael Jordan in blue letters, MJ on front cover, red shirt, Shaq back cover, illustrations by Deborah Max, Script by John DiMeola (5.111)	Part 2	15.00
96	Space Jam DC Comics by D.C. Weiss (5.112)	cover	10.00

Year   **Consumer Reports Magazine**
| 8/91 | Who's Got the Right One, Baby (5.113) | cover | 15.00 |

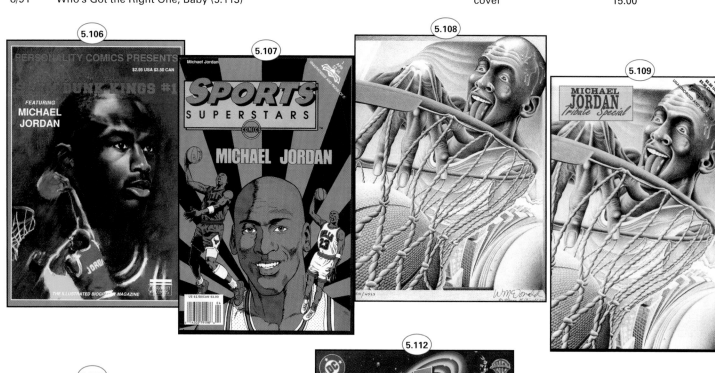

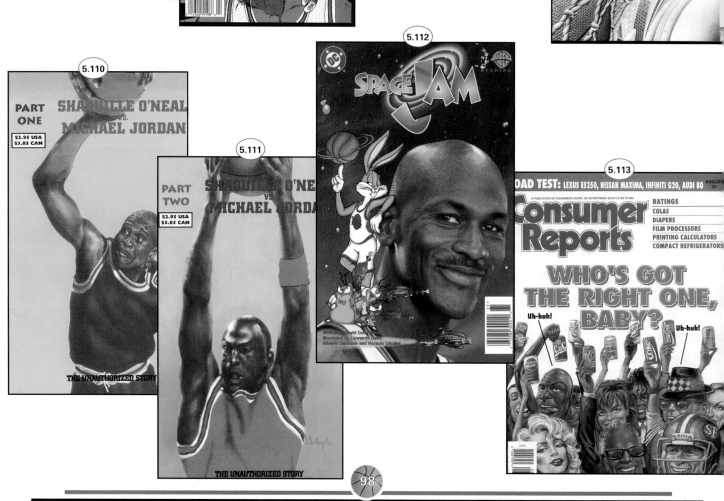

Year	Cracked Magazine	mag #		
1/92	Win a MJ Rookie Card (5.114)	#269	6.00	

Year	Disney Magazine	mag #		
11/91	Disney Adventures, One on One with MJ, 1st Anniversary Issue (5.115)	V2 N1	5.00	10.00

Year	Eastbay Magazine	mag #		
97	MJ inside	cc97	3.00	
97	MJ inside	hh97	3.00	
97	MJ inside	0498	3.00	

Year	Ebony Magazine	mag #		
8/91	How Black Creativity Is Changing America (5.116)	cover	18.00	
11/91	MJ & Juanita (5.117)	cover	18.00	
8/92	Winning, From J. Robinson to MJ (5.118)	cover	15.00	
12/93	The MJ Nobody Knows (5.119)	cover	12.00	
5/97	Michael's Mom: We Didn't Set Out To Raise A Superstar (5.120)	cover	12.00	

Year	Ebony Man Magazine	mag #		
4/91	Do Women Manipulate Men?, MJ on cover (5.121)	V6 N6	18.00	

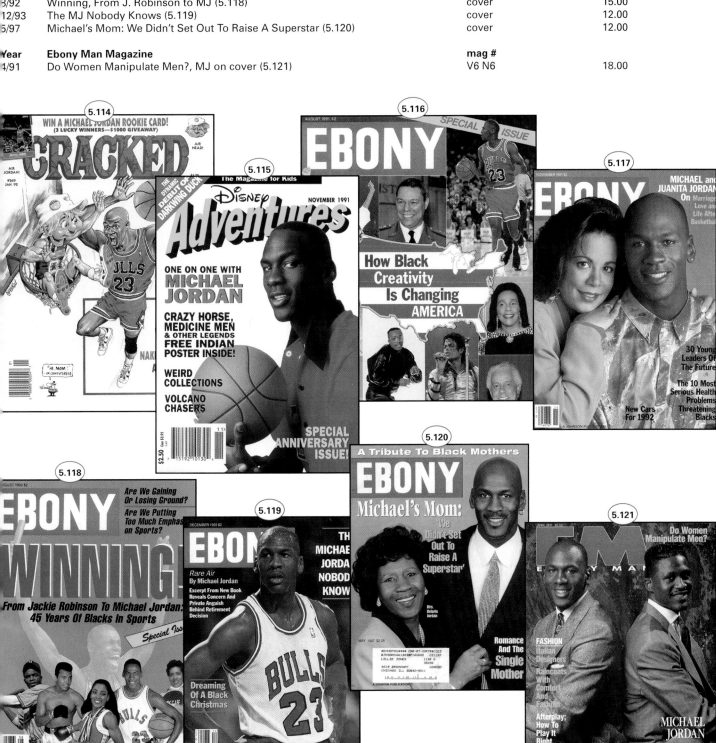

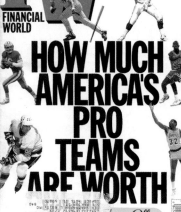

Year	Game Programs of Other Teams	item #	
11/12/86	Hoops, Washington Bullets, MJ dunking right hand, white 23, yellow signature (5.130)	cover	35.00
2/87	Full Court Press, New Jersey Nets, cover, 2 hand shot (5.131)	V7 N1	25.00
1990	The Fifth Quarter, Indy Pacers, MJ on back cover (5.132)	V5 N6	20.00
6/7/91	Tonight's Game, Lakers vs. Bulls, MJ & Magic front (5.133)	V9 D1	35.00
6/9/91	Today's Game, Lakers vs. Bulls, MJ & SP front (5.134)	V9 D2	35.00
11/96	Magazine, plus Game Program vs. Clippers, MJ running and holding ball, NBA at 50, blue cover (5.135)	cover	10.00

Year	Gold Collectors Series Magazine		
96	Magic vs. Bulls		4.00
96	Chicago 70 Souvenir Edition		4.00
96	MJ 1996 MVP Tribute		4.00
96	Michael & Chicago Go for Four		4.00
96	Jordan, Simply the Best (5.136)	cover	10.00
97	1997 Playoff Preview, Chicago The Bulls Will Dominate the Court (5.137)	cover	8.00

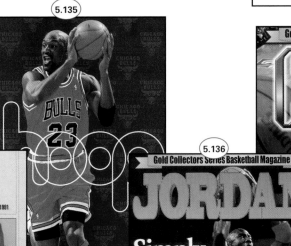

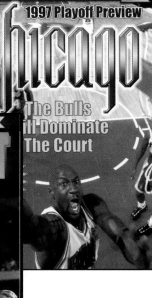

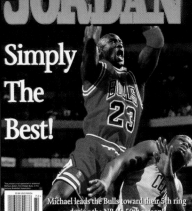

98	Michael Jordan, Chicago Loves MJ!, white #45	cover A	8.00
98	Michael Jordan, Chicago Loves MJ!, Trophy & MJ	cover B	8.00
98	Michael Jordan, Chicago Loves MJ!, blue AS #23	cover C	8.00

Year	HBO Magazine		
9/97	HBO Guide, We're All Ears About Space Jam (5.138)	cover	2.00

Year	Heroes of the Game Magazine	issue#	
95	Collector's Edition, gold foil, MJ white 45 front, MJ Barons back, # of 7,500 issued (5.139)	20	20.00
95	Collector's Edition, gold foil, MJ white 23 front, MJ red 45 back, # of 7,500 issued (5.140)	29	10.00
95	Collector's Edition, MJ autograph insert issue, MJ white front, MJ red 45 back, sealed, Certificate of Authenticity, # of 200 issued (5.141)	29	125.00
96	Collector's Edition, gold foil, MJ red 23 front, MJ black 23 back, # of 4,000 issued (5.142)	38	10.00
96	Collector's Edition, platinum foil, MJ red 23 front, MJ black 23 back, # of 1,500 issued (5.143)	38	15.00
96	Collector's Edition, gold foil, MJ on back cover, Rodman on front cover, # of 4,000 issued (5.144)	48	10.00
96	Collector's Edition, platinum foil, MJ on back cover, Rodman on front cover, # of 975 issued	48	15.00

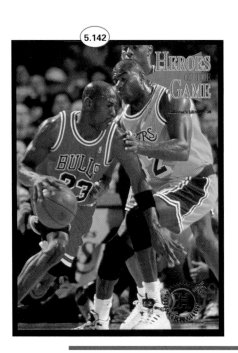

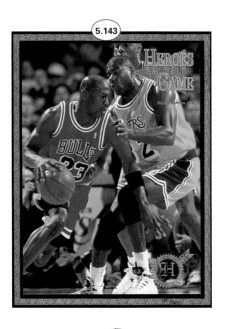

Year	Hollywood Collectible Magazine	mag #	
93	Michael! A Career Tribute, H & S Media (5.146)	cover	15.00
	—-MJ poster		
94	Michael! A Baseball Photo Album, H & S Media (5.147)	cover	15.00
	—-MJ poster		

Year	Inside Sports Magazine	mag #	
11/85	NBA Preview, Laker Repeat, Ewing & MJ Showtime in NBA	V-7	40.00
11/86	Annual NBA Preview, MJ Air Awesome, MJ cover (5.149)	V-8	35.00
6/87	NBA Playoffs, MJ cover (5.150)	V-9	30.00
12/87	Pro/College Basketball Ratings, MJ Raging Bull at Crunch Time (5.151)	V-9	30.00
5/88	Playoffs, NBA, MJ his Bulls are a Long Shot (5.152)	V-10	25.00
11/88	NBA Preview, Chicago's MJ (5.153)	V-10	25.00

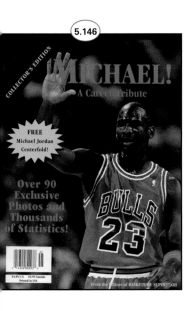

5.146

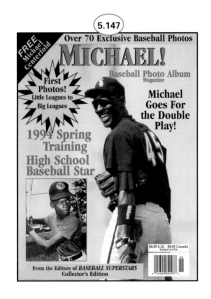

5.147

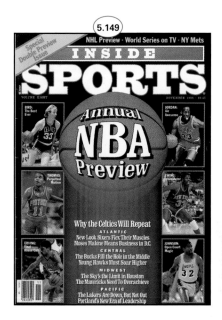

5.149

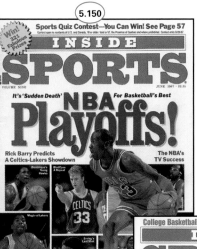

5.150

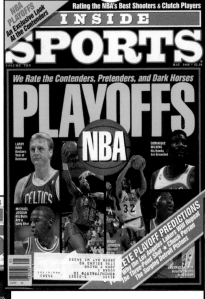

5.152

5.151

5.153

4/91	Sports Salaries (5.162)	V 13	18.00
5/91	NBA Playoffs Preview (5.163)	cover	15.00
10/91	MJ World Champions (5.164)	cover	15.00
11/91	91-92 NBA & College Preview (5.165)	V 13	15.00
12/91	David Robinson	cover	15.00
5/92	Malone: This is Our Year! (5.166)	cover	14.00
6/92	US Olympic Team is Out to Conquer the World (5.167)	cover	14.00
10/92	3 Peat! (5.168)	cover	14.00
11/92	NBA and College Preview (5.169)	cover	14.00
12/92	How good are the Bulls?, MJ & Wilt (5.170)	cover	14.00
2/93	NBA Insiders Poll Tells All (5.171)	cover	12.00

5/93	NBA Playoffs Preview (5.172)	cover	12.00
11/93	Head to Head, sealed with NBA Guide (5.173)	cover	12.00
93	End of an Era	cover	12.00
93/94	Pro Basketball Yearbook, For Patrick, It's Catchy (5.174)	cover	10.00
1/94	Our Sportsman of the Year; Crunch Time NFL (5.175)	cover	10.00
12/94	NBA Hot Questions (5.176)	cover	10.00
5/95	NFL's Perfect Man, Montana (5.177)	cover	9.00
6/95	Shaq Believe the Hype, MJ Hologram, on front (5.178)	cover	9.00
10/95	The Next Jordan? (5.179)	cover	9.00
11/95	95-96 NBA Preview (5.180)	cover	9.00
12/95	Hair & Air (5.181)	cover	9.00

5.172 5.173 5.174 5.175

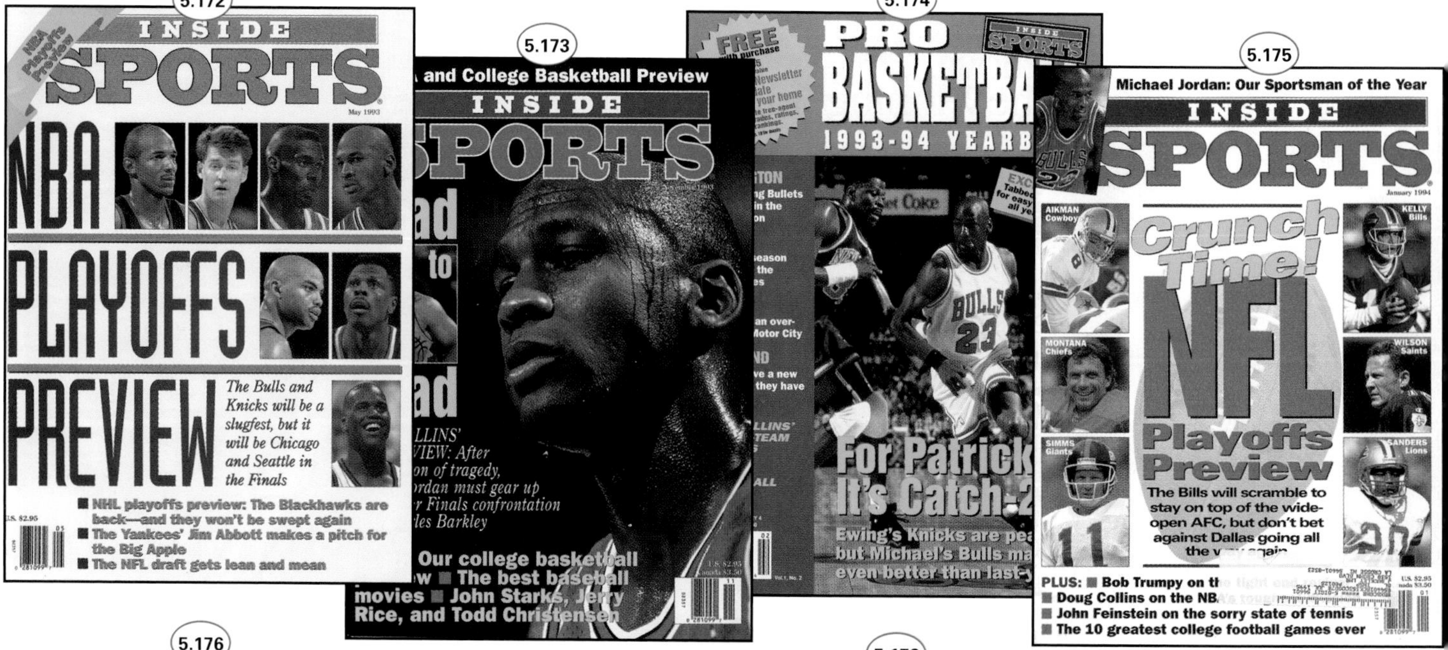

5.176 5.177 5.178 5.179

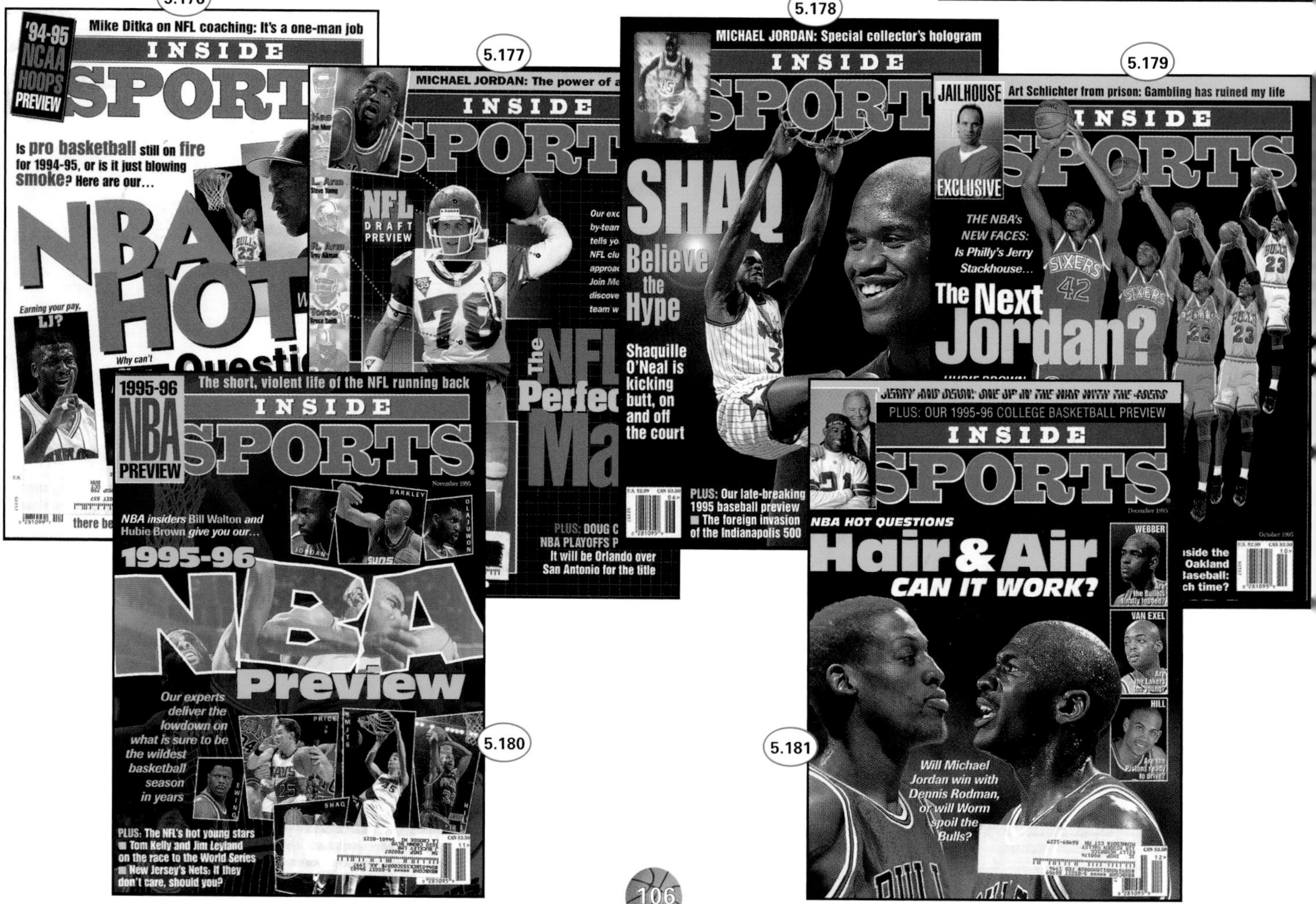

5.180 5.181

4/96	The Best...and the Busts (5.182)	cover	7.00
6/96	Bulls Can Be Beaten (5.183)	cover	7.00
96	The Bulls Rewrite History	cover	7.00
11/96	The Drive For Five (5.184)	cover	7.00
2/97	The Real NBA Ratings (5.185)	cover	5.00
11/97	Who Can Beat the Bulls	cover	5.00

Year	Jet Magazine		
6/12/89	Michael Jordan Leaps to Success (5.186)	cover	20.00
10/9/89	Michael Jordan Takes a Bride: Juanita Vaney (5.187)	cover	20.00
4/29/91	MJ: The Most Exciting Pro BB Player Ever (5.188)	cover	18.00
7/1/91	MJ Leads Chicago To NBA Crown (5.189)	cover	18.00
7/6/92	MJ Leads Chicago Bulls to #2 NBA Title (5.190)	cover	15.00
8/12/92	Blacks Who are Best Bets to Win Gold in Olympics	cover	15.00

87	Avon Superstars, McHale & Jordan, Avon Books owned by Heart Pub (5.206)	cover	35.00
12/96	30 Year Celebration Brochure (5.207)		2.00
96/97	Athlon Sports Pro Basketball Annual, Chicago's Bargain at $30 Million (5.208)	Vol. 3	6.00
97-98	Athlon Sports Pro Basketball Annual, Would MJ+Anyone=NBA		4.00
2/93	Baseball Hobby News, Issue 166, MJ The World's Most Exciting Player	V15 N2	6.00
91-92	Basketball Almanac	cover	20.00
91	Basketball Sportlines, MJ, Ewing, & Mikan on cover	book	18.00
96	Bull Run by Addax, Limited Edition of 21, 771		10.00
97	Celebrity Golfer, The 1997 Official Guide to the World of Celebrity Golf, MJ, Bing Crosby and Bob Hope on cover (5.209)	cover	12.00
96-97	Celtics Yearbook, MJ tipoff on center court (5.210)	cover	10.00
Sp 94	Champs Sports, Glory Days (5.211)		12.00
4/95	Champion Sports Memorabilia		10.00
7/95	Champion Sports Memorabilia, DiMaggio cover		10.00
	—MJ insert card	8	8.00
9/28/	92-Card News, Dan Marino NFL Iron Man Shows No Sign of Slowing Down	V11N20	12.00
2/89	Chicago, MJ Against Himself, Bulls in Transition (5.212)	V38 N2	15.00
10/96	Chicago Calendar of Events, Tourism Office (5.213)	cover	5.00

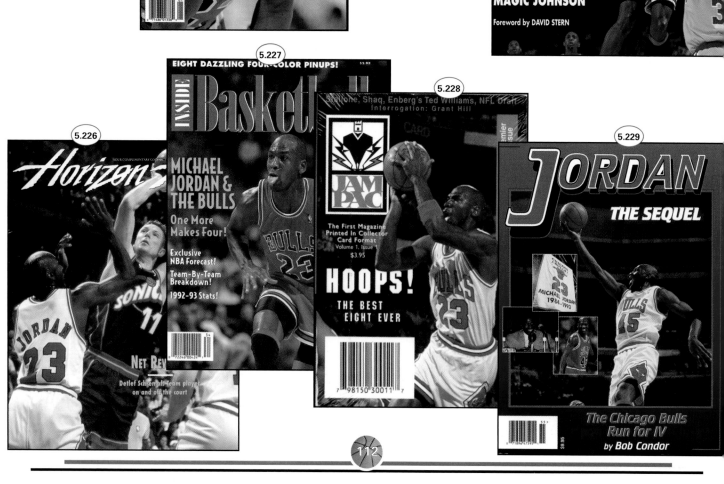

11/94	MJ A Salute To, 11/1/94 (5.238)	cover	20.00
1994	MJ A Shooting Star, George Beahm, book (5.239)	cover	25.00
93	MJ A Tribute to, Commemorative Edition by Bob Sakamoto, published by Publications International (5.240)	1	15.00
94	MJ Basketball Great, Sean Dolan, Chelsea House (5.241)	book	15.00
88	MJ Basketball's Soaring Star by Deegan, First Ave. Editions (5.242)	cover	20.00
96	MJ Basketball Superstar, S. Dolan, Chelsea Juniors (5.243)	book	8.00
89	MJ & Magic, R. Brenner (5.244)	cover	10.00
91	MJ MVP and NBA Champ, Bob Sakamoto (5.245)	cover	8.00

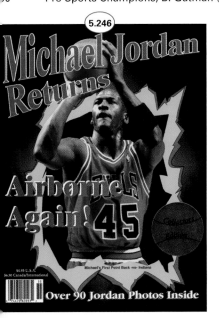

5.246

5.247

5.249

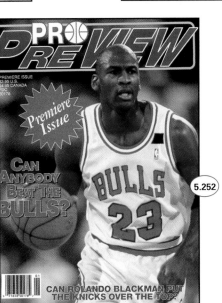

5.248

 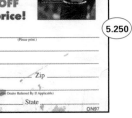

5.250

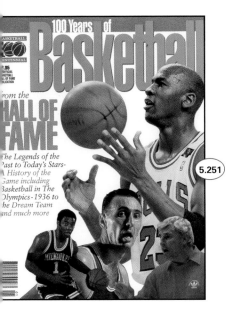

5.251

5.252

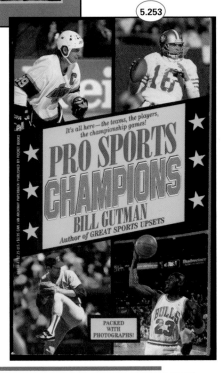

5.253

96	Raging Bulls 72 Victories, Barnes & Noble, hardcover (5.254)	cover	10.00
2/94	Salute, MJ cover (5.255)	V10N1	4.00
91	Sanchez Comprehensive Yearly Price Guide in Basketball (5.256)	2nd ed.	15.00
10/96	Satellite Orbit, Winter Sports Special	V15 N4	12.00
10/84	Sports Mirror, "MJ Will He Make it in Chicago? (5.257)	cover	65.00
97	Sports Playbook	cover	8.00
95	Sports Stars MJ Beyond Air, Brooks (5.258)		8.00
3/96	Swing, Zen Masters & The Bulls		6.00
92	Taking to the Air, J. Naughton	book	12.00
1994	Target the Family (5.259)	cover	15.00
8/90	Team Sports Business Magazine (5.260)	V3 N8	20.00
92	The Golden Boys, C. Stauth, US Olympic BB Team	book	15.00
1/31/90	The National, MJ over skyline, Chicago area distribution only	cover	30.00
1/93	The Jordan Rules, Sam Smith	book	10.00
96-97	Ultimate Sports	cover	5.00
97-98	Ultimate Sports	cover	4.00
2/97	Vibe, Fresh Air With Chris Rock	cover	6.00
91	Welcome Back Michael (5.261)	book	15.00
2/92	YSB, Air Jordan Takes It All to the Hoop, Young Sisters & Brothers Mag. (5.262)		10.00

Year	5 Majeur French Magazine & Items	mag #		
-	cover	HS-N1	75.00	
-	cover & poster	HS-N4	70.00	
-	cover	HS-N7	65.00	
-	cover	HS-N9	60.00	
-	cover	N-2	75.00	
-	cover	N-5	70.00	
-	cover	N-11	65.00	
-	cover	N-14	60.00	
-	cover	N-15	65.00	
10/92	Shaq & Magic in All-Star Game, Dream Team Poster with MJ	N-18	75.00	
-	poster	N-23	70.00	
-	cover	N-26	65.00	
-	cover	N-27	60.00	
91	MJ cover, holding ball, white 23 (5.263)	N-13	60.00	
	—MJ & I. Thomas Poster			
	—Sally card, 4 x 6			
	—Scott card, 4 x 6			
	—Elliot card, 4 x 6			
	—Wingate card, 4 x 6			
	—Robertson card, 4 x 6			
	—McDaniel card, 4 x 6			
	—Levingston card, 4 x 6			
	—Bird card, 4 x 6			
12/92	MJ cover, hands on knees, white 23 (5.264)	N-20	40.00	
	—Olajuwon & Barkley Poster			
	—Drexler USA Olympic Dream Team card, 4 x 6			
	—Pippen USA Olympic Dream Team card, 4 x 6			
	—Ewing USA Olympic Dream Team card, 4 x 6			
	—Willis USA Olympic Dream Team card, 4 x 6			
	—Owens USA Olympic Dream Team card, 4 x 6			
	—Johnson USA Olympic Dream Team card, 4 x 6			
	—Kersey USA Olympic Dream Team card, 4 x 6			

Year	Mastro & Steinbach Catalog			
3/27/97	Auction Catalog	inside	5.00	
8/27/97	Auction Catalog	inside	5.00	
11/20/97	Auction Catalog	inside	5.00	

Year	Money Card Collector Magazine	mag #		
4/96	Money Card Collector, cover, phone card mag. (5.265)	V3 N4	3.00	8.00
1/97	Money Card Collector, cover, phone card 50 minutes (5.266)	V4 N1	8.00	15.00
3/97	Money Card Collector, cover, Space Jam phone card (5.267)	V4 N3	8.00	15.00

5.263 5.265 5.267 5.264 5.266

Year	National Sports Review Magazine	mag #		
91	Best & Worst of 1991 (5.268)	V VI	15.00	20.00
93	Best & Worst of 1993 (5.269)		10.00	15.00
95	1995	cover	8.00	12.00
95-96	Pro Basketball 95-96	cover	6.00	10.00
97	Preview Special 97-98 NBA	cover	4.00	6.00

Year	NBA Inside Stuff Magazine			
12/95		cover	10.00	15.00
95	NBA Inside Stuff Magazine Offer Coupon, receive a Reggie Miller card on, MJ on coupon	cover	10.00	18.00
97	Subscription Offer Coupons, Special NBA Offer!, 2 coupons, Sports Illustrated Magazine-2 coupons attached together (5.270)		1.00	2.00
97	Subscription Offer Form, Drive for Five!	front	2.00	4.00
5/97	Drive for 5	cover	5.00	10.00
	—-MJ Poster	NNO		

Year	NBA...Magazines			
96	Finals Magazine, Focus Corporation	cover	15.00	20.00
97	Finals Magazine, Bulls/Jazz, PSP Sports		10.00	15.00
93	Jam Session Book Offer for NBA Dunk Coupon, back 92-93 checklist, coupon with MJ, Drakes book offer		5.00	10.00

Year	Newsweek Magazine			
7/6/92	Team Dream (5.271)		15.00	20.00
10/93	Greatest Ever (5.272)		4.00	8.00
3/20/95	Hoop Dreams (5.273)		3.00	6.00

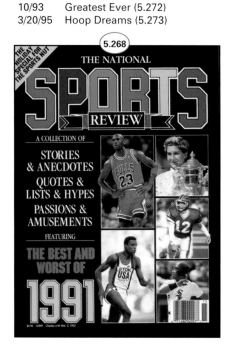

5.268

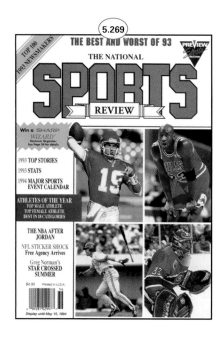

5.269

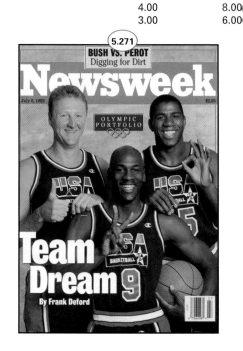

5.271

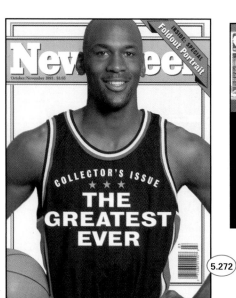

5.272

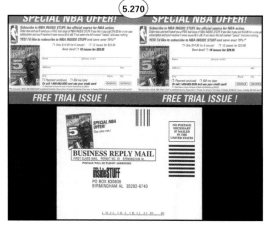

5.270

5.273

Year	People Magazine	mag #		
12/18/89	The Sexiest Man Alive Sexiest Athlete (5.274)	cover	20.00	30.00
Sum 91	50 Most Beautiful People in the World 1991	cover	15.00	25.00
8/30/93	Richest Women in Show Biz	cover	10.00	15.00
10/10/93	The Sexiest Couple Alive	cover	10.00	15.00

Year	Petersons Magazines			
89	Preview 89-90, Michael's Bulls for a Title		20.00	25.00
90-91	Preview 90-91 & poster	cover	15.00	20.00
91	Preview 91-92, Champion Chicago (5.275)	cover	15.00	20.00
93-94	Pro Basketball, Shaq Attack, Shaq hologram, Sports Series, blue cover, sealed	cover	10.00	15.00
9/96	Pro Basketball	cover	6.00	10.00
96	Pro Basketball Action, Are the Bulls da Bomb?	cover	6.00	10.00
96	Pro Basketball, Bulls, the Best Team Ever	cover	6.00	10.00
97	Pro Basketball, The Bulls, Back for Another	cover	4.00	6.00

Year	Pocket Pages Magazines	mag # card #		
93	Card, MJ & Barkley, 93 NBA MVP's, "Bonus" on front bottom right in red letters yellow stripe, MJ on back, magazine back cover bonus card, 10,000 produced	BC-3	10.00	15.00

Year	Pro Basketball...Magazines			
90-91	Annual, Basketball Today, MJ overhead shot	cover	12.00	25.00
92	Complete Handbook, Celebrating a Century of Hoop	cover	12.00	25.00
91-92	Illustrated, NBA Champion Chicago, Bulls One More Time (5.276)	cover	10.00	20.00
92-93	Illustrated, NBA Scoring Champ & MVP	cover	8.00	15.00
93-94	Illustrated, NBA's Top Gun!, 7 Time Scoring	cover	6.00	12.00
94	Illustrated, MJ 85-93 A Final Tribute	cover	12.00	20.00
	—-12 MJ 8.5 x 11 sheets			
	—-4 MJ posters			
95	Illustrated	cover	10.00	15.00
	—-18 MJ 8.5 x 11 sheets			
	—-4 MJ posters			
90-91	Scene Annual, MJ close up	cover	20.00	25.00
91-92	Scene Annual, MJ & Ewing, Barkley Robinson		15.00	15.00
92-93	Scene Annual, Jordan How He Rates With All	cover	12.00	15.00
93-94	Scene Season Preview, In-Depth Analysis of 27 Teams	cover	10.00	15.00
90	Today	cover	25.00	30.00

Year	Rare Air Book			
93	Softcover		15.00	20.00
93	Hardcover		25.00	30.00

Year	Scholastic Magazines & Books	mag #		
91	Sports Shots Collectors Book (5.277)	1	2.00	4.00
92	Sports Shots, revised & updated	18	5.00	10.00
93	Michael Jordan, Chip Lovitt	book	5.00	10.00
95	Sports Shots, MJ Premium Edition #1, revised and updated	35	5.00	10.00
97	NBA by the Numbers, B. Brooks	inside	10.00	15.00
97	NBA Megastars, B. Weber	inside	10.00	15.00
97	NBA Slam Dunk Champions, J. Layden	inside	10.00	15.00

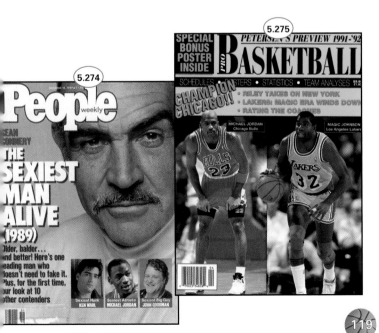

Year	Sears Catalogs			
5/31/91	The Starting Lineup	back	15.00	20.00

Year	Slam Magazine	mag #		
7/95	Mike! Be Like Mike on side (5.278)	6	12.00	
	——poster, MJ front white #45, Dennis Rodman on back			
7/96	Mike, The Interview		5.00	
8/97	The Real top 50 Players of All Time	cover	5.00	
9/97	Bow Down	cover	5.00	
10.97	Slam Presents Michael Jordan	cover	5.00	

Year	Space Jam Magazines & Books	mag #		
96	Collectors Pop-Up, SJLAN-18		4.00	8.00
96	Hello Reader, L-3, Grade 1&2, SJSC-21, soft cover, Scholastic		2.00	4.00
96	Jumbo Jam Coloring/Activity,SJLAN-8, soft cover		2.00	4.00
96	Jumbo Jam Coloring/Activity,SJLAN-8-k, Edition-soft cover		2.00	4.00
96	Jumpin' Jumbo Jam, SJLAN-17, soft cover		2.00	4.00
96	Lola Bunny Don't Ever Call Me Doll, SJLAN-10, soft cover		2.00	4.00
96	Lola's Time In Sticker Book, SJLAN-9h, hard cover		2.00	4.00
96	Lola's Time In Sticker Book, SJLAN-9s, soft cover		3.00	6.00
96	Look & Find, MJ in Space Jam, Pub. Intl., LTD	31872	6.00	12.00
96	Mask Book, purple cover, MJ 3:00 position, Modern Pub	SJM031	4.00	8.00
96	Mask Book, green cover, MJ 7:00 position, Modern Pub	SJM032	4.00	8.00
96	MJ Secret Stuff, SJLAN-12		2.00	
96	Sound, MJ/Bugs Bunny in Space Jam, BB & 8 sounds, Pub Int.	31966	10.00	20.00
96	Sound, MJ/Bugs Bunny in Space Jam, sound panel right side	31872	10.00	20.00
96	Space Jammin', 10.25 x 10.25, hard cover		10.00	15.00
96	Story Album with 66 stickers, Baio Company (5.279)	84653	5.00	10.00
	——MJ Stickers—17 different		10.00	15.00
96	Sufferin' Succotash (on back cover), soft cover, Scholastic	SJSC17	3.00	6.00
96	Swackhammers Mean Team BB, SJLAN-11W, Ed., soft cover		2.00	4.00
96	Swackhammers Mean Team BB, SJLAN-11, soft cover		2.00	4.00
96	The Monstars Go To Court, SJLAN-16h, hard cover		3.00	6.00
96	The Monstars Go To Court, SJLAN-16s, soft cover		2.00	4.00
96	The Ultimate Game, 17 x 22", SJLAN-13, poster inside		3.00	6.00
96	Tune Squad vs. Monstars, SJSC-18, hard cover, Scholastic		10.00	15.00
96	Tune Squad vs. Monstars poster book, SJSC-19, 15 posters, Scholastic		5.00	10.00
96	What's Up Doc? (on back cover), SJSC-16, soft cover, Scholastic		4.00	8.00

Year	Sport Magazine	mag #		
3/82	The Fight Holmes vs. Cooney, NC Tar Heels: Can They Win the Title	inside	45.00	65.00
3/87	Spring Training Warm-Up, cover	V78 N3	35.00	45.00
6/87	Who Makes What In Sports, 5th 100 Best Salary Survey (5.280)	cover	35.00	45.00
7/87			35.00	45.00
11/88	Jordan of the Chicago Bulls Changing of the Guard (5.281)		25.00	35.00

11/89	89-90 Pro Basketball Preview	cover	20.00	25.00
6/90	Top 100 Earners in All of Sports (5.282)	cover	15.00	20.00
37-19				
10/90	100 Best in Sports (5.283)	cover	15.00	20.00
37-18				
1/91	Air to the Throne	cover	12.00	15.00
11/91	NBA Preview	cover	12.00	15.00
12/91	"Michael, The Price of Fame"		12.00	15.00
91	Ad Flyer, "MJ Prince of Fame"	cover	3.00	5.00
6/92	Can Bulls be Beaten?	cover	12.00	15.00
8/92	Subscription Order Form, foldout back cover	inside	2.00	4.00
1/93	Top 40	cover	10.00	12.00
5/93			10.00	12.00
11/93	NBA Preview	cover	10.00	12.00
12/93	Ten Years of MJ		10.00	12.00
1/94	Top 40 The Best in Sports	cover	8.00	12.00
11/94	NBA Preview Issue 94-95	cover	8.00	12.00
4/95	Baseball's Future?	cover	8.00	12.00
6/95	Jordan's Back	cover	8.00	12.00
7/95	Slam		8.00	12.00
11/95	Pro Basketball Preview Issue	cover	8.00	12.00
1/96	Jordan's Next Jump	cover	6.00	10.00
5/96			6.00	10.00
9/96	MJ Player of the Half Century		6.00	10.00
11/96	America's Teams		6.00	10.00
6/97	I'm Better Than Ever-MJ Exclusive	cover	5.00	8.00
12/97		cover	5.00	8.00

Year	Sporting News			
83-84	BB Yearbook, College & Pro, MJ in NC uniform (5.284)		60.00	75.00
85-86	Pro & College Yearbook, MJ & David Rivers	cover	50.00	60.00
87-88	Pro Basketball Yearbook, High & Mighty (5.285)	Series 4	40.00	50.00
87/88	Official NBA Register	cover	30.00	40.00
88/89	Official NBA Guide (5.286)	cover	20.00	30.00
89-90	Official NBA Register	cover	15.00	25.00
91/92	Official NBA Guide	cover	15.00	25.00
92/93	Official NBA Guide, SP & MJ vs. Drexler	cover	12.00	20.00
89/90	Pro Basketball Yearbook, Thriller	cover	12.00	20.00
92-93	Pro Basketball Yearbook, Three Peat	cover	10.00	20.00
93-94	Pro Basketball Yearbook, Bull Run	cover	10.00	15.00

5.282

5.283

5.284

5.285

5.286

Year	The Sporting News Newspaper			
3/28/83	Player of the year, NC's MJ	cover	60.00	75.00
2/13/84	NC...Nothin' Could Be Finer	cover	50.00	60.00
3/26/84	Player of the Year, MJ is Head & Shoulders Above the Rest	cover	50.00	60.00
10/29/84	The Next Dr. J, MJ is Ready to Operate in the NBA	cover	50.00	60.00
12/8/86	Making Point	cover	45.00	55.00
3/23/87	(Show) Business As Usual, MJ & Dr. J	cover	40.00	50.00
5/18/87	Manager Pete Rose, MJ TSN All-Star	cover	35.00	45.00
5/23/88	The Last Hurrah?, MJ Player of Year	cover	30.00	40.00
3/20/89	One Man Gangs, Barkley & MJ	cover	25.00	30.00
5/28/90	Taking Bulls by Their Horns	cover	20.00	25.00
3/4/91	Keep the DH, AL to Fay	cover	15.00	20.00
5/6/91	It's In the Stars	cover	15.00	20.00
6/10/91	Michael & Magic A Dream Matchup	cover	15.00	20.00
6/24/91	Bulls! Jordan & Co. Bury Lakers	cover	15.00	20.00
7/22/91	Power of Appeal	cover	15.00	20.00
1/6/92	Man of the Year	cover	15.00	20.00
2/17/92			15.00	20.00
6/15/92	Rising to the Occasion	cover	15.00	20.00
6/28/93			10.00	15.00
10/18/93	What Now? Report on MJ Retirement	cover	10.00	15.00
10/18/93	The Next Dr. J		10.00	15..00
3/20/95	The One and Only	cover	8.00	12.00
5/15/95	Knockout Round	cover	8.00	12.00
11/06/95			8.00	12.00
5/13/96			8.00	12.00
6/17/96			8.00	12.00
9/96	Mike the Magnificent, 96/97 Yearbook	cover	5.00	10.00
4/28/97			5.00	10.00
6/2/97			5.00	10.00
6/23/97			5.00	10.00

Year	Sports Card Collectors Magazine			
6/96	17th NSCC Convention, regular, Anaheim, CA-No MJ Cover		5.00	10.00
6/96	17th NSCC Convention, gold issue, Anaheim, CA-No MJ Cover		10.00	15.00

Year	Sports Cards Price Guide	mag #		
6/95	Welcome Back Mike!, Issue 117	V15 N6	8.00	12.00
1/96			6.00	10.00
6/96	MJ Pointing to a 4th NBA Title	V16 N6	6.00	10.00
7/97	Ad Card, MJ Hungry to Win a Fifth NBA Title, black #23, dribbling RH, card like cover, back sending for free trial issue (5.287)		10.00	
1/98	Drew Bledsoe, MJ on back cover	V18 N1	5.00	7.00

Year	Sports Card Trader Magazine	mag #		
5/90	Exclusive! 2nd Year Sports Cards, Can Make You Rich	V1 N1	15.00	20.00
11/90	Air Jordan Cards Take Off, MJ on cover	V1 N7	15.00	20.00
11/91	MJ King of the Court & Cards, MJ on cover	V2 N7	12.00	18.00
12/92	What's Hot, MJ on cover	V3 N8	10.00	15.00
11/93	Shaq and MJ, Battle for Supremacy, MJ on cover	V4 N7	10.00	15.00
12/94	Top 10 Most Collected Sports Stars, Issue #56, MJ on cover	V5 N8	8.00	12.00
3/96	Exclusive Jason Kidd, MJ cover	I-71	5.00	8.00

Year	Sports Collectors Digest Items	mag #		
7/28/89	Michael Jordan Interviewed	V16N30	25.00	30.00
1/4/91	MJ at free throw line		15.00	25.00
91	Ad sheet, Krause Publications	cover	3.00	6.00
4/92	Sports Cards Price Guide, no MJ card inside	cover	5.00	10.00
6/92	Price Guide-MJ Cards Keep Climbing	cover	15.00	25.00
7/92	Sport Card Price Guide, 8 insert cards	52	15.00	25.00
	—MJ Card, red 23 holding ball, green & back	41	6.00	12.00
10/92	Price Guide, Dream Team		10.00	15.00
7/93	7/30/93, Preview of 14th NSCC newspaper		7.00	12.00
4/94		cover	6.00	11.00
3/95	Price Guide #84, Can MJ Save Baseball		5.00	10.00
3/96	Price Guide		3.00	6.00
4/96	National Convention Map & Schedule, NSCC	inside	2.00	4.00
4/96	NSCC Dealer Directory, NSCC	cover	2.00	4.00
8/96		cover	4.00	8.00
11/8/96	Entertainment, MJ & Space Jam, insert of SCD	cover	2.00	8.00
11/96	11/29/96, newspaper	cover	4.00	8.00
3/97	3/21/97, newspaper	cover	4.00	8.00
4/97	4/11/97, newspaper	cover	4.00	8.00
5/29/98	Supplement to SCD, "1998 Guide to SLU and other Figurines"	cover	2.00	4.00

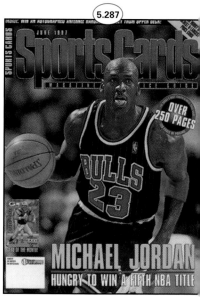

Year	Sports Illustrated Magazine			
3/29/82	Tar Heels on a Tear	inside	20.00	30.00
11/2883	No 1 UNC, MJ/Perkins	cover	70.00	100.00
7/23/84	UP Up For LA Olympics	cover	65.00	95.0
12/10/84	A Star is Born	cover	60.00	90.00
11/17/86	One Man Gang	cover	55.00	85.00
86	Poster Ad Sheet, vendor issue, has 2 MJ posters, laminated, 3 holes, football posters one side, BB posters other side (5.288)	8.5 x 11	40.00	65.00
	—-dunking with 2 Laker #21 & #32, red 23	4453-2		
	—-dunking, white 23	4453		
86	Poster Ad Sheet, vendor issue, has 3 MJ posters, football posters one side, BB posters other side (5.289)	8.5 x 11	45.00	70.00
	—-dunking with 2 Laker #21 & #32, red 23	4454		
	—-dunking, white 23	4453		
	—-hook dunk, red 23, scoreboard in background	4465		
11/9/87	Special NBA Preview	cover	40.00	50.00
12/28/87	Year In Pictures	cover	40.00	55.00
5/16/88	Sky High vs. Cavs.	cover	35.00	45.00
6/16/88	MJ/Bulls	cover	35.00	40.00
3/13/89	How High Can He Fly	cover	30.00	40.00
5/15/89	Raging Bull	cover	30.00	40.00
8/14/89	Jordan's My Name, Golf's My Game	cover	30.00	40.00
11/6/89	Can Anyone Shut Michael Down?, MJ/Joe Dumars	cover	30.00	40.00
5/21/90	Show Time	cover	25.00	35.00
12/17/90	Another Bull Run	cover	25.00	35.00
1990	35 Years of Covers, 1954-1989	cover	25.00	35.00
2/18/91	Dream Team	cover	20.00	25.00
5/21/91	MJ 1st Cover Track	cover	20.00	25.00
6/3/91	Finally, NBA Finals	cover	20.00	25.00
6/10/91	Magic and Michael	cover	20.00	25.00
6/17/91	Air Power, NBA Finals	cover	20.00	25.00
6/24/91	Insert MJ's Crowning Glory	cover	20.00	25.00
8/5/91	The Black Athlete	cover	20.00	25.00
11/11/91	Man in the Middle	cover	20.00	25.00
12/23/91	Sportsman of the Year	Hologram	20.00	25.00
1991	Sportsman of the Year Hologram Proof Card, larger than the hologram on the magazine	2 sided	20.00	30.00
91	Order Form, video offer "Come Fly with Me"	cover	20.00	25.00
5/11/92	On Collision Course vs. Drexler	cover	18.00	25.00
5/25/92	Busting Loose vs. Knicks	cover	18.00	25.00
6/15/92	Yesss!	cover	18.00	25.00
6/22/92	How Sweet It Is To Repeat	cover	18.00	25.00
92	Sports Almanac and Record Book, MJ on back cover		10.00	15.00
6/7/93	Hanging Tough, NBA Finals	cover	15.00	20.00
6/21/93	Head To Head vs. Barkley	cover	15.00	20.00
6/28/93	3!. with cover	cover	15.00	20.00
6/28/93	Collector Edition-3 Seasons to Savor	cover	15.00	20.00
10/18/93	Why, MJ Retires	cover	15.00	20.00

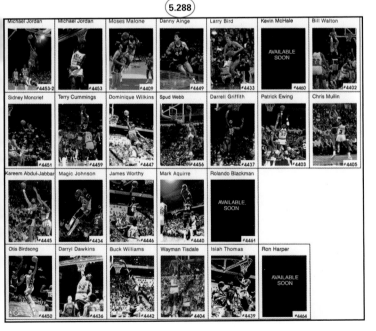

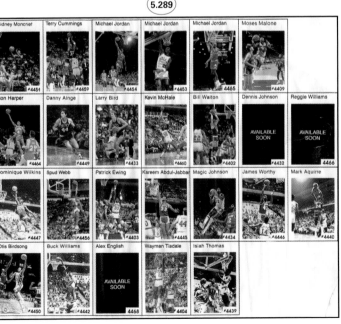

93	Sports Almanac		20.00	30.00
3/14/94	Bag It Michael!	cover	12.00	17.00
9/19/94	40 For the Ages	cover	12.00	17.00
3/20/95	It's Super Michael	cover	10.00	18.00
3/27/95	I'm Back, #45 Jersey vs. Pacers	cover	10.00	18.00
5/22/95	Battle of Titans vs. Shaq	cover	10.00	18.00
10/23/95	Air & Space, Rodman	cover	10.00	18.00
95	The Year in Pictures	cover	10.00	18.00
95/96	Presents Pro Basketball Premier Edition, Presents "Eyes On the Prize," Regional Issue	cover	10.00	15.00
5/27/96	The Running of the Bulls	cover	8.00	12.00
6/3/96	Chicago Fires vs. Orlando	cover	8.00	12.00
6/17/96	Bulls Whipped, NBA Finals	cover	8.00	12.00
6/19/	The Best		8.00	12.00
11/96	"The Best"-Chicago Bulls 95-96 A Special Collector's Edition, sent to SI subscribers	47156	8.00	12.00
12/96-97	"Presents Pro Basketball 96-97," Drive for Five	cover	10.00	15.00
3/10/97	Are The Bulls So Good They're Bad for the NBA	cover	6.00	10.00
3/17/97	Family Portrait, "BB-A History of the Game"	cover	6.00	10.00
5/19/97	Guarding Jordan	cover	6.00	10.00
6/9/97	Gimme Five	cover	5.00	8.00
6/23/97	Is the Jordan Dynasty the NBA's	cover	5.00	8.00
6/25/97	Presents Chicago Bulls 96-97 Champs	cover	5.00	8.00
9/97	SI Presents The Fantastic 5, Gatorade Cap Mail In Offer	inside	5.00	8.00
97	SI Order Form, Save Up to 80% with Educational Discount	folder	5.00	8.00
97	Presents Pro Basketball: One More Time		5.00	8.00
2/16/98	Don't Bag It, Michael		4.00	6.00
5/11/98			4.00	6.00
6/8/98	The Last Stand		4.00	6.00
6/15/98			4.00	6.00

Year	Sports Illustrated for Kids Items	mag #		
89	Ad Promo-MJ with fan, Matt Russell, "Our Best Young Athletes Tell Us your Favorite Team...," 4 page promo for SIK	cover	10.00	15.00
89	Order Form with 1st issue	inside	1.00	2.00
1/89	Jump! Premier Issue-MJ cover	V1 N1	50.00	75.00
2/90	Whoa! Snow!	V2 N2	20.00	25.00
	——MJ Poster, part 1		10.00	15.00
3/90	Fast Company	V2 N3	20.00	25.00
	——MJ Poster, part 2		10.00	15.00
4/90	Play Ball!	V2 N4	20.00	25.00
	——MJ Poster, part 3		10.00	15.00
5/90	The Right Stuff	V2 N5	20.00	25.00
	——MJ Poster, part 4		10.00	15.00
10/90	Monster Bash, 4 McDonald's Cards, MJ comic inside	V2 N10	20.00	25.00
	——The Layup	1	2.00	4.00
	——The Blocked Shot	2	2.00	4.00
	——The Backup Dribble	6	2.00	4.00
	——The Jump Shot	7	2.00	4.00
12/90	Triple Dribble, 4 McDonald's Cards	V2 N12	20.00	25.00
	——The Chest Pass	3	2.00	4.00
	——The Drive	4	2.00	4.00
	——The Speed Dribble	5	2.00	4.00
	——The Free Throw	8	2.00	4.00
90/92	Michael Jordan, Now Includes 91 NBA Finals, Berger & Rolfe	book	10.00	15.00
5/92	Michael Mania!, MJ on cover	V4 N5	10.00	15.00
11/93	Goal Rush!, MJ in Foldout NBA Ad	V5 N11	8.00	12.00
6/94	Card Sheet from Soccer Madness!	270	8.00	12.00
12/94	Everything You Want to Know About Sports, Encyclopedia	cover	8.00	12.00
94	Michael Jordan and Others, 20 Most Amazing Athletes of the 90's	cover	10.00	15.00
1/95	Amazing Sports Photos	cover	7.00	10.00
5/95	Hoopmania!	cover	7.00	10.00
5/95	Look What's Inside, MJ on cover	V7 N5	7.00	10.00
8/95	MJ Collectors Issue	cover	8.00	10.00
	——McWorld Poster		4.00	8.00
3/96	Jammin' with Mike, MJ on cover	V8 N3	8.00	10.00
	——MJ Poster		4.00	8.00
12/96	L.J. Comes to Play, MJ on cover	V8 N12	6.00	8.00
12/96	Inside Space Jam, Special Collector Edition	cover	6.00	8.00
	——MJ Space Jam Poster		3.00	5.00
1996	Sports Encyclopedia and CD Rom Kit		30.00	45.00
	——The Everything You Want to Know About Sports Encyclopedia	CD Rom		
8/95	——Special Collector Issue Magazine-8/95, Michael!	cover		
	———McWorld Poster inside			
1/97	Sack Man, MJ in AD & page 40, 53	V9 N1	4.00	6.00
2/97	An American Hero, MJ on cover	V9 N2	4.00	6.00

3/97	Small Wonder, MJ on page 76	V9 N3	4.00	6.00
97	Subscription Order form, MJ front, SIK Book	4.25 x 5	4.00	6.00
Spr 98	The 50 Greatest Athletes of Today	cover	4.00	6.00
6/15/98	MJ Rises Again	cover	4.00	6.00
98	Greatest Teams	cover	10.00	15.00
98	Extra: The 1997 Spectacular Sports Yearbook	cover	5.00	8.00
98	Big Shots, book	cover	10.00	15.00
98	Funny Sports Photos	cover	10.00	15.00
Year	**Sports & Soaps Brochures**	**mag #**		
5-6/92	Dominick's "MJ Airs Talent in NBA Playoffs," Dick Wickstrom Chevy (5.290)	SIL-113	8.00	10.00
4/96	Andronico Park Shop Magazine (5.291)		2.00	4.00
5-6/98	Dominicks "NBA Playoffs, Michael Jordan, Shaquille O'Neal" (5.292)		1.00	2.00
Year	**Sports Wrap Magazine**	**mag #**		
97	Catalog (5.293)	No. 4	2.00	
97	Catalog (5.294)	No. 5	2.00	
Year	**Spring Training Magazine**			
94	Chicago White Sox	inside	5.00	10.00
95	Michael! Baseball Yearbook	cover	10.00	15.00
Year	**Street and Smith Magazine**			
86-87	College, Pro, Prep Basketball, Can MJ & Bulls Bounce Back (5.295)	cover	35.00	50.00

5.290

5.291

5.292

5.293

5.294

5.295

88	Pro BB, Who's The Greatest?, Inaugural Issue (5.296)	cover	35.00	40.00
89	MVP Michael Jordan	cover	30.00	35.00
90/91	Michael's Too Much! Bulls Star Still on the Rise	cover	25.00	30.00
91/92	Michael Jordan NBA's MVP	cover	20.00	25.00
92/93	Olympic Uniform	cover	15.00	20.00
93/94	Jordan Soars Bulls Drive for 4	cover	10.00	15.00
95/96	Rare Air	cover	6.00	10.00
9/96	Unstoppabul! MJ's Drive for 5	cover	6.00	10.00
97	The Last Dance?	cover	4.00	5.00

Year	Team Sports Magazine			
8-9/90		cover	20.00	25.00

Year	Telephone Books	size		
82	Chapel Hill Cover		10.00	15.00
82	Chapel Hill (5.297)		20.00	35.00
11/91	Directories America, Area Code 708, red cover, 91/92, Bartlett, etc., MJ+5 Bulls (5.298)	8.5 x 11	15.00	20.00
1/92	Directories America Sprint Yellow Pages, Area Code 708, red cover, January 1992, Aurora MJ + 5 Bulls (5.299)	8.5 x 11	10.00	15.00
3/92	Directories America Sprint Yellow Pages, Area Code 708, red cover, March 92/93, Homer Township, MJ+ 5 Bulls (5.300)	8.5 x 11	10.00	15.00
92/93	Directories America, Crestwood, Tinley Park		8.00	12.00
92/93	Directories America Sprint Yellow Pages, Area Code 708, red cover, North Shore, Bannockburn, MJ + 5 Bulls (5.301)	8.5 x 11	7.00	10.00
92/93	Directories America Sprint Yellow Pages, Area Code 708, red cover, 92/93, Alsip, MJ + 5 Bulls (5.302)	6 x 9	7.00	10.00
92/93	Directories America Sprint Yellow Pages, Area Code 708, red cover, 92/93, SW Suburban, Brookfield, MJ + 5 Bulls (5.303)	8.5 x 11	7.00	10.00
92/93	Directories America Sprint Yellow Pages, Area Code 708, 92/93, Darien, Downers Grove, Lisle, Westmont (5.304)		10.00	15.00

Year   **The National Sport Daily**   **mag #**

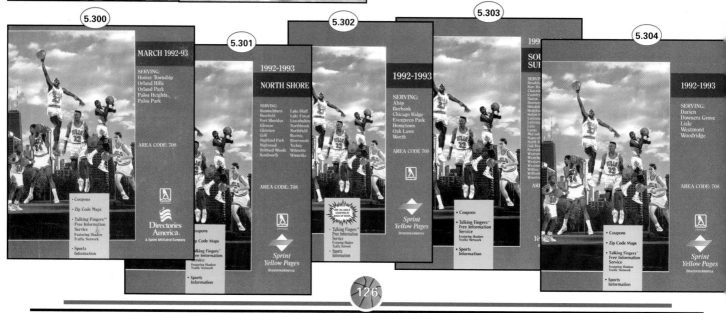

1/31/90	America's Bullish on Michael (5.305)	Prem. Ed.	45.00	60.00
12/18/90	Most Influential People in Sport	V1 N269	40.00	50.00
12/26/90	Chicago's Holiday Air	V1 N274	40.00	50.00
1/15/91	Central Showdown	V1 N287	35.00	45.00
3/28/91	New Monsters of the Midway	V2 N41	25.00	35.00
4/25/91	In This Season to Smile	V2 N61	35.00	45.00
5/20/91	Rare Jordan	V2 N78	35.00	45.00
5/28/91	Jordan Finally!	V2 N83	35.00	45.00
5/31/91	Michael vs. Magic	V2 N86	35.00	45.00
6/3/91	Err Jordan	V2 N87	30.00	40.00
6/6/91	Bulls Storm Back	V2 N90	25.00	35.00
6/7/91	Look Out, Bulls! You're in Magic's Kingdom Now	V2 N91	25.00	35.00
6/8/91	Bulls Air Out LA, 3-1	V2 N92	25.00	35.00
6/13/91	We Had a Ball	V2 N95	25.00	35.00

Year	Trading Cards Magazines			
12/91	Can Jordan Keep Soaring?	Cover	25.00	35.00
	—2 sided sheet insert			
8/93	Inside Scoop Beckett Honest Reporting on Price	cover	20.00	25.00
93	Tribute to MJ The World's Greatest Athlete and Stuff	1st edition	20.00	25.00
	—MJ Poster		10.00	15.00
1/94	End of an Era	cover	15.00	20.00
4/94	MJ's Field of Dreams	cover	15.00	20.00
6/95	Best of Best	cover	10.00	15.00

Year	Tuff Stuff Magazine & Cards	mag #		
12/89	Up in the Clouds over Michael Air Jordan	V-69	30.00	35.00
7/90	Ryan, large 2nd issue, No MJ	V 76	25.00	30.00
7/91	Jr.-Ken Griffey cover, No MJ	V1 N1	20.00	25.00
8/91	Jr.-Frank Thomas cover, No MJ	V1 N2	20.00	25.00
9/91	Card, red #23, white back, blue border	25	20.00	24.00
2/92	Jr.-Michael Jordan	V1 N8	18.00	24.00
3/92	Jr.-David Robinson cover, No MJ	V1 N9	18.00	24.00
7/92	Barcelona Bound, Team Picture	V9 N3	18.00	24.00
12/92	Michael Jordan, King of the Court	V9 N8	18.00	24.00
	—J. Elway, Collector's Edge Card	TS-1		
3/94	Is Shaq the New Jordan?		15.00	20.00
5/94	Piazza on cover, The Jordan Frenzy		15..00	20.00
6/94	Shaq's Magic, No MJ	V11 N2	15.00	20.00
5/95	Sweet! Behind the Scenes at Air Jordan's Relaunch	V12 N2	12.00	15.00
5/95	Starting Lineup, Jordan Hotter Than Ever	V3 N1	12.00	15.00
6/95	Number 45		12.00	15.00
1/96	Jam, Air Waves It's Jordan Show Again!		10.00	15.00
	—MJ & Shaq Poster		4.00	8.00
6/96	Jordan, Nobody Can Beat My Bulls	V13 N2	8.00	12.00
7/97	Michael! Scorching the NBA		5.00	8.00

Year	TV Guide Magazine			
12/26/92	MJ Olympic Flier or Ad for Hire (5.306)	cover	2.00	5.00
4/12/97	Kings of the Court, Can Any One Beat MJ? (5.307)	cover	5.00	10.00

5.305

5.306

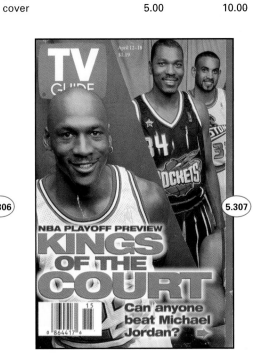

5.307

Year	US News & World Report			
3/24/97	Are Pro Sports Bad for Black Super America?	cover	4.00	6.00

Year	Video Games Magazines	mag #		
4/92	Game Players-Sega Genesis Strategy Guide Michael! MJ vs. Bird, Bulls vs. Lakers	V3 N2	50.00	65.00
11/92	Game Player PC Entertainment+insert, Jordan Goes Digital, 1	V6 N5	45.00	60.00
5/92	Game Pro-MJ vs. Bird 16 bit EH	cover	45.00	60.00
5/93	Game Pro-Sports! + Sports insert, Championship Sports Guide	cover	40.00	50.00
5/92	Video Games & Computer Equipment, Jordan vs. Bird	VVI N5	45.00	60.00
9/94	SNES-Mortal Kombat II, MJ Chaos in the Windy City-Pak Watch Section, MJ on page 110	V-64	40.00	50.00
12/94	SNES-Earthworm Jim, MJ Chaos in the Windy City-Now Playing Section, MJ on page 104	V-67	40.00	50.00
6/95	SNES-Weaponlord, MJ Chaos in the Windy City-Classified Information Section, MJ on page 68	V-73	35.00	45.00

MAGAZINES WITH MICHAEL JORDAN CARDS

Year	Ballstreet Magazines	mag # card #		
3/91	Magazine, Journal, Bo Jackson, bimonthly (5.308)	V2 N2	25.00	30.00
	—-Card, MJ swinging bat, red shirt, white pants, blue "C" cap, green back, story, trivia quiz, 4 x 6 (5.309)	19	5.00	10.00
1/92	Magazine, MJ in red 23, jump shot, bimonthly (5.310)	V2 N1	15.00	20.00
	—-Card, Magic & Michael, white & tan back, 4 x 6	9	5.00	10.00
	—-Card, MJ same as cover, white & tan back, 4 x 6	10	5.00	10.00
5/92	Magazine, MJ in white #9 USA, bimonthly (5.311)	V2 N5	15.00	20.00
	—-Card, MJ same as cover, white & tan back, 4 x 6	nno	5.00	10.00
7/92	Magazine, Shaq in LSU #33, bimonthly (5.312)	V2 N7	10.00	15.00
	—-Card, MJ with trophy, white & tan back, 4 x 6	nno	3.00	5.00
	—-Card, MJ & Pippen, white & tan back, 4 x 6	nno	3.00	5.00
9/92	Magazine, Joe Montana on cover, bimonthly (5.313)	V2 N9	8.00	12.00
	—-Card, Dream Team/MJ, white & tan back, 4 x 6	nno	3.00	4.00
	—-Card, MJ with flag on shoulder	nno	3.00	4.00

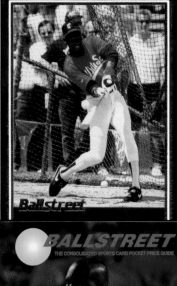

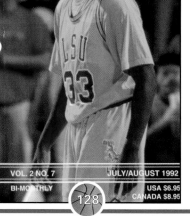

11/92	Magazine, E. Smith on cover, bimonthly (5.314)	V2N11	10.00	15.00
	—-Card, MJ hands on knees, red 23, white & tan back, 4 x 6	nno	3.00	5.00
12/92	Magazine, Shaq in Magic #32 white, bimonthly (5.315)	V2N12	15.00	20.00
	—-Card, MJ in USA 9, holding ball, white & tan back, 4 x 6	nno	3.00	5.00
	—-Card, MJ with flag on shoulders, 2 fingers raised, 4 x 6	nno	3.00	5.00
	—-Card, Dream Team/MJ, white & tan back, 4 x 6	nno	3.00	5.00
1/93	Magazine, News, Premier Issue, Shaq cover, gold "B" & circle on cards, 25,000 issued (5.316)	V1 N1 806	10.00	15.00
	—-Card, MJ walking, red #23, small head picture on back (5.317)	nno	5.00	10.00
1/93	Magazine, News, Premier Issue, Shaq cover, platinum "B" & circle on cards, Platinum Issue Numbered 20,000 to 25,000 (5.318)	V1 N1	10.00	15.00
	—-Card, MJ walking, red #23, small head picture on back (5.319)	nno	5.00	10.00
3/93	Magazine, News, Ripkin cover, gold "B" & circle on cards, 20,000 issues produced (5.320)	V1 N2	3.00	6.00
	—-Card, MJ dribbling, tongue out, small head picture on back (3.321)	nno	2.00	3.00

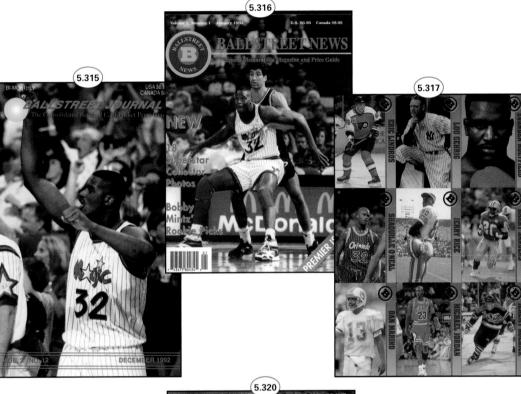

3/93	Magazine, News, Ripkin cover, Platinum Edition, gold stripe on right side, 5,000 issues produced (3.322)		V1 N2	12.00	15.00
	—Card, MJ dribbling, tongue out, small head picture on back (5.323)		nno	8.00	12.00
7/93	Magazine, News, MJ cover, gold "B" & circle on cards, 20,000 issues produced (5.324)		V1 N4	5.00	10.00
	—Card, MJ dribbling, #23 white (5.325)			3.00	5.00
7/93	Magazine, News, MJ cover, Platinum Edition, platinum stripe on right side card, 5,000 issues produced (5.326)		V1 N4	10.00	15.00
	—Card, MJ dribbling, #23 white (5.327)		nno	8.00	10.00
9/93	Magazine, News, Joe Montana cover, gold "B" & circle on cards, 20,000 issues produced (5.328)		V1 N5	5.00	10.00
	—Card, MJ jumping to dunk, For Promotional Use Only-back (5.329)		nno	2.00	5.00

		mag #	card #		
/93	Magazine, News, Joe Montana cover, Platinum Edition, platinum stripe on right side on card, 5,000 issues produced (5.330)	V1 N5		10.00	15.00
	——Card, MJ jumping to dunk, For Promotional Use Only-back (5.331)	nno		5.00	10.00
Year	**Baseball Card Magazine**				
2/91	Presents Superstar & Rookie Special, strip with Mattingly, MJ, Ripkin, back with red top, pink bottom, black outline, quiz (5.332)			12.00	20.00
	——MJ insert card, tan top, blue bottom, hold ball, red 23, black signature (5.333)	19		5.00	12.00
2/92	Presents "Basketball 93 Yearbook & Card Preview," Shaq Attack (5.334)	V3 N5		15.00	20.00
	——MJ Card, red 23, holding ball, white/black border & blue background front, "Bulls" bottom, black orange & white back, quiz on back (5.335)	1		10.00	15.00
1/93	Presents "Basketball 94 Yearbook & Card Preview," Shaq's Back (5.336)	NNO		15.00	20.00
	——MJ Card, red 23, hands on hips, black/white/red border & blue edge front, "Bulls" & basket on bottom, red, black, pink card back, information & card values (5.337)	NNO		10.00	15.00

5.330

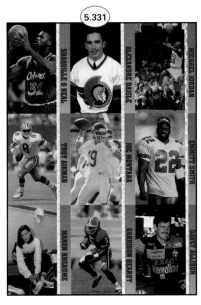

5.331

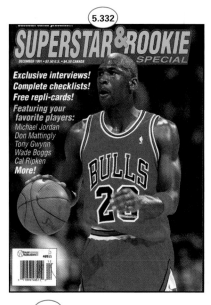

5.332

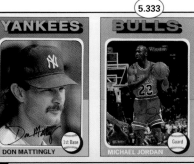

5.333

5.334

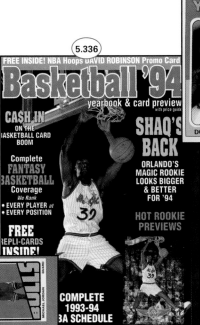

5.336

5.337

5.335

1/94	Presents "Sports Cards," Issue 101-8 insert + Robinson Skybox cards, Shaq: Should You Invest in His Cards (5.338)	V14 N1	15.00	20.00
	——MJ Card, red 23, holding ball, basket bottom right, brown border, white black & yellow back, information & card values (5.339)	8	7.00	15.00

Year	Cartwrights Magazine	mag # card #		
92	Roger Clemens cover, summer large size issue (5.340)	V1 N3	4.00	8.00
	——MJ Card, Player Choice, red 23, tongue out, dribbling	9	2.00	4.00
93	Nolan Ryan cover, 1st Anniversary Issue (5.341)	V2 N1	10.00	20.00
	——MJ Card, Players Choice, red 23, gold foil cards, standing with hands on hips	7	4.00	8.00
93	Nolan Ryan cover, 1st Anniversary Issue, Special Collector's Edition	V2 N1	30.00	40.00
	——MJ Card, Players Choice, red 23, blue foil cards, standing with hands on hips	7	15.00	25.00

Year	Collectors Chronicle Magazine	card #		
8/7/92	Olympic Basketball Preview, 50,000 print run (5.343)	cover	15.00	
	——MJ Card, 2 poses, shooting with left hand & running; white USA uniform with no number, stars on bottom front, red border & blue background on front, American Flag on back, 92 USA Barcelona on back (5.344)	USA 3	7.00	10.00
	——Team Card/MJ, 5 players, 5" x 7.5" (5.345)	NNO	3.00	5.00

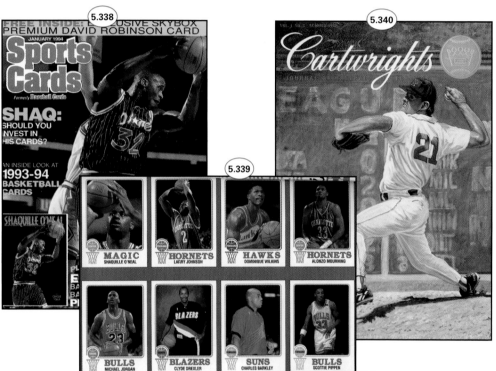

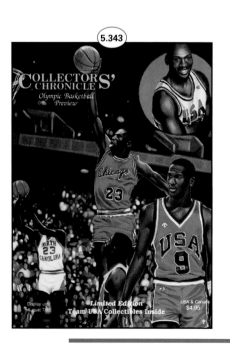

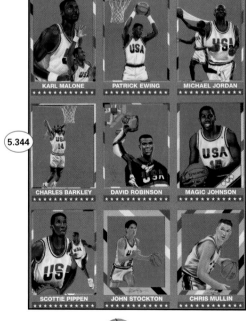

Year	Comic Books	mag #	card #	
90's	Personality Comics Presents Sports Personalities MJ, 2 views, closeup in red t-shirt, white uniform holding ball, #293 of 600, sealed pack (5.346)	13	18.00	25.00
	—MJ Card, blue t-shirt, "Michael Jorden" misspelling (5.347)	nno	10.00	15.00
1/92	Celebrity Books, Bo Jackson vs. MJ, gray background, suits on both, Limited Trading Card Edition, #1, 2 Kirks back cover with no writing, 3,000 produced (5.348)		20.00	25.00
	—Bo Jackson vs. MJ, Bo batting, blue background (5.349)	nno	4.00	6.00
	—Bo Jackson vs. MJ, MJ red 23, dribbling, front shot (5.349)	nno	4.00	6.00
	—Bo Jackson vs. MJ, Bo batting, yellow background (5.349)	nno	4.00	6.00
	—Bo Jackson vs. MJ, 2 shots of MJ, head shot, flying in air (5.349)	nno	4.00	6.00
5/92	Celebrity Books, Bo Jackson vs. MJ, purple & yellow front cover, 2 Kirks back cover with writing, 2,000 produced (5.350)		15.00	

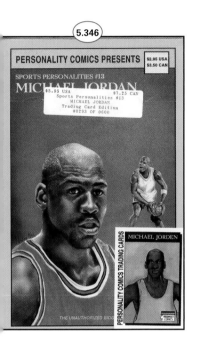

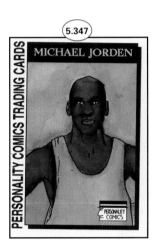

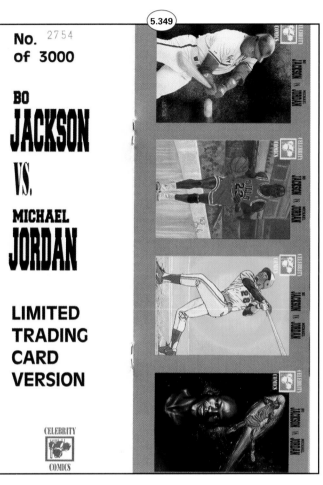

	—-MJ 23 dribbling with right hand, front view, blank back, b&w (5.351)	nno	5.00	
	—-MJ 23 layup with left hand, blank back, b&w (5.351)	nno	5.00	
2/93	Revolutionary Comics Sports Superstars Annual (5.352)	1	10.00	
	—-Cover Card, Series 1, cards 1,2,3 (5.353)		2.00	
	—-MJ Card, 84-85 Rookie Year, white 23 (5.354)	S1 C1	2.00	
	—-MJ Card, Sports Superstars Annual, red 23, 2 views (5.353)	S1 C2	2.00	
	—-MJ Card, Greatest Moment, red 23, 2 views (5.353)	S1 C3	2.00	
Year	**Diamond Sports Memorabilia Magazine**	**mag #**		
3/4/92	MJ on cover, light blue foil cards, 40,000 issue (5.355)	V1 N2	15.00	
	—-MJ Card, holding ball, white 23	12	8.00	12.00
Year	**Hoops**			
89-90	Sheet & Program, NBA All-Star Game, Houston 2/10/89, Issued at 2/9/90 Miami Game, 15,000 produced, perforated sheet (5.356)	4 of 4		
		6 cards		
		1 book	45.00	
	M. Eaton	174		
	M. Jordan	21	15.00	25.00
	J. Worthy	219		
	P. Ewing	159		
	C. Drexler	69		
	C. Barkley	96		

Year	Investors; Focus, Journal, & Analyst	mag # card #		
10/94	Focus-MJ on cover, #997, gold foil, 5,000 issues produced	I-1	20.00	25.00
	—-MJ Cover Card, red 23, running, no ball	nno		
	—-MJ Card, white 23, holding ball	6		
	—-MJ Card, White Sox Uniform, leaning on bat	9		
10/94	Focus-MJ on cover, Platinum Issue, # S, platinum foil on cards, 500 issues produced	I-1	50.00	60.00
	—-MJ Cover Card, red 23, running, no ball	nno		
	—-MJ Card, white 23, holding ball	6		
	—-MJ Card, White Sox Uniform, leaning on bat	9		
11/91	Journal, Premiere Edition, Eric Lindros Hockey Cover, 10,000 issued	V1 I1	10.00	15.00
	—-MJ Card, dunking, red 23	3		
1/92	Journal, Canadian Connection, gold foil on cards, 17,500 issued, 13,000 distributed	V2 I2	20.00	25.00
	—-MJ Card, golf swing, white hat, purple shorts	14		
3/92	Journal, MJ on cover with hair, gold foil on cards, 17,500 issued	V2 I3	15.00	20.00
	—-MJ Card, red 23 dribbling	23		
	—-Magic Card/MJ red 23	31		
3/92	Journal, MJ on cover with hair, silver foil on cards, #S of 1,750 issued	V2 I3	35.00	40.00
	—-MJ Card, red 23 dribbling	23		
	—-Magic Card/MJ red 23	31		
5/92	Journal, Ryne Sandberg, gold foil on cards, 24,000 issued	V2 I4	10.00	15.00
	—-MJ Card, red 23 jumping with ball	43		
5/92	Journal, Ryne Sandberg, blue foil on cards, #B of 2,400 issued	V2 I4	20.00	25.00
	—-MJ Card, red 23 jumping with ball	43		
7/92	Journal, Shaquille O'Neil, gold foil on cards, 17,500 issued	V2 I5	15.00	20.00
	—-MJ Card, red warmup jacket	59		
7/92	Journal, Shaquille O'Neil, purple foil on cards, #P of 1,750 issued	V2 I5	25.00	30.00
	—-MJ Card, red warmup jacket	59		
9/92	Journal, Mickey Mantle, gold foil on cards, 17,500 issued	V2 I6	15.00	20.00
	—-MJ Card, dunking over Lakers	73		
9/92	Journal, Mickey Mantle, red foil on cards, 1,750 issued	V2 I6	25.00	30.00
	—-MJ Card, dunking over Lakers	73		
11/92	Journal, Magic Johnson, gold foil on cards, 17,500 issued	V2 I7	15.00	20.00
	—-MJ Card, black 9, shooting	100		
11/92	Journal, Magic Johnson, light blue foil on cards, #B of 1,750 issued	V2 I7	25.00	30.00
	—-MJ Card, black 9, shooting	100		
12/92	Journal, Cal Ripken, Jr., gold foil on cards, 12,000 issued	1st Ann.	15.00	20.00
	—-MJ Card, white 9, dribbling	116		
12/92	Journal, Cal Ripken, Jr., copper foil on cards, #C of 1,200 issued	1stAnn	25.00	30.00
	—-MJ Card, white 9, dribbling	116		
1/93	Journal, Clyde Drexler, gold foil on cards, Issue 8, 2,500 issued	V3 I1	15.00	20.00
	—-MJ Card, red 23, passing, black back, yellow outline	2		
1/93	Journal, Clyde Drexler, rainbow foil on cards, Issue 8, 500 issued	V3 I1	50.00	75.00
	—-MJ Card, red 23, passing, black back, yellow outline	2		
1/93	Journal, Manon Rheaume, gold foil on cards, Issue 8, 17,500 issued	V3 I1	15.00	20.00
	—-MJ Card, red 23, passing, black back, yellow outline	2		
1/93	Journal, Manon Rheaume, holofoil foil on cards, Issue 8, 750 issued	V3 I1	35.00	40.00
	—-MJ Card, red 23, passing, black back, yellow outline	2		
1/93	Journal, Manon Rheaume autograph edition, blue foil on cards, Issue 8, autograph edition, 1,000 issued, Certificate of Authenticity-1/20/94	V3 I1	45.00	60.00
	—-MJ Card, red 23, passing, black back, yellow outline	2		
5/93	Journal, Shaq, gold foil on cards, 10,000 issued	I-9	10.00	15.00
	—-MJ Card, standing, red 23, hands on hips	35		
5/93	Journal, Shaq, blue foil on cards, #B of 1,000 issued	I-9	40.00	65.00
	—-MJ Card, standing, red 23, hands on hips	35		
5/93	Journal, Charles Barkley, gold foil on cards, 2,500 issued	I-9	15.00	20.00
	—-MJ Card, standing, red 23, hands on hips	35		
5/93	Journal, Charles Barkley, blue foil on cards, 500 issued	I-9	60.00	75.00
	—-MJ Card, standing, red 23, hands on hips	35		
5/93	Journal, Jamal Mashburn, gold foil on cards, 2,500 issued	I-9	10.00	15.00
	—-MJ Card, standing, red 23, hands on hips	35		
5/93	Journal, Jamal Mashburn, blue foil on cards, 500 issued	I-9	60.00	75.00
	—-MJ Card, standing, red 23, hands on hips	35		
9/93	Journal, MJ, gold foil on cards, 17,500 issued	I-10	10.00	15.00
	—-MJ Card, high 5 Barkley, red 23	37		
9/93	Journal, MJ, red foil on cards, #R of 1,750 issued	I-10	30.00	45.00
	—-MJ Card, high 5 Barkley, red 23	37		
6/94	Journal, MJ, Gretzky, Ripken, Drexler, gold foil on cards, 5,000 issued	I-11	15.00	25.00
	—-MJ Front Cover Card, Sox Uniform, white batting, tape on hands	nno		
	—-MJ Back Cover Card, Golfing, swinging club, purple shirt			
	—-MJ Card, Sox Uniform, black, holding bat	8		
	—-MJ Card, holding ball, red 23	18		
	—-MJ 8 x 10 picture, Sox Uniform, white, batting			

6/94	Journal, MJ, Gretzky, Ripken, Drexler, silver foil on cards, 500 issued	I-11	60.00	75.00
	——MJ Front Cover Card, Sox Uniform, white batting, tape on hands, batting, tape on hands	nno		
	——MJ Back Cover Card, Golfing, swinging club, purple shirt			
	——MJ Card, Sox Uniform, black, holding bat	8		
	——MJ Card, holding ball, red 23	18		
	——MJ 8 x 10 picture Sox Uniform, white, batting			
3/95	Journal, gold foil on cards	I-12	10.00	15.00
	——MJ Front Cover Card, dunking, white 23, gold cross hatch	C-3		
	——MJ Back Cover Card, dripping, white 23, 95 Sport Super Star	TP-3		
	——MJ Back Cover Card, shooting, white 23, gold circles	TP-2		
3/95	Journal, silver foil on cards	I-12	30.00	45.00
	——MJ Front Cover Card, dunking, white 23, gold cross hatch	C-3		
	——MJ Back Cover Card, dripping, white 23, 95 Sport Super Star	TP-3		
	——MJ Back Cover Card, shooting, white 23, gold circles	TP-2		
6/95	Journal, gold foil on cards, 2,000 issued	I-14	10.00	15.00
	——MJ Front Cover Card, white 45, hands on knees	TP-2		
	——MJ Back Cover Card, white 45, holding ball left side	C-1		
	——MJ Back Cover Card, white 45, dribbling with left hand	HP-3		
	——MJ Back Cover Card, white 45, standing with finger pointing	M-2		
6/95	Journal, silver foil on cards, 200 issued	I-14	75.00	100.00
	——MJ Front Cover Card, white 45, hands on knees	TP-2		
	——MJ Back Cover Card, white 45, holding ball left side	C-1		
	——MJ Back Cover Card, white 45, dribbling with left hand	HP-3		
	——MJ Back Cover Card, white 45, standing with finger pointing	M-2		
7/95	Journal, gold foil on cards, 2,000 issued	I-15	10.00	15.00
	——MJ Front Cover Card, red 45, hands stretched to sides	AB-1		
	——MJ Back Cover Card, white 45, hands over head	MP-1		
	——MJ Back Cover Card, white 45, walking, hands at sides	TP-1		
	——Shaq Back Cover Card/MJ, white 45, MJ's back view, hands over head	AP-1		
	——MJ & Shaq Back Cover Card	HP-2		
7/95	Journal, silver foil on cards, 200 issued	I-15	75.00	100.00
	——MJ Front Cover Card, red 45, hands stretched to sides	AB-1		
	——MJ Back Cover Card, white 45, hands over head	MP-1		
	——MJ Back Cover Card, white 45, walking, hands at sides	TP-1		
	——Shaq Back Cover Card/MJ, white 45, MJ's back view, hands over head	AP-1		
	——MJ & Shaq Back Cover Card	HP-2		
8/95	Journal, gold foil on cards, 2500 issued	I-16	15.00	20.00
	——MJ Front Cover Card, white 45, dribbling with left hand	TP-1		
	——MJ Front Cover Card, white 45, red 23, two poses	MP-2		
	——MJ Back Cover Card, red 45, shooting, star in background	CP-1		
	——MJ Back Cover Card, red 23, walking, looking to right	MP-1		
8/95	Journal, silver foil on cards, 250 issued	I-16	75.00	100.00
	——MJ Front Cover Card, white 45, dribbling with left hand	TP-1		
	——MJ Front Cover Card, white 45, red 23, two poses	MP-2		
	——MJ Back Cover Card, red 45, shooting, star in background	CP-1		
	——MJ Back Cover Card, red 23, walking, looking to right	MP-1		
8/95	Journal, copper foil on cards, Special Issue made for Don Losack, 125 issued	I-16	100.00	125.00
	——MJ Front Cover Card, white 45, dribbling with left hand	TP-1		
	——MJ Front Cover Card, white 45, red 23, two poses	MP-2		
	——MJ Back Cover Card, red 45, shooting, star in background	CP-1		
	——MJ Back Cover Card, red 23, walking, looking to right	MP-1		
9/95	Journal, gold foil on cards, 2500 issued	I-17	15.00	20.00
	——MJ Front Cover Card, white 23, shooting, hearts-background	CP-1		
	——MJ Front Cover Card, red 45, shooting, BB-background	TP-1		
	——MJ & Smith & Thomas Back Cover Card, white 45, dribbling	AP-1		
	——MJ Back Cover Card, white 23, shooting, "Jordan" background	HP-2		
9/95	Journal, silver foil on cards, 250 issued	I-17	75.00	100.00
	——MJ Front Cover Card, white 23, shooting, hearts- shooting, hearts-background	CP-1		
	——MJ Front Cover Card, red 45, shooting, BB-background	TP-1		
	——MJ & Smith & Thomas Back Cover Card, white 45, dribbling	AP-1		
	——MJ Back Cover Card, white 23, shooting, "Jordan" background	HP-2		
1/96	The Analyst, Premier Issue, gold foil on cards, 2000 issued	I-1	10.00	15.00
	——MJ Front Cover Card, white 23, white WS & golfing	FF		
	——MJ Back Cover Card, white 45, holding ball overhead	HP		
1/96	The Analyst, Premier Issue, copper foil on cards, 200 issued	I-1	75.00	100.00
	——MJ Front Cover Card, white 23, white WS & golfing	FF		
	——MJ Back Cover Card, white 45, holding ball overhead	HP		

Year	Kayes Magazine & Cards	mag #		
10/91	Sports Cards News & Price Guide, silver foil & orange border cards (5.357)	N1 cover	20.00	30.00
	—-MJ Card, rebounding, red 23 (5.358)	2	4.00	8.00
	—-MJ Portrait Cover Card, 3 views of MJ, 5 x 8	2	6.00	10.00

Year	Legends Magazines	mag #		
90	Clark & Ott, cover #10	V3 N3	10.00	15.00
	—-MJ Card, dunking over Laker, red 23, gold foil	16		
90	Mattingly & DiMaggio, cover #11	V3 N3	25.00	30.00
	—-MJ Card, dunking over Laker, red 23, gold foil	16		
5/91	Rickey Henderson, cover #16	V4 N2	10.00	15.00
	—-MJ Card, hands on knees & chin, red Nike shirt, silver foil	11		
5/91	Michael Jordan, cover #17	V4 N2	25.00	30.00
	—-MJ Card, hands on knees & chin, red Nike shirt, silver foil	11		
7/92	Holyfield, Pendleton, Wilkins, Sanders, cover #32, red foil cards	2 13th NSCC	15.00	20.00
	—-MJ Card on Sheet with Clemens, Henderson & Hall, Commemorative Sheet #4, 30,000 produced	C-14		
9/92	Darryl Strawberry, cover #36, red foil on cards	V5 N5	8.00	15.00
	—-MJ Card, closeup, red 23	48		
9/92	Mark Messier, cover #37, red foil on cards	V5 N5	4.00	10.00
	—-MJ Card, closeup, red 23	48		
9/92	Michael Jordan, cover #38, Limited Edition Cover, gold foil on cards, randomly inserted 1-2 copies for every 40 regular issues ordered	V5 N5	55.00	70.00
	—-MJ Card, closeup, red 23	48		
11/92	Roberto Alomar, cover #39, red foil on cards	V5 N6	7.00	15.00
	—-MJ Archives Postcard	C6 C17		
11/92	Emmitt Smith, cover #40, red foil on cards	V5 N6	25.00	30.00
	—-MJ Archives Postcard	C6 C17		
7/93	MJ + Chicago Sports Stars, cover #49, silver foil on cards, 14th National	V6 N4 14th NSCC	8.00	15.00
7/93	MJ + Chicago Sports Stars, cover #49, silver foil on cards, autograph issue	V6 N4 14th NSCC	40.00	50.00
7/93	MJ + Chicago Sports Stars, cover #49, 1993 Limited Gold Edition, gold foil on cards	V6 N4 14th NSCC	40.00	50.00
9/93	Shaq, cover #51	V6 N5	10.00	15.00
	—-MJ Archive Post Card			
7/98	MJ, cover #84	V10 N3	10.00	1400
	—-MJ & R. Jackson card sheet, 6 MJ cards, gold borders, non perforated			
	—-MJ & R. Jackson Archives post card sheet, 2 MJ post cards, non perforated			
7/98	Reggie Jackson, cover #85	V10 N3	5.00	7.00
	—-MJ & R. Jackson card sheet, 6 MJ cards, gold borders, non perforated			
	—-MJ & R. Jackson Archives post card sheet, 2 MJ post cards, non perforated			

Year	Little Basketball Big Leaguers			
91	Leaguers, Nash & Zullo (5.359)	cover	35.00	
	—-MJ Card, kid picture	nno		

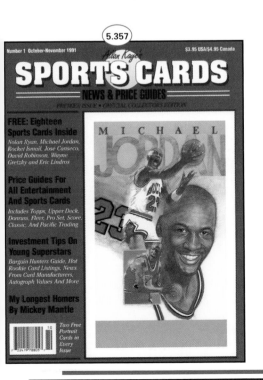

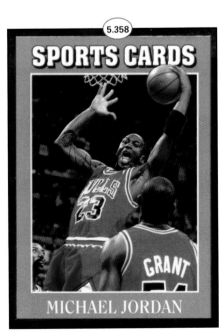

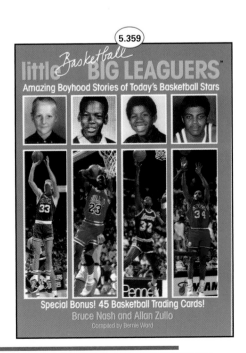

Year	5 Majeur French Magazine	mag #		
-	card	N-10		
1/93	Shaq cover	N-21	65.00	
	——MJ USA Olympic Dream Team Card, 4 x 6			
	——Ad Card/MJ, 4 x 6 (number add card) (5.360)			
	——Malone USA Olympic Dream Team card, 4 x 6			
	——Mullin USA Olympic Dream Team card, 4 x 6			
	——Price USA Olympic Dream Team card, 4 x 6			
	——Anderson USA Olympic Dream Team card, 4 x 6			
	——Rodman USA Olympic Dream Team card, 4 x 6			
	——Wilkens & Pistons Poster			
9/93	MJ cover, plain clothes red top & white bottom (5.361)	N-28	60.00	
	——MJ Card, red 23, 4 x 6			
	——MJ & Shaq Poster			
	——Paxson card, 4 x 6			
	——Armstrong card, 4 x 6			
	——Williams card, 4 x 6			
	——Jackson card, 4 x 6			
	——Pippen card, 4 x 6			
	——Grant card, 4 x 6			
	——Cartwright card, 4 x 6			

Year	Miscellaneous Issues			
7/95	Champion Sports Memorabilia, DiMaggio cover		15.00	20.00
	——MJ insert card	8		

Year	McDonald's			
9/24/92	Book, NBA Fantasy Packs Bluebook, sales promotion book for extra value meals, highlighting strategy for the promotion of 2/26-3/25/93, MJ written up inside, blue cover		25.00	35.00
	——Insert sheet, 92 UD card #44 reproduction			

Year	MVP Magazine	mag # card #		
1/92	M. Jordan cover, Premier Issue (5.362)	V1 N1	15.00	20.00
	——MJ Card, red 23 holding ball, 4 x 6 card, 50,000 issued (5.363)		10.00	15.00

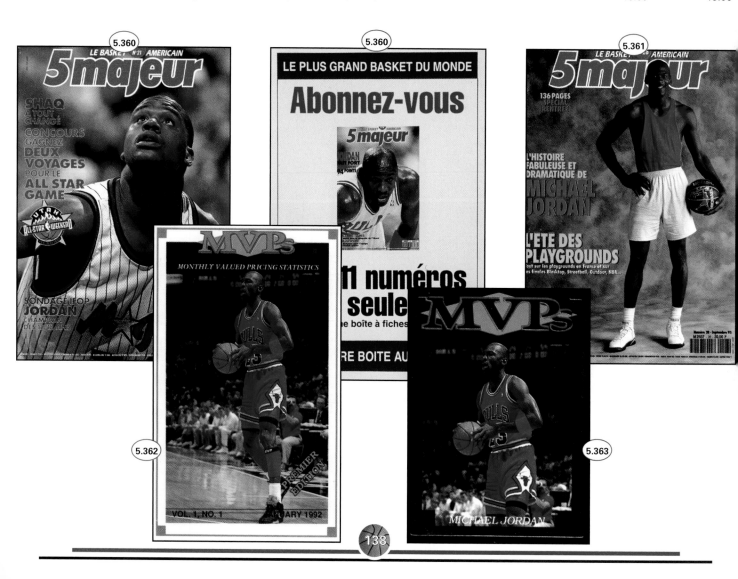

Year	NBA Inside Stuff Magazine			
11/93	1,2,3,4, Michael? (5.364)	cover	6.00	10.00
	—93-94 Fleer NBA Commemorative Sheet, 8.5 x 11, No MJ , Pippen, Hardaway, Manning, Ainge, Rivers, Coleman, Adams, Kemp			
	—92-93 Fleer Ultra NBA Jam Session Card/MJ, Perry, Causwell, Pippen, Parish, Augmon-front, Jordan, Malone, Williams, Grant, Woolridge-back (5.365)	nno	2.00	3.00
	—92-93 Fleer Ultra NBA Jam Session Card/No MJ, Robinson, Mutombo, Thorpe, Olajuwon, Kemp-front, Barkley, Ellison, Morris, Daugherty, Coleman-back	nno		
7/94	Global Giants		5.00	10.00
	—MJ USA Basketball Highlights Commemorative Sheet, 8.5 x 11, UD Issue, World Championship of Basketball, 8/4/94-8/14/94 (5.366)	nno	2.00	5.00
12/96	Rising Stars, different cover (5.367)		2.00	5.00
	—MJ UD "Still The Best" Commemorative Sheet, 8.5 x 11, 95-96 UD MJ #23 card on sheet	nno		
12/96	Jordan Rules Again, different cover (5.368)		8.00	15.00
	—MJ UD "Still The Best" Commemorative Sheet, 8.5 x 11, 95-96 UD MJ #23 card on sheet (5.369)	nno		
5/97	Drive for 5 (5.370)	cover	3.00	
	—MJ Poster	nno		

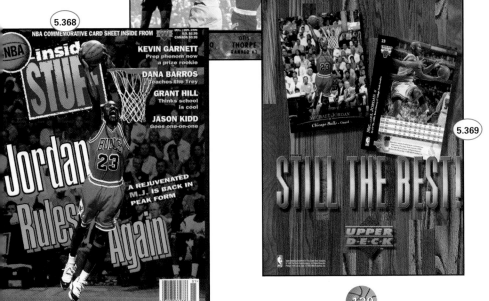

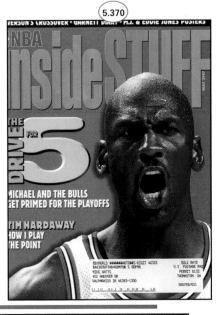

Year	Olympic Magazines	card #		
92	Book, USA Basketball Stickers-15, Golden Pub. #2398	cover	10.00	15.00
	—MJ Sticker	10		

Year	Petersons Magazines			
92-93	Sport Basketball Pro Review/92 MVP Holoview Card on orange cover		20.00	45.00
92-93	Sport Basketball Pro Review/92 MVP Holoview Card on yellow cover		20.00	45.00

Year	Pocket Pages Magazines	mag # card #		
9/92	MJ USA Basketball cover, USA black #9	V2-N3	15.00	20.00
	—MJ Card, USA BB, white #9, tongue out, holding ball	18		
9/92	Nolan Ryan Cover		10.00	15.00
	—MJ Card, USA BB, white #9, tongue out, holding ball	18		
8/93	Chris Webber cover	V3-N4	10.00	15.00
	—MJ Card, white 23, arms & hands in air, fists tight, silver foil on card top	48		
8/93	Mike Piazza Cover		10.00	15.00
	—MJ Card, white 23, arms & hands in air, fists tight, silver foil on card top	48		
1/94	MJ cover, white 23, shooting ball overhead	V4-N1	15.00	20.00
	—MJ Card, Ryan & MJ, white 23, silver foil on card top	56		
	—MJ Card, dribbling, white 23, silver foil on card top	58-A		
1/94	Wayne Gretzky Cover		15.00	20.00
	—MJ Card, Ryan & MJ, white 23, silver foil on card top	56		
	—MJ Card, dribbling, white 23, silver foil on card top	58-A		
4/94	MJ cover, White Sox white & black uniform	V4-N1	10.00	20.00
	—MJ Card, two views, white 23 & black & white WS uniform, silver foil on card top	64		
4/94	Frank Thomas Cover		20.00	30.00
	—MJ Card, two views, white 23 & black & white WS uniform, silver foil on card top	64		

Year	Scholastic Magazines	mag #		
97	Ultimate NBA Postcard Book, Mitch Richmond, MJ, L. Super MJ inside Vaught,	back cover	10.00	15.00

Year	Sport Educational	card #		
91-92	Magazine, Basketball Edition		8.00	12.00
	—MJ Card, dribbling right hand, tongue out, red 23, white back, blue statistics, 2 player picture	1		

Year	Sporting Magazine	mag #		
95-96	Magazine from England		35.00	45.00
	—MJ Pop-up			

Year	Sport Action Basket (French Magazine)	card #		
	—Issue # 53, Fling Machine, wearing jersey #23.	5317	35.00	75.00
	—Issue # 54, Star Planetair, golfing	5404	35.00	75.00
	—Issue # 54, Gold Medal, wearing jersey # 9	5413	35.00	100.00
	—Issue # 56, Batman, White Sox uniform	5615	35.00	75.00

Year	Sports Cards & Value Line Review Price Guides	mag #		
9/92	Jordan, Michael Takes His Show to Barcelona!	V2 N9		
		cover	10.00	15.00
	—MJ Card, Prime Pics, red 23, set shot, blue, red, yellow back, 91-92 NBA Hoops MVP card on back	45		
4/93	1992 In Review-6 insert cards	V3 N4	15.00	20.00
	—MJ Card, Prime Pics, red 23, jumping to shoot, dunk, mouth open, blue, red, yellow back, 91/92 Fleer AS Team card on back	16		

Year	Sports Collectors Digest	mag # card #		
11/90	Baseball Card Price Guide, 5 insert cards	32	15.00	20.00
	—MJ Card, white WS shirt, holding bat on right shoulder, C on dark cap, white & red back	51		
91	Football, Basketball & Hockey Price Guide, orange cover with Namath, MJ & W Gretzky on front	cover	15.00	20.00
	—MJ Repli Card for '75 Topps BB Set, holding ball, red 23, tan top blue card bottom, black signature, red top pink bottom on back, quiz at top, perforated card	nno		
11/91	Football Basketball & Hockey Collector with Price Guide	cover	10.00	15.00
	—91 Fleer Sheet, MJ card	236		
7/92	Sport Card Price Guide, 8 insert cards	52	15.00	20.00
	—MJ Card, red 23 holding ball, green & gray back	41		
7/93	Sports Card Price Guide, 8 insert cards	64	15.00	20.00
	—MJ Card, white shirt, blue pants, holding ball, blue/white front, blue stripe on left, quiz on back, red black & white back	55		
1/94	Sports Card Price Guide, inserts	70	10.00	15.00
	—MJ Card, dunking, red 23, blue stripe on left front, blue/white front, blue stripe on left, quiz on back, red black & white back	102		

Year	Sports Illustrated for Kids	mag #	card #		
2/89	It's Air Gretzky!	V1 N2		45.00	65.00
	—MJ Card, holding ball, tongue out, red 23, aqua border, quiz on back		16	25.00	40.00
1/92	Bo! Wrestles with His Future in Sports	V4 N1		35.00	40.00
	—MJ Card, MJ holding ball to shoot, red 23, aqua border, quiz on back		4	15.00	20.00
6/94	Soccer Madness!	V6 N6		20.00	30.00
	—MJ Card, WS uniform, catching a ball, tongue out		270	10.00	15.00
3/95	Shaq!	V7 N3		15.00	20.00
	—MJ Card, kid picture batting		349	5.00	10.00
6/95	Rockin!	V7 N6		10.00	15.00
	—MJ Card, layup, white 45		374	4.00	8.00
4/97	Here Comes Baseball Catch It!	V9 N4		8.00	12.00
	—MJ Card, golfing, red shirt		571	3.00	5.00
Sum 98	Extra: Totally Michael; Special Collectors Edition	cover		4.00	6.00
	—1969 Ogden Elementary School	1			
	—1978 Laney High School	2			
	—1984 University of North Carolina	3			
	—1985 Rookie of the Year	4			
	—1991 Playing Golf	5			
	—1992 US Olympic Team	6			
	—1994 Birmingham Barons	7			
	—1995 The Comeback	8			
	—1996 Chicago Bulls: The Best Team Ever	9			

Year	Sports Report Magazine	mag #	card #		
92	MJ cover, gold foil on cards, 10,000 issued	V1 I1		15.00	25.00
	—MJ Card, shooting, red 23, ball overhead		16		
92	MJ cover, silver foil on cards, 1,000 issued	V1 I1		40.00	55.00
	—MJ Card, shooting, red 23, ball overhead		16		
93	Shaquille O'Neal cover, gold foil on cards, 7,500 issued	V1 I2		45.00	60.00
	—MJ Card, dunking, white 23		23		
93	Shaquille O'Neal cover, silver foil on cards, 750 issued	V1 I2		50.00	65.00
	—MJ Card, dunking, white 23		23		

Year	Spot Light Magazine				
4/94	Spot Light Magazine Card Strip	3 cards		6.00	12.00
	—T. Aikman	3		2.00	4.00
	—MJ Card	2		2.00	4.00
	—N. Ryan	6		2.00	4.00

Year	Top Stars Magazine	card #			
8/9/93	Top Stars Magazine Card Strip, "Hot Stars"	3 cards		15.00	20.00
	—MJ Card, jumping to dunk, 23 red	4			
	—F. Thomas	5			
	—N. Ryan	6			

Year	Trading Cards Magazines	mag #	card #		
3/96	MJ cover, 3 insert cards			5.00	8.00
	—MJ Card, 95-96 UD		23		
	—MJ Poster				

Year	Tuff Stuff Magazine	mag #	card #		
2/91	MJ on cover, large size issue	V7 N10		10.00	15.00
	—MJ Cover Card, 3 x 5 card		5		
	—MJ Card, 3 x 5 card		6		
9/91	Jr-Joe Montana cover	V1 N3		10.00	15.00
	—MJ Card		25		
10/91	Jr-Cal Ripkin cover-WOW!	V1 N4		10.00	15.00
	—MJ Card, MJ & J Erving, Doctors of Dunk		28		
11/91	Jr-Barry Sanders cover	V1 N5		10.00	15.00
	—MJ Card, 91 Fleer AS, promotional sample sheet		236		
	—MJ Card, Tuff Stuff Jr. MJ Contest Card, MJ jump shot, side-front view, red 23, ball in right hand, blue border with red, yellow and green spots on back the card was submitted by Mark T. Laposky, from Cherokee, IA, Age 16, Why I Chose This Player: "Because I believe...		nno		
91	Jr-Special Issue, The 1991 NBA Finals	cover		6.00	12.00
	—MJ Card, On Tempo, red & gold front borders	1			
	—MJ Card, On Basketball, tan & white backs	2			
	—MJ Card, On Magic Johnson	3			
	—MJ Card, On Perception	4			
	—MJ Card, On His Favorite Fan	5			
	—MJ Card, On the Future of the Game	6			
	—MJ Card, On His Success Formula	7			
	—MJ Card, On Role Models	8			
	—MJ Card, 1991 Finals Record	9			

——Magic Card/MJ, On Learning BB, purple & gold front borders	10
——Magic Card/MJ, On Passing, tan & white backs	14
——Magic Card/MJ, On His Moves	17
——Magic Card/MJ, 91 Finals Record	18
——Phil Jackson Card/MJ	21
——Cliff Levingston Card/MJ (5.371)	23
——Vlade Divac Card/MJ	24
——Team Play Card/MJ	27
——Byron Scott Card/MJ	36

Year	USA BB Mark & See Books	mag #		
91-92	"You Call The Play," book & pen (5.372)	22381		
		cover	25.00	35.00
	——USA Olympic Basketball Team Picture Card/MJ front, 3 pictures, Skybox perforated cards, 2 x 2.5	544, 545, 546		
	——MJ Card, #9 white, hands on hips, Skybox perforated card, 2 x 2.5	534		
91-92	"Superstars & Super Stats," book & pen, MJ not on cover	22382	20.00	30.00
	——USA Olympic Basketball Team Picture Card/MJ front, Skybox perforated card, 7.25 x 3.5	nno		
91-92	"You Call The Play," book & pen, no cards inside, Bull vs. Bullets	22361		
		cover	25.00	35.00

Year	Magnets-miscellaneous	mag #	
90's	Waist high closeup, red 23, hands on hips, hair (5.373)	NNO	10.00
90's	Jump shot on Dumars #4, red #23 (5.374)	NNO	10.00
90's	Layup, white #23 (5.375)	NNO	10.00

Year	Magnetables		
89	Bulls MJ, red #23,"Bull" top right, dunking, side view (5.376)		25.00
89	Pistons Rodman/MJ, Phoenix (5.377)		5.00

5.371
5.372
5.373
5.374
5.375
5.376
5.377

Year	McDonald's & Upper Deck Related Items	card# item #		
80's	Ad display, Help McDonald's Fight Muscular Dystrophy, MJ with a lot of hair (5.378)		20.00	30.00
85-86	School Folder, MJ & Bulls, 20th Bulls Season, D.L. Strouse Business card on front, group ticket sales packet, layup on front & dunk on back, white 23, schedule inside	McD-14084 9" x 3"	100.00	150.00
	—Bumper Sticker, "Chicago Bulls" & Bulls Logo, white background			
	—Entry Blank, 1985-86 McDonald's Discount Night			
	—Schedule, Bulls			
	—Order form, Group Ticket Sales & schedule			
	—Letter, Community & Organizational Program, 20th Season			
	—Photo, 20th Season Chicago Bulls, "Group A whole new breed of entertainment," MJ, Stan Albeck, & 3rd man all around a desk, yellow/black Saltzman sticker lower right			
5/6-90	Crew Pages-2, MJ pictures, folded brochure		15.00	20.00
	—MJ on cover (5.379)			
	—MJ on page 3 (5.380)			
90	Sheet, "Catch Michael's Best Moves" (5.381)	8 cds	6.00	10.00
	—The Layup			
	—The Blocked Shot			
	—The Chest Pass			
	—The Drive			
	—The Speed Dribble			
	—The Backup Dribble			
	—The Jump Shot			
	—The Free Throw			
90	Window Ad, MJ dunking, red color, 2' x 3'		45.00	60.00
91	Ad Poster, Sport Fitness Fun Happy Meal, Collect all 8 toys! While Supplies Last, red to yellow background, eight toys pictured, FC# MCD-299	14 x 14 McD# 91-138	25.00	40.00
91	Bag, Sport Fitness Fun Happy Meal, quiz on back (5.382)		2.00	4.00
91	Disc, It'll Be Sweet 2 Repeat, Free when you buy a McJordan Combo-back, Not Intended for children under 8. While supplies last-on back	12"	15.00	25.00
91	Pin, "It'll Be Sweet 2 Repeat," MJ sitting on bb, red shirt, black shorts, free with McJordan Combo	3"	2.00	5.00
91	Sticker, It'll Be Sweet 2 Repeat, Free when Buying McJordan Combo, 2 discs joined (5.383)	4"	8.00	12.00
91	Sticker, It'll Be Sweet 2 Repeat, Only __cents Off With Any Purchase, 2 discs joined (5.384)	5"	15.00	20.00

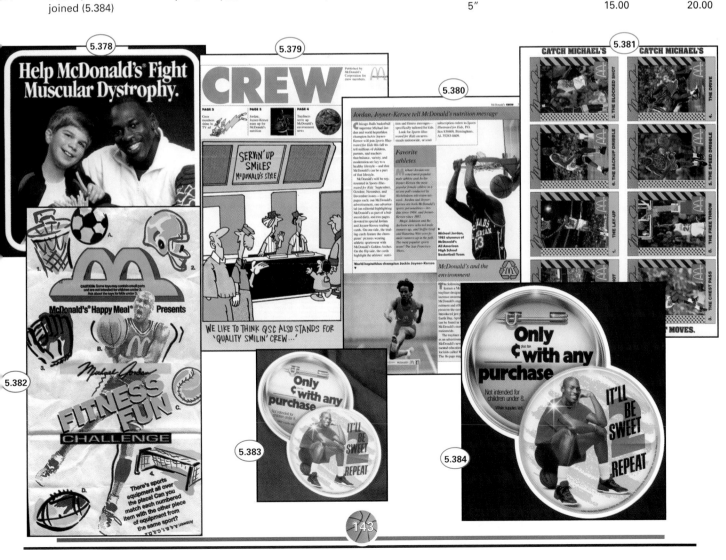

91-92	Ad poster, Collect al 62! NBA Hoops Limited Edition BB Cards, Get 4 Cards Free!, BB background, yellow bottom, MJ MVP shooting red 23	14 x 14 McD# 91-150	15.00	20.00
91-92	Card, Hoops '92 USA Basketball Team, back #55 in orange basketball (5.385)	55	2.00	4.00
91-92	Card, Hoops MVP, back #5 in orange basketball (5.386)	5	1.00	3.00
91-92	Card Strip, Hoops MVP Factory, uncut	10 cards	20.00	30.00
	—-5 MJ cards with #5, numbers in basketball			
	—-5 Wilkins cards with #1, numbers in basketball			
91-92	Card, Upper Deck French Issue, number in arches	15	15.00	25.00
91-92	Set, McJordan Special Items		75.00	90.00
	—-Pin, MJ head view, "Try A McJordan Special" head view (5.387)	3"	35.00	45.00
	—-BB Hoop & Backboard, "Try A McJordan Special" (5.388)		40.00	45.00
9/92	Kemper Lakes Country Club, Ronald McDonald's Children's Charities Celebrity Golf Championship, September 5-7, 1992			
	—-Pin, 1992 Event Pass, red border (5.389)	3"	15.00	20.00
	—-Placement with photo (5.390)	14 x 11	10.00	15.00
	—-Brochure (5.391)		2.00	4.00
	—-Luggage Tag (5.392)		15.00	25.00

	—Program (5.393)	8.5 x 11	15.00	20.00
	—Pairing guide, 9/7/92, foldout (5.394)	4.5 x 11	15.00	20.00
	—Color photo, MJ swinging club, Chicago Tribune (5.395)	8 x 10	5.00	10.00
	—Envelope with invite		10.00	15.00
	—Poster	21 x 30	40.00	60.00
92	Ad Display, Free McDonald's NBA Fantasy Pack When You Buy an Extra Value Meal, MJ with ball in RH over head on left side; pack, MJ, Stockton & Ewing cards on right side, blue and red background, American Airline plane bottom	26 x 44 McD# 92-173	35.00	50.00
92	Ad Poster, Gold Metal Meal, MJ on cup, triple cheeseburger, large fries, $4.33, gold background & coin	15 x 17	15.00	20.00
92	Ad Poster, McJordan Special Meal Includes: Large Fries Medium Soft Drink, black background, red outline top and right, burger, fries & coffee, only $3.19 pictured, FC# MCDA-788	22 x 22 McD# 92-184	15.00	20.00
92	Ad Sheet, "Burger of the Month McJordan Special Meal"		20.00	25.00
92	Cup, USA Basketball	5 of 10	4.00	8.00
92	Drink container, MJ handprint & signature, Bulls Logo, black bottle with green cap		25.00	30.00
92	Drink container, MJ handprint & signature, Bulls Logo, red with black top & straw		25.00	30.00
92	Pin, "It'll Be Sweet 2 Repeat," MJ sitting on BB, red shirt, black shorts, free with McJordan Combo	3"	2.00	4.00
92-93	Ad poster, Fantasy Pack, "Free pack with Extra Value Meal," American Airlines plane, MJ jumping, MJ card, red & blue, white bottom (5.396)	9 x 10	15.00	20.00
92-93	Ad poster, Fantasy Pack, "Free pack with Extra Value Meal," American Airlines plane, MJ jumping, MJ card, red & blue background, orange price diamond	14 x 14	10.00	15.00
92-93	Ad poster, "Win An NBA Fantasy Instantly, One-on-One with MJ, NBA European Vacations" 92-93 UD card on left MJ dunk, American Airline plane on right, red background	22 x 28 McD# 92-137	25.00	35.00
92-93	Card, UD MJ Hologram 91-92 NBA MVP, standing shooting the ball, McDonald's name & logo front, blank back	NNO	10.00	15.00
92-93	Cards, UD Chicago Team Set, arches as logo back	12 cards	4.00	8.00
	—MJ	CH-4	2.00	4.00
92-93	Cards, UD Chicago & Regular Set, arches as logo back	62 cards	20.00	30.00
	—MJ	P-5	4.00	8.00
	—Hersey Hawkins/MJ front	P-30	4.00	8.00
92-93	Cards, UD Fantasy Set	102cards		
	—MJ (5.397)	P-5	1.00	2.00
	—MJ (5.398)	CH-4	2.00	4.00
	—Hersey Hawkins/MJ front	P-30	1.50	2.00
	—Denis Scott/MJ front	OR-8	1.50	2.00
92-93	Placemat, NBA Fantasy Pack, Net A Set of NBA Cards		3.00	6.00
8/26-	29/93-MJ & Ronald McDonald Children's Charities Celebrity Golf Classic Event Ticket, Seven Bridges Golf Club, Woodridge, Illinois, MJ swinging club (5.399)	2.5 x 5	10.00	15.00
93-94	Card, Upper Deck Holojam Regular, French Issue McDonald's Holol) logo back (5.400)	29	100.00	150.00

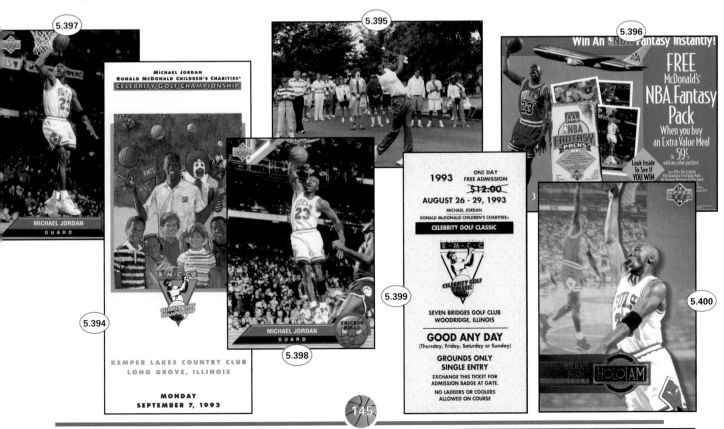

93-94	Cards, Upper Deck Team Card Set, French Issue	27 cards	4.00	8.00
	—-Bulls Team Card, MJ on front, rear view (5.401)	4		
93-94	Cup, Nothing But Net MVP	1 of 6	4.00	8.00
93-94	French Fry Holder, Nothing But Net, 5 x 7	Set of 6	15.00	20.00
	—-MJ Holder (5.402)		5.00	10.00
6/9-12/94	-Schedule, MJ & Ronald McDonald Children's Charities Celebrity Golf Classic Event Ticket, Seven Bridges Golf Club, Woodridge, Illinois, MJ swinging club, green (5.403)	5.5 x 8.5	5.00	10.00
94	Ad Poster, "Double Big Mac Super-Size Meal, Includes Super size Fries, Large Soft Drink in MVP Cup," MJ on cup and Nothing but Net MVP french fry holder, picture of burger, FC# MCDA 888	22 x 22 McD# 94-018	15.00	20.00
94	Ad Poster, "Free MVP Cup When You Super Size an Extra Value Meal," acetate, 6 cups shown, "Nep All 6," FC# MCDA 888	14 x 14 McD# 94-018	10.00	15.00
94	Menu, UD/NBA Playoffs with sticker, French Issue		2.00	4.00
94	Menu, UD/NBA Playoffs with no sticker, French Issue		3.00	6.00
94	Sheet, UD/NBA Playoffs Collection, French Issue (5.404)		3.00	6.00
94-95	Cards, UD Nothing But Net Jumbo Set			
	—-MJ card, # of 20,000 produced, 3 x 5 (5.405)	5	10.00	15.00
	—-MJ, Bird & Barkley card, # of 20,000 produced, 3 x 5	12	8.00	12.00
	—-MJ card, # of 20,000 produced, 3 x 5 (5.406)	13	10.00	15.00
94-95	Cards, UD Nothing But Net Set, sealed	16 cards	15.00	20.00
	—-Bird Card, # of 20,000 produced, 3 x 5	6		
	—-1 UD Pack			
	—-MJ Card	1		
	—-Mt. Rushmore Presidents/MJ	4		
	—-MJ Card	5		
	—-MJ Card	7		

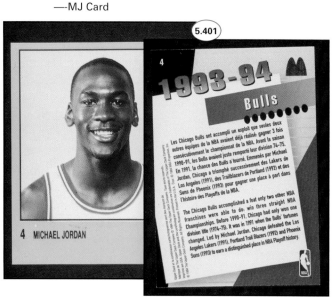

5.401

4 MICHAEL JORDAN

1993-94 Bulls

Les Chicago Bulls ont accompli un exploit que seules deux autres équipes de la NBA avaient déjà réalisé: gagner 3 fois consecutivement le championnat de la NBA. Avant la saison 1990-91, les Bulls avaient juste remporté leur division 74-75. En 1991, la chance des Bulls a tourné. Emmenés par Michael Jordan, Chicago a triomphé successivement des Lakers de Los Angeles (1991), des Trailblazers de Portland (1992) et des Suns de Phoenix (1993) pour gagner une place à part dans l'histoire des Playoffs de la NBA.

The Chicago Bulls accomplished a feat only two other NBA franchises were able to do: win three straight NBA Championships. Before 1990-91, Chicago had only won one division title (1974-75). It was in 1991 when the Bulls' fortunes changed. Led by Michael Jordan, Chicago defeated the Los Angeles Lakers (1991), Portland Trail Blazers (1992) and Phoenix Suns (1993) to earn a distinguished place in NBA Playoff history.

5.402

MICHAEL JORDAN 1988

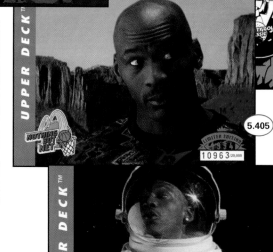

5.403

MICHAEL JORDAN - RMCC CELEBRITY GOLF CLASSIC

JUNE 9 - 12, 1994
SEVEN BRIDGES GOLF CLUB

SCHEDULE OF EVENTS

THURSDAY, JUNE 9
- 18 Hole Celebrity-Amateur Competition
- Women's Golf Clinic 1:30 pm
- Wilson Junior Golf Clinic 4:00 pm

FRIDAY, JUNE 10
- First Round Celebrity Tournament
- Ram Celebrity Long Drive Contest 5:00 pm

SATURDAY, JUNE 11
- Second Round Celebrity Tournament

SUNDAY, JUNE 12
- Third Round Celebrity Tournament

5.405

5.406

5.404

DU 16 MARS AU 12 AVRIL 1994

MENU BASKET

DECOUVREZ LES 27 EQUIPES NBA

L'EQUIPE

	—-MJ Card		9		
	—-MJ Card		12		
	—-MJ Card		13		
94-95	Cards, UD Nothing But Net Set, sealed		16 cards	20.00	25.00
	—-Barkley Card, # of 20,000, 3 x 5		10		
	—-1 UD Pack				
	—-MJ Card		1		
	—-Mt. Rushmore Presidents/MJ		4		
	—-MJ Card		5		
	—-MJ Card		7		
	—-MJ Card		9		
	—-MJ Card		12		
	—-MJ Card		13		
94-95	Cards, UD Nothing But Net Set, sealed		16 cards	20.00	25.00
	—-MJ, Bird & Barkely Card, # of 20,000, 3 x 5		12		
	—-1 UD Pack				
	—-MJ Card		1		
	—-Mt. Rushmore Presidents/MJ		4		
	—-MJ Card		5		
	—-MJ Card		7		
	—-MJ Card		9		
	—-MJ Card		12		
	—-MJ Card		13		
94-95	Cards, UD Nothing But Net Set, sealed		16 cards	20.00	25.00
	—-MJ Card, # of 20,000, 3 x 5		13		
	—-1 UD Pack				
	—-MJ Card		1		
	—-Mt. Rushmore Presidents/MJ		4		
	—-MJ Card		5		
	—-MJ Card		7		
	—-MJ Card		9		
	—-MJ Card		12		
	—-MJ Card		13		
94-95	Cards, UD Nothing But Net Set, sealed		16 cards	15.00	20.00
	—-Bird Card, # of 20,000, 3 x 5		14		
	—-1 UD Pack				
	—-MJ Card		1		
	—-Mt. Rushmore Presidents/MJ		4		
	—-MJ Card		5		
	—-MJ Card		7		
	—-MJ Card		9		
	—-MJ Card		12		
	—-MJ Card		13		
94-95	Cards, UD Nothing But Net Set, sealed		16 cards	20.00	25.00
	—-MJ Card, # of 20,000, 3 x 5		5		
	—-1 UD Pack				
	—-MJ Card		1		
	—-Mt. Rushmore Presidents/MJ		4		
	—-MJ Card		5		
	—-MJ Card		7		
	—-MJ Card		9		
	—-MJ Card		12		
	—-MJ Card		13		
94-95	Cards, UD Nothing But Net, regular size cards		15 cards	12.00	20.00
	—-MJ & Bird Card (5.407)		1	2.00	3.00
	—-Mt. Rushmore Presidents/MJ (5.408)		4	2.00	3.00
	—-MJ Card (5.409)		5	2.00	3.00
	—-MJ & Bird Card (5.410)		7	2.00	3.00

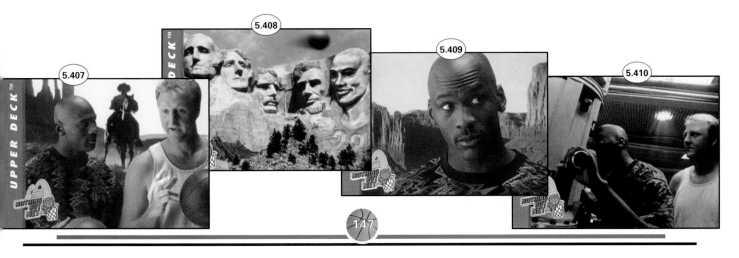

	——MJ & Bird Card (5.411)	9	2.00	3.00
	——MJ, Bird & Barkley Card (5.412)	12	2.00	3.00
	——MJ Card (5.413)	13	2.00	3.00
95	Ad Poster, McBacon Deluxe, Super Size Meal Includes Super Size Fries and a Large Soft Drink in a Showdown Cup, red top stripe, blue background, MJ on french fry holder, Barkley on cup, burger pictured, "only $3.88"	22 x 22 FC# MCDA-963	20.00	25.00
95	Ad poster, McBacon Deluxe, MJ Favorite!, Super Size Meal, MJ on french fry holder	22 x 22	2.00	4.00
95	Ad poster, "Showdown Cups Get Your Cup when you Super Size and Extra Value Meal. These are all Mine, Mine, All Mine!," MJ, Bird & Ewing on cups, red & blue background, Daffy holding cups	22 x 22 FC# MCDA-963	15.00	20.00
95	Ad poster, Taste of the Month, McBacon Deluxe Meal, MJ Favorite!	15 x 15	2.00	4.00
95	Cup, NBA Looney Tunes All-Star Show		5.00	10.00
95	Placement, NBA Looney Tunes, "Get Your Hands on the Most Amazing Hoop Action of All Time!," MJ & Bugs on a cup, seven cups pictured-Kemp, Ewing, Barkley, Bird, Miller, Johnson; red background	14 x 11	15.00	20.00
95	Ad Poster, "McBacon Deluxe Try This Big Bacon Taste in a Super Size Meal," MJ and Bugs on french fry, Charles Barkley on cup	T9508VP 29 x 38	20.00	25.00
95-96	Ad poster, McBacon Deluxe "Seelight," MJ on french fry holder, red & blue background, Barkley on cup	14 x 14	15.00	20.00
95-96	Ad poster, McBacon Deluxe "Seelight," MJ on french fry holder, red & blue background, Barkley on cup	22 x 22	15.00	20.00
95-96	French fry holder, Scouting Report, 5 x 7	Set of 6	25.00	35.00
	——MJ Holder (5.414)		5.00	8.00
10-11-12/96	Magazine, "Management News America's Favorite Fries," MJ inside on french fry holder, french fry holder on front cover	page 8	10.00	15.00
96	Ad Display Board, Space Jam, Plush Looney Tunes Characters, MJ top left leaning on "Plush" backboard and Bugs sitting on backboard, Daffy, Lola, Blank, Nerdlucks, Taz and Bugs pictured in actual size	20" x 4' FC# MCDA-152-52	25.00	35.00
96	Ad Display Board, Space Jam, Plush Looney Tunes Characters, MJ left side of "Plush" backboard and Bugs on right side of backboard Daffy, Lola, Blank, Nerdlucks, Taz and Bugs pictured in actual size	4' x 20" FC# MCDA-152-52	25.00	35.00
96	Ad Sheet, Space Jam, French Issue	14" x 7"	20.00	30.00
96	Ad Poster, Space Jam Toddler Toy Set, "Collect and Connect All 8!," toys on BB court pieces, MJ looking over left shoulder	Part # 1524	25.00	35.00
96	Bag, Space Jam Happy Meal, MJ on bag (4.415)		2.00	4.00
96	Box, Happy Meal, Space Jam, MJ on left side of punch-out backboard looking over right shoulder, blue background, punch-out net & BB, "Help Michael and The Tune Squad Beat The Monstars?" on adjoining side (4.416)	4.5 x 4.5 x 7"	10.00	15.00
96	Box, Happy Meal, Space Jam, MJ on right side of punch-out backboard looking over left shoulder, red background, punch-out net & BB, "Score with Michael and The Looney Tunes!" on adjoining side, MJ shooting 2 hands over head (5.416a)	4.5 x 4.5 x 7"	10.00	15.00
96	Box, McNuggets 20 piece, MJ, SP, & AH, The Double Team (4.417)		5.00	10.00

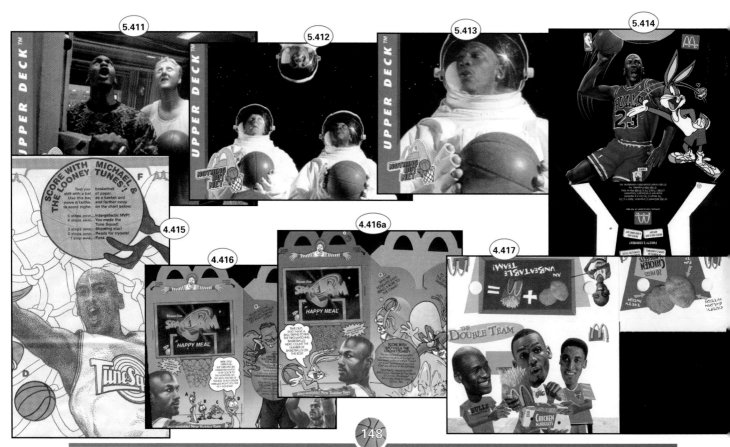

96	Cup, Space Jam, "McDonald's is the Place for Space Jam Stuffed Characters," MJ, Taz with BB, Daffy, Bugs with hearts in eyes, Lola Bunny with BB		6.00	10.00
96	French fry holder, All-Star Guy, 5 x 7	Set of 6	15.00	25.00
	—MJ & Barkley Holder (4.418)		2.00	4.00
	—MJ, Barkley, A. Hardaway Holder (4.419)		2.00	4.00
96	French fry holder, Space Jam, baseball, MJ at plate holding bat, white 45 baseball uniform, "Whew! That's Some fast ball!!, back two Monstars talking "We seek the one they call Bugs Bunny" (4.420)	13146	10.00	15.00
96	French fry holder, Space Jam, MJ slam dunk with blue Blank Monstar, "Let me show you my stuff, Monstar!" Back: Blanko blue Monstar saying "Whatcha lookin' at?" (4.421)	13159	7.00	10.00
96	French fry holder, Space Jam, MJ dribbling with Taz, "Set the screen, Taz! I'm going for two! Back: Taz saying, "#$%>&*()!!!"(4.422)	13146	7.00	10.00
96	French fry holder, Space Jam, MJ with Bugs, Sylvester, rooster & Daffy drinking "Michael's Secret Stuff" Back: Daffy saying "Hey, watch me shoot from Downtown!" (4.423)	13159	7.00	10.00
96	French Fry holder, Space Jam, MJ sitting with Bugs, "Where am I, Bugs?" "You got a hole-in-one!" Back: Bugs saying, "This oughta be one hare-raisin' game." (4.424)	13159	10.00	15.00
96	French fry holder, Space Jam, MJ holding ball, Bugs and Lola, "I'd like to try out for the team" Back: Lola saying "I'll do my taking on the court!" (4.425)	29097	7.00	10.00

96	Package, Space Jam, Plush Looney Tune Characters Set, sealed package, 6 toys from Happy Meals		
	—-Blanko, blue, black "O" uniform (4.426)		15.00
	——-insert Blanko card		
	——-insert $5.00 refund on Space Jam video, MJ looking over shoulder		
	——-package top, MJ looking over shoulder		
	—-Lola, pink gym bag		15.00
	——-insert Lola card (4.427)		
	——-insert $5.00 refund on Space Jam video, MJ looking over shoulder		
	——-package top, MJ looking over shoulder		
	—-Nerdlucks, purple one & orange one (4.428)		15.00
	——-insert Nerdlucks card		
	——-insert $5.00 refund on Space Jam video, MJ looking over shoulder		
	——-package top, MJ looking over shoulder		
	—-Taz, in Space Jam uniform (4.429)		15.00
	——-insert Taz card		
	——-insert $5.00 refund on Space Jam video, MJ looking over shoulder		
	——-package top, MJ looking over shoulder		
	—-Bugs		15.00
	——-insert Bugs card		
	——-insert $5.00 refund on Space Jam video, MJ looking over shoulder		
	——-package top, MJ looking over shoulder		
	—-Daffy		15.00
	——-insert Daffy card		
	——-insert $5.00 refund on Space Jam video, MJ looking over shoulder		
	——-package top, MJ looking over shoulder		
96	Toys & BB Court & Background toys issued with Happy Meals, Space Jam Toddler Toy Set,		10.00 / 15.00
	—-background, MJ holding basket ball in left hand overhead		
	—-clear plastic basketball court with markings for toy placement		
	—-sign for basketball court front edge, "Collect & Connect all 8!"		
	—-basketball nets, green	4 nets	
	—-hockey like sticks, green	2 sticks	
	—-Lola with bb in RH, BB court on toy bottom	1	
	—-Bugs leaning on basket, BB court on toy bottom	2	
	—-Martian standing on basketball, BB court on toy bottom	3	
	—-Daffy with hands out, BB court on toy bottom	4	
	—-Taz leaning on basketball hoop, BB court on toy bottom	5	
	—-Sylvester with Tweety on BB, BB court on toy bottom	6	
	—-Green Monstar with hands over head, BB court on toy bottom	7	
	—-Blue Monstars in purple coat, BB court on toy bottom	8	
96	Window Ad, Acetate, MJ reaching with ball in RH, red 23, "Vote for 'Em Here... All-Star Guys McDonald's NBA All-Star Balloting," red backgound, McD logo bottom left	MCDA-171-17 28 x 42"	40.00 / 60.00
97	Coupon sheet, Space Jam, French (4.430)		18.00 / 25.00

(4.426)

(4.430)

(4.427)

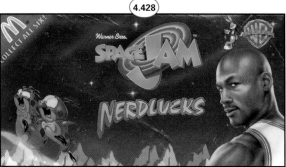
(4.428)

(4.429)

Year	Description	Size		
97	Cup, Space Jam, paper, Germany, MJ & Space Jam characters	0.5L	20.00	35.00
97	Growth Chart, Space Jam 198 cm, French Issue (4.431)		18.00	25.00
97	Placemat, Space Jam, French Issue (4.432)	8" x 12"	10.00	15.00
97	Placemat, Space Jam, French Issue	14" x 10"	20.00	30.00
97	Placemat, Space Jam, German Issue, ad for compact disc movie music, MJ looking over shoulder, 2 CD covers MJ pictures	14 x 10	20.00	30.00
-	Ad Sticker Sheet, "Michael Jordan's Favorite!" with orange basketball, store location stated; counter mat, drive-through translite, store translite, totm window merchandiser	13.5 x 15 7 stks	45.00	55.00
1/1/??	Instruction Sheet, for placement of "Michael Jordan's Favorite! McBacon Deluxe" stickers, 4 locations drawings on sheet, "On April 1, Michael Jordan in coming back to McDonald's!" on top Counter mat, driver-thru translite, totm window merchandiser, & in-store translite store areas listed on right side of sheet		25.00	30.00
-	Window Ad, acetate, MJ reaching with ball in LH, coming out of UD card, NBA & McD logo on ball, UD card with Paxson, and Lakers, CB logo bottom right, McD logo bottom left, "Michael Jordan" bottom right	14.5" x 45"	40.00	60.00

Year   McDonald's Toys with MJ Insert Photo Cards

There were 8 different Michael Jordan Toys issued, one with each Happy Meal Order. In addition, there was a different color insert photo of Michael Jordan (3" x 4") inside each toy pack. The back of each photo contained a different quote by Michael Jordan. Note: Most toys are found loose with the basketball being the rarest. The stopwatch and Frisbee toys have a color photo of Michael Jordan on them. (4.433)

Year	Description	Size		
91	Toys & Cards, Sport Fitness Fun Challenge Happy Meal, MJ Photo and story on each card. Sealed bag.	16 items	65.00	110.00
	—-Baseball Pack with insert		5.00	10.00
	———Baseball		3.00	5.00
	———Jordan on Sports, swinging bat, red shirt, white pants		2.00	3.00
	—-Basketball Pack with insert		20.00	30.00
	———Basketball		15.00	20.00
	———Jordan on Good Sportsmanship, closeup with towel, white uniform		2.00	3.00
	—-Football Pack with insert		5.00	10.00
	———Football Pack		3.00	5.00
	———Jordan on Effort, closeup in red uniform		2.00	3.00
	—-Frisbee Pack with insert		10.00	15.00
	———Frisbee		5.00	10.00
	———Jordan on Winning, sitting with ball on leg in warmups		2.00	3.00
	—-Jump Rope Pack with insert		5.00	10.00
	———Jump rope		3.00	5.00
	———Jordan on Practice, blue shorts, white t-shirt, foul line shot		2.00	3.00
	—-Soccer Ball Pack with insert		5.00	10.00
	———Soccer Ball		3.00	5.00
	———Jordan on Teamwork, MJ & Paxson, standing with hands on hips		2.00	3.00
	—-Stop Watch Pack with insert		10.00	15.00
	———Stop watch		5.00	10.00
	———Jordan on Doing Your Best, red McDonald's hat, white McDonald's shirt		2.00	3.00
	—-Water Bottle Pack with insert		5.00	10.00
	———Water bottle		3.00	5.00
	———Jordan on Being in Shape, red 23, jumping with ball		2.00	3.00
91	Set of Insert Color Photo Cards	8 items	16.00	24.00

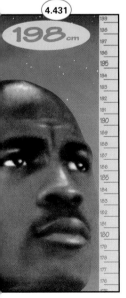

(4.431) (4.432) (4.433)

Year	MC Sports			
-	Bumper Sticker, Michael Forever! MC	13 x 3"	1.00	2.00

Year	Measure Up			
87	Standee, "1987 Measure Up Standee," MJ holding ball in RH, white 23, 6'6" scale on right side, Official NBA Product		50.00	75.00

Year	Michael Jordan Celebrity Golf Challenge, Hilton Head Island-9/93			
	Cabana Straw Hat, black, red, blue, teal		20.00	25.00
	Color Sweatshirts, white, gray, black		40.00	45.00
	Crew Neck Sweatshirt, white, gray, black		40.00	45.00
	Hat, white, gold, blue, black, red, teal		15.00	20.00
	Putter, 231		75.00	85.00
	Shirt, white, gold, green, black, red, teal,		30.00	35.00
	Towel, 241		12.00	15.00
	T-shirt, white, gray, black		12.00	15.00
	Video, 281		18.00	25.00

Year	Michael Jordan Foundation			
93	Newsletter, "Air Mail," MJ & young boy (Donnel Gates) with McDonald's "It will be sweet to Repeat" pin, MJF "Making a Difference," red/orange cover	V-3	20.00	25.00
9/19/92	"1993 Datebook" from the Third Annual Gala Extravaganza, MJ dribbling with LH on cover, red 23, Souvenir Datebook, 23 MJ pictures inside (4.434)		25.00	35.00
94	Datebook, 8 MJ pictures		25.00	35.00
95	Ruler with 3D glasses, sold at Target Stores, sealed package (4.435)		10.00	15.00
95	Ruler with no 3D glasses, sold at Target Stores, sealed package (4.436)		5.00	10.00
-	Ad Sheet, cut from magazine		2.00	4.00
-	Sweatshirt, white 111, red 112, gray 113, black 114		15.00	28.00
-	T-shirt, white 101, red 102, gray 103, black 104		10.00	15.00

Year	Michael Jordan Signature 23 Junior Golf Set			
98	Bag, red and black with two side pockets, signature on large pocket (4.437)		150.00	175.00
	Golf club, #1 wood, signature and #23 on bottom and shaft			
	Golf club, #5 iron, signature and #23 on bottom and shaft			
	Golf club, #6 iron, signature and #23 on bottom and shaft			
	Golf club, #7 iron, signature and #23 on bottom and shaft			
	Golf club, putter, signature and #23 on bottom and shaft			
	Golf club cover, signature and #23 on bottom and shaft			

Year	Michael Jordan Golf Center	size or # item		
96	Brochure, Everyone Can Play, foldout with inserts		5.00	8.00
96	Gift Packet-coaster, tees, cleat cleaner, ball markers	1 box	10.00	15.00
96	MJ Picture in Pewter Frame, sitting on bucket of balls		18.00	20.00
96	MJ Picture, same as pewter frame, sitting on bucket of balls, purple border		4.00	8.00
96	Merchandise Catalog, MJ pictures		4.00	8.00
96	Opinion Survey Card, MJ inside sitting on bucket	foldout	4.00	8.00
96	Plastic Bags, 2 small, 1 large, Golf Center bags	3 bags	2.00	6.00
96	Post Cards			
	——Be Like Mike, Play Golf, red/white, MJ head picture		5.00	10.00
	——Be Like Mike, Play Golf, white, MJ sitting on bucket of golf balls (4.438)		5.00	10.00

Year				
	—-MJ sitting on Bucket of Balls, green border		5.00	10.00
	—-Michael Jordan Golf, white with hole, pin, flag, green, & basketball		5.00	10.00
	—-Michael Jordan Golf, white with BB, golf ball halves, flagpin		5.00	10.00
	—-Picture of Shop Inside, big basketball on golf tee		5.00	10.00
96	Promotion Sheets of the Centers events	7 sheets	15.00	20.00
96	Wilson Ultra 500 Golf Balls, white MJ picture box	3 ball	12.00	15.00
96	Wilson Ultra 500 Golf Balls, orange MJ picture box	3 ball	12.00	15.00
96	Display, Win $1,000,000 Hole-in-One Shoot Out, Golf Center & Chicago Sun-Times	15 3/4" x 11"	15.00	20.00

Year **Michael Jordan Restaurant**

Year				
94	Restaurant Package		100.00	150.00
	—-Dessert Menu in holder, 6.25 x 9.25			
	—-Dinner menu	7.5 x 11		
	—-Fast Break Bar & Grill menu (4.439)	8.5 x 11		
	—-Fetzer wine list, 4.5 x 6.5			
	—-The Starting Lineup, drink menu	4 x 6		
	—-Illinois Special Olympics Raffle flyer, pictures of MJ, Barnett, Hampton, Santo	4 x 6		
	—-Ticket, MJ R 3rd Birthday, 2.75 x 7.5			
4/93	Basketball, Opening Night, 4/23/93, Wilson, gold lettering, red stamp of restaurant and 150, MJ Professional BB in gold and red, 150 produced	B1261	200.00	300.00
4/93	Invitation, Opening Night, 4/23/93, two piece, greeting card & entrance ticket, MJ photo in tux on both parts		60.00	75.00
95	Ad, Gizzae Upstairs at MJ's		2.00	4.00
-	Bag, large shopping, orange BB, paper bag		2.00	4.00
-	Bag, small shopping, orange BB, paper bag		2.00	4.00
-	Menu, adults, front red signature		10.00	20.00
-	Menu, children's, games and writing inside		2.00	4.00
-	Menu, children's, basketball shaped (4.440)		10.00	15.00

Year **Michael Jordan's Senior Flight School**

Year				
8/97	Brochure, BB camp adults of 35, Bally's in Las Vegas, NV	cover	10.00	15.00

Year **Michael Jordan Softball Celebrity Challenge, Comiskey Park-7/25/93, MJ Air Force/M Bolton Bombers**

Year				
93	Hats, softball, white with black bill 311, black with cream bill 312		25.00	40.00
93	T-shirt, Air Force, black 302		15.00	25.00

Year **Michael Jordan Tux, 2 piece**

Year				
94	Bugatchi Uomo for Michael Jordan, made in China (4.441)		350.00	450.00

4.439

4.440

4.441

Year	Miller Brewing			
93	Brochure, Maximum Basketball NBA Playoffs and Finals		5.00	10.00
97	Brochure, 50 Fantasy Matchups handout 97 All-Star Game (4.442)	inside	1.00	2.00

Year	Miscellaneous			
91	Ad insert, "MJ on the Pursuit of Excellence," 2 cutout bottom for mounting on a box (4.443)	6 x 7	5.00	10.00
91	Ad display, NBA Eye Wear, All-Star Game, Photo by A.D. Bernstein, produced by Society Optiks, MJ in photo		10.00	15.00
89-90	Cards, Caesar's Lake Tahoe Celebrity cards in box attached to an invitation holder to Golf Association,	8 cards	1,500.00	2,000.00
	—MJ, white & black marble border, Roman column left, "Heavy Hitter" top left-front, MJ in white Wilson golf hat, MJ in blue golf shirt; back "Celebrity Golf Association" #1 in golf ball, line for autograph	1	1,200.00	1,800.00
	—Checklist	8	50.00	100.00
95	Card, Basketball USA Magazine, from Germany, walking white 45, black left arm band, 3.75 x 5.5, purple border		50.00	75.00
-	Clock, MJ likeness Figure, 2 piece, legs move, red #23 uniform, battery operated, plastic		20.00	25.00
89	Cooler, Puppet Kooler, double size, shaped like MJ, cardboard box (4.444)	24 oz.	100.00	150.00
	—Instructions			
	—Certificate of Authenticity from Puppet Kooler Industries			
92	Drinking Glass, Bulls Championship Team Glass, MJ listed on back in roster & records		15.00	20.00
-	Drawing, of 90 Fleer Card by Ward, # of 100		10.00	20.00
-	Jersey, Champion, white #9 USA, size 48 (4.445)		35.00	70.00
91	Plates, UD 3D Printing, 6 plates of 3 players		600.00	1,000.00
-	Puzzle, American Pro Stickers		100.00	150.00
-	Sunvisor, Woodridge & MJ & Kids, Seven Bridges Golf Club, 8/26-29th, orangish to pinkish with white border		20.00	30.00
93	T-Shirt, 3 Time NBA World Champs		10.00	20.00

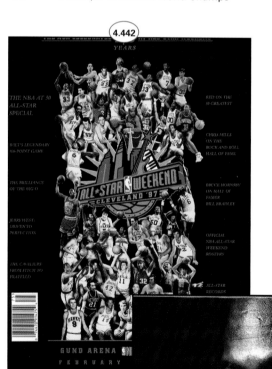

4.442

4.443

Michael Jordan
on the Pursuit
of Excellence

4.444

4.445

N

Year	NBA Jam Session Items, Slam Dunk			
92	Puzzle, NBA Inside Stuff Slam Dunk, Sky Jams, MJ, Shawn Kemp, Tom Champers, 200 piece puzzle with Magazine Coupon Offer, listed in the Golden Puzzle Section	5474C	75.00	125.00
92-93	Book, Photo Salute of the NBA Dunk, Intro-D Stern, Drakes Offer		15.00	25.00
94	Calendar, 16 month, Day Dream Calendar		10.00	25.00
-	Sticker Book, purple cover, Golden Pub.		15.00	20.00
-	Book, Fleer Mark & See, Pen, Golden Pub., yellow cover		20.00	25.00
-	Marker Book, tear out pages, Golden Pub., blue cover		20.00	25.00

Year	NBC Items			
9/91	Sheet, NBC/Toys R Us $10,000 Shopping Spree (6.1)		2.00	

Year	Nestle Products			
96	UD CC Card, Slam Dunk Series, MJ Card, unissued set, vs. New York, white 23, dunking (6.2)	4 of 40	500.00	1000.00
96	UD CC Card, Slam Dunk Series, Eddie Jones/MJ front, unissued set, vs. Lakers, white 23	16 of 40	25.00	50.00
97	UD Card, Crunch Time Series, MJ Card, red 23, vs. Blazers, black & white background	CT-05/40	10.00	15.00
97	UD Card, Slam Dunk, red 23 (6.3)	SD 22/40	5.00	10.00

Year	Newspapers, Inserts-miscellaneous			
6/13/91	The Courier News, Making Us Bull-ieve		3.00	6.00
9/26/91	The New American Newspaper Magazine, MJ, Magic, Ewing on cover	V31N39	3.00	6.00
1/1/92	Basketball Times Newspaper Magazine, MJ & Best of the NBA	V14N12	5.00	10.00
3/30/93	National Enquirer, Di: How I Beat Bulimia	cover	4.00	8.00
4/27/93	Kid News Insert, Flying with Air Jordan		3.00	6.00
11/21/93	Daily Herald, The Triple Crown	cover	5.00	10.00
1/1/95	Magazine, Section 10, The Year: Word & Pictures	cover	3.00	6.00
4/13/97	The Times Parade Mag, newspaper insert	cover	3.00	6.00
6/14/97	Vidette Times, 5 Golden Rings	front	3.00	6.00
-	Newspaper Clipping, MJ HS photo		10.00	15.00
3/10/98	Chicago Flame, MJ on page 6	inside	2.00	4.00
2/5/98	Daily News Special Section, The Stars Come Out	cover	2.00	4.00
6/98	Newspaper, S.L.A.M. Mega'ine	cover	2.00	4.00

6.1

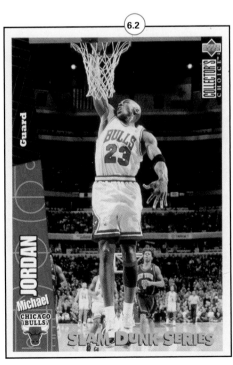

6.2

6.3

Year	Nike	card #		
84	Pin, Air Jordan Flight, "Flight" in black, red MJ, cream background	3/4" x 3/4"	60.00	90.00
84-85	Ad Cards, came in a box marked Nike Poster Sports, black box with 3 thumb tacks, box distributed from Nike Retail Poster Program			
	——"Air Jordan," jumping to basket with red and black clothes, night shot of Chicago skyline, name and number on back	290850	50.00	100.00
	——"Jordan Blue & Black," standing on road with bb under right hand, blue and black outfit, name and number on back	290858	50.00	100.00
	——"Jordan Freeze Frame," 4 MJ shots on film strip going up to dunk, old red 23, name and number on back	290851	50.00	100.00
84-85	Sport Cards Set, 3 x 5	6 cards	25.00	45.00
	——Title Card with 4 balls, MJ face in basketball			
	——MJ flying to dunk, Chicago skyline, red & black outfit			
	——D. Gooden			
	——L. Parrish			
	——J. McEnroe			
	——J. Lofton			
85	Annual Report, 2 pictures on cover		45.00	75.00
85-86	Ad card, "Black & Blue," standing on runway in blue Air Jordan gear		35.00	60.00
85-86	Ad card, "Freeze Frame," 4 shots of MJ on film during dunk contest, laminated cardboard		35.00	60.00
85	Newsletter, Air Jordan Flight Club, 9000 S.W. Nimbus Drive, Beaverton, OR;	V-I	100.00	150.00
86	Newsletter, Air Jordan Flight Club, 9000 S.W. Nimbus Drive, Beaverton, OR;	V-II	90.00	
87 Spr	Newsletter, Air Jordan Flight Club, 9000 S.W. Nimbus Drive, Beaverton, OR; MJ closeup with white shirt, gray stripe background, old "Air Jordan" logo & white "NEWSLETTER" on top (6.4)	V-III 9 x 13"	85.00	
88 Spr	Newsletter, Air Jordan Flight Club, 9000 S.W. Nimbus Drive, Beaverton, OR; ST-12k-2/88 on back, red AJFC logo flying in air BB over head in LH in center, black background, top gray "NEWLETTER" (6.5)	V-IV 9 x 13"	75.00	
88 Fal	Newsletter, Air Jordan Flight Club, 9000 S.W. Nimbus Drive, Beaverton, OR; ML-12k-8/88 on back, blue sky & cloud cover, knees down on top right front, AJFC logo & Flight on bottom right front, red "NEWSLETTER" top (6.6)	V-V 9 x 13"	65.00	
88	AJFC Membership Kit, shipped in white box			
	——sheet with membership card & sticker "Don't Be Stupid, Stay in School" (6.7)		35.00	
	——copy of AJFC Newsletter (6.8)		65.00	
	——T-shirt		20.00	
	——member welcome letter (6.9)		5.00	

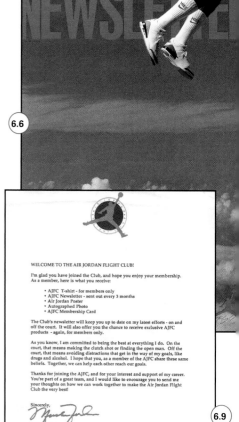

—-Air Jordan poster		20.00
—-Air Jordan photo		20.00
—-environment letter with questionnaire on back (6.10)		5.00
89 Spr Newsletter, Air Jordan Flight Club, 9000 S.W. Nimbus Drive, Beaverton, OR; ST-15k-3/89 on back, MJ going for slam with group of players in street, ball, gray brick wall with graffiti, red "NEWSLETTER" top, red AJFC logo and "Flight" bottom right (6.11)	V-VI 9 x 13"	55.00
89 Fal Newsletter, Air Jordan Flight Club, 9000 S.W. Nimbus Drive, Beaverton, OR 97005, white cover, AJFC logo in middle, "NEWSLETTER" on top, T. Zimmerman cartoon on back (6.12)	V-I 8.5 x 11	65.00
12/89 Brochure, "Nike Flight Collection Fall 1990," clothing ads and AJFC membership joining coupon, MJ shooting with three others in a gym, MJ on right with purple and blue shirt/shorts (6.13)	REF# 1004	30.00
89 Ad, Sport Tees, shirts, MJ face on red t-shirt shaped ad, hole upper left, back " For the man who has everything, there's always something more from Nike. Sport tees...Nobody does it better-Michael and Nike" (6.14)	M5944I 5 x 4	35.00
90 Spr Newsletter, Air Jordan Flight Club, 9000 S.W. Nimbus Drive, Beaverton, OR, black cover, red "NEWSLETTER," AJFC logo	V-II 8.5 x 11	45.00
6/90 Newsletter, Air Jordan Flight Club, 9000 S.W. Nimbus Drive, Beaverton, OR, gray cover, closeup, red "NEWSLETTER," t-shirt with AJFC logo	V-III 8.5 x 11	40.00
10/90 Brochure, "Nike Basketball Collection," clothing ads, MJ reverse dunk RH, black shirt, red shorts, brick wall background (6.15)	IH-63K	20.00

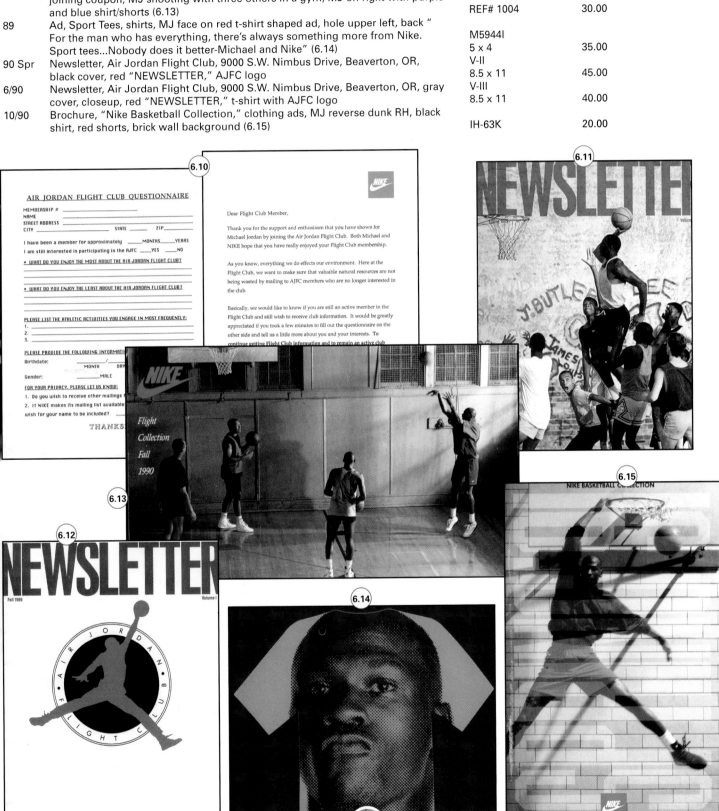

10/90	Newsletter, Air Jordan Flight Club, One Bowerman Drive, Beaverton, OR, black cover, AJFC logo bottom right, LH in front, jumping with ball in RH in back, red "NEWSLETTER," AJFC uniform	V-IV 8.5 x 11	35.00	
90	Ad card, "Is It the Shoes?," (Jordan, Lee), 36" x 24," white background, 5 x 7	290837	25.00	75.00
90	Ad card, "Is It The Shoes?," (Jordan, Lee), 36" x 24," 5 x 7, black background	290838	15.00	
90	Ad card, "Orbit," (Jordan, Lee, Professor, 22" x 36"), 5 x 7	290848	25.00	75.00
90	Ad cards, "Jam 'N Slam"	290922	25.00	75.00
90	Ad card, "Super Jordan," (Cartoon drawing of MJ soaring)	290946	25.00	75.00
90	Ad card, "Art of Dunk," (Jordan flying through air), 36" x 24," 5 x 7	291005	25.00	75.00
90	Ad card, "Wings," ad card, heavy paper stock	292335	25.00	75.00
90	Ad card, "Best on Earth/Mars," (Spike Lee & MJ), heavy paper stock		25.00	75.00
90	Pennant, Nike, MJ & Griffey		75.00	100.00
90	Send Away Sheet, Fan Club-color, 5 x 7		2.00	4.00
90-91	Sheet, Applications for AJFC, Bo and Andre Clubs		3.00	6.00
2/91	Newsletter, Air Jordan Flight Club, One Bowerman Drive, Beaverton, OR, AJFC logo on bottom right, closeup in black jacket, hands on ball, red cover, black "NEWSLETTER"	V-V 8.5 x 11	25.00	40.00
91 Spr	Newsletter, Air Jordan Flight Club, One Bowerman Drive, Beaverton, OR, AJFC logo top left, white cover, red "NEWSLETTER" top, red "AIR JORDAN FLIGHT CLUB" middle, flying hands front and back	V 6 6 x 11"	20.00	35.00
	——Poster, foldout of front & back covers, AJFC			
91 Sum	Newsletter, Air Jordan Flight Club, One Bowerman Drive, Beaverton, OR, AJFC logo & "MJ MVP 1990-91" bottom center, red shirt, black pants, black cover, red "AIR JORDAN FLIGHT CLUB" top, red "NEWSLETTER" bottom left, running holding ball, gray "MVP" middle right	V-7 6 x 11"	20.00	35.00
91 Fal	Newsletter, Air Jordan Flight Club, One Bowerman Drive, Beaverton, OR, AJFC logo top left, blue/gray & black cover, white letters, waiting for ball, white 23, vs. Lakers, 3 pictures on bottom kissing trophy, head against trophy, trophy	V-8 6 x 11"	20.00	35.00
	——Poster, foldout front and back covers, Road Map to Playoff			
91	Calendar, Air Jordan Flight Club Wheaties on back		15.00	20.00
91	Box, MJ/Spike Lee Cards	cover	5.00	10.00
91	Cards, MJ/Spike Lee Set (6.16)	6 cards	10.00	15.00
	——Box, MJ & Lee, front & back	NNO		
	——Earth/Mars, MJ & Lee, front & back	1		
	——High Flying, MJ & Lee, front & back	2		
	——Air Jordan from Nike, MJ & Lee, front & back	3		
	——Stay in School, MJ & Lee, front & back	4		
	——No title, Lee & Little Richard, MJ on back	5		
	——MJ Flight School, MJ & Lee, front & back	6		
92	Calendar, Air Jordan Flight Club, dunking, black shirt, red shorts, brick wall	290953		
92 Spr	Newsletter, Air Jordan Flight Club, One Bowerman Drive, Beaverton, OR, AJFC logo top right, white t shirt with "Air Jordan & logo, red/black shorts, standing holding ball in RH with Bugs holding carrot on right finger, orange and black cover	V-I X 6 x 11"	15.00	30.00
92 Sum	Magazine, Air Jordan Flight Club Presents The Athlete Connection, "On the Set with Michael," MJ behind camera, purple cover, magazine with MJ, Bo & Andre A.	premier, issue	10.00	15.00

92 Win	Magazine, Air Jordan Flight Club Presents The Athlete Connection, "MJ off the Court," MJ shooting over head, black cover, magazine with MJ, Bo & Andre	issue two	10.00	15.00
92	Fan, "Hare Jordan," Bugs kissing MJ, Looney Tunes & Warner Bros., red circles, blue middle, with handle	12"	50.00	75.00
92-93	Calendar, Hare Jordan, Day Dream 1993	3-1502	10.00	15.00
93	Key Chains, Aerospace, 6 different kinds			
	----Bugs, MJ holding Space Man, SKU #00427781		10.00	15.00
93	Newsletter, Air Jordan Flight Club		15.00	30.00
93	Pins, Aerospace, 14 different kinds			
	----MJ flying with BB in LH, blue	3" x 2"	4.00	8.00
	----Bugs, MJ holding Space Man, SKU #00427799	3" x 2"	10.00	15.00
	----MJ flying with BB in LH, SKU #00427773	1.5"	10.00	15.00
	----Bugs, Yipes!, MJ, SKU #00427773	1.5"	10.00	15.00
	----MJ in Roman Helmet, SKU #00427773	1.5	10.00	15.00
93	Stickers, Warner/MJ Set in CD case	12 stickers	10.00	20.00
	----Greetings Earthlings, Spaceman with BB & dog			
	----MJ holding Martian & Bugs with basketball, red t-shirt, black shorts			
	----MJ/Bugs in #23 space ship, white t-shirt			
	----MJ Aerospace, ball in left hand, flying, white t-shirt, black shorts			
	----MJ The Scream Team, MJ & Bugs, center court with monsters			
	----MJ name listed on Warnings: Martian			
	----Dog & Martian hanging from 1/2 moon			
	----The Best on Earth The Best on Mars, Martian hanging on S			
	----What's up Jock?, Bugs with BB flying			
	----Nice Shoes Indeed!, Dog & Martian			
	----J-J-Just Do It. Porky Pig			
	----"That's All Folks," Porky Pig in Space Ship			
93	Stickers, Mini, Aerospace, SKU 00428904	9 stickers	10.00	20.00
	----Space Man with BB, disc			
	----MJ flying with BB in left hand disc			
	----Bugs with BB, disc			
	----Porky, Just Do It, rectangle			
	----MJ/Bugs in #23 Spaceship rectangles			
	----MJ/Bugs/Space man, rectangle			
	----Spaceman, rectangle			
	----MJ/Bugs with green giants rectangle			
	----Nike, square			
93	Stickers Mini, Aerospace	8 stickers	10.00	20.00
	----Space Man with BB			
	----MJ flying with BB in left hand			
	----Bugs with BB			
	----Porky, Just Do It			
	----MJ/Bugs in #23 Spaceship			
	----MJ/Bugs/Spaceman			
	----Spaceman			
	----MJ/Bugs with green giants			
93	Stickers Notebook, Aerospace, 6 different kinds		5.00	10.00
	----MJ in white t-shirt, black shorts, 11.5 x 3, MJ flying in air, left hand with ball	SKU00428888		
93	Stickers Trading, Aerospace Pack	6 stickers	10.00	20.00
	----MJ/Bugs in #23 spaceship, white t-shirt			
	----MJ holding Martian & BB/Bugs, red t-shirt, black shorts			
	----Dog & Martian hanging from half-moon			
	----The Best on Earth, The Best on Mars, Martian hanging on S			
	----Greeting Earthlings, Spaceman with basketball & dog			
	----"That's All Folks," Porky Pig in Space Ship			
93	Stickers Trading, Aerospace Pack	6 stickers cover	10.00	20.00
	----MJ The Scream Team, MJ & Bugs center court with Monstars			
93	Stickers Trading, Aerospace Pack	6 stickers cover	10.00	20.00
	----MJ Aerospace, ball in left hand flying, white t-shirt,			
11/94	Mailer, "MJ Emperor of the Air," MJ Fan Club	2 item	4.00	8.00
	----UDA MJ Tribute Retirement Card, 3 poses, blank back, 3 x 5			
94	Ad Card, 84 MJ pictures, MJ, shoes, jerseys, newspaper clippings, black border, hardwood floor border, printed in China	5 x 10	75.00	125.00
94	Cards, UD Original Poster Set, black metal box with orange center, 3 x 5	9 cards	15.00	30.00
	----M. Jordan, Jumpman-1984			
	----D. Dawkins, Chocolate Thunder-1981			
	----P. Westphal, Goin' Home-1981			
	----R. Fingers & Bruce Sutter-1986			
	----G. Perry, K-Lord-1986			
	----H. Long, Lethal Weapon-1987			
	----M. Malone, Moses-1980			
	----G. Gervin, Iceman-1978			
	----D. Griffith, Dr. Dunkenstein-1986			
94	Newsletter, Air Jordan Flight Club		15.00	25.00
95	Newsletter, Air Jordan Flight Club		15.00	25.00

94	Poster Sample Card, 84 MJ pictures, MJ, shoes, jerseys, newspaper clippings, black border, hardwood floor border, printed in China	3 x 5	1.00	15.00
95	Postcard, 2 front pictures, 3 x 5		10.00	20.00
1/96	Mailer, red #23 shooting, MJ Fan Club		4.00	8.00
6/96	Mailer, "The Jump Man Rules," MJ Fan Club-white t-shirt	3 item	4.00	8.00
	—-MJ Book Mark			
	—-Autographed Poster, dunking in street clothes			
8/96	Mailer, "Jordan" hands on face, MJ Fan Club	3 item	4.00	8.00
	—-Trophy Poster, 2 sided			
	—-8 Time Scoring Champion Card, blank back, 3 x 5			
11/96	Mailer, "Jumpman," MJ Fan Club	2 items	4.00	8.00
	—-Autographed Picture, closeup, black & white, 3 x 5			
	—-Poster inside cover of mailer, Practice Hard Jordan			
4/97	Poster, Mailer, red "23" + MJ flying, black front, MJ Fan Club-details about 97 MJ Basketball Camps		4.00	8.00
9/97	Mailer, gray, MJ in black t-shirt, MJ Fan Club	3 item	4.00	8.00
	—-UDA card, jump shot, red 23, BB on right edge, Fan Club			
	—-Nike Air Jordan Sticker			
97	Shoes, First Jordan X ll	size-1c	25.00	35.00
-	Ad Brochure, "Air Jordan Hi" shoes, MJ flying across Chicago skyline, BB in LH overhead, old "Air Jordan" logo left side, MJ in red & black shirt and long pants, gray undershirt, inside shoe information, black is back with "Nike" upper left, hole upper left corner	fold out	5.00	10.00
-	Ad Card, Any Questions? (MJ inside of ? mark)		5.00	10.00
-	Ad Card, Sky Jordan (MJ dunking with sky background)		5.00	10.00
-	Ad Card, Return Flight (MJ suspended in air in shorts & t-shirt)		5.00	10.00
-	Ad Card, That's All Folks (MJ & Bugs)		5.00	10.00
-	Ad Card, Imagination (MJ in white jumpsuit, heavy paper stock)		20.00	30.00
-	Ad Card, MJ/Genie (Spike Lee, Little Richard & MJ), heavy paper stock		20.00	30.00
-	Ad Card, High Flying 360 (Spike Lee & MJ), heavy paper stock		20.00	30.00
-	Ad Card, 1988 MVP (jumping from freethrow line)		5.00	10.00
-	Ad Card, Reverse Dunk (MJ dunking in empty gym)		5.00	10.00
-	Ad Card, Evolution (blue toned with various pictures of MJ)		5.00	10.00
-	Ad Card, Air Jordan Shoes & Accessories Poster, old Nike/Air Jordan logo top left, MJ in black shirt/pants, red & black shoes over shoulder, blue lettering on shoes & accessories		5.00	10.00
-	Ad Sheet, Nike Baby Jordan, "The Baby Jordan. What did you think the Air Jordan looked like when it was a baby?" black and red shoe under magnifying glass (6.17)	8 x 10	25.00	
-	Book cover, "What if there were no Sports," purple background (6.18)		5.00	10.00
-	Book cover, "Do What Michael Says: Stay in School," red, yellow, black (6.18)		5.00	10.00
-	Cup, AJFC, black with gold logo	248241	10.00	15.00
-	Cup, AJFC, white with red/black logo		10.00	15.00
-	Hat, baseball style, black brim and two side sections, one with red "Nike" and logo, two red front and back sections, front section has black AJFC logo, back section has black "Jordan," inside label "Authentic Jordan by Nike"	toddler size	20.00	30.00
-	Hoop, AJFC Junior Jammer Indoor & Outdoor Set, blue stand, white pole, white backboard with AJFC logo, red hoop, red white & blue net	248322	75.00	
-	Jersey, Red #23, size 44 (6.19)		30.00	60.00
-	Keychain, acrylic, AJFC	248195	10.00	
-	Keychain, brass, AJFC	248194	10.00	

(6.17)

(6.18)

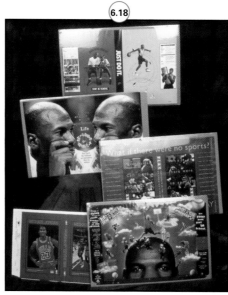

(6.19)

Year	Description	No./Size	Price	Price
	Lapel Pin, "Air Jordan Flight Club" in red letters with gold trim, black background	292754	15.00	
	Lapel Pin, AJFC, red MJ, black inner circle, gold outer circle with letters AJFC	248242	15.00	
	Magazine Sheets, "Things they might have said but never did"	2 sheets	20.00	
	Magnet, MJ & Spike & World, 1.75 x 2.75"		20.00	
	Magnet, Hare Jordan, MJ & Bugs, 4 x 6"		20.00	
	Magnet, Jam & Slam, 4 x 6"		20.00	
	Magnet, Jordan, Pippen, Joint Chief of Stuff, 4.25 x 6.25"		20.00	
	Photo, Air Jordan Flight Club, white t-shirt, black shorts & autograph		30.00	
	Pin, insert with first "Air Jordan Shoes," bronze, rectangle with loop on top, player flying in air with BB in RH & legs spread, "Nike" logo on bottom, edge has orange peel finish and cutouts, uniform has orange peel finish	1.5 x 2	45.00	75.00
	Room Decoration Kit	248422	30.00	45.00
	——Metal Trash Can/Net/Backboard	19 x 10"		
	——Logo Sheet	19 x 36"		
	——Wallpaper Border	6" x 20'		
	Wall Ball, Air Jordan Flight Club Ohio Air Jordan, MJ is backboard with AJFC Sticker		20.00	35.00
	Water bottle, AJFC, red, black logos	248196	15.00	25.00
	Water bottle, AJFC, white, red letters, black and red logo	248419	15.00	25.00
	Watch, AJFC adult, black band loop & buckle, round face, black face with white inner circle, "AJFC" on white inner circle, no bezel, red AJFC logo on face, white hands	248151	50.00	75.00
	Watch, AJFC child, black band loop & buckle, round face, black bezel with white number & lines, red case around bezel, black face with white inner circle, AJFC on white circle, white hands, red AJFC on face, red dot on second hand	248150	50.00	75.00
	Watch, AJFC Elite, black band loop & buckle, round face, red bezel, black & white AJFC & red logo on face, red hands, Bulova	230001	50.00	75.00
	Watch, AJFC, black band & loop, silver buckle, round black face, no bezel, AJFC logo on face, white hands & circle		50.00	75.00
	Watch, AJFC, black band loop and buckle, round face, red bezel, "Air Jordan Flight Club" & AJFC logo on face, black hands		50.00	75.00

Nintendo Electronic Games

Year	Description	No./Size	Price	Price
88	Jordan vs. Bird One on One, Milton Bradley (6.20)	4980	45.00	60.00
92	Super, Bulls vs. Blazers, no MJ on Box, MJ in game		15.00	25.00
94	Super, MJ Chaos in the Windy City, MJ on box, made by Electronic Arts	7048	45.00	60.00
94	UD "Chaos In the Windy City" on front of card, MJ in street clothes holding ball with fire, MJ in blue and white shadow-front, back-2 windows playing basketball, round and square windows, "MJ & Chaos in the Windy City" Super Nintendo Game (6.21)	cut out card	350.00	550.00

Norman James Sheets

Year	Description	No./Size	Price	Price
89	Sheets, Canadian issue, sealed bag	8 x 10	10.00	15.00
	——MJ vs. Lakers, dunking, red 23, Pepsi sign in background (6.22)		8.00	
	——Akeem Olajuwon, red 34, Houston Rockets			
89	Sheet, MJ shooting, red 23 vs. Lakers (6.23)		8.00	

Year	ODDBALL CARDS			
	Oddball-NBA Items			
86-87	Fleer			
	-Uncut Sheet, complete card set		1200.00	1,800.00
87	Fleer			
	Fleer Uncut Sheet, complete set		1000.00	1,600.00
89-90	Fleer			
	-Rack Packs Strip	43 cards	15.00	20.00
	——MJ Sticker	3		
89-90	Hoops			
	-Sealed Pack	15 cards	10.00	15.00
	——MJ Card in front	200		
90-91	Fleer			
	-Card Set	50 cards	10.00	15.00
	——MJ Card on top	26		
90-91	Hoops			
	-AS East Weekend, Miami, card sealed in plastic, Factory Show Card, Feb/9-11/1990, NBA HOOPS sealed in bottom	5	60.00	100.00
	-Collect A Book, Series 1 Box (6.24)	1-12	6.00	10.00
	——MJ Book (6.25)	#4	3.00	5.00
	-100 Superstars Box, gray box with yellow star, sold only at Sears, 1990	100 cards	10.00	15.00
	——MJ Card (6.26)	12	4.00	8.00
91-92	Fleer			
	-3D Plastic Card Wrapper		.01	.05
	-3D Plastic Card Regular Card, wrapper mail-in card	29	250.00	35.00
	-3D Plastic Card, Joe Dumars/MJ, wrapper mail-in card	59	25.00	50.00
	-3D Plastic Card, All-Star Team, MJ, wrapper mail-in card	211	225.00	325.00
	-3D Plastic Card League Leader, wrapper mail-in card	220	225.00	325.00
	-3D Plastic Card, Stockton/MJ, wrapper mail-in card	221	25.00	50.00
	-3D Plastic Card/All-Star Game/MJ, wrapper mail-in card	233	25.00	50.00
	-3D Plastic Card/All-Star Game/MJ, wrapper mail-in card	236	25.00	50.00
	-3D Plastic Card/All-Star Game/MJ, wrapper mail-in card	237	25.00	50.00
	-3D Plastic Card/All-Star Game/MJ, wrapper mail-in card	238	25.00	50.00
	-3D Plastic Card/Team Leader, wrapper mail-in card	375	225.00	325.00
	-3D Plastic Card Pro Vision, wrapper mail-in card	2 of 6	225.00	325.00
	-Pro Vision	2 of 6	1.00	2.00
	-Tony's Pizza, same as regular #29, different number (6.27)	S-33	60.00	90.00
	-Fleer Pro Vision Factory Uncut Error Strip from sheet, K. Malone front, MJ back		35.00	50.00
	——5 MJ card backs			
	-Fleer Pro Vision Factory Uncut Error Strip from sheet, MJ front, K. Malone back		35.00	50.00
	——5 MJ card fronts			
91-92	Hoops			
	-All-Star Weekend Charlotte, card sealed in plastic, Factory Show Card, 2/8-10/91, NBA HOOPS in bottom of holder	253	60.00	100.00
	-92 USA Basketball Team, 2 send-in cards, BB with world map, "Sent the World Spinning," MJ name in quiz on card back	NNO	15.00	25.00
	-100 Superstars, copper box with red star & white background, gold star in "A" on box front & back, sold only at Sears, dated 1991	100 cards	50.00	75.00
	——MJ Card (6.28)	13	30.00	40.00

Year	Description		Low	High
91-92	Sky Box			
	-Rack Pack	62 cards	25.00	35.00
	—-MJ Card, top card	39		
	—-MJ vs. Magic, Great Moments from the NBA, top card	333		
	-Canadian Minis Set, in wrappers	50 cards	15.00	25.00
	—-MJ Card	7	5.00	10.00
91-92	Upper Deck			
	-Locker Series Sealed Box 1 of 6, MJ on box	84 cards	6.00	10.00
	-Locker Series Sealed Box 2 of 6, MJ on box	84 cards	6.00	10.00
	-Locker Series Sealed Box 3 of 6, MJ on box	84 cards	6.00	10.00
	-Locker Series Sealed Box 4 of 6, MJ on box	84 cards	6.00	10.00
	-Locker Series Sealed Box 5 of 6, MJ on box	84 cards	6.00	10.00
	-Locker Series Sealed Box 6 of 6, MJ on box	84 cards	6.00	10.00
92-93	Fleer			
	-Drake's Bakery, reprint of #32 Fleer (6.29)	7	35.00	50.00
	-Slam Dunk, Tony's Pizza, same as #273, NBA Jam Session (6.30)	NNO	15.00	25.00
92-93	Hoops			
	-100 Superstars Set, copper box with red star, white star in letter, "A" on box front/back, sold only at Sears, dated 1992	100 cards	75.00	100.00
	—-MJ Card (6.31)	14 MVP	45.00	60.00
92-93	Skybox			
	-Metal Can	4"	25.00	35.00
92-93	Upper Deck			
	-Locker Series Card, blank back	NNO	4.00	8.00
93-94	Upper Deck			
	-Locker Talk Series One, Sealed Locker Style Box	88 cards	20.00	25.00
	-Locker Talk Series Two, Sealed Locker Style Box	88 cards	20.00	25.00
	-Pro View—3D Glasses, MJ middle of frame		3.00	6.00
94-95	Upper Deck			
	-Rare Air Set Ad Brochure		5.00	10.00
	—-letter			
	—-envelope			
	-Launch Tour 94 Invitation, 1/20/94		15.00	20.00
95-96	Fleer			
	-Sheet, Metal Slick Silver, 9 MJ card fronts with 9 other players on sheet	28 x 40		
95-96	SP MJ Popup Display		15.00	20.00
95-96	SP			
	-Ad Foldout		10.00	15.00
	—-MJ Sample Card	23		
	-UDA SP Regular Card, gold left back & signature, QVC #C337840, 1000 produced	23	100.00	150.00
	-UDA SP NBA All-Star, silver top strip, gold signature front, Home Shopping Network Card, nick & scratch back, black back, holding trophy, #654 of 1,000 produced	AS-2	100.00	150.00
95-96	Stadium Club		200.00	300.00
	-Members Only Proof Sheets, two sheets	200 cards		
	—-MJ Card			
	—-MJ Card			
95-96	Topps			
	-World Class, Canadian Issue (6.32)	WC-1	45.00	65.00

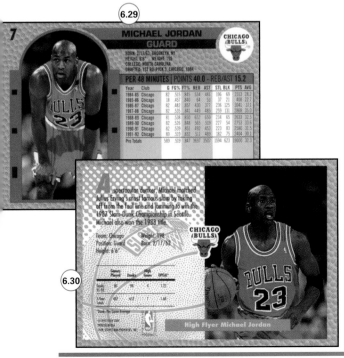

163

95-96	Upper Deck			
	-UDA "95-96 Chicago Bulls" top, "72 Wins 1996 NBA Champions" bottom, gold stripe top & bottom on front, porcelain card, team picture & names & record stats, no stripes on back, 2,500 produced, regular size		35.00	50.00
	-UD Refuse to Lose Sealed Pack Set		5.00	10.00
	——MJ metal slammer	#18		
	——"Bulls Win 70 Games" red border, SP, MJ, DR on front, SK, RH, TK on back, 3 x 5	NNO	5.00	10.00
	——Upper Deck Collector Choice	15 cards		
	-UD Basketball Card Kit, Fenton Hill Manufacturer		15.00	25.00
	——96-97 Collector Choice, 4 packs sealed	40 cards		
	——Collector Album plus sheet, MJ on cover	1 item	5.00	10.00
	——Six nine-card sleeves	6 items		

Oddball-UD NBA Foreign Issued Cards

94-95	UD Collector's Choice-French			
	-Wrapper (6.33)	front	.25	.50
95-96	Collector's Choice Sticker Album-England, poster inside		10.00	15.00
95-96	Collector's Choice Stickers-England			
	-85 Rookie of Year (6.34)	MJ-1	1.50	2.50
	-86/87 1000 points	MJ-2	1.50	2.50
	-88 Defensive Player of Year	MJ-3	1.50	2.50
	-Jordan Collection	MJ-4	1.50	2.50
	-#45 He's Back	MJ-5	1.50	2.50
	-#45 He's Back	MJ-6	1.50	2.50
	-#45 He's Back	MJ-7	1.50	2.50
	-#45 He's Back	MJ-8	1.50	2.50
	-#45 He's Back	MJ-9	1.50	2.50
	-Regular Card	120	3.00	5.00
95-96	UD Collector's Choice Series I Basketball Collector's Album, 3 packs of binder insert sheets		10.00	15.00

Oddball Baseball Major League Cards

94-95	Upper Deck			
	-Scouting Report Sealed Pack, plus '94 Minor League Pack	17 cards	8.00	12.00
	——MJ Card, White Sox Top Prospect, 3 x 5	MJ-23		
	-Scouting Report Sealed Pack, plus '94 Minor League Pack	17 cards	8.00	12.00
	——MJ Card, Hitting, 3 x 5	SR-1		
	-Scouting Report Sealed Pack, plus '94 Minor League Pack	17 cards	8.00	12.00
	——MJ Card, Fielding, 3 x 5	SR-2		
	-Scouting Report Sealed Pack, plus '94 Minor League Pack	17 cards	8.00	12.00
	——MJ Card, Throwing, 3 x 5	SR-3		
	-Scouting Report Sealed Pack, plus '94 Minor League Pack	17 cards	8.00	12.00
	——MJ Card, Speed, 3 x 5	SR-4		
	-Scouting Report Sealed Pack, plus '94 Minor League Pack (6.35)	17 cards	8.00	12.00
	——MJ Card, Summary, 3 x 5	SR-5		

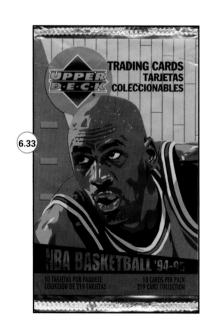

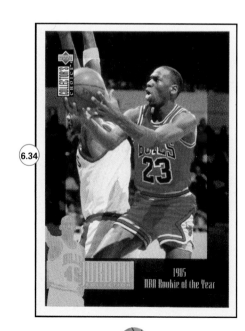

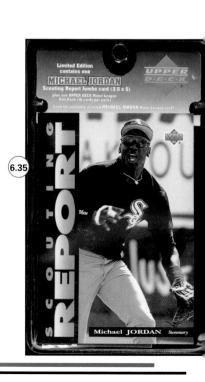

Oddball-Baseball Minor League Cards

Year				
95	**Upper Deck** Metal Cards, "Michael Jordan Tribute Set" on left side, "Embossed Metal Collector Cards" on bottom, black, gray and gold can, 2 view batting in black Barons shirt, on base in white Barons uniform #45 raised view, Metallic Impressions Baseball Set (6.36)	5 cards	20.00	25.00
96	**Upper Deck** Sealed Set, Treat Entertainment, Manufacturer			
	—2 Topps Finest Baseball Packs	24 cards	4.00	8.00
	—MJ Card, Season Highlight, Extends Hit Streak to 13, 3 x 5	MJ-3	4.00	8.00
	Sealed Set, Treat Entertainment, Manufacturer			
	—4-1995 Minor League Packs	16 cards	6.00	10.00
	—MJ Card, Decade of Dominance, 3 x 5		3.00	5.00
	—MJ Coin, #45		2.00	3.00

Oddball Cards-Star Company

Year				
84-85	Uncut Sheet, All Rookie Team, 2-1st year MJ's	11 cards	400.00	600.00

Ohio Art Sports Games

Year				
90	Lil' Sport Hoops, Over the door, On the wall, Anywhere BB, Slam Dunk Champ (6.37)	671M	50.00	90.00
90	MJ Wall Ball Game, front red, MJ picture, MJ back board picture, ball, net, basket, numbers front/back bottom	672	25.00	40.00
90	Jr. Jammer, round backboard (6.38)	678	40.00	75.00
90	Jordan Jammer	690	40.00	75.00
90	Lil'Sport MJ Electronic Countdown Basketball	691	50.00	90.00
90	Magazine Sheet, Lil' Sport MJ Electronic Countdown BB Game, MJ picture in old #23 red and black signature	8.5 x 11	3.00	6.00
90	Jordan Pro Basketball Set, 4 to 6' stand, 7" ball	692	50.00	90.00
92	Mike & Me Talking Basketball Set, two talking modes (6.39)	673	75.00	125.00
94	Michael Jordan, Jr. Jammer, square backboard	676	60.00	90.00
94	MJ 45 Wall Ball Basketball Set, MVP Gamecap Bonus, MJ portrait for backboard	668M	25.00	35.00
-	Ad Sheet, Lil'Sport, for Jordan Jammer, MJ Hoops, and MJ Sports Locker, Free MJ poster with every purchase		2.00	4.00
-	Lil'Sport, Jordan Jammer, hoop, pole and backboard, 2 MJ pictures on white backboard with red center square	7'	75.00	125.00
	Locker, Lil'Sport, Sport Locker, red		25.00	50.00

Olympic Magazines

Year		card #		
4/17-22/84	Program, 1984 USA Olympic Basketball Trials, Bloomington, IN, MJ picture and biographical article (6.40)	inside	75.00	
6/84	Program, Olympic Trials, Indiana, Univ. Alumni vs. USA Olympians	cover	50.00	125.00
7/84	Program, Hoosier Dome Indianapolis USA BB, Olympic Trials, 7/9/84, World's Largest BB Game, red white & blue cover	cover & inside	50.00	125.00
5/92	Book, Team USA by Devra Speregen, posters, Scholastic	cover		
92	Yearbook, "The Official USA BB, Dream Team," MJ, Bird, Magic		15.00	25.00
92	Book, USA Basketball Stickers-15, Golden Pub. #2398	cover	10.00	15.00
	—MJ Sticker	10		
92	Book, USA BB America's Team Poster Book, Barcelona '92, gold cover, Western Publishing Company, Golden Books	12412	5.00	10.00
92	Book, USA BB America's Dynasty Poster, 1936-1992, red, white, blue, Western Publishing Company, Golden Books	12413	5.00	10.00

6.36 6.37 6.38 6.39 6.40

USA

1984 OLYMPIC BASKETBALL TRIALS

Bloomington, Ind.   April 17-22

92	Sheet, US Olympic Summer Team Collection Ad Sheet for posters	36 USC 380	4.00	8.00
96	Ad sheet, Lightweight Backpack from Coach's Olympic Game Collection, MJ in blue shirt and blue jeans	8 x 10	3.00	6.00

Year	**Organ & Tissue Donation**			
96	Pamphlet Holder, MJ front (6.41)		10.00	25.00
	—-Pamphlet, MJ front & inside (6.42)			

Year	**OVERSIZED CARDS**			
	Oversize NBA Cards			
91-92	Upper Deck			
	-Blowup of card #44, 8.5" x 11"	44	20.00	30.00
92-93	Upper Deck			
	-UD Salutes Chicago Bulls Back-to-Back World Champions, CBS & Fox Video Card, Back-to-Back 90-91, 91-92, World Champions, team picture on back, 3 x 5 (6.43)	11378	75.00	100.00
93-94	Upper Deck			
	-Pro View Box	110cards		
	—-MJ Card on Box Bottom, 4 x 6		3.00	6.00
	-MJ Flight Team Jumbo Cards, 3 x 5	5 cards	40.00	60.00
	—C. Barkley, 3 x 5	FT-2	8.00	12.00
	—D. Brown, 3 x 5	FT-4	8.00	12.00
	—C. Drexler, 3 x 5 `	FT-7	8.00	12.00
	—K. Malone, 3 x 5	FT-13	8.00	12.00
	—A. Mourning, 3 x 5	FT-15	8.00	12.00
	-MJ Flight Team Suns Team Set	26 cards	15.00	20.00
	—-1 clear pack of cards			
	—-1 foil pack of cards			
	—-Barkley Flight Team/MJ back, 3 x 5	FT-2	8.00	12.00
	—-Mitch Richmond, 3 x 5	64		
	-MJ Flight Team Hornets Team Set	26 cards	15.00	20.00
	—-1 clear pack of cards			
	—-1 foil pack of cards			
	—-Mourning Flight Team/MJ back, 3 x 5	FT-15	8.00	12.00
	—-Calbert Cheaney, 3 x 5	487		
	-MJ Flight Team Celtics Team Set	26 cards	15.00	20.00
	—-1 clear pack of cards			
	—-1 foil pack of cards			
	—-D. Brown Flight Team/MJ back, 3 x 5	FT-4	8.00	12.00
	—-Anfernee Hardaway, 3 x 5	382		
	-MJ Flight Team Blazers Team Set	26 cards	15.00	20.00
	—-1 clear pack of cards			
	—-1 foil pack of cards			
	—-Barkley Flight Team/MJ back, 3 x 5	FT-7	8.00	12.00
	—-Chris Webber, 3 x 5	483		
	-MJ Flight Team Jazz Team Set	26 cards	15.00	20.00
	—-1 clear pack of cards			
	—-1 foil pack of cards			
	—-Malone Flight Team/MJ back, 3 x 5	FT-13	8.00	12.00
	—-Shaquille O'Neal, 3 x 5	LT3		

(6.41) (6.42) (6.43)

-UDA "MJ Team MVP," blowup of 1992-1993 hologram card #4, 7,500 produced, 5 x 7		35.00	50.00
-UDA "Jerry West Selects Best All Around Player," blowup of 92-93 JW-8 card, 5,000 produced, 8.5 x 11		20.00	30.00
-UDA "All NBA Team," blowup of 1992- 1993 card #AN1, 10,000 produced, 8.5 x 11		20.00	30.00
-UDA "Mr. June Jordan's 3 Peat," blowup of 1993-1994 card #MJ-9, 5,000 produced, 8.5 x 11	NNO	20.00	30.00
-UDA "Team MVP," blowup of 1992-1993 card #TM-5, 2,500 produced, 8.5 x 11		45.00	60.00
-UDA "NBA 3 Time Champs," JP, MJ, & SP-front, 7,500 produced, 3 x 5		25.00	40.00
-UDA "UD Salutes MJ Retirement," 3 poses: shooting, trophy, dribbling, back story and shooting 10,000 produced, 3 x 5		25.00	35.00
-UDA "NBA All-Stars East," I. Thomas, MJ, & Shaq back, M. Price, L Johnson, S. Pippen front, 20,000 produced, 3 x 5		10.00	20.00
-UDA "NBA All-Stars West," back Hardaway, Drexler, Stockton; D. Robinson, Malone, Barkley, 20,000 produced, 3 x 5		10.00	20.00
-UDA "An Expert's Guide to Card Collecting," MJ front & back, Gretzky, Montana, MJ, R. Jackson front, 3 x 5 (6.44)		10.00	20.00
-Hobby Box, 36 packs, sealed box	432 cards	30.00	35.00
—MJ Card on box bottom, 4 x 6		6.00	10.00
-Retail Box, 36 packs, sealed box	432 cards	20.00	25.00
—MJ Card on box bottom, 4 x 6		6.00	10.00

94-95	Upper Deck			
	-Basketball Heroes Jumbo Set	10 cards	60.00	120.00
	—Basketball Heroes, 3 x 5	37	6.00	12.00
	—Basketball Heroes, 3 x 5	38	6.00	12.00
	—Basketball Heroes, 3 x 5	39	6.00	12.00
	—Basketball Heroes, 3 x 5	40	6.00	12.00
	—Basketball Heroes, 3 x 5	41	6.00	12.00
	—Basketball Heroes, 3 x 5	42	6.00	12.00
	—Basketball Heroes, 3 x 5	43	6.00	12.00
	—Basketball Heroes, 3 x 5 (6.45)	44	6.00	12.00
	—Basketball Heroes Checklist, 3 x 5	45	6.00	12.00
	—Basketball Heroes Header Card, 3 x 5	JH	6.00	12.00
	-#45 He's Back Collectors Edition Card, MJ vs. Pacers, 3 x 5	NNO	8.00	12.00
	-#45 He's Back Collectors Edition Card, MJ vs. Hawks, gray signature right side, 3 x 5	NNO	8.00	12.00
	-#45 He's Back Collectors Edition Card, MJ vs. Hawks, gray signature bottom center, 3 x 5	NNO	8.00	12.00
	-#45 He's Back Commemorative Set	21 cards	12.00	18.00
	—Series I pack			
	—Series II pack			
	—MJ Card, white 45 uniform left front, gray signature bottom middle front, 3 x 5		8.00	12.00
	-#45 He's Back Commemorative Set	21 cards	12.00	18.00
	—Series I pack			
	—Series II pack			
	—MJ Card, white 45 uniform right front, gray signature right front, red 45 uniform left front, 3 x 5		8.00	12.00
	-#45 He's Back Commemorative Set	21 cards	12.00	18.00
	—Series I pack			
	—Series II pack			
	—MJ Card, red 45 uniform in 3 front positions gray signature bottom front, 3 x 5		8.00	12.00

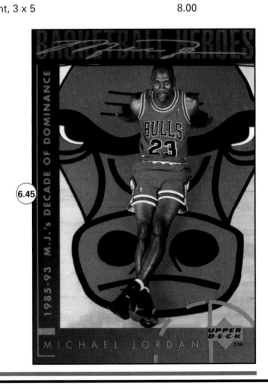

-Decade of Dominance Rare Air Card, towel over head, Set of 5, 3 x 5	1 of 5	5.00	8.00
-Decade of Dominance, back to basket dunk with right hand, back "Two of the most Memorable moments...," 3 x 5	2 of 5	5.00	8.00
-Decade of Dominance, jumping holding ball, red shirt black short, "Kareem Abdul-Jabbar is the NBA's all...," 3 x 5	3 of 5	5.00	8.00
-Decade of Dominance, dribbling in mirror with reflections, "Reflecting back on his NBA career,...," 3 x 5	4 of 5	5.00	8.00
-Decade of Dominance, shooting over New York Knicks, P. Ewing, "MJ didn't just win seven," 3 x 5	5 of 5	5.00	8.00
-Full Shot Sealed Set	21 cards	10.00	15.00
——Two 94-95 Series II packs			
——MJ Card, Rare Air, 3 x 5	1 of 5	5.00	8.00
-Full Shot Sealed Set	21 cards	10.00	15.00
——Two 94-95 Series II packs			
——MJ Card, Decade of Dominance, 3 x 5	2 of 5	5.00	8.00
-Full Shot Sealed Set	21 cards	10.00	15.00
——Two 94-95 Series II packs			
——MJ Card, Decade of Dominance, 3 x 5	3 of 5	5.00	8.00
-Full Shot Sealed Set	21 cards	10.00	15.00
——Two 94-95 Series II packs			
——MJ Card, Decade of Dominance, 3 x 5	4 of 5	5.00	8.00
-Full Shot Sealed Set	21 cards	10.00	15.00
——Two 94-95 Series II packs			
——MJ Card, Decade of Dominance, 3 x 5	5 of 5	5.00	8.00
-Mr. June Commemorative Jumbo Set	10 cards	40.00	60.00
——Jordan's Steal, 3 x 5	MJ-1	4.00	6.00
——MJ's High Five, 3 x 5	MJ-2	4.00	6.00
——1991 NBA Finals MVP, 3 x 5	MJ-3	4.00	6.00
——35 Points in One Half, 3 x 5	MJ-4	4.00	6.00
——Three Point King, 3 x 5	MJ-5	4.00	6.00
——Back-to-Back Finals MVP, 3 x 5	MJ-6	4.00	6.00
——55 Point Game, 3 x 5 (6.46)	MJ-7	4.00	6.00
——Record Scoring Average, 3 x 5	MJ-8	4.00	6.00
——Third Straight MVP, 3 x 5	MJ-9	4.00	6.00
——Checklist, 3 x 5	MJ-10	4.00	6.00
-Rare Air Set, Box Insert Cards	4 cards		
——10,120 of 30,000, under basket looking at ball, 3 x 8		8.00	15.00
——23,558 of 30,000, passing the ball, 3 x 8		8.00	15.00
——304 of 55,000, dribbling the ball in a crowd, 3 x 8		6.00	12.00
——1,506 of 60,000, reaching for ball vs. Lakers, 3 x 8		5.00	10.00
-Launch Tour Changing the Game Forever Card/MJ front & back, Hobby Series, 10,000 produced, 3 x 5 (6.47)		75.00	100.00
-Launch Tour Changing the Game Forever Card/MJ front & back, Tour Series, 2,000 produced, 3 x 5		100.00	150.00
-"UDA Salutes MJ's Return to the NBA" top front, gold signature & story on back, 45,000 produced, 3 x 5		20.00	25.00
-UDA "'95 Playoff Heroes top, 1995 NBA Playoffs" bottom front, AH, HO, MJ front, 5,000 produced, 3 x 5		45.00	60.00

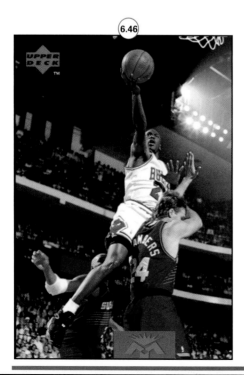

6.46

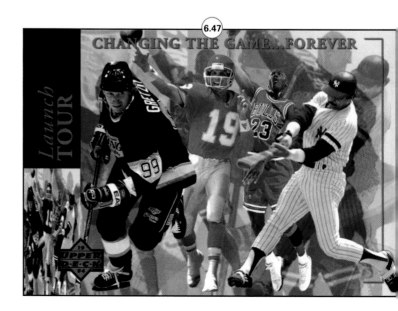

6.47

CHANGING THE GAME...FOREVER

95-96				
	Collector's Choice			
	-UD Slam Jam Jumbo MJ card included with Factory Set purchase, 5 x 7	352	5.00	10.00
	-#45 He's Back MJ Champion, 5 x 7	M-1	25.00	40.00
	-#45 He's Back MJ Champion, 5 x 7	M-2	25.00	40.00
	-#45 He's Back MJ Champion, 5 x 7	M-3	25.00	40.00
	-#45 He's Back MJ Champion, 5 x 7	M-4	25.00	40.00
	-#45 He's Back MJ Champion, 5 x 7	M-5	25.00	40.00
95-96	SP Championship			
	-UDA 94/95 SP Championship, #41, 7,500 made, 5 x 7		15.00	20.00
95-96	Stadium Club			
	-Spike Says Oversized Proof Card	SS-1	35.00	45.00
	-Members Only oversized proof card from 50 cards, Members Only Set, 2-3/4 x 3-3/4	20	35.00	45.00
95-96	Upper Deck			
	-USA Olympic Champions Olympicards Set, 5 pictures-1 MJ, 3 x 8	155 cards	15.00	20.00
	-USA Olympic Champions Passing the Torch, MJ & AH, 5 x 7 (6.48)	NNO	12.00	18.00
	-USA Olympic Champions Passing the Torch, MJ & AH, 5,000 produced, 3 x 5		25.00	35.00
	-UDA "Rare Air" 24k facsimile gold signature, blowup, 5,000 produced, 8 x 11		35.00	45.00
	-UDA "Rare Air," blowup, 5,000 made, 8 x 11	NNO	35.00	45.00
	-UDA "MJ First Championship," NC die-cut, gold top stripe and signature-front, MJ on floor back, 5,000 produced, 3 x 5 (6.49)		25.00	35.00
	-UDA "MJ First Championship," NC die-cut, silver top stripe and signature-front, MJ on floor back, 5,000 produced, 3 x 5		25.00	35.00
	-UDA "Bulls Best Ever NBA Start Chicago Bulls," 2 gold stripes front top & bottom, RH, TK, LL back, gold top red bottom stripes-back, 4,103 produced, 3 x 5		25.00	35.00
	-UDA First 70 Win Season Set, 2 cards & holder			
	—-red card, "Chicago Bulls" in top red stripe, "First 70-Game Winners" in bottom red stripe TK, MJ, SP, DR-front, SK, RH, LL-back, 2,500 produced, 3 x 5,		40.00	60.00
	—-gold card, "Chicago Bulls" in top gold stripe, "First 70-Game Winners" in bottom gold stripe, TK, MJ, SP, DR-front, SK, RH, LL-back, 1,000 produced, 3 x 5		50.00	75.00
	-UDA 70 Wins "Chicago Bulls" on top front gold stripe, "70 Game Winners" on bottom front, "70-Game Winners" on back gold top stripe, 7,096 produced, 3 x 5	#1	20.00	30.00
	-UDA 70 Wins "95-96 70 Wins Bulls" on top-front, big BB on front, Bull Logo-back, die-cut gold color, gold bottom/top borders front, no back border, 10,000 produced, 3 x 5		20.00	25.00
	-UDA 70 Wins "Chicago Bulls 1st 70-Win Season" on 2 gold side stripes on front, die-cut, black with gold border around six pictures-back, MJ-front, 15,000 produced, 3 x 5		20.00	25.00
	-UDA 70 Wins "Chicago Bulls First 70 Game Winners" on top and bottom red stripes front, April 16, 1996, top front below red border red bottom/ top borders-front, red top border-back, DR, MJ, SP-front, 14,300 produced, 3 x 5	#5	20.00	25.00
	-UDA "70 Victory Season '95-96 Chicago Bulls" on top & bottom front, gold border top and bottom front, red border bottom-back, SP, DR, MJ-front, 7,096 produced, 3 x 5	#6	20.00	35.00
	-UDA "National Hero MJ Chicago Bulls', die-cut, card #NH-15,000 produced, 3 x 5,		25.00	40.00
	-UDA "Eastern Conference Finals Magic vs. Bulls" black/silver on front, Grant, Scott, Anderson, Kukoc, Rodman, Pippen, 5,000 produced, 3 x 5		25.00	40.00
	-UDA "1996 Eastern Conference Finals Orlando Magic vs. Chicago Bulls" gold stripes on top & bottom, gold on front, black back, gold top stripe-back, MJ/AH-front, 5,000 produced, 3 x 5		25.00	40.00
	-UDA "1996 NBA Finals" Bull & Sonics, gold strip top and two sides on front, SK ,MJ-back, top/sides gold stripes-back, 5,000 produced, 3 x 5		25.00	40.00
	-UDA "1996 NBA Champions" on gold top & side strips, 2 basketballs top corners on front, LL, TK, SP, DR, DH on black back, gold stripes top & sides-back, 20,000 produced, 3 x 5	#1	10.00	15.00

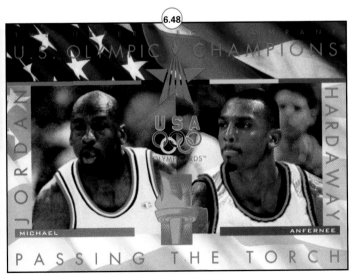

(6.48)

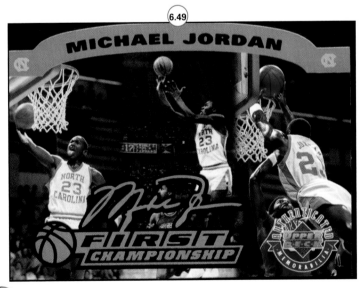

(6.49)

Description	No.	Low	High
-UDA "Chicago Bulls 4th NBA Championship," die-cut, 2 gold side strips, Bulls logo top front DR, SP, TK, RH, LL, SK. on back, each player framed-25,000 produced, 3 x 5	#2	10.00	15.00
-UDA "95-96 Chicago Bulls" top, "72 Wins 1996 NBA Champions" bottom, gold stripe top & bottom front, die-cut, team picture/names, "95-96 Chicago Bulls," top gold stripe-back, 10,000 produced, 3 x 5	#3	15.00	20.00
-UDA "95-96 Chicago Bulls" top, "72 Wins 1996 NBA Champions" bottom, gold stripe top & bottom front, die-cut, team picture/names, "95-96 Chicago Bulls," top gold stripe-back, 10,000 produced, 8.5 x 11		15.00	20.00
-UDA "Chicago Bulls Fourth NBA Championship," black front, gold top stripe on front, top gold stripe-back, DR, MJ, SP-front, Bull's logo all corners-front & back, 10,000 produced, 3 x 5	#4	15.00	25.00
-UDA "Chicago Bulls 4th NBA Championship" gold top & bottom stripe on front, TK, LL, SK,RH on black back, 10,000 produced, 3 x 5		15.00	25.00
-UDA "8 Time Scoring Champ," blank back, 3 x 5	NNO	10.00	15.00
-UDA "8 Time Scoring Champ," die-cut, gold strips each side front, MJ with towel-back, 5,000 produced, 3 x 5		20.00	35.00
-UDA "MVP Most Valuable Player," gold signature on front, die-cut, 3 pictures, stats, story-back, 2,500 produced, 3 x 5		30.00	45.00
-UDA "MJ 25,000 points" die-cut, red front, 3 poses, QVC-black back, MJ back pose, 5,000 produced, 3 x 5		25.00	40.00
-UDA "Jordan Command Performers," die-cut, silver front, gold signature, 5,000 produced, 3 x 5		25.00	40.00
-UDA MJ framed 4-Up uncut Holographic Scoring Leader Cards, 25,000 issued, 6 x 10	10203 4 cards	25.00	40.00
-UDA MJ framed 4-Up uncut Holographic MVP Cards, 25,000 issued, 6 x 10	10204 4 cards	25.00	40.00
-UDA MJ 2 card uncut Hologram Display-Scoring Leader card #AW1, 25,000 issued, 3 x 5	10206 2 cards	15.00	25.00
-UDA MJ 2 card uncut Hologram Display-MVP card #AW4, 25,000 issued, 3 x 5	10207 2 cards	20.00	35.00
-UDA Legends of '95, Montana, Marino, MJ shirts front, blue background, gold line border, MJ rare air towel picture on top back, 5,000 produced, 3 x 5	251	40.00	55.00
-1996 Jordan Collection, 3 x 5	25 cards	35.00	50.00
—-	JC-1	1.50	2.00
—-	JC-2	1.50	2.00
—-	JC-3	1.50	2.00
—-	JC-4	1.50	2.00
—-	JC-5	1.50	2.00
—-	JC-6	1.50	2.00
—-	JC-7	1.50	2.00
—-	JC-8	1.50	2.00
—-	JC-9	1.50	2.00
—-	JC-10	1.50	2.00
—-	JC-11	1.50	2.00
—-	JC-12	1.50	2.00
—-	JC-13	1.50	2.00
—-	JC-14	1.50	2.00
—-	JC-15	1.50	2.00
—-	JC-16	1.50	2.00
—-	JC-17	1.50	2.00
—-	JC-18	1.50	2.00
—-	JC-19	1.50	2.00
—-	JC-20	1.50	2.00
—-	JC-21	1.50	2.00
—-	JC-22	1.50	2.00
—-	JC-23	1.50	2.00
—-	JC-24	1.50	2.00
—-8th Season Scoring Champion	NNO	1.50	2.00
-UD MJ 95-96 NBA Season Magic Memories, Meet the Stars Trivia Challenge, trade card, die-cut, UDC-red/ black card, blurred background, MJ jumping through air, ball in right hand, 4 x 6		8.00	12.00

Oversized NBA UD Foreign Issued Cards

94-95	UD Collectors Choice-Japanese			
	Series 2 Wax Box Trade Card for 3 x 5 Japanese MJ Retirement Card, front 3 poses of MJ just like 3 x 5, back "Congratulations!" + Japanese	T-1	65.00	90.00
	-MJ Retirement Card, exchanged for the Series 2 Wax Box Trade Card, front 3 poses of MJ, blank back, 3 x 5 card (6.50)	NNO	15.00	30.00

Oversized Baseball Major League Cards

94-95	Collector's Choice			
	-Blow Up Baseball, round UD logo on back, 5 x 7	23	8.00	12.00
	-Blow Up Baseball, not autographed, star UD logo on back, 5 x 7	23	8.00	12.00
	-Blow Up Baseball, autograph, star UD logo on back, 5 x 7	23	3500.00	4500.00
94-95	Upper Deck			
	-Star Rookies Electric Diamond, 3 x 5	19	4.00	8.00
	-Scouting Report WS Top Prospect, 3 x 5	MJ-23	4.00	8.00
	-Scouting Report Hitting, 3 x 5 (6.51)	SR-1	4.00	8.00
	-Scouting Report Fielding, 3 x 5	SR-2	4.00	8.00
	-Scouting Report Throwing, 3 x 5	SR-3	4.00	8.00
	-Scouting Report Speed, 3 x 5	SR-4	4.00	8.00
	-Scouting Report Summary, 3 x 5	SR-5	4.00	8.00
	-Scouting Report Summary, 3 x 5	SR-5	4.00	8.00
95-96	Collectors Choice			
	-UDA 94-95 Rookie Class Card #661, gold signature, 2,500 produced, 5 x 7	1894	50.00	75.00

Oversized Baseball Minor League Cards

94-95	Upper Deck			
	-White Sox Prospects, 3 x 5	MJ23	5.00	10.00
95	Upper Deck			
	-Season Highlights, White Sox Welcome MJ to Spring Training, from mail-in wrappers, 3 x 5 (6.52)	MJ-1	5.00	8.00
	-Season Highlights, MJ Supplies Offense at Classic, from mail-in wrappers, 3 x 5	MJ-2	5.00	8.00
	-Season Highlights, MJ Extends Hitting Streak to 13, from mail-in wrappers, 3 x 5	MJ-3	5.00	8.00
	-Season Highlights, MJ Hits First Home Run, from mail-in wrappers, 3 x 5	MJ-4	5.00	8.00
	-Season Highlight, MJ Does Extracurricular Baseball, from mail-in wrappers, 3 x 5	MJ-5	5.00	8.00
	-Star Rookie '94, blowup, 4 x 6	19	15.00	20.00

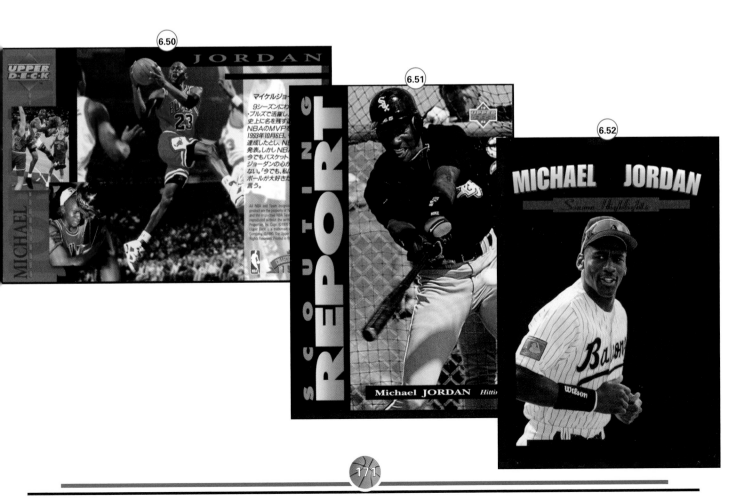

Panini Stickers & Album Sets

There were 6 sets manufactured from 1987 through 1992 and distributed only in European countries. The first and last 2 years are the most difficult to find. Special Note: Panini also made 2 different versions for distribution in Europe in '91 and '92.

Year	Panini Stickers & Album Sets	sticker# or #of stickers		
87	Set, "Panini Supersport," Spanish Version	161 sticks	275.00	400.00
	---MJ Sticker	4		
	---Album, yellow, blue, orange & green strip cover		20.00	30.00
87	Set, Panini SuperSport, multisport, Spanish Version	204 sticks	250.00	350.00
	---MJ Sticker	141		
	---Album, yellow cover		20.00	30.00
89	Set, "Panini Basketball NBA '89," Spanish Version	292 sticks	275.00	325.00
	---MJ Sticker	76		
	---MJ Sticker	261 AS		
	---MJ Sticker	285 AS West		
	---Album		15.00	25.00
90	Set, "Panini Basketball NBA '90," Spanish Version	272 sticks	250.00	300.00
	---MJ Sticker	67		
	---MJ Sticker	254 AS		
	---B. Benjamin Sticker/MJ front	197		
	---Album		10.00	20.00
90-91	Set, "Panini Basketball 90-91...," American Version	170 sticks	15.00	20.00
	---MJ Sticker, on a sticker sheet	91		
	---MJ Sticker, on a sticker sheet	G-AS		
	---MJ Sticker, on a sticker sheet	K		
	---Album, "Premiere Edition"		2.00	4.00
91	Set, "Panini Basket NBA '91'," European Version	217 sticks	225.00	275.00
	---MJ Sticker	61	75.00	100.00
	---MJ Sticker (7.2)	205	50.00	75.00
	---MJ Sticker (7.2)	206	50.00	75.00
	---Album		10.00	15.00
91-92	Set, "Panini Basketball 91-92," American Version	192 sticks	20.00	25.00
	---MJ Sticker	96 AS		
	---MJ Sticker	116		
	---MJ Sticker, All NBA	190		
	---Album, "Panini Basketball 91-92"		3.00	5.00
91-92	Set, "Panini Basketball 91-92," European Version	192 sticks	200.00	250.00
	---MJ Sticker front, BJ Armstrong, #118 on back (7.3)	96 AS	35.00	50.00
	---MJ Sticker front, JR Reid #107 on back	116	35.00	50.00
	---MJ Sticker front, Spanish information on back, All NBA (7.4)	190	35.00	50.00
	---Album, "Panini Basketball 91-92"		10.00	15.00

(7.2)

(7.3)

MICHAEL JORDAN
CHICAGO BULLS 96

(7.4)

92-93	Set, "Panini Basketball 92-93...Collectable," American Version	192 sticks	20.00	30.00
	---MJ Sticker	12		
	---MJ Sticker	13		
	---MJ Sticker	14		
	---MJ Sticker	15		
	---MJ Sticker	16		
	---MJ Sticker	17		
	---MJ Sticker	18		
	---MJ Sticker	19		
	---MJ Sticker	20 MVP		
	---MJ Sticker	102 FF		
	---MJ Sticker	128		
	---McDaniel Card/MJ front	177		
	---Album, "Panini Basketball 92-93"			
95-96	Set, "Panini NBA Basketball 95-96," American Version	288 sticks	25.00	35.00
	---MJ Sticker	83		
	---Album, 64 pages			
95-96	Set, "Panini NBA Basketball 95-96 Starter Set," American Version	60 sticks	10.00	15.00
	---10 packs of 6 stickers			
	---Album, 64 pages			
95-96	Sticker, MJ, 6 languages on back, Italian Version	83	25.00	35.00

Year	**Phame Phone Net Inc. Telephone Card**	**# minu**		
11/1/94	MJ Retirement, MJ in a brown sport coat, green pants, colorful tie, gold "#23" bottom right, SN 006490 (7.5)	23 min 2 x 3.25	25.00	
	---envelope, card information on front			

Year	**Photographs/Team Photos**	**size**		
90-91	Bulls 1st NBA Championship, Official Team Photo	8 x 10	20.00	25.00
91-92	Bulls Repeat NBA Championship, Official Team Photo	8 x 10	15.00	20.00
92	The Official USA Olympic Dream Team Men's Basketball Team Photo, by Andrew Bernstein, 12 man squad & coaches	8 x 10	12.00	15.00
92-93	Bulls Three-Peat Championship, Official Team Photo	8 x 10	15.00	20.00
92-93	Official NBA Team Set Promotional Photos, 27 Teams, b & w	2-3/8 x 10	10.00	15.00
93-94	Official NBA Team Set Promotional Photos, 27 Teams, b & w	2-3/8 x 10	10.00	15.00
94-95	Official NBA Team Set Promotional Photos, 27 Teams, b & w	2-3/8 x 10	10.00	15.00
94-95	Bulls Official Team Photo	8 x 10	15.00	20.00
95-96	Bulls Game Handout, dunking, 23 white, B. Gossage photograph (7.6)	8 x 10	12.00	15.00
95-96	Bulls 30 Year Official Team Photo (7.7)	8 x 10	12.00	15.00
96	MJ Statue at United Center, by W. Barry	16 x 11	15.00	20.00
96-97	Bulls Official Team Photo	8 x 10	10.00	12.00
96-97	"The 90's Dynasty," 5 photos of 90-91, 91-92, 92-93, 95-96, 96-97 Championship Teams, list of players	11 x 14	12.00	15.00
-	MJ Photo with Joe Dumars #4, NBA Licensed Photo (7.8)	8 x 10	10.00	15.00
-	MJ/SP/DR cartoon like, sitting on bench with towel (7.9)	3 x 5	6.00	12.00

Year	Pins & Buttons-miscellaneous	size		
88	"Michael Jordan" Caricature, holding ball in right hand, running, MJ with hair, Bulls logo, red 23, Sold at '88 AS Miami Game, black signature	2"	15.00	20.00
80's	"Michael," jumping for dunk, red #23, MJ with hair, red arm band on left forearm	3"	15.00	30.00
80's	"Michael Jordan" on red bottom, closeup, white uniform, MJ with hair, Bulls Logo top right, red stripe behind MJ	3"	15.00	30.00
80's	"Michael Jordan MVP," 2 views, red 23, dribbling left hand, holding ball, MJ with hair, white background, black, white and red stripe, Bulls logo in center (7.10)	6"	25.00	40.00
80's	"Michael Jordan MVP," 2 views, red 23, dribbling left hand, holding ball, MJ with hair, white background, black, white and red stripe, Bulls logo in center	3"	15.00	30.00
80's	MJ pictures-4, Bulls logos-2, MJ with hair, black cardboard backing with stand and pin	6"	25.00	40.00
80's	MJ pictures-4, Bulls logos-2, MJ with hair, black cardboard backing with stand and pin	3.5"	20.00	35.00
90-91	"World Champions," Team Picture, red top, black bottom	6"	25.00	40.00
90-91	"World Champions" Team Picture, red top, black bottom	3.5"	20.00	25.00
92	Dream Team Pin Collection	6 pins	25.00	40.00
94	Sharp's Lapel Pin, 4/24/94 Ticket, Bulls vs. Knicks, Sharps mounting card for pin	1-3/4" x 3/4"	15.00	20.00
-	Lapel pin, ball overhead, white "Bulls 23" red shoes, tongue out, tan skin color, white left arm band	1.5	10.00	15.00
-	Lapel pin, ball overhead, red 23, white elbow & knee pad, big head with hair	1-3/4"	10.00	15.00
-	Lapel Pin, "Air Jordan," red silhouette jumping, ball left hand	1"	10.00	10.00
-	Lapel Pin, "Jordan" on bottom, dribbling right hand, red 23, red elbow pad	1-7/8"	10.00	10.00
-	Peter David Pin of MJ, gold background, red 23, MJ dribbling with ball in right hand		25.00	35.00

Year	Pogs, miscellaneous			
-	Sheet of 6 pogs (7.11)	6 pogs	10.00	15.00
	---dunking RH, white 45			
	---reaching RH, red 45, Bill Cartwright background			
	---shooting, red 45			
	---two hand dunk, white			
	---"Jordan 45"			
	---layup RH, white			
-	Sheet of 6 pogs	6 pogs	10.00	15.00
	---Jordan, red 23, ball behind head shooting			
	---Armstrong			
	---Pippen			
	---Kukoc			
	---Perdue			
	---Harper			
-	Sheet of 6 MJ pogs	6 pogs	10.00	15.00
	---3 fingers up, locker room, BB, white cap,			
	---dunking with RH, red 23			
	---holding ball with RH, All-Star uniform			
	---hands in air, white 23			
	---layup, red 23			
	---closeup, looking, hands on knee, white uniform			
-	Pog, Hang Time, red figure, BB in right hand		5.00	10.00
-	Metal, MJ layup LH, white 23, red, left arm band, front view		2.00	4.00
-	Metal, MJ shooting, white 23, rear view, graphic background		2.00	4.00

Year	Polaroid Sheet	sheet type		
90	Polaroid Photo Night March 24, 1990, MJ front & inside, royal blue front, Polaroid One Film & Osco Drug back (7.12)	fold out	20.00	

Polaroid Photo Night   March 24, 1990

Year	Popular Sports Stars			
0	Reading Study Cards, Order #8525, Media Materials Inc.		45.00	65.00
	---Box (7.13)		10.00	15.00
	---MJ Card, Portrait, 72183-43, back MJ, 5 questions (7.14)		30.00	40.00
	---Sports Stars Card, 72183-13, back MJ, facts (7.15)		5.00	10.00

Year	Postcards			
9	NBA 1987-1988 Art Map with players, MJ #23 white uniform, middle front, produced by World Impressions for NBA, postcard 4 x 6 (7.16)	50PST-BK7SG3PO	15.00	20.00
0	CHIARoScURO's Furniture, MJ sitting on chair holding ball in RH, red 23 large pants, feet crossed, "PORTRAIT CHAIRS by Phillip Grace CHIARoScURO's 1990 Collection, opening 6/15, 750 N. Orleans Chicago, IL (312) 988.9253, hours, chair auction item of MJ Foundation 9/15/90 (7.17)	3 x 5	15.00	20.00
4	The Gallery of Sports Art, "When The Loudest Cheer Stopped" by Tim Spransy, "Sample" on front, PO Box 381, Greendale, WI 53129; MJ walking with ghost to basket, inside Chicago Stadium, no time or score, banners on ceiling (7.18)	3 x 5	15.00	20.00
6	United Center & MJ's Statue, Terrell Publishing (7.19)	3 x 5	3.00	6.00
	BY DESIGN, 4 pictures on front Montana, Nickolas, baseball player, MJ in white 23 over Hawks player head, on back BY DESIGN 221 McHenry Ave. Modesto, CA 95354, 209 523 8998, Sport Art by Daniel M. Smith (7.20)	4 x 6	15.00	20.00

7.13

POPULAR
SPORTS STARS
Reading Study Cards

- 30 career highlights of great athletes
- 30 picture cards
- Teacher's guide

7.14

Michael Jordan

7.15

MICHAEL JORDAN
Basketball Player
School: University of North Carolina
Position: Forward
Team: Chicago Bulls
Birthdate: February 17, 1963

The fans call him "Air" Jordan for the way he flies th the air, *defying* opposing players and slam-dunking h into the record books.

Michael is not only a great basketball player. He a colorful character whose friendly smile and wide-ope of play have made him a tremendous drawing card for p sional basketball.

Michael is only 6-foot-6 in a game where 6-foot above is normal, but he is so quick and skillful that oppe have a difficult time blocking him from the basket.

He was voted the National Basketball Associa (NBA) Rookie of the Year in 1985 after being drafted on t round by the Chicago Bulls.

He signed a new contract in 1988 worth $25 millio eight years. That's about $3.1 million a year, and puts M Jordan up among the leaders in salary in the NBA. Patrick Ewing and Magic Johnson make the same amount each year.

Michael Jordan is an *avid* golfer and tries to play the top 10 golf courses in the country each year

©1991 Media Materials, Inc.
Baltimore, MD 21224. Printed in U.S.A.

7.16

BK7SG3 edition has been discontinued.
A new edition will be released mid 1989.

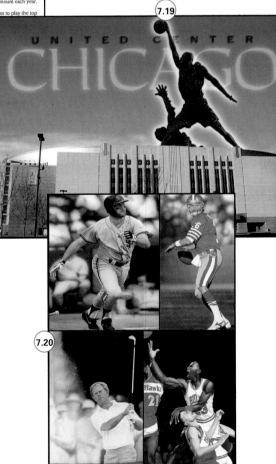

7.17

PORTRAIT CHAIRS
by Phillip Grace

7.18

7.19

7.20

Year	Poster Ad and Sample Cards-misc.	size		
-	NBA Aerial Assault, Chicago skyline background MJ flying through air, ball at tips of right hand (7.21)	4 x 6	8.00	12.00
-	NBA Jam Session Slam Dunk Champions 1984-1993, 8 players pictured (7.22)	4 x 6	8.00	12.00
-	Salem 1993 3-Time World Champions Chicago Bulls, cartoon like team, picture, MJ popping out of center, 3 fingers up (7.23)	4 x 6	8.00	12.00
-	Skyline Dream Team Made in Heaven, blue border/background pictures (7.24)	3 x 5	8.00	12.00

POSTER SECTION

Year	Poster-Amateur Basketball Association	size		
84	Poster, "Double Gold Los Angeles-1984," seven pictures of men's & women's BB teams, 3 MJ pictures, Team picture, crowded around each other, coach on shoulders (7.25)	22 x 30	95.00	

Year	Poster-Amoco Oil Company	size		
97	Posters, United Way, Mounted, MJ/SP/DR on cover	40 x 30	75.00	150.00

Year	Poster-Bart & Ninja Turtles	size		
88	Display Board, MJ/Bart/Ninja Turtles, "Chill Out Dude!" middle center, The backboard on bottom left, white blank back, MJ dunking, Bart blocking, die-cut round top, display slits on fans silhouette bottom (7.26)	16 x 11	125.00	175.00

Year	Posters-Book, miscellaneous			
92	MJ, Jack Clary	cover	15.00	
	---insert poster like cover, MJ doing reverse dunk, red 23 (7.27)	18 x 25	15.00	

Year	Poster-Boy Scouts of America			
90-91	BSA Poster, Chicago Area Council, MJ Says Stay in School, It's Your Best Move (7.28)	14 x 18	20.00	

Poster-Bull's Eye Barbecue Sauce

Year		Size		
87	Poster, "Big Bold Stuff," 8 photos, MJ in bottom left, Paxson, Oakley, Sellers, Pippen, Corzine, Grant, MJ, Vincent, tan background, bottle in lower right, Techtron Imaging Network, Ridges Finer Foods Inc. (7.29)	16 x 25 884418	60.00	

Poster-Chicago Transit Authority

Year		size		
88-89	Poster, "The Bulls, Chicago & CTA, A Perfect Three Point Play," team on bus looking out window, three players on steps-MJ BC, SV, Perdue, Paxson, Davis, Hodges, Corzine, Sellers, Haley, Jordan, Cartwright, Vincent (7.30)	24 x 17	60.00	

Posters-Chevrolet & General Motors

Year		size		
91	Poster, '91 Eastern Conference Champions, 25th Anniversary, Starline Product (7.31)	23 x 38	20.00	
95-96	Poster, It's The Drive		12.00	
/98	Poster, "The Greatest," MJ & Ali, Chevy Dealers handout (7.32)	37 x 23	10.00	

Posters-Chicago Sun Times Newspaper

Year				
85-87	Poster, "Your Hometown Sports Authority, Catch it Today, Just $.35," MJ going for layup, "CST It's a Smart Move to Make"	11.5 x 15.5"	60.00	85.00
6/13/91	Poster, "Bulls Win It," front page	cover	15.00	20.00
6/15/92	Poster, "Champs!" front page	cover	15.00	20.00
6/21/93	Poster, "3 Fest!" front page	cover	12.00	20.00
3/19/95	Poster, "I'm Back!" front page	cover	4.00	8.00

Posters-Chicago Tribune Newspaper

Year				
87	Poster, Slam Dunk Contest , April 8, 1987 (7.33)	11 x 17	60.00	
80's	Poster, MJ flying to basket, red 23, like Slam Dunk Contest with 3:51 on clock poster, "Chicago Tribune Chicago's Best Sports Section" on bottom right	17 x 11	35.00	
6/13/91	Posters, front page, High Five! Bulls Are Champs		10.00	15.00
6/15/91	Posters, front page, Two For Two Still Champs		10.00	15.00
91-92	Poster, "1991-92 Chicago Bulls," MJ left front, white 23, WACE, team, (March 30) (7.34)	18 x 21	35.00	
92-93	Poster, 1992-93 Chicago Bulls, MJ right front white 23, team view, (April 12) (7.35)	18 x 26	45.00	
6/21/93	Posters, front page, Three Mendous		8.00	15.00
10/13/93	Posters, front page, Thanks for the Memories		8.00	15.00
3/20/96	Posters, front page, Relaunched		5.00	10.00
4/17/96	Posters, front page, 70 Booklet		5.00	10.00
6/17/96	Posters, front page, Ring Masters		5.00	10.00

7.29 7.30 7.31 7.32 7.33 7.34 7.35

Year	Posters-Coca Cola	size		
86-87	Poster, Chevy Blazer, Hot Tops, 23 jersey (7.36)	18 x 26	50.00	
89	Poster, "Share The Dream" top, "Lifelong Careers Begin With Education, Dr. J, I. Thomas, MJ, Classic, Coke, diet Coke, cherry Coke, Sprite, Minute Maid logo on bottom (7.37)	18 x 20	50.00	
90	Poster, "No Brain No Gain," "Stay in School," MJ in white shirt & gray tie, sitting at desk, books in background Coke logo bottom right (7.38)	18 x 24	45.00	
90	Poster, "The Coca Cola Company 1990," MJ dunking 6 pack of coke, white 23, Chicago skyline in background (7.39)	18 x 24	45.00	

Year	Posters-Cologne			
5/98	Poster Sticker, "at Carson Pirie Scott," cologne bottle on left site, advertised on Chicago Transit Authority Buses, made by FLEXcon BUSmark	6 ft. x 30 inches	75.00	125.00
5/98	Poster Sticker, "MICHAEL JORDAN cologne," silhoutte on left site, advertised on Chicago Transit Authority Buses, made by FLEXcon BUSmark	6 ft. x 30 inches	75.00	125.0
5/98	Poster Sticker, "MICHAEL JORDAN cologne at Carson Pirie Scott," silhouette on left side, cologne bottle on right side, advertised on Chicago Transit Authority Buses, made by FLEXcon BUSmark (7.40)	6 ft. x 21 inches	50.00	75.00

Year	Posters-Costacos			
93	Poster, "Invincibulls" top center, "Back-to-Back NBA World Champions," Team in warmups, lined up near foul line (7.41)	30 x 12	30.00	
95	Poster, "Space 2," door size, shooting overhead, red 23	26 x 74"	15.00	
96	Poster, "Year of the Bull," 1996 NBA Champions, MJ in 4 pictures, 12 pictures on poster (7.42)	23 x 35	10.00	

7.36

7.37

7.38

7.39

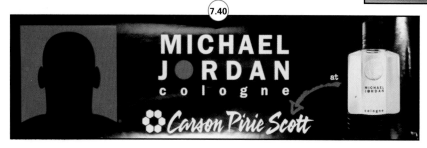
7.40

7.42

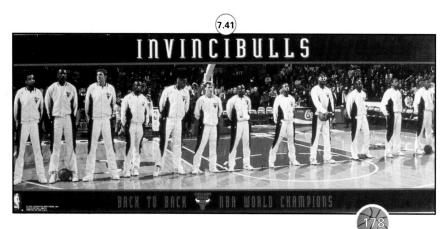
7.41

Year		size		
97	Poster, "The Eighth Wonder of the World, 11 MJ pictures, black 23, From 1985 through 1996 (7.43)	23 x 35	6.00	
-	Poster, "Dream"	23 x 35	3.00	5.00
-	Poster, "Count Down"	23 x 35	3.00	5.00
-	Poster, "Enter the Zone"	23 x 35	3.00	5.00
-	Poster, "Return Flight"	23 x 35	3.00	5.00
-	Poster, "Out of the World"	23 x 35	3.00	5.00
-	Poster, "Space"	23 x 35	3.00	5.00
-	Poster, "Great Chicago Flyer"	23 x 35	3.00	5.00
-	Poster, "Pure Energy"	23 x 35	3.00	5.00

Year	**Poster-Enterprise Rental Car**	size		
1997	Poster, "Join the Celebration, 1957-1997, Celebrate 40 Great Years," MJ head view in gray 1997, Tahoe, five vehicles listed from '57 Bel Air to '97 Tahoe (7.44)	26 x 35	45.00	

Year	**Poster-Ferrara Pan Candy Company**			
89-90	Sheet, Chicago Bull, Ferrara Pan Candy Company & Lemonhead, Chicago Sports Magazine, 1 MJ picture (7.45)	2 picture 11 x 37	25.00	35.00

Year	**Poster-First Chicago Bank**	size		
86	Poster, "Spectacular Performance is Nothing New to Chicago," b&w, MJ jumping to dunk, #23, "Performance has always been a Chicago Tradition, First Chicago," on bottom (7.46)	16 x 23	65.00	

Year	**Poster-French**	item #		
95-96	Poster, Sport Action Basket, Mini, red 23 uniform standing (7.47)	12 x 18"	10.00	15.00
	Poster, "Basket Action," MJ dunking, closeup from behind the hoop, white 23	23 x 32	15.00	

Year	**Poster-Fugi**	item #		
91	Poster, "CB Fugi The Bulls and Fuji Film" on left, film strip pictures across page, Kieffer-Nolde Poster, photo by Bill Smith, SP, Grant, Cartwright, MJ, Paxson, BJ in separate pictures, purple background (7.48)	39 x 12	45.00	
94	Poster, "CB, The Short, The Block, 1991-1992-1993 World Champions," MJ jumping hands overhead, Fugi Film & logo bottom right	24 x 18	40.00	

7.43

7.46

7.44

7.48

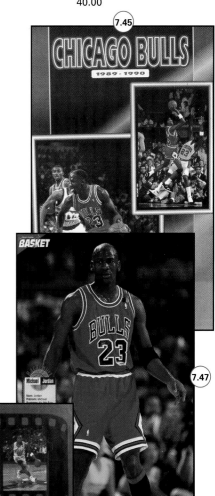

7.45

7.47

Year	Posters-Gatorade	size	
91	Display, It's All You Thirst For, two sided and top and bottom half, for 3-D book (7.49)	24 x 36	40.00
92	Poster, "Be Like Mike," white 23, dunking, NBA Property (7.50)	S-VC	
		17 x 25	20.00
92	Poster, "Be Like Mike," USA BB #9, dunking, USA BB Inc. (7.51)	S-VC	
		17 x 25	15.00
92	Poster, "Dream Team"	12 x 18"	20.00
93	Poster, "Michael Jordan" on left vertical, "Gatorade. For That Deep, Down Body Thirst" on bottom, white 23, layup, Stokely-Van Camp, Inc. (7.52)	18 x 26	15.00
93	Poster, "MJ Ready to Slam," promotional poster	18 x 24	30.00
93	Poster, "Nothing Beats Gatorade" left side, MJ layup, white 23, on front side of poster, back side of poster MJ dribbling waist up view, red 23	17 x 24	
		S-VC	20.00
93	Poster, "Nothing Beats Gatorade" bottom, MJ reverse layup, red 23, on front side poster, back side of poster MJ dribbling waist down view, red 23	17 x 24	
		S-VC	20.00
94	Poster, "Quench It," towel on shoulder		10.00
95	Poster, "45," MJ dunking, red 45, Gatorade logo lower right, Starline Inc. (7.53)	22 x 34	20.00
95	Poster, "I'm Back." "Reaching for More," black signature March 24, 1995, MJ in black t-shirt, arm stretched out with Gatorade cup (7.54)	30 x 11	15.00
95	Poster, "Drive, Skills, Guts, Passion=Life (7.55)	14 x 22	15.00
95	Poster, "Life is Sport," MJ head view, promotional	15" x 23	10.00
97	Poster, "It's a Sport, Drink it Up," 7/Eleven Stores (7.56)	14 x 37	45.00

Year	Posters-Hanes			
93	Store Display, MJ holding BB in street clothes, sport coat, white t-shirt, Hanes logo upper right, black signature & " Michael Jordan for Hanes" lower right, blue background (7.57)	31 x 39	60.00	90.00
97	Store Display, MJ in sport coat and white t-shirt, Hanes logo upper left, "Unconditionally Guaranteed" lower left, earring in left ear, brown stripe background (7.58)	38 x 41.5	60.00	90.00

Year	Poster-Hang Time Gum			
92	Poster, Life Size Michael Jordan		35.00	35.00

Year	Poster-Illinois Items			
89	Poster, Lottery, MJ Hang Time, $.50 off coupons on bottom, Flying over Skyline, calendar on bottom (7.59)	1 picture 11 x 37	35.00	

Year	Poster-Inside Sports Magazine			
85-86	Poster of 11/85 Magazine Cover, MJ & Ewing (7.60)	18 x 25	65.00	

Year	Poster-John Wooden Award			
91	Sheet, Wooden cards, 2 MJ cards, printers proof, 21 x 26 (7.61)	#12 21 x 26	75.00	125.00

Year	Poster-Jump, Gibson & Cleo			
93	Poster, MJ dribbling left hand on highway with yellow strip, red 23, white tape on right index finger, 12 month calendar on bottom, Cleo on bottom left, #260-7017 (7.62)	260-7017 24 x 36	45.00	

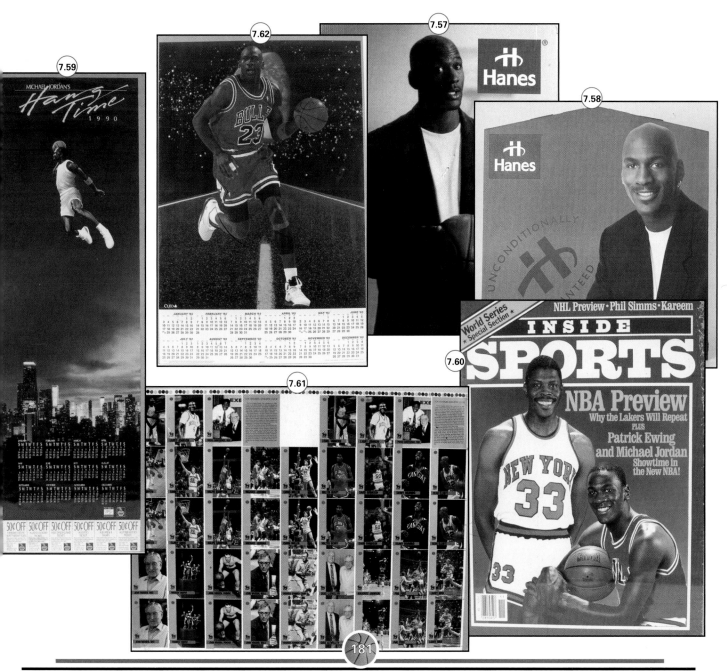

Year	Posters-Kodak Film	size		
87-88	Poster, Larry Bird white signature & Boston Celtics logo top right, MJ background blocking Bird, Kodak video pack on bottom left, film pack bottom right	14 x 22		35.00

Year	Poster-Kraft Products	size		
96	Poster, Macaroni & Cheese, Space Jam, mail in poster (7.64)	24 x 36		15.00

Year	Posters-5 Majeur French Magazine			
91-92	Poster, red 23, looking	No 2		25.00
93	Poster, 2 sided, standing in red warmups, looking, "MJ L'Homme De L'anne" upper right; standing in red t-shirt, white shorts, holding Wilson BB in LH, "MJ" upper right	22 x 32		20.00
93	Poster, 2 sided, layup, blue All-Star uniform #23, white uniform, All-Star players looking, "MJ AS Game 93" upper right; MJ in black shirt and shorts, holding basketball in right hand, looking down, left hand on hip (7.65)	22 x 33		20.00
94	MJ with red #45 (7.66)	22 x 32		25.00
94	Poster, 2 sided, standing in blue USA warmup suit, looking, "MJ Dream Team 92" upper right; dunking in red 23, mouth open, Blaylock #10 looking, "CB MJ" upper left (7.67)	22 x 33	25.00	

Year	Posters-McDonald's			
89	McDonald's made a three-piece, two sided poster set. Each part has a different action photo of MJ on the front. When put together the three backs make up on growth chart of Michael.	27 x 81	70.00	
	---Poster, MJ jumping with ball between legs, white 23, yellow border	1 of 3		
		27 x 27	25.00	
	---Poster, MJ jumping to dunk, red 23, blue border	2 of 3		
		27 x 27	25.00	
	---Poster, MJ backward jumping to dunk, red 23, red border	3 of 3		
		27 x 27	25.00	
92	Poster, Ron McDonald's Celebrity Golf Championship, September 5-7, 1992, pictures were Michael Jordan, Ronald McDonald and kids, blue and yellow letters, Nike, UA, Hanes, UD & McDonald's logos on bottom (7.68)	40 x 50	125.00	175.00

92	Poster, Ron McDonald's Celebrity Golf Championship, September 5-7, 1992, pictures were Michael Jordan, Ron McDonald and kids, blue and yellow letters, Nike, UA, Hanes, UD & McDonald's logos on bottom (7.69)	21 x 30	45.00	
93	Poster, Win an NBA Fantasy Instantly (7.70)	22 x 28	60.00	
12/93	Poster, Planete Mac #1, Le Journal Des Equpiers De McDonald's En France, MJ reaching RH, red 23, Lancement du N 1 de Planete Mac le journal des equipiers de McDo, French McDonalds (7.71)	23 x 36	65.00	90.00
95	Poster-Mc Bacon Deluxe, MJ photo on french fry holder (7.72)	29 x 38	25.00	
96	Ad Poster, Vote for 'em here, All-Star Guys (7.73)	28 x 41	45.00	

Year	Poster-Michael Jordan Foundation	size		
12/91	Poster, 12 MJ pictures with months of the year, MJF t-shirts, sweatshirts and datebook order form, bottom left, Soodik Printing Company, J&O Wace USA (7.74)	27 x 35	75.00	
-	Poster, LeRoy Neiman, #122	25 x 37"	65.00	100.00

Year	Posters-Michael Jordan Golf Center	size		
96	Poster, Win $1,000,000 Hole-in-One Shoot Out, 1 of 100 distributed, Golf Center & Chicago Sun-Times, hung in underground "L" Stations	22" x 27"	60.00	90.00
97	Poster, "Win a trip to Chicago and MJ Golf Center to Meet MJ," sweepstakes ends 10/25/97, yellow background, MJ with club at tee, black shirt, brown pants, double sided (7.75)	22 x 28	45.00	65.00

Year	Posters-Miller Brewing	size		
90-91	Poster, Chicago Stadium inside view, MJ center court, "Compliments of Miller Genuine Draft" lower right, Poster by Wace, USA, Photo by LaPayne Photography (7.76)	29.5 x 9	45.00	

91	Poster, "Chicago Bulls, 1991 NBA Champions," Grant, SP, Paxson, MJ, BJ, Cartwright, Genuine Draft Bottle, skyline (7.77)	30 x 20	45.00	
	Posters-Miscellanous	**size**		
85	Midas Muffler Poster-MJ vs. Bucks, coupons on bottom		60.00	100.00
85-86	Poster, "Chicago Bulls 20th Season, 1 MJ photo out of 8 pictured, orange color, Sports Phone 976-1313 on bottom (7.78)	19 x 25	65.00	
85-86	Poster, "Chicago's Newest Generation of Winners!, Sports Vision," Ed Olczyk-Blackhawks, MJ, Kar Heinz Granitza-Sting pictured, "Chicago's Winners on Cable" schedule listed for each sport, Odyssey Productions, Chicago, Bradley Printing (7.79)	22 x 28	65.00	
86	Bill Clark Litho, 5 player set, NBA licensed, SFI Tampa, FL Magic, Bird, Dr. J, Kareem	16" x 20"	market	price
87	MJ Personality Poster, 17 x 2, 2 sided		45.00	
90	"Air Michael Jordan" foldout, Publications Intl. (7.80)		25.00	
90-91	Poster, Focus on Sports, two sided, "Michael Jordan" top left in white and yellow letters, hands on knees, white 23, closeup; back cartoon like MJ in red 23 slam dunking with hand on rim, head bigger hand body, way above court, ball through net, "Michael Jordan" lower right, white & yellow letters	16 x 21		50.00
90-91	Ron Dumas' Serigraph & Nike, 723 autographed by artist, Nike's Certificate of Authenticity	24" x 30"	market	price
90-91	Ron Dumas' Serigraph & Nike, 723 autographed by artist, 23 signed by MJ, Nike's Certificate of Authenticity	24" x 30"	market	price
91	Nobody Does BB Like UD, MJ jumping hold ball, white 23, shiny on gray background with letters		15.00	
91	Michael 'n' Magic Poster Book, Kids Books Inc. (7.81)		10.00	
91	Break Away Slam Dunk, 91 Finals vs. Lakers	16 x 20	25.00	
92	MJ Poster Book, A Book of 12 Tear Out Posters, sealed packet	12 posters	30.00	
92-93	Poster, MarketCom, "Chicago Bulls," SP, MJ JP, HG, SK & BC, six individual pictures with white signature (7.82)	20 x 16 6463	40.00	

93	Basketball Superstars Album, by R. Brenner (7.83)	16 posters	25.00
93	Poster, "Skinnies!," "Parody Basketball Cards that Uncover the Real NBA, On Sale Here," Ewing & Johnson also shown, MJ in Gatorade shirt, holding Wheaties, McD, wearing Hanes shorts & Nike shoes (7.84)	11 x 17	20.00
95	NSCC Promo, MJ with ball overhead, mouth open, red 23, blue signature by Robert Hurst	22" x 11.5	market / price
96	Poster, Toronto Raptors, "New 12 Games for the Price of 11, from $115.50, MJ and Shaq on poster, "The Joint's Always Jumpin," call (416) 366-Dunk, 12 game mini pack includes MJ or Shaq (7.85)	20 x 28	12.00
96	Poster, Cable TV & Radio, 12 Game Mini Pack Tickets, Raptors vs. Bulls, MJ red 23 & Shaq	20 x 28	12.00
96	Print, MJ dunking, closeup and holding BB out with RH, by Frank Nareau	11" x 14	market / price
96	Prints, MJ dribbling LH, by Frank Nareau	11" x 14	market / price
97	Litho, Kelly Russell, Chicago Bulls	11" x 14	market / price
90's	Wall hanging, MJ jumping over skyline, BB in LH over head, red 23, lots of hair, "Michael Jordan" upper left, background blue to purple, Nylon, Manufactured by Nikry Company, Van Nuys, CA 71405 (7.86)	3' x 5'	150.00 / 250.00
-	Litho, "MJ Returns," by Angelo Marion, 5 MJ views, signed by MJ and artist, 4,500 issue, AAU Authenticated		market / price
-	Litho ad sheet, "Jordan Promo," Litho Series Ltd. (7.87)	8 x 11	2.00 / 4.00
-	Poster, UNC Dunk, MJ as a sophomore	16 x 20	market / price
-	Poster, Jordan & Magic From Above	16 x 20	market / price
-	Print, "Baby Dream Team," MJ, Bird, Magic, Ewing, by K Gatewood	35 x 24	market / price
-	Print, "Chairman of the Boards," MJ, Barkley, O'Neal, by K Gatewood	33 x 26	market / price

Year	Poster-Newsweek Magazine	size	
93	Poster, "Newsweek" upper right, MJ blue USA #9 with BB in RH (7.88)	16 x 20	15.00

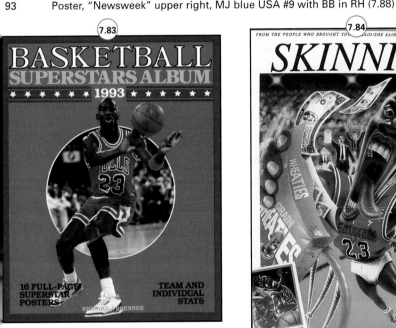

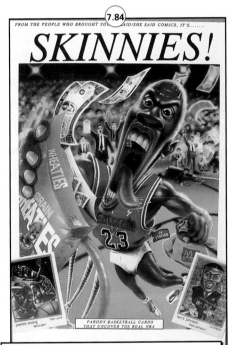

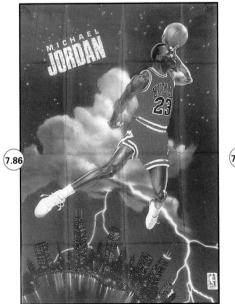

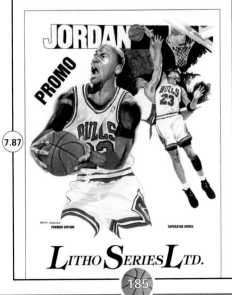

Year	Posters-Nike	size	
85-86	Poster, red "Air Jordan" bottom left, jumping to basket in playground with red and black clothes, night shot of Chicago skyline, metal BB net and poles, red "Nike" logo bottom right (7.89)	29 x 24	65.00
86-87	Poster, Air Jordan 4 Frame Slam Dunk, getting ready to dunk, dunking wearing, 23 on jersey, in early Air Jordans with red body, black trim (7.90)	22 x 36"	60.00
86-87	Poster, Nike Air Jordan, 5 action photos or running, jumping and dunking, wearing white top and bottom sweatsuit (7.91)	21 x 36	60.00
88-89	Poster, "A High Flying 360 Slam Dunk, Death Defying," MJ and Spike Lee (7.92)	36 x 24	45.00
88-89	Poster, "Slam Dunk Championship," MJ flying to dunk, red 23, gray stripe on bottom with "1988 NBA MVP, Defensive Player of the Year, Slam Dunk Champion, All-Star MVP Leading Scorer," crowd in the background, 3:51 on clock, red "Nike" logo bottom right (7.93)	35 x 23 290883	45.00
1/90	Poster, "Nice Shoes as Seen On TV," 'I've never ever seen anything like it,' pictures of Gretzky, McEnroe, Strange, Jordan, & Bo; bottom of poster has Albert, Michaels, Caray, Heinsohn, Summerall, Vitale, Enberg in purple strip, "Holy cow!" Four shoes pictured Air Jordan, Air Trainer SC, Air Max, Air Tech Challenge II (7.94)	024673 24 x 32	40.00
91	Poster, MJ kneeling on left knee, white AJFC t-shirt, black shorts, left hand on Wilson BB, right hand on right knee, "Nike" red in upper right corner (7.95)	24 x 36	40.00
91	Poster, "Evolution, A Process of Change from a Lower Simpler Form to a More Complex or Better State," jumping ball in RH (7.96)	24 x 24	20.00

92	Poster, "Slam Dunk Championship," MJ flying to dunk, red 23 crowd in the background, 3:51 on clock (7.97)	5284 35 x 23	12.00
92	Poster, "Art of the Dunk," MJ going to dunk with light lines, red 23, black background, red "Nike" logo upper right (7.98)	5228 35 x 23	12.00
92	Poster, "Hare Jordan" in red on bottom, MJ & Bugs with carrot, AJFC t-shirt and red/black shorts, blue Nike & logo upper right (7.99)	16 x 20 85229	12.00
93	Poster, Warner/MJ Sticker Set CD		20.00
93	Poster, Spike Lee/MJ, "Mars, Blackman," black & white	32 x 22	30.00
93	Poster, "In the unlikely event of a water landing, this poster can be used as a Flotation Device," white 23, MJ dunking the ball, "Nike Inc." and logo bottom center (7.100)	5356 23 x 35	35.00
93	Poster Book, Aerospace, 8 images		35.00
93	Poster, "Great Moments in Flight," 4 MJ pictures, other astronauts and pilots, black background, white "Nike" logo bottom (7.101)	23 x 35 5360	12.00
93	Posters, Aerospace, 6 different kinds		
	---"Earth The Best on Mars," MJ holding Martian & BB, Bugs next to MJ, MJ in red t-shirt, black shorts, red "Nike" logo upper left (7.102)	5336 23 x 35	35.00
	---"Aerospace," BB in LH, flying in air, white t-shirt, black shorts, white "Nike" logo upper left (7.103)	5337 23 x 35	35.00
	---	5338 23 x 35	
	---MJ & Bugs in space ship, Toon characters hanging on edge, Porky in space ship, "That's All Folks" on bottom, red "Nike" logo upper right (7.104)	5339 23 x 35"	35.00
	---	5340 23 x 35	

187

93	---"Stargazer," "MJ Abducted by Aliens," MJ in Martian hat, red "Nike" logo bottom right, "Air Jordan Pattern Found" (7.105)	5341	23 x 35"	35.00
95	Poster, "?," "The Jump. The Spin. The Jam. Any Questions?," question mark in center filled with photos, red logo bottom (7.106)	5492	35 x 23	15.00
97	Poster, "The Master," MJ dribbling ball on white background, black shirt and gray shorts, lines from center circle (7.107)	5518	23 x 35	6.00
90's	Poster, slide strip with 4 shots of MJ, red "Nike" logo bottom left, red "Chicago Bulls" logo bottom right		36 x 17	30.00
80's	Poster, slide strip with 4 shots of MJ, red "Nike" logo bottom left, red "Air Jordan" logo bottom right, one slide strip over another		36 x 22	45.00
90's	Poster, "Commemorative"			20.00
90's	Poster, "Earth to Mars," 22 x 36	290874		20.00
90's	Poster, "Earth to Orbit," 22 x 36	290848		20.00
90's	Poster, "Imagination," 5 pictures of MJ dunking, white sweatsuit, white "Air Jordan" logo bottom right, gray background		38 x 21	45.00
90's	Poster, "Is It the Shoes?" 24 x 36	290838		20.00
90's	Poster, "Playground," 24 x 36	290891		20.00
90's	Poster, "Reverse Jam," 24 x 24	290909		20.00
90's	Poster, "Sky Jordan"			20.00
90's	Poster, "Super Jordan," 24 x 36	290946		20.00
90's	Poster, "Wings," door size, horizontal, 75 x 24	292335		35.00
90's	Poster Sample Book-Reverse Dunk, Orbit, Wings, Playground, MVP, Shirts & Skins, Is It The Shoes-white, Is It The Shoes-black, High Flying 360, Earth & Mars, Jam & Slam, brown cover with hole and "poster" spelled out			25.00

Year	Poster-Nintendo and Electronic Arts			
94-95	Poster from Michael Jordan game, Chaos in the Windy City		16 x 12	10.00

Year	Poster-Ohio Art Sports Games		size	
87-88	Poster, Lil'Sport, with each purchase, MJ in white shirt & pants slam dunking ball with right hand, tan background, "Lil'Sport" in bottom right (7.108)		11 x 17	45.00

Year	Posters-Olympic Magazines		size item #
84	Poster, Sports Page, "Gunnin' for the Gold," MJ shooting over Mexican Team in Olympics, 7/23/84, newspaper format, cardboard stock, details the 1984 Olympics in LA	23" x 37"
84	Poster, USA Olympic BB Team, men's & women's team	22 x 30

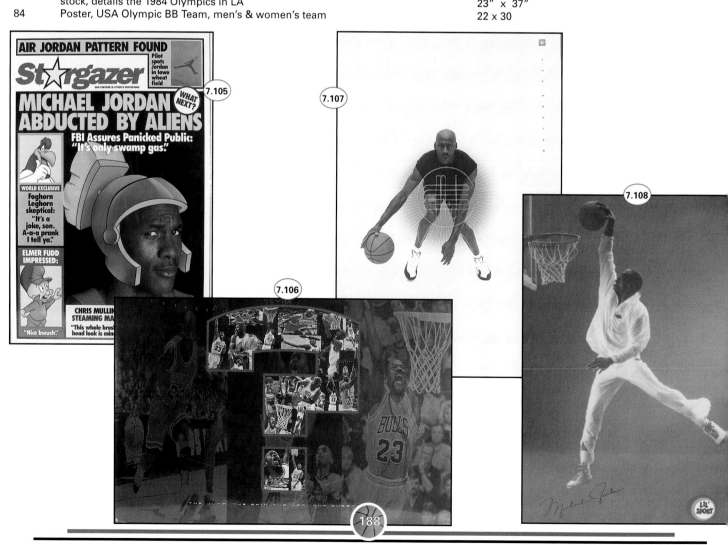

Year		Size		
92	Poster, "Barcelona '92," team line up, USA BB item (7.109)	34 x 22	10.00	
92	Poster, "USA Dream Team," USA BB (7.110)	34 x 22	10.00	
92	Poster, "Shooting for Gold 1992 US Olympic Team," MJ hookshot vs. 10, drawing like picture, USA BB item, Fine Art LTD, St. Louis, MO, USA Olympic Committee Licensee (7.111)	28 x 22 36USC380	25.00	

Year	**Poster-Organ & Tissue Donation**			
96	Poster		15.00	20.00

Year	**Poster-Playboy Magazine**	size		
82-83	Poster, "Playboy's 1982-1983 All America Team," photo by Bill Arsenault, players Rivers, Ellis, Ewing, Holland, Bowie, Sundvold, Whatley, MJ, Perkins, Lee, Sampson (7.112)	16 x 11	25.00	

Year	**Posters-Pro Star Cereal**			
91	Cereal Box Poster, Michael Jordan throwing Spaceball, tongue out (7.113)	4.5 x 24	10.00	
91	Poster, Michael Jordan throwing Spaceball, all teeth (7.114)	13 x 24	30.00	

Year	**Poster-Quaker Chewy Granola Bars**	size		
87	Poster, Sports Illustrated Poster,#23 white, expires 12/31/87, send-in, poster #4453	11 x 17	60.00	

Year	**Poster-Rayovac Battery**			
95	Photo, Chicago Tribune Newspaper, Basketball Offering (7.115)	11 x 14	10.00	
95	Poster, "Play it Smart," head view of MJ, white signature & red "Rayovac" bottom right corner, lighting bolt in ear & in Rayovac (7.116)	3' x 2'	15.00	

			size		
97	Ad Display, "Maximum Power Maximum Value," red background, MJ holding lightning bolt, MJ in orange polo shirt, batteries in Sega like electronic game jaws (7.117)		9 x 25	20.00	

Year   **Poster-Rust-Oleum and Handy Andy**
1-92   Lithograph, 4/13, 3 MJ photos (7.118)   11 x 14   35.00

Year   **Poster-Sega Genesis**   size
96   Poster, Space Jam Game, MJ 3 photos (7.119)   25 x 20   20.00

Year   **Posters-Skybox Sheets**   size
90   Commemorative Press Proof Inaugural Edition, white 23   20.00

Year   **Poster-Sony**   size
85-86   Poster, "1985-86 Chicago Bulls," 20th Season logos top corners, team picture, blue background, "Sony Tape. The Official Video Tape of the NBA" bottom, video tape on left, audio tape on right (7.120)   25 x 19   65.00

Year   **Posters-Space Jam**   size
96   Poster, pre movie release   10.00   15.00
96   Poster, movie, MJ & Bugs, head views, Russian version (7.121)   27 x 38   45.00
96   Poster, movie, MJ, Bugs & cartoon characters on ring, " In Theaters Everywhere" on bottom (7.122)   27 x 40   20.00   35.00
96   Poster, MJ and Bugs looking over shoulders (7.123)   24 x 36   10.00   15.00
96   Poster, MJ, Bugs, purple monster with tiny BB, yellow monster with MJ shooting ball overhead, Bugs with basketball (7.124)   16 x 20   10.00   15.00

7.117

7.119

7.118

7.120

7.124

7.121

7.122

7.123

96	Round Poster, "Music From and Inspired by the Motion Picture," MJ/Bugs front, orange basketball back		10.00	15.00

Year	Posters-Sports Channel TV	size	
94	Poster, F. Thomas, MJ, hockey, stadium handout (7.125)	16 x 27	35.00
94	Poster, "Ten Sport Channel Years," MJ hands out, Paxson, Pippen (7.126)	18 x 26	40.00

Year	Posters-Sports Illustrated Magazine		
89	Poster, MJ passing ball right hand, vs. Pistons, "Michael Jordan" red bottom right, white signature, red 23 (7.127)	11 x 17 7484	40.00
89	Poster, "How does it feel to play a bunch of mortals?" white 23, "SI Get The Feeling" in lower left, MJ jumping over Atlanta Hawks player with hand in face	59 x 45"	50.00
91	Poster, "Michael Jordan" on top left, dunking, white 23, white signature, Licensed by NBA Properties, NBA Players Association, Copyright Marketcom/St. Louis, photo by Focus on Sports, " A Sports Illustrated Poster" (7.128)	4453 23 x 35	60.00
91	Poster, MJ dunking with right hand, red 23, white signature right side, crowd in background, Marketcom/St Louis, Photo by Nathaniel Butler	7465 21 x 32	45.00
93	Poster, SI The Glory Years, Bird, Magic & MJ, Issue 5 Volume 5, Mercury ad on bottom "A Great Bench with a Lot of Depth" (7.129)	19 x 37	45.00
96	Poster, Special Commemorative Edition, SI Presents 5, Chicago Bulls, NBA Champs, 96-97, On Sale Now, Red with MJ in Champions hat, holding trophy, bandage on index finger (7.130)	16 x 24	30.00

7.125 7.126 7.127

7.128

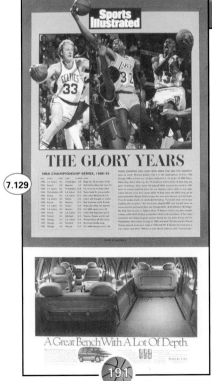

7.129

7.130

Year	Posters-Sports Illustrated For Kids		
90	Set of 4 Posters Distributed over 4 issues	21 x 32	55.00
	---2/90 Issue, Part 1, MJ's right hand with basketball (7.131a)	10.5 x 16	12.00
	---3/90 Issue, Part 2, MJ's right foot with crowd in background (7.131b)	10.5 x 16	12.00
	---4/90, Issue, Part 3, MJ from waist down jumping in air (7.131c)	10.5 x 16	12.00
	---5/90, Issue, Part 4, MJ from waist up jumping in air (7.131d)	10.5 x 16	12.00

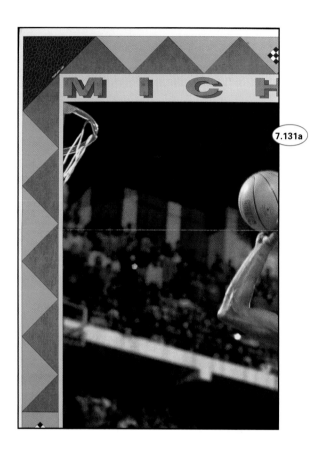

7.131a

7.131b

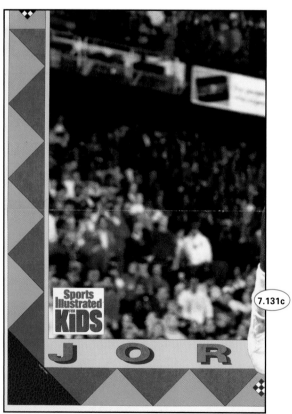

7.131c

7.131d

Year	Posters-Starline	size		
88	Poster, MJ layup right hand, red 23, crowd in background, "Michael Jordan" top center, photo by Noren Trotman (7.132)	16 x 20	35.00	
90	Poster, "Jordan," 5 MJ pictures, "CB" & logo center	41 x 58	45.00	
90	Poster, "Jordan," on left vertical, white 23, red & black striped on left vertical and bottom dunking,	16 x 20	40.00	
90	Poster, "Michael Jordan" in red 7 black flag on bottom, red 23, dunking, tongue out, vs. Clippers #20 (7.133)	8 x 24	25.00	
92	Poster, "America's Team," team players with flag in background, MJ in white USA #9 dunking	16 x 20	20.00	
92	Poster, "America's Team," USA BB logo lower left, team players with flag in background (7.134)	22 x 34.5	25.00	
95	"1995," poster		5.00	10.00
96	"1996," poster		4.00	8.00
	"Home-Red Uniform," poster		3.00	6.00
	"Home-White Uniform," poster		3.00	6.00
	"Soaring," poster		3.00	6.00

Year	Posters-Starting Lineups			
92	Poster-Walking with basketball (7.135)	11 x 14	25.00	
92	Poster-Soaring to Jam (7.136)	11 x 14	25.00	

Year	Poster-The Plain Dealer Newspaper			
97	Poster, insert in the Cleveland newspaper from All-Star Weekend, 7/97, matched front page (7.137)	11 x 17	15.00	

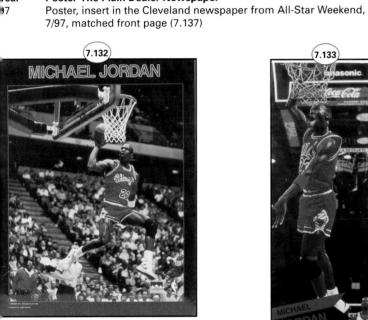

7.132

7.133

7.134

7.135

7.136

7.137

Year	Poster-Time, MJ & Guy Laroche	size		
85	Poster, white signature, "Time Jordan by Guy Laroche," MJ closeup, with hand on BB, red and black stripe watch band, 2 red stripes on black face, red square at 6:00 position (7.138)	23 x 34.5	100.00	

Year	Posters-Upper Deck	size		
93	Poster, "3-D: A New Dimension from the UD Company," red 23, 1994 3-D Pro-View NBA Basketball Cards" (7.139)	22 x 34	20.00	
93	Poster, "UD Company Present, Adventures in 'Toon World," 2 MJ cards out of 3, blue to purple background (7.140)	22 x 34	20.00	
93-94	Poster, "Series Two 1993-94 Basketball Cards," white 23, MJ shooting, red foul line key in background (7.141)	22 x 34	15.00	
94	Poster, "NBA Trading Card Line Up!! '94-95," All 440 cards, Rare Air Cards, Basketball Heroes Cards, Japanese Poster (7.142)	33 x 23	20.00	
94	Poster, "Even Michael's Up for It," The World Cup USA Set. Only from UD," jumping in sky, red shorts, ball in RH, white shirt (7.143)	20 x 28	45.00	
94-97	Poster, Autographed Nike "Wings," framed, 11 x 36, 500 issued	13988	550.00	700.00
94-97	Poster, unsigned Nike "Wings," framed, 11 x 36, 4,500 issued	13611	200.00	350.00
95	Poster, laminated, "The UD Jordan Center," die-cut like, "45" (7.144)	29 x 20	45.00	
96	Halloween Treats display (7.145)	6 x 9	20.00	

Year	Posters-Video	size		
88	Michael Jordan's Come Fly With Me Poster, "The Whole MJ Story on Videocassette. See It To Believe It!" (7.146)	25 x 38	55.00	
90	Michael Jordan's Playground, Whole Grain Wheaties The Breakfast Of Champions Poster "Now on Video" (7.147)	25 x 38	50.00	

Year	Posters-Wheaties Cereal Box	size		
86	Poster, Slam Dunk Contest Action photos (7.148)	16 x 23	60.00	
89	Nike posters were attached to Wheaties boxes with series numbers 43, 56, 57, 18 oz. There were four different 2 sided posters. The back of the posters show a photo of all four posters and has the following quote, "Collect All Four"	8' x 12'	45.00	
	---Poster, Nike, jump shot next to brick wall, red shirt and black shorts, shooting with six kids, graffiti on white part of wall	16 x 24"	10.00	
	---Poster, Nike, dribbling next to brick wall, white shirt and black shorts, dribbling alone, graffiti on brick wall, MJ looking at camera	16 x 24"	10.00	
	---Poster, Nike, dunk shot in air, red #23 uniform, 1 camera man on floor, 2 referees on floor, side view, camera shot from under the basket, Jordan's name on scoreboard	16 x 24"	10.00	
	---Poster, Nike, flying through air to dunk shot, front-side view, 3:51 on clock, side view	16 x 24"	10.00	
89	Wheaties attached 3 different, 4 sided posters, to cereal boxes with series numbers 73z. When the backs are assembled they made one large action photo of MJ dunking	24 x 48	15.00	
	---Poster, MJ Bursting Out of Box, blue strip on cover, top poster section with head shot dunking on inside poster (7.149)	8 x 12	5.00	
	---Poster, MJ Bursting Out of Box, green strip on cover, middle poster section with chest and hip section on inside poster (7.149)	8 x 12	5.00	
	---Poster, MJ Bursting Out of Box, purple strip on cover, bottom section with knees and feet section on inside poster (7.149)	8 x 12	5.00	
89	Poster, MJ Bursting Out of Box, blue strip on cover, proof poster, top poster section with head shot dunking on inside poster		100.00	150.00
89	Poster, MJ Bursting Out of Box, green strip on cover, proof poster, middle poster section with chest and hip section on inside poster		100.00	150.00
89	Poster, MJ Bursting Out of Box, purple strip on cover, proof poster, bottom section with knees and feet section on inside poster		100.00	150.00

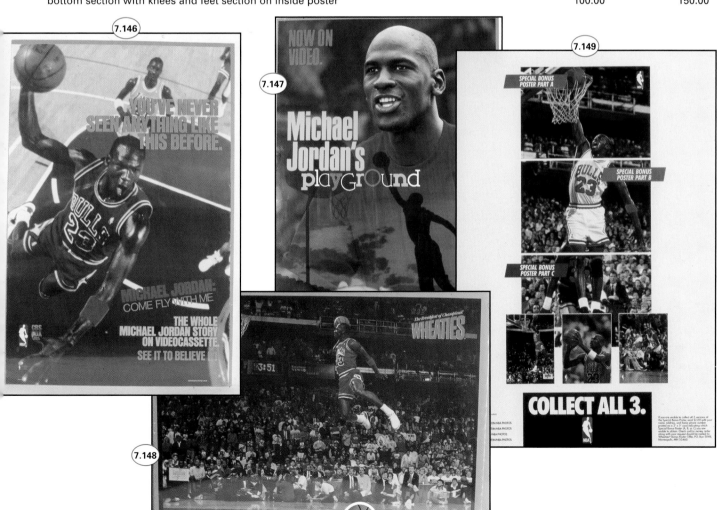

Year	Posters-Wilson	size		
86-87	Poster, red/white "Wilson" top, white outline around MJ, jumping to basket, BB in RH, old red 23, rubber bands around neck, white MJ signature with "Member, Wilson Advisory Staff" (7.150)	12 x 18	45.00	
88	Poster, "MJ Limited Edition BB Backboard, Flexible Goal and Rapid Adjust Pole All in One Kit," #s on bottom WCTN 00020 105, WLBL0002800, MJ bending over, tongue out, red 23, 2 pictures of boards, white signature (7.151)	21 x 24	50.00	
88	Backboard, "MJ Limited Edition BB Backboard, Flexible Goal and Rapid Adjust Pole All in One Kit," #s on bottom WCTN 00020 105, WLBL0002800, MJ bending over, tongue out, red 23, 2 pictures of boards, white signature		250.00	300.00
88	Poster, "Wilson" on left vertical, MJ reaching, red 23, tongue out, black signature & "Wilson Celebrating 75 years as Brand of Pros" bottom left (7.152)	19 x 26	40.00	
91-92	Poster, "Michael & Wilson" on left side, "23 MVP" on right top, red Wilson & Wilson Sporting Good Co., on bottom right, "Michael Jordan" on bottom left center, blue background (7.153)	22 x 30	40.00	

Year	Posters-World Book	size item#	
84-85	Poster, 1st year with Bulls, old uniform, pre Air Jordan shoes, regional piece,	18" x 26"	65.00
85-86	Poster, "Partners in Excellence, You can soar to new heights by reading books," white 23, sitting on bench holding book, "read" on headband on BB, orange, black, white borders (7.154)	22 x 28 PUB 4715	50.00
86-87	Poster, "Partners in Excellence, You can soar to new heights by reading books," white 23, sitting on bench holding book, "read" on headband on BB, like 7.154 except white, orange, blue, white borders	22 x 28 SC 8358N	45.00
94	Poster, "Read and pursue your dreams!" top, "World Book" bottom, MJ in color print shirt, MJ on baseball field with Wilson bat, golf clubs and bag, stack of WB on table (7.156)	22 x 28 2S601041	40.00

(7.150)

(7.151)

(7.152)

(7.153)

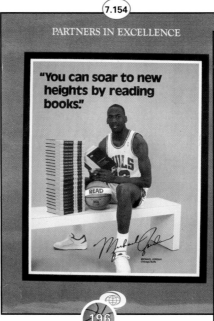

(7.154)

(7.15

Year	Profiles Icon Sports	card #		
3	Card, MJ from Magic Johnson's Gold Set, MJ in USA white #9, Barcelona, Spain Basketball Commemorative Edition (7.157)	SP-1	35.00	50.00
3	Cards, MJ Gold Set, Dream Team Edition Series 1, Barcelona, Commemorative, # of 25,000 produced	19 cards	60.00	85.00
	---MJ	13	5.00	8.00
	---MJ	14	5.00	8.00
	---MJ	15	5.00	8.00
	---MJ	16	5.00	8.00
	---MJ	17	5.00	8.00
	---MJ	18	5.00	8.00
---MJ	Bonus 5		5.00	8.00
	---MJ	Bonus 6	5.00	8.00
	---Checklist	BC001	2.00	3.00
	---Sid Bingham Autograph Card, MJ, random insert	SP-1	100.00	150.00
3	Card, MJ from Magic Johnson's Purple Set, MJ in USA white #9, Barcelona, Spain Basketball Commemorative Edition, # of 1,000 produced (7.158)	SP-1	75.00	100.00
3	Cards, MJ Purple Set, Dream Team Edition Series 1, Barcelona, Commemorative, # of 1,000 produced	19 cards	125.00	175.00
	---MJ	13	15.00	20.00
	---MJ	14	15.00	20.00
	---MJ	15	15.00	20.00
	---MJ	16	15.00	20.00
	---MJ	17	15.00	20.00
	---MJ	18	15.00	20.00
	---MJ	Bonus5	15.00	20.00
	---MJ	Bonus6	15.00	20.00
	---Checklist	BC001	5.00	10.00
	---Sid Bingham Autograph Card, MJ, random insert	SP-1	200.00	250.00

PROMO CARD SECTION

Year	Promo-Action Packed Cards	card #		
0	Gold border, MJ & Bill Cartwright & Sonic player, MJ in golf hat & "sample" on back (7.159)	NNO	175.00	300.00

Year	Promo-Arena Holograms			
1	Arena Hologram, 12th NSCC	3		

Year	Promo-Ballstreet Items	mag # card #		
1	Sheet, 4 promo cards, like (7.160) but silver border	NNO	10.00	15.00
	---MJ			
	---K. Griffey Jr.			
	---Lemieux & B. Errey			
	---J. Montana			

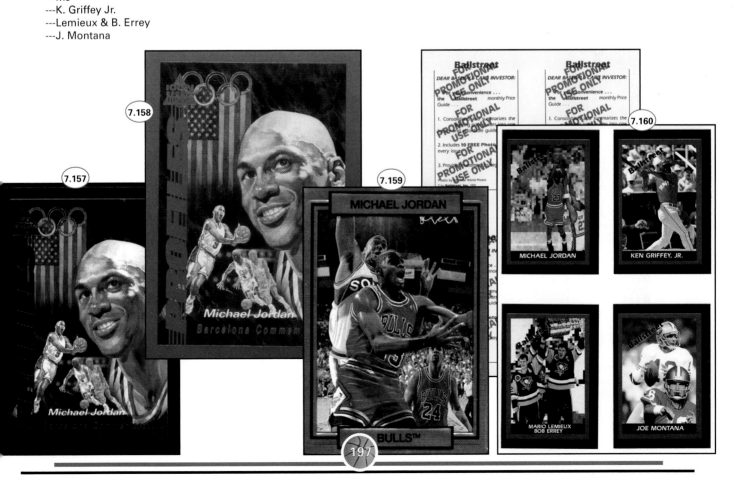

7.158
7.157
7.159
7.160

MICHAEL JORDAN

BULLS™

Michael Jordan

Michael Jordan
Barcelona Commem

MICHAEL JORDAN
KEN GRIFFEY, JR.
MARIO LEMIEUX BOB ERREY
JOE MONTANA

91	Sheet, 4 promo cards, silver border (7.161)	1621	10.00	15.00
	---MJ			
	---K. Griffey Jr.			
	---Lemieux & B. Errey			
	---J. Montana			
91	Sheet, 4 promo cards, like (7.162) but red border	2086	10.00	15.00
	---MJ			
	---K. Griffey Jr.			
	---Lemieux & B. Errey			
	---J. Montana			
91	Sheet, 4 promo cards, gold border (7.163)	NNO	10.00	15.00
	---MJ			
	---K. Griffey Jr.			
	---Lemieux & B. Errey			
	---J. Montana			
91	Sheet, 4 promo cards, like others but multi-color border	NNO	10.00	15.00
	---MJ			
	---K. Griffey Jr.			
	---Lemieux & B. Errey			
	---J. Montana			
91	Card, promo, shining silver foil & blue border, jump shot, 1-92, Ballstreet Journal information on white back, "For Promotional Use Only" (7.165)		2.00	5.00

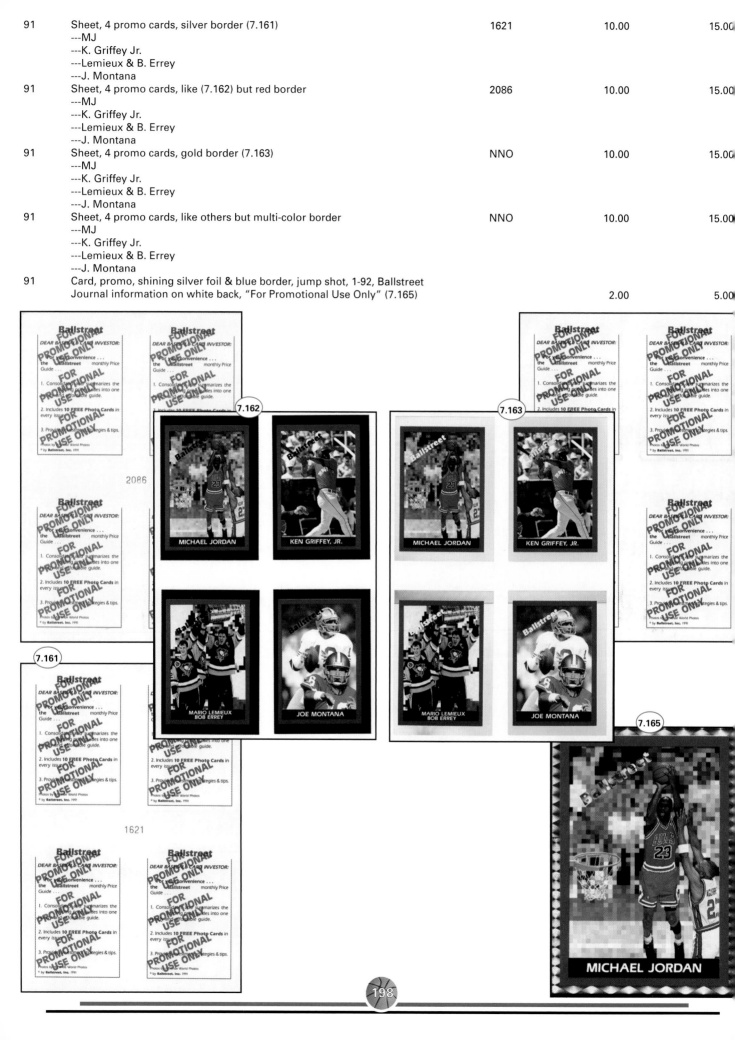

91	Card, promo, multi-color foil & blue border, jump shot, 1-92, Ballstreet Journal information on white back, "For Promotional Use Only" (7.166)	2.00	5.00
91	Card, promo, gold foil & blue border, jump shot, 1-92, Ballstreet Journal information on white back, "For Promotional Use Only" (7.167)	2.00	5.00
91	Card, promo, red foil & blue border, jump shot, 1-92, Ballstreet Journal information on white back, "For Promotional Use Only" (7.168)	2.00	5.00
91	Card, promo, silver foil & blue border, jump shot, 1-92, Ballstreet Journal information on white back, "For Promotional Use Only" (7.169)	2.00	5.00
91	Card, promo, gold foil & blue border, 1992 Premier Edition, jump shot, 1-92, Ballstreet Journal information on white back, 2 yellow stripes on front (7.170)	2.00	5.00
91	Card, promo, red foil & blue border, 1992 Premier Edition, jump shot, 1-92, Ballstreet Journal information on white back, 2 yellow stripes on front	2.00	5.00
91	Card, promo, shiny silver foil & blue border, 1992 Premier Edition, jump shot, 1-92, Ballstreet Journal information on white back, 2 yellow stripes on front (7.171)	2.00	5.00
91	Card, promo, silver foil & blue border, 1992 Premier Edition, jump shot, 1-92, Ballstreet Journal information on white back, 2 yellow stripes on front (7.172)	2.00	5.00

91	Card, 1992 Premier Edition, multi-color card with Advertisement Flyer, flyer attached, card with issue #3 on front (7.173)		2.00	5.00
5/92	Card, USA white #9 holding ball, gold border, white back with Ballstreet information (7.174)	promo	3.00	6.00

Promo-Baseball Minor League Cards

96	SP-Top Prospect Promo	NNO	20.00	30.00

Year	Promo-Broader Baseball Cards			
92-93	"Michael Jordan Rare Air," gold swirls, Barons uniform, standing, 10,000 produced	promo	1.50	2.00
92-93	"Michael Jordan Rare Air," gold background with swirls, black WS uniform, close up, red/black back, MJ picture, stats from 86-93, 10,000 produced	promo	5.00	8.00
93	Sports Images, negative like front with MJ holding bat, tape on fingers, Two Sport Superstars, "Sports Images," blue top white bottom, 92-93 stats, information	proto type	1.50	2.00
94	Royal Air, MJ with hand in glove, silver lettering, Royal Air Silver Foil Edition, blue top white bottom	promo	1.50	2.00
94	"Summer of 94," MJ in WS pinstripe uniform, looking at ball after swinging, sunset in background, blue & gold border, gold signature, blue back border, blue dot upper left, 92-93 stats, story, "Collectible Promo Card"	promo	1.50	2.00

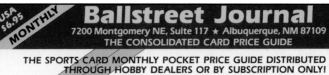

Year	Promo-Broader Basketball Cards	cd #	#of cds	
90-91	Slam Dunk Promo Card, side view jumping with ball in hand overhead, fire trail on ball, red #23, back "Slam Dunk Cards," Promo Cards, MJ, "Best of Best," 1990-1991	1 of 3	10.00	15.00
90-91	Slam Dunk Promo Card, side view slam dunk over Lakers, red #23, back "Slam Dunk Cards," Promo Cards, MJ, "Best of Best," 1990-1991	2 of 3	10.00	15.00
90-91	Slam Dunk Promo Card, side view, MJ in UNC uniform, going for dunk, blue and white #23, back "Slam Dunk Cards," Promo Cards, MJ, "Best of Best," 1990-1991	3 of 3	5.00	10.00
90-91	Slam Dunk 3 in 1 Promo Card, side view jumping with ball in hand overhead, red #23, back MJ in #23 UNC blue uniform dunking, red #23 dunking over Laker player, "Jammin, Slammin...Flyin High"		10.00	15.00
92	Pacific Coast Sportcards, closeup drawing of Sports Heroes, 3 of 4 prototype, 10,000 printed MJ head & shoulders		1.50	2.00
92	Pacific Coast Sportcards, closeup drawing of MJ head & shoulders, Sports Heroes, 3 of 4 prototype	sheet	15.00	20.00
92	Raging Chicagoians, Prestige & Sterling, 1992 prototype, 60,000 produced, cartoon-like card		3.00	6.00
92-93	"Michael Jordan Rare Air," dunking, red and white top bottom strips, red #23, 10,000	promo	2.00	3.00
92-93	"Michael Jordan Rare Air," one hand shooting, red & white top & bottom strips, red #23, 10,000	promo	2.00	3.00
92-93	"Michael Jordan Rare Air," gold swirls, one hand shooting, red #23, 10,000 red uniform	promo	2.00	3.00
92-93	"Michael Jordan Rare Air," gold swirls, right hand shooting, white #23, 10,000 white uniform	promo	2.00	3.00
93	"America's Best Michael Jordan," jumping with ball in right hand, "Michael Jordan, Prototype, Forward Chicago Bulls," Chicago National Show	proto	5.00	10.00
93	"Celebration of Greatness," Retirement Tribute in lower right, silver name & signature, MJ walking away in red #23, insert swinging bat, blue box upper left, 92-93 stats, silver foil edition, 1,750 produced	promo	2.00	3.00
93	"Hot Stars MJ," MJ dunking over New York, red 23, card for NSCC in Chicago, 7/22-25/93	promo	2.00	3.00
93	"Hot Stars MJ," MJ jumping to dunk, red 23, NSCC, Chicago, IL, July 22-25, 1993	promo	4.00	8.00
93	Headliners, "New Flash Jordan Retires 10/6/93," closeup in red shirt, white back with blue border, "Three-Peat!," story	promo	1.50	2.00
93	"Retirement Commemorative: October 6, 1993" gold foil and signature, "Jordan The Legend Continues"	promo	4.00	8.00
93	"Retirement Commemorative: October 6, 1993" silver foil and signature, "Jordan The Legend Continues," 3,000 issued	promo	5.00	10.00
93	Slammers, MJ flying in air with ball in right hand, tongue out, red #23, cloud-like background, gold lettering, Slammers on top, blue and white back, 92-93 stats, personal info	promo	1.50	2.00
93	Sports 2000, "Tribute 10/6/93 Retirement," yellow stripes, red top, blue background, MJ dunking, white #23, blue box right top back, 92-93 stats, personal info	promo test issue	1.50	2.00
93	3rd Super Show Annual, MJ in USA blue #9, tan border, August 25-29, St Paul MN, Downtown Pavilion,	promo	4.00	6.00
93	US Legends, #23 MJ, closeup view with black t-shirt, gold signature and border, blue box with US Legends, personal info, 92-93 stats, white back	prototype	1.50	2.00
8/4-7 94	Sports Sensations, MJ Retired 10/6/93, shiny gold signature & border, shooting a jump shot over Barkley, 15th National Sports Collectors Convention, Houston, Texas	promo card	3.00	6.00
8/4-7 94	Sports Sensations, MJ Retired 10/6/93, plain gold signature & border, looking to his side, 15th National Sports Collectors Convention, Houston, Texas	promo card	3.00	6.00
8/4-7 94	Sports Sensations, MJ Retired 10/6/93, shiny gold signature & border, looking to his side, 15th National Sports Collectors Convention, Houston, Texas	promo card	3.00	6.00
8/4-7 94	Sports Sensations, MJ Retired 10/6/93, shiny gold signature & border, 15th National Sports Collectors Convention, Houston, Texas	promo card	3.00	6.00
-	Champions Magazine, MJ dribbling, back Promotional, Champions Magazine, Sports Memorabilia	8	35.00	40.00
-	Collector Quarterly, MJ USA #9, holding world, flag background with gold bottom, red & yellow back, "Collectors Quarterly MJ US Olympian"	#3 prototype	3.00	6.00
-	"Dare To Dream," MJ gold signature, dunking on Chicago Skyline, red #23, back MJ basketball picture/yellow half back	promo	1.00	2.00
-	"Dare To Dream," MJ gold signature, 2 poses, UNC Blue uniform, black White Sox top, back MJ baseball picture/yellow half back	promo	1.00	2.00
	Krown International, orange backs	promo	1.50	2.00
	---layup, basket view, red #23, red foil	1 of 4	1.50	2.00
	---passing ball, red #23, red foil	2 of 4	1.50	2.00
	---standing above ball on floor, red foil	3 of 4	1.50	2.00

---hands on hits, B&W, red foil	4 of 4	1.50	2.00
---layup, basket view, red #23, silver foil	1 of 4	1.50	2.00
---passing ball, red #23, silver foil	2 of 4	1.50	2.00
---standing above ball on floor, silver foil	3 of 4	1.50	2.00
---hands on hips, B&W, silver foil	4 of 4	1.50	2.00
---layup, basket view, red #23, gold foil	1 of 4	1.50	2.00
---passing ball, red #23, gold foil	2 of 4	1.50	2.00
---standing above ball on floor, gold foil	3 of 4	1.50	2.00
---hands on hips, B&W, gold foil	4 of 4	1.50	2.00
- MJ hands in air, red #23, "Promo" on black strip upper left corner, "Bottom of the Net Promotions" on white back		1.50	2.00
- MJ hands on knees, gold signature and border, red #23, blue & white back, 25,000 produced	promo	2.00	3.00
- MJ holding trophy, gold border & signature, black & white back, 25,000 produced	promo	2.00	3.00
- "Michael Jordan Premier Sports," silver border, USA Olympic, flowers, blue back, same front picture	promo	1.50	2.00
- "National Sports Michael Jordan," silver border, layup, red #23, blue back, same front picture	promo	1.50	2.00
- "Promo" on back, MJ shooting layup with right hand under basket, red #23, "Promo" on back, nothing else	promo	4.00	6.00
- Sport Art Images, MJ reaching with Bulls logo in background, white #23, drawing like picture, "Michael Jordan #23 Guard," MJ is a leader of his team again, on back	promo 22	4.00	6.00
- Sport Art Images, MJ dribbling, red #23, drawing like picture, "Michael Jordan #23 Guard," MJ is a member of USA Olympic Team that won a Gold Metal in 1992, on back	promo 23	4.00	6.00
- "Michael Jordan Sports Edition," silver border, cigar, white T-shirt, blue back, same front picture, info	promo	1.50	2.00
- "Michael Jordan Sports Edition," silver border, dunking white uniform, blue back, same front picture, info	promo	1.50	2.00
- "Michael Jordan Sports Edition," MJ with red and black warmups, silver border, blue back with b&w insert of front picture	promo	3.00	5.00

Year	Promo-Broader Golf Cards			
94	"MJ Retired October 6, 1993," swinging club, straw hat, silver signature & border, Sports Sensations, 15th-NSCC, 8/4-7/94, Houston, T X , 5,000 produced	promo	4.00	6.00
94	"Retired October 6, 1993,"shooting bb, red #23 on left side of card/ swinging club, straw hat, silver signature on right side of card, silver border, Sports Sensations, 15th-NSCC, 8/4-7/94, Houston, T X , 5,000 produced	promo	4.00	6.00
94	"Summer of 94," MJ in golf clothes, sunset in background, blue & gold border, gold signature, blue back border, blue dot upper left, 92-93 stats, story, "Collectible Promo Card"	promo	4.00	6.00

Year	Promo-Broader Miscellaneous Cards	cd #		
94	"A Man for All Seasons," MJ golfing, #45 baseball, #23 basketball, personal stats, 92-93 Chicago stats, Pro Totals, story-"With Two 400 foot drives, Michael "Home Run"...	proto	4.00	8.00

Year	Promo-Chris Martin Enterprises Magnets			
93	1993 Dog Tag Plus, #23 white, stats & picture on back, hole punched top center, less than 100 issued, Chris Martin Enterprises on back (7.175)	Prototype	125.00	200.00

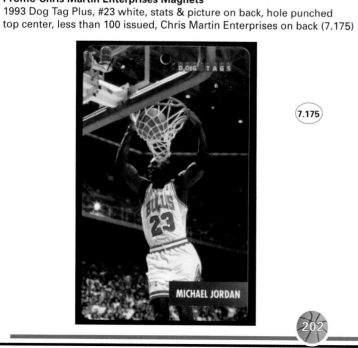

94	Pro Mag, #23 white, Bulls logo in circle lower left front, blank back, same as Dog Tag but closeup view with red outline, less than 100 issued (7.176)	Prototype	75.00	125.00

Year	**Promo-Collegiate Collection**	6 cds	45.00	75.00
90	Cards, Collegiate Collection Finest Promo Set, "Say No to Drugs, Yes to Life," on back bottom	6 cds	45.00	75.00
	---MJ (7.177)	NC-1		
	---Joe Namath	AL-1		
	---Bart Starr	A-12		
	---Bo Jackson	AU-1		
	---Herschel Walker	GA-1		
	---Johnny Unitas	LOU-1		
92	Card, Collegiate Collection, MJ & Magic, 12th National	NNO		

Year	**Promo-Diamond Sport Memorabilia Magazine**			
92	MJ Card, holding ball, white 23, white edge border, plain back with number stamped on bottom "No. 343," Given out at San Francisco in 2/92 at National , 2,000 issued (7.178)	promo	65.00	

Year	**Promo-Hoops Sheet**	item #		
90-91	Sheet, NBA Promo, blue top strip, white bottom half, blank back (7.179)	NNO		
	---I. Thomas	8.5 x 11	10.00	
	---M. Jordan			
	---P. Ewing			
	---L. Bird			
	---R. Parish			
	---C. Drexler			

Year	**Promo-MVP Magazine**			
91	N. Ryan cover, Prototype Issue		20.00	25.00
	---MJ Card, red 23 & black shirt, 4 x 6 card		15.00	20.00

	Promo-NBA Cards			
90-91	Skybox			
	-Prototype (7.180)	41	45.00	75.00
	-Julie Moran card, MJ on back with Julie for interview	NNO	25.00	50.00

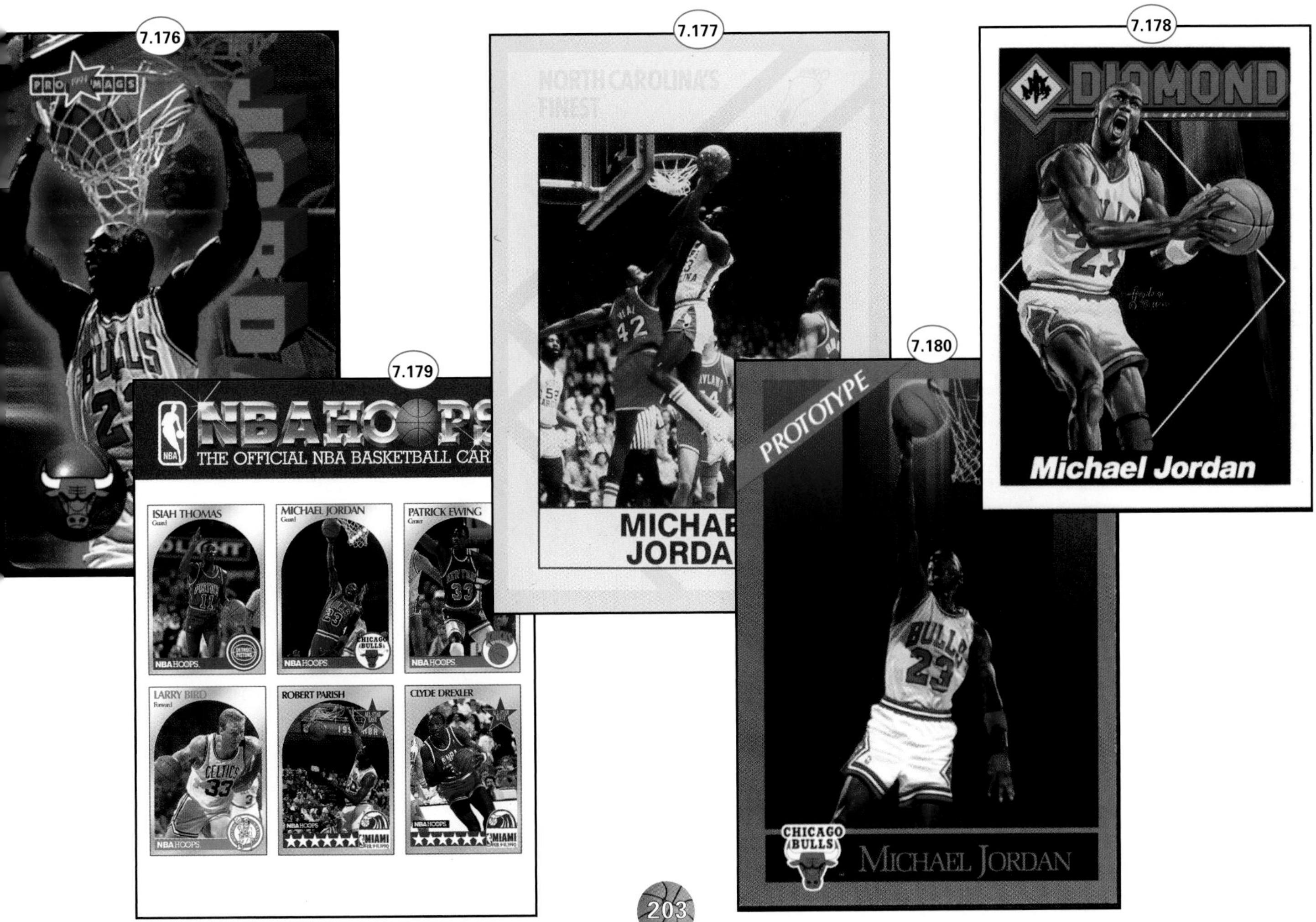

7.176

7.177

7.178

7.179

7.180

91-92	Fleer				
	-All-Star Game Promo/MJ front, promo written on back	236	5.00	10.00	
91-92	Hoops				
	-Prototype 00 (7.181)	004	60.00	80.00	
91-92	Upper Deck				
	-Promo MJ (7.182)	1	20.00	25.00	
	-Promo David Robinson	400			
93-94	Sky Box				
	-Promo "93-94" Edition Set	6 cards	10.00	15.00	
	---MJ Card	NNO			
	---Shaq, The Center Stage	NNO			
	---C. Laettner, All Rookie Team	NNO			
	---Showdown Series, Mourning & Ewing	NNO			
	---D. Robinson	NNO			
	---D. Majerle	NNO			
93-94	Stadium Club				
	-Triple Double, promo, gold "Michael," blue "Jordan"	1	15.00	25.00	
93-94	Upper Deck				
	-Promo Card-G, light top right front corner, MJ name in red stripe on back goes half way, Born: Feb. 17, 1963, 88/93 stats on back	23	20.00	30.00	
	-Promo Card-G with line in middle of G, light top right front corner, MJ name in red stripe on back goes half way, Born: Feb. 17, 1963, 88/93 stats on back (7.183)	23	25.00	35.00	
	-Holojam Promo, UD logo left front, back logo touches bottom blue line (7.184)	H-4	25.00	35.00	
	-Pro View, 3D Promo, small picture + 5 shoes on back	23	25.00	35.00	
94-95	SP				
	-Promo, gold side	23	15.00	25.00	
94-95	Upper Deck				
	-Rare Air Promo	NNO	10.00	15.00	
95	SP Championship Promo European, He's Back	41	10.00	15.00	
95-96	SP				
	-Promo, gold left back	23	20.00	30.00	
95-96	SP X				
	-Promo Set		250.00	300.00	
	---MJ Card				
	---A. Hardaway Card				
	---Folder				

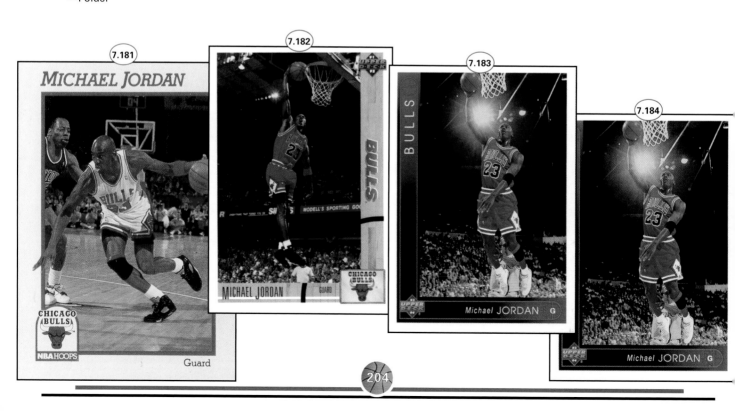

Promo-NBA UD Foreign Issued Cards

Year		card #		
93-94	Upper Deck-French -Promo Card	NNO	25.00	45.00
93-94	Upper Deck-German -Promo Card	NNO	25.00	45.00
93-94	Upper Deck-Italian -Promo Card	NNO	25.00	45.00
93-94	Upper Deck-Spanish -Promo Card	NNO	25.00	45.00

Year	**Promo-Pocket Pages Magazines**	card #		
93	Card, silver top, "Promo" on left side red letters yellow stripe, fist in the air, "Free Sample" back	48	2.00	4.00
1/94	Card, promo, MJ dribbling with left hand, white 23, bent over, yellow stripe top left with "Promo" free send-in card offer, black back, "Free Sample" next to number, "Michael Jordan, Chacago Bulls, Off the Air?," misspelled Chicago on card,	58-A	20.00	30.00
1/94	Card, promo, MJ & N. Ryan, yellow stripe top left with "Promo," free send-in card offer, black back, "Free Sample" next to number, "Thanks for the Memories"	56	20.00	30.00
4/94	Card, foil promo, MJ baseball & basketball pictures, yellow stripe top left with "Promo," free send-in card offer, black back, "Free Sample" nex to number, "Out of His League?"	64	20.00	30.00
94	Sheet, proof, no names or foil, MJ cover for 4/94, two #64 MJ cards, two #64 MJ cards for the "Promo Strip"	20 x 26	75.00	125.00
94	Sheet, printers proof, MJ cover for 4/94, two #64 MJ cards, two #64 MJ cards for the "Promo Strip"	20 x 26	45.00	65.00

Year	**Promo-Pro Set**	card #		
91-92	Card, Pro Set Prototypes	000	1000.00	1500.00

Year	**Promo-RBI Magazine**	card #		
91	Regional Baseball Index Prototype	cover	15.00	20.00
	---MJ Card, batting, red WS shirt, white pants, blue hat with "C," 4 x 6 card	1-P	8.00	12.00

Year	**Promo-Showtime**			
-	Showtime Promo Sheet (7.185)	8 x 10		5.00

Year	**Promo-Skybox Sheets**			
90	Commemorative Press Proof Inaugural Edition, white 23, blank back (7.186)			60.00

Year	**Promo-Space Jam**	item #		
95-96	Card & folder, UD All-Star Cast, Bugs, MJ, & Sylvester, promo card	SJ-1	10.00	15.00
95-96	Card, UD All-Star Cast, Bugs, MJ, & Sylvester, promo	SJ-1	6.00	12.00

(7.185)

Michael Jordan

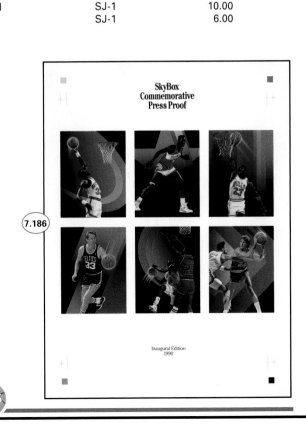

(7.186)

SkyBox
Commemorative
Press Proof

Inaugural Edition
1990

Year	Promo-Sport Educational	card #		
92	Card, MJ dribbling, red 23, black & gold border, white & blue back with black "1992 National Promo, Booth #6210" insert	promo #1	2.00	4.00

Year	Promo-Sports Report Magazine	mag # card #		
6/92	Frank Thomas cover, gold foil on cards, 15,000 issued	proto	15.00	25.00
	---MJ Card, holding ball, red 23	8		
6/92	Frank Thomas cover, silver foil on cards, 1,500 issued	proto	45.00	60.00
	---MJ Card, holding ball, red 23	8		

Year	Promo-Spotlight Magazine	mag # card #		
4/94	Prototype Issue, MJ cover in White Sox Uniform, white, 5,000 issued batting, l-1		20.00	25.00
	---MJ Card, same as cover, White Sox Uniform, white, batting, completing swing, looking at ball, bat in left hand, side	P-1	2.00	4.00
	---MJ Card, White Sox Uniform, black & white, pitching, shot on a gym floor	P-14	2.00	4.00

Year	Promo-Star Company Ad Cards	card #		
90	MJ & Chicago Ad Card red border, white letters on front, white back with red letters (7.187)	NNO	25.00	45.00
90	MJ & Chicago Ad Card red border, white letters, glossy finish white back with red letters,	NNO	15.00	35.00
90	Chicago Ad Card, MJ red to black border, white letters, white back with red letters	NNO	15.00	25.00
90	MJ & Chicago Ad Card white border, red letters, white back with red letters (7.188)	NNO	20.00	35.00
90	MJ & Chicago Ad Card white border, red letters, glossy finish, white back with red letters	NNO	35.00	60.00
90	MJ & Chicago Ad Card gray border, red letters, white back with red letters	NNO	15.00	30.00
91	MJ & Chicago Ad Card white border, black letters, white back with black letters	NNO	20.00	35.00
91	MJ & Chicago Guard black border with white letters, white back with black letters	NNO	20.00	35.00
92	Chicago Ad Card & MJ, gray border, red letters, white back with red letters	NNO	15.00	25.00
92	MJ & Chicago Ad Card, blue border, white letters, white back with blue letters	NNO	15.00	25.00
92	MJ & Chicago, Forward, Ad Card, yellow to blue border, blue to yellow letters, white back with blue letters	NNO	15.00	25.00

Year	Promo-Star Company Promo Ad Cards	card # # cards		
91	MJ & Chicago Prototype, yellow border, red letters, white back with red letters	NNO	20.00	45.00
91	Jordan Promos, yellow to red border, red to yellow letters, white backs, red border, black letters, 1,000 sets produced	5 cards	40.00	60.00
	---MJ & Chicago Career Statistics from 84-91	1 of 5	8.00	12.00
	---MJ & Chicago Playoff Statistics from 84-91	2 of 5	8.00	12.00
	---MJ & Chicago All-Star Statistics from 85-91	3 of 5	8.00	12.00
	---MJ & Chicago Career Information from 86-91	4 of 5	8.00	12.00
	---MJ & Chicago Personal Information birth to Bull	5 of 5	8.00	12.00

(7.187)

STAR

MICHAEL JORDAN   **CHICAGO** Ad Card

(7.188)

STAR

MICHAEL JORDAN   **CHICAGO** Ad Card

Year		mag #/card #		
91	MJ & Chicago Prototype, red border with white letters, white back with black letters	NNO	20.00	45.00
92	Jordan Promo Set, black to red border, white letters, white back with black letters	5 card set	25.00	40.00
	---MJ & Chicago Career Stats, Statistics from 1984-1991, 1,000 sets produced	1 of 5	5.00	8.00
	---MJ & Chicago Playoff Stats, Statistics from 1984-1991	2 of 5	5.00	8.00
	---MJ & Chicago All-Star Stats, Statistics from 1985-1991	3 of 5	5.00	8.00
	---MJ & Chicago Career Info, Career Info from 1986-1991 on back	4 of 5	5.00	8.00
	---MJ & Chicago Personal Info, MJ personal information birth to Bulls	5 of 5	5.00	8.00
92	MJ & Chicago Prototype, red to yellow border, yellow to red letters, white back with red letters	NNO	15.00	25.00
92	MJ & Chicago Prototype, purple border, white letters, white back with purple letters	NNO	15.00	25.00
92	MJ & Chicago Prototype, purple to yellow border, yellow to purple letters, white back with purple letters	NNO	15.00	25.00

Year	Promo-The National Sport Daily	mag #		
89	MJ & Ewing jump shot, blue back with NSD information	promo	50.00	75.00

Year	Pro Star Cereal Box Cards and Painted Cels-Canada			
91-92	Cereal Box Card Set, Mail in offer, English/French backs	9 cards		
	---Michael Jordan (7.189)		25.00	
	---Wayne Gretzky/MJ front (7.190)		10.00	
	---MJ & Bo Jackson & Wayne Gretzky (7.191)		10.00	
91-92	Animation Hand Painted Original Production Cel by DIC Entertainment			
	---Pencil drawing, with red lines for centering, of MJ, Wayne Gretzky, & Bo Jackson, sketch for color #D cel (7.192)	9 x 11	150.00	250.00
	---Color 3D cel of MJ, Wayne Gretzky and Bo Jackson standing in a room in front of a door, looking to their right, all in Pro Star uniforms (7.192)	9 x 11	150.00	250.00
	---Pencil drawing of MJ, Wayne Gretzky and Bo Jackson underwater with SCUBA gear and being squeezed by octopus's tentacles (7.193)	9 x 11	150.00	250.00
	---Color 3D cel of MJ, Wayne Gretzky and Bo Jackson underwater with SCBA gear and being squeezed by octopus's tentacles (7.193)	9 x 11	150.00	250.00

(7.189) MICHAEL JORDAN

(7.190) WAYNE GRETZKY

(7.191) PRO STARS

(7.192)

(7.193)

Year	Rayovac Battery	item #	# item	
5/95	Brochure, Battery Ad, 2 x 7, gatefold 6-sided ad with 3 photos of MJ	W-194	5.00	8.00
12/24/95	Chicago Tribune Ad, "Play It Smart," handprint BB and poster offer, 36" x 24" (7.194)	11 x 14	10.00	15.00
96	Coupon, Play It Smart Basketball Hand Print Basketball offer	CP190	1.00	2.00
96	Store Display Card	8.5 x 11	15.00	20.00
96	Coupon, Rebate & Handprint	CP238	1.00	2.00
3/96	Coupon, Free Poster Offer	CP186	1.00	2.00
6/96	AAA Reusable Battery Pack, MJ "Play It Smart" Sticker, no border around "Play It Smart" orange sticker	45050	8.00	12.00
6/96	AAA Reusable Battery Pack, MJ "Play It Smart" Brochure, white border around "Play It Smart" brochure	45050	8.00	12.00
6/96	AA Reusable Battery Pack, MJ "Play It Smart" Sticker, no border around "Play It Smart" orange sticker	45048	8.00	12.00
6/96	AA Reusable Battery Pack, MJ "Play It Smart" Brochure, gray border around "Play It Smart" brochure	45048	8.00	12.00
6/96	C Reusable Battery Pack, MJ "Play It Smart" Sticker, no border around "Play It Smart" orange sticker	45047	8.00	12.00
6/96	C Reusable Battery Pack, MJ "Play It Smart" Brochure, gray border around "Play It Smart" brochure	45047	8.00	12.00
6/96	D Reusable Battery Pack, MJ "Play It Smart" Sticker, no border around "Play It Smart" orange sticker	45046	8.00	12.00
6/96	D Reusable Battery Pack, MJ "Play It Smart" Brochure, gray border around "Play It Smart" brochure	45046	8.00	12.00
6/96	Renewal Power Station, AA & AAA, borderless orange sticker	45051	16.00	20.00
6/96	Renewal Power Station, AA & AAA, borderless blue sticker	45051	12.00	15.00
6/96	Renewal Power Station, AA, AA, C, D, borderless black sticker	45052	32.00	35.00
6/96	Renewal Power Station, AA, AAA, C, D, borderless orange sticker	45052	30.00	35.00
6/96	Renewal Power Station, AA, AAA, C, D, borderless blue sticker	45052	22.00	25.00
8/96	Coupon, Renewal for DM X Subscribers	X -180	1.00	2.00
8/96	Coupon, Basketball, $10 Check MJ signatures	CP237	1.00	2.00
96	"Jammin Pack" Box (7.195)		60.00	
	---Coupon Book			
	---Official Size BB with MJ hand prints			
	---4 AA Rechargeable Batteries			
	---Renewal Power Station for AA or AAA Batteries			
96	Booth #1149, McCormick Place, MJ in black shirt, red background, "The Game has Changed, Jordan & Rayovac Join our Team at Booth 1149"	cover	10.00	15.00
96	Booth #1149, McCormick Place, MJ in Space Jam t-shirt, "Find Out How to Jam with Jordan"	cover	10.00	15.00
97	Booth #11801, McCormick Place Business Show		10.00	15.00
3/97	Coupon, Poster Offer, small card		1.00	2.00
6/97	Coupon, Save $5.00, "Play It Smart"		1.00	2.00
6/97	Coupon, Save $10.00, "Play It Smart"		1.00	2.00
12/97	Coupon Ad, Walgreens, Save $2.00, MJ & Arnold. Palmer			1.00
97	Ad Display, "Maximum Power Maximum Value," red background, MJ holding lightning bolt, MJ in orange polo shirt, batteries in Sega like electronic game jaws	B360 22 x 13"	50.00	75.00
97	Ad Display, "Maximum Power Maximum Value," red background, MJ holding lightning bolt, MJ in orange polo shirt, batteries in Sega like electronic game jaws	B361 35 x 13"	50.00	75.00
97	Coupons-2, Save $3.00 & $1.00, MJ picture, Space Jam "Meet Mike" Entry Form	2 forms	2.00	3.00
97	Entry Form, Space Jam "Meet Mike," MJ name, 4 forms	CP 280	1.00	2.00
97	Coupon, Save $3.00 Space Jam Video, MJ picture, 3 forms	CP 281	1.00	2.00
98	AA Alkaline Battery Pack, "All the Power...For Less" with MJ insert	815-8C	4.00	5.00
98	Coupon and Display Board		4.00	6.00
	---Display MJ holding AA pack	SS447		
	---Coupon, Save $.55, No MJ			

Year	**Retirement Night**			

On Nov. 1, 1994, there was a retirement ceremony for Michael Jordan at the United Center in Chicago. The items below were distributed to everyone who attended in the Nike duffel bag. Inside the bag was an Environment bronze coin mail-in form, which most people didn't redeem. These coins are very rare. There was also a 5 x 7 red or white card, # of 18,000. The red versions are very rare. The items, marked with a "*" were not part of the handout but were made available later. (7.196)

Complete Set of Items Listed

	Item		Low	High
	---Ameritech Magnet, orange BB		10.00	20.00
	---Ball Park Frank Pennant, white, 23, logo, 26,000 issued		15.00	25.00
	---Chicago Sun Time Print of 1st, 2nd, 3rd Championships, logo	2 sheets	5.00	10.00
	---Chicago Tribune/Sport Channel Ticket Holder, no logo		10.00	20.00
*	---Environment bronze coin, retirement logo, 25,000 issued	NNO	75.00	100.00
	---Environment bronze coin mail-in form		1.00	2.00
	---Gatorade Water Bottle retirement logo, green		10.00	20.00
	---McDonald's Pin, white 23, logo, on backing, 26,000 issued		15.00	25.00
*	---Magazine, MJ A Salute To Michael Jordan, hands on knees, white 23, retirement logo, 11/1/94	cover	20.00	25.00
	---Nike Book with MJ Shoes, logo, was attached to bag		15.00	25.00
	---Nike Duffel Bag, logo, black, red seams, zipper, & strap		60.00	90.00
*	---Pass, sealed red, "All Access," retirement logo		10.00	20.00
*	---Pass for Media, MJ photo		10.00	20.00
*	---Pass for Media, MJ & Phil J. photo		10.00	20.00
	---Ohio Art Sports Tray, logo red & black, Home of the Stars		10.00	20.00
	---Rotblatt-Amrany Statue Order Form, retirement logo		5.00	10.00
*	---Ticket Stubs, receipt, United Center envelope		20.00	25.00
	---Wheaties Key Chain, MJ ball over head, retirement logo		10.00	20.00
	---Wilson #23 Golf Ball, retirement logo		10.00	25.00
	---Wincraft button & card, 23 white, red/black background, signature		10.00	20.00
	---UD MJ Tribute Night Red Card, 18,000 issued, 5 x 7		125.00	200.00
	---UD MJ Tribute Night White Card, 18,000 produced, 5 x 7		15.00	25.00
	---UD Rare Air Promo Card, towel head	NNO	5.00	10.00

Year	**Richard Rush**			
96	Above the Crowd Poster, 5,000 produced (7.197)	2083	20.00	35.00
	---Above the Crowd Certificate, Jireh Publishing Int.			
	---Above the Crowd Letter, R. Rush			
	---Folder			
96	MJ vs. Magic, Sheet & Folder (7.198)		20.00	35.00
	---MJ vs. Magic Certificate, Jireh Publishing Int.			
	---MJ vs. Magic Letter, R. Rush			
	---Folder			
-	MJ vs. Magic Postcard (7.199)		10.00	15.00

7.196

7.198

7.199

7.197

Year	Salvino Figurines-MJ			
95	Baseball #2004, facsimile signature, certificate, original generation, 8 issued, black uniform	master mold	1200.00	1500.00
95	Baseball #2004, facsimile signature, certificate, 16-20 issued, black uniform	prototype	1000.00	1300.00
95	Baseball #2004, facsimile signature, swinging bat black uniform, 2500 issued		175.00	250.00
95	Baseball #2005 SP, facsimile signature, certificate, original generation, 8 issued, pinstripe uniform	master mold	1200.00	1500.00
95	Baseball #2005 SP, facsimile signature, certificate, 16-20 issued, pinstripe uniform	prototype	1000.00	1300.00
95	Baseball #2005 SP, facsimile signature, swinging bat, pinstripe uniform, 343 issued		250.00	350.00
95	Baseball #2005 SP, hand signature, swinging bat, pinstripe uniform, 25 issued		1300.00	1500.00
95	Basketball #1074 UDA, facsimile signature, 2 poles, knees straight, 8 issued, red uniform, original generation certificate	master mold	1200.00	1500.00
95	Basketball #1074 UDA, facsimile signature, 2 poles, knees straight, 16-20 issued, red uniform, certificate	prototype	1000.00	1300.00
95	Basketball #1074 UDA, facsimile signature, 2 poles, knees straight, red uniform, 2500 issued		175.00	250.00
95	Basketball #1074 UDA, facsimile signature, 2 poles, knees straight, 8 issued, white uniform, certificate, original generation	master mold	1200.00	1500.00
95	Basketball #1074 UDA, facsimile signature, 2 poles, knees straight, 16-20 issued, white uniform, certificate	prototype	1000.00	1300.00
95	Basketball #1074 UDA, facsimile signature, 2 poles, knees straight, white uniform, 2500 issued		175.00	250.00
95	Basketball 700 UDA, facsimile signature, 1 pole, knees bend, 8 issued, white uniform, jumping, certificate, original generation	master mold	1200.00	1500.00
95	Basketball 700 UDA, facsimile signature, 1 pole, knees bend, 16-20 issued, white uniform, jumping, certificate	prototype	1000.00	1300.00
95	Basketball 700 UDA, facsimile signature, 1 pole, knees bend, white uniform, jumping, 318 issued		325.00	425.00
95	Basketball 700 UDA, hand signature, 1 pole, knees bent, white uniform, jumping, 50 issued		1300.00	1500.00
95	Basketball 700 UDA, facsimile signature, 1 pole, knees bent, 8 issued, red uniform, jumping, certificate, original generation	master mold	1200.00	1500.00
95	Basketball 700 UDA, facsimile signature, 1 pole, knees bent, 16-20 issued, red uniform, jumping, certificate	prototype	1000.00	1300.00
95	Basketball 700 UDA, hand signature, 1 pole, knees bent, red uniform, jumping, 368 issued		225.00	300.00

Year	Schick			
1992	USA Basketball Team Guide, BB Tournament of the Americas, 6/27-7/5, Portland, OR, sealed pack		8.00	10.00
	---David Robinson, on same card as Assistant Coach	5		
	---Assistant Coaches, on same card as #5	NNO		
	---Charles Barkley, on same card as #8	14		
	---Scottie Pippen, on same card as #14	8		
	---MJ, on same card as #15 (8.1)	9	3.00	4.00
	---Magic Johnson, on same card as #9	15		
	---Team Picture/MJ (8.2)	NNO	3.00	4.00

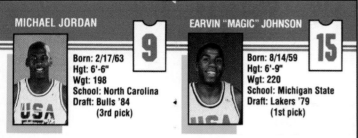

8.1

8.2

---John Stockton, on same card as Head Coach		12		
---Head Coach, on same card as #12		NNO		
---Chris Mullin, on same card as #7		13		
---Larry Bird, on same card as #13		7		
---Patrick Ewing, on same card as #11		6		
---Karl Malone, on same card as #6		11		

Year	School Folder			
89	School Folder, "Introducing Chicago Bulls Sponsorship Opportunities," inside Bulls vs. Celtics on scoreboard, team in warmups huddled together front, back crowd shots, inside MJ, Jackson, SP, Bull-et, Mascot & full court view	fold out	15.00	20.00

Year	Seat Belt			
	Ad Sheet, Seat Belts, holding seat belt in car, jump shot, yellow signature, MJ with hair, Ill. Safety Council, "The Winning Combination," Ill. Governor's Task Force (8.3)		5.00	
	Ad Sheet, Seat Belts, holding seat belt in car, jump shot, yellow signature, MJ with hair, UNC Highway Safety, NC Governors, NC HSAA, NC Seats Belts for Safety (8.4)		5.00	

Year	Sega Genesis			
92	NBC Sports Barcelona 92 Olympic Games		40.00	60.00
92	Game, Team USA Basketball, MJ cover, made by Electronic Arts	7148	40.00	60.00
92	Jordan vs. Bird, made by Electronic Arts (8.5)	7051	40.00	60.00
92	Box & directions, Bulls vs. Lakers and the NBA Playoffs, MJ on box, made by Electronic Arts	7099	40.00	60.00
93	Bulls vs. Blazers, no MJ on box, MJ in game		20.00	30.00
94	NBA Showdown 94, MJ on cover maybe		15.00	25.00

Year	Showtime			
	Showtime MJ Card, holding ball, red 23, silver border, black back with "Showtime" written on back (8.6)		5.00	

Year	Southtown Newspapers			
6/15/92	Economist, sports section only	cover	15.00	20.00
6/16/92	Daily Economist, "Twice is Nice, Chicago Bulls Do It Again"	inside	15.00	20.00
6/22/93	Daily Special Sports Section, "Bulls Champ"	inside	10.00	15.00
6/17/96	Daily, "Time 4 Rejoicing"	cover	6.00	8.00
	Sheet, Economist, "Fast Breaking Coverage"	cover	2.00	4.00

Year	Space Jam	item # or # items		
95-96	Ad flyer, MJ jumping, ball in RH with Tweety on top	8.5 x 11	4.00	8.00
95-96	Box, 60 Card Set, empty		1.00	2.00
95-96	Card, UDA MJ & Tune Squad, die-cut, 2 gold sparkle side stripes, gold sparkle signature, QVC-MJ/Tune characters back, black bottom stripe, border 3 sides, 5,000 produced, 3 x 5	#1	20.00	35.00
95-96	Card, UDA Space Jam MJ, Bugs & Skull, silver signature & border, MJ/Tune characters back, gold border around die-cut, 5,000 produced, 3 x 5	#2	20.00	35.00
95-96	Card, UDA Filmstrip, MJ/Bugs front, QVC-50,000 produced, 5 x 7		10.00	25.00
95-96	Card, UD Space Time, Half Time Heart Break	45	3.00	4.00

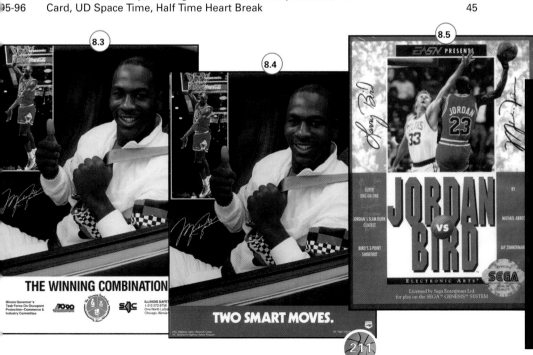

95-96	Cards, UD Jumbo Set, 3 x 5 cards	20 cards	20.00	30.00
95-96	Cards, UD Set, Series 1	60 cards	15.00	25.00
	---MJ on 19, 23, 34, 38, 41, 43, 45, 51, 52, 63, 54, 55, 57, 60			
	---Limited Edition Commemorative Sheet			
95-96	Cards, UD Set, Series 2	60 cards	25.00	35.00
	---MJ on 68, 73, 74, 79, 81, 83, 85, 88, 92, 96, 100, 103, 104			
95-96	Stickers, Space Jam, Baio	66 stickers	25.00	35.00
	---MJ on 6, 7, 8, 22, 24, 25, 26, 28, 29, 31, 38, 46, 49, 51, 57, 60, 63, 64, 65, 66			
95-96	Stickers, Cosmic Showdown, CS 1 through CS 30	30 stickers	15.00	20.00
	---MJ on 1, 3, 5, 6, 7, 8, 9, 11, 13, 15, 17, 19, 21, 23, 25, 26, 27, 29			
95-96	Cards, Jordan Silver Screens, JS 1 through JS 15	15 cards	75.00	125.00
95-96	Cards, Space Jam Scratchers, SC 1 through SC 9	9 cards	10.00	15.00
	---MJ	SC 2		
	---MJ	SC 7		
	---MJ	SC 8		
95-96	Cards, UD Sealed Packet	10 item	5.00	10.00
	---one 8 card pack			
	---1 collectible figure			
	---commemorative card, 5 x 7			
11/15/96	Newspaper, Scottsdale Life, "Air and the Hare"	cover	5.00	10.00
96	Ad, Playmates & WB Toys Items	foldout	2.00	4.00
96	Band Aid, open & packaged		3.00	6.00
96	Band Aid Box		1.00	2.00
96	Bath Set Label		2.00	4.00
96	Beverage Napkins, MJ picture, 9.87" x 9.87"	16 nap	3.00	5.00
96	Book Mark, MJ shooting overhead	26-504	3.00	5.00
96	Book Mark, MJ holding all Super Characters	26-505	3.00	5.00
96	Box, from JC Penny, Save $10.00 Coupon, Maze on bottom (8.7)		1.00	2.00
96	Cassette + 28 Page Book	2 items	10.00	15.00
96	Cards, UD Jam Time, Australian, connect to Ayala Center Air Pass & a raffle coupon, puzzles on card packs		60.00	75.00
	---Michael Gets a Physical	1	20.00	25.00
	---The Monstars Meet Their Match	2	20.00	25.00
	---The Rabbit is Revealed	3	20.00	25.00
96	Card, "Tune Squad Starting 5," Taz, Bugs, Daffy, Lola, MJ with hands on hips, brown BB court in background, MJ Bugs Lola, Taz, Daffy on back with positions by name (8.8)	3-3/8x 2-1/8 6-2221	5.00	10.00
96	Card, "Space Jam," Bugs, Daffy, Willy, with MJ head in background on right side, back with 4 "Ball Handling Tips" (8.9)	3-3/8 x 2-1/8 6-2222	5.00	10.00
96	Card, "Space Jam," purple Monstar, yellow Monstar, Bugs, & MJ shooting on right side, back with 3 "Shooting Drills" (8.10)	3-3/8 x 2-1/8 6-2223	5.00	10.00
96	CD Movie Soundtrack		15.00	20.00
96	Coin, MJ Bugs, Tweety & ?, with movie, 77 & 78 on back		5.00	10.00
96	Coupon, Aklaim, SJ The Video Game $5.00 Rebate		1.00	2.00
96	Coupon, Free T-Shirt/Poster, purple		1.00	2.00
96	Coupon, Slam In, Jamm In, Mail In Rebates, with movie		1.00	2.00

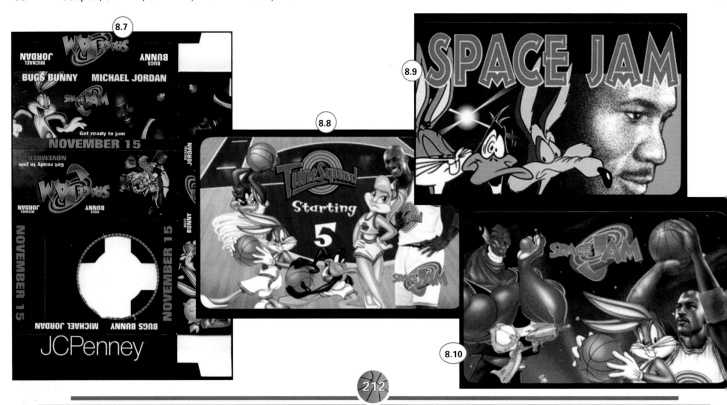

96	Dessert Plates, MJ picture, 7" diameter	8 plates	3.00	5.00
96	Flashlight, disposable, red, MJ on light	cover	5.00	10.00
96	Game, MJ's Cosmic Court, Playmates, Asst# 19010	19057	5.00	10.00
96	Hoop Set, Strato Slammer, ball net, basketball with slam meter		10.00	15.00
96	ID Card, MJ holding all characters	6-2225	2.00	.00
96	Pointed Banner, MJ picture	6 feet	10.00	15.00
96	Loot Bags, MJ picture, 6" x 7.25"	8 bags	3.00	5.00
96	Luncheon Napkins, MJ picture, 12.87" x 12.87"	16 nap	3.00	5.00
96	Luncheon Plates, MJ picture, 8.75" diameter	8 plates	3.00	5.00
96	Magnet, Space Jam Tune Squad-Bugs, Daffy, MJ, Road Runner		3.00	5.00
96	Mug, Ceramic Figural, Applause Inc.		6.00	12.00
96	Paper Cone Hats, Bugs popout ears	8 hats	3.00	5.00
96	Paper Cups, MJ picture, 9 oz.	8 cups	3.00	5.00
96	Party Pack, 6 Pin Set	81005	3.00	5.00
	---Bugs, Happy Birthday		20.00	25.00
	---MJ, Happy Birthday			
	---Daffy, Happy Birthday			
	---Space Man, Happy Birthday			
	---Taz, Happy Birthday			
	---She Rabbit, Happy Birthday			
96	Pillow, Poster Bed Pillow, black & multi-colored	17x17"	10.00	15.00
96	5 Pin Set, 2,500 produced		35.00	45.00
	---MJ & Bugs with BB, square like 3 sides			
	---MJ with BB & Taz with BB, oval like			
	---MJ & Porky with BB, oval like			
	---MJ with BB & Daffy, rectangle like			
	---Bugs, Girl Bunny, MJ & #, long rectangle			
96	Pin, closeup side view, basketball court in background	1681	3.00	5.00
96	Pin, MJ & Bugs, closeup		3.00	5.00
96	Pin, MJ & Bugs, closeup, 11/15		3.00	5.00
96	Placemat, 3 views, layup, 2 dribbling		3.00	5.00
96	Pog Set, Tazo, from Japan, one inserted in a snack bag, 2/jumbo, Movie Motion 3D pogs, slits on edge	80 pogs	45.00	75.00
	---"MJ Gets Kidnapped," 3D, purple back	1		
	---"Bugs Kisses Michael," 3D, purple back	2		
	---"Daffy The Ducktor," & MJ, 3D, purple back	3		
	---"MJ's Headache," 3D, purple back	4		
	---"Nerdlucks Jump 4 Joy," 3D, purple back	5		
	---"Monstars Mean Team," 3D, purple back	6		
	---"MJ Jams," 3D, purple back	7		
	---"Lola vs. Pound," 3D, purple back	8		
	---"MJ Plays Basketball," 3D, purple back	9		
	---"Bupkus Loses His Head," 3D, purple back	10		
	---"Sylvester vs. Tweety," 3D, purple back	11		
	---"Tweety Gets Flicked," 3D, purple back	12		
	---"Bang, Headbutts, Foghorn," 3D, purple back	13		
	---"The Tune Squad," 3D, purple back	14		
	---"Bugs Grows Muscles," 3D, purple back	15		
	---"Michael Jams #2," 3D, purple back	16		
	---"MJ Victory," 3D, purple back	17		
	---"Blanko & MJ," 3D, purple back	18		
	---"Yosemite Gets Zapped," 3D, purple back	19		
	---"MJ vs. Nawt," 3D, purple back	20		
	---"Bang," blue & green back	21		
	---"Bupkus," orange back	22		
	---"Blanko," purple & orange back	23		
	---"Pound," green back	24		
	---"Nawt," blue & green back	25		
	---"Monstars," pink back	26		
	---"Bang," blue & green back	27		
	---"Bupkus," orange back	28		
	---"Blanko," purple back	29		
	---"Pound," green back	30		
	---"Nawt," blue & green back	31		
	---"Nerdlucks," pink back	32		
	---"Space Jam," blue back	33		
	---"Space Jam," green back	34		
	---"Space Jam" & MJ, blue back	35		
	---"Tune Squad," orange back	36		
	---"Taz," brown back	37		
	---"Michael Jordan," purple back	38		
	---"Space Jam" & MJ, purple back	39		
	---"Tune Squad" & MJ, blue, red tan, & black back	40		

	Description		Low	High
	---"Michael Jordan," blue back	41		
	---"Space Jam" & MJ, green & yellow back	42		
	---"Space Jam" & MJ, yellow, pink & blue back	43		
	---"Michael Jordan," green back	44		
	---"Space Jam" & MJ, pink back	45		
	---"Space Jam" & MJ, green & pink back	46		
	---"Space Jam," blue back	47		
	---"Monstars," yellow back	48		
	---"Michael Jordan," pink, purple, yellow back	49		
	---"Michael Jordan," green back	50		
	---"Michael Jordan," orange back	51		
	---"Tune Squad," green back	52		
	---"Nerdlucks," green back	53		
	---"Bugs & Lola," blue back	54		
	---"Lola Bunny," pink back	55		
	---"Marvin the Martian," blue back	56		
	---"Swackhammer," purple back	57		
	---"Moron Air," purple back	58		
	---"Moron Mountain," purple back	59		
	---"Sludge Summit," brown back	60		
	---"Bang," 3D, blue back	61		
	---"Bupkus," 3D, green back	62		
	---"Blanko," 3D, pink back	63		
	---"Pound," 3D, purple back	64		
	---"Nawt," 3D, green back	65		
	---"Bang," 3D, blue back	66		
	---"Monstars," 3D, blue back	67		
	---"Nawt," 3D, green back	68		
	---"Nawt," 3D, blue back	69		
	---"Swackhammer," 3D, green back	70		
	---"Minion," 3D, purple back	71		
	---"Bugs & Lola," 3D, pink back	72		
	---"Looney Tunes," 3D, pink back	73		
	---"Space Jam," 3D, blue back	74		
	---"Taz," 3D, blue back	75		
	---"Marvin the Martian," 3D, orange back	76		
	---"Michael Jordan," 3D, red back	77		
	---"Michael Jordan," 3D, green back	78		
	---"Michael Jordan," 3D, blue back	79		
	---"Tune Squad" & MJ, 3D, pink back	80		
96	Puzzle, Playmates, 100 pieces	19060 & 19062	15.00	20.00
96	Sheet, magazine, Toys R Us, Playmates Toys		3.00	5.00
96	Shooting Drills Card, MJ shooting, Super tips on back	6-2223	3.00	5.00
96	Spiral Mobile	030352	3.00	5.00
96	Statue, Playmates, basketball, Blue uniform		5.00	10.00
96	Statue, Playmates, basketball, red left arm band, white shirt with Tune Squad Logo in middle, black shorts		5.00	10.00
96	Statue, Playmates, basketball, blue left arm band, white uniform with Tune Squad Logo in middle of shirt		5.00	10.00
96	Statue, Playmates, baseball, ready to swing bat, white pants, black cap & shirt with Tune Squad Logo in middle of shirt		5.00	10.00
96	Statue, Playmates, swinging golf club, gray pants, pink shirt, golf hat		5.00	10.00
96	Statue, Sports Figures, holding golf club left hand pink shirt & hat, gray pants, black stands	9"	10.00	15.00
96	Statue, Sports Figures, holding basketball right hand, white with red trim uniform, black stands	9"	10.00	15.00
96	Statue, Sports Figures, holding baseball bat right hand, black helmet & shirt, white pants, black stands	9"	10.00	15.00
96	Statue, Sports Figure Set, golf swing, dribbling, baseball swing, on one black stand	9" 17680	10.00	15.00
96	Statue, Sports Figure Set, Spanish with English Version, golf swing, dribbling, baseball swing, on one black stand	9" 1768090	10.00	15.00
96	Statue, Talking MJ, white with red & blue trim	14"	30.00	60.00
96	Statue, cloth, ACE Play By Play Company, #35306-95013	12"	20.00	30.00
96	Statue, Trophy Treats Basketball Gumballs-brown MJ head, Creative Confections Concepts		3.00	5.00
96	Statue, & Key Chain, holding ball	3"	3.00	5.00
96	Statue, holding ball	3"	3.00	5.00
96	Sticker, "Space Jam Get ready to jam," "November 15," MJ half face & name on left side, advertisement on Chicago Transit Authority Buses, made by FLEXcon BUSmark on right side, Bugs half face	12 feet x 30 inches	75.00	125.00
96	UD Poster, MJ & Bugs, mail in offer		5.00	10.00
96	UDA Jumbo Card, 1,000 produced	8.5x11	25.00	40.00

Year	Description	cd #		
96	Movie Folder		150.00	200.00
	---"Opening Announcement" sheets, "Space Jam, Starring MJ and BB to Open Here"	3 sheets		
	---"Warner Bros. Presents" sheet, "An Ivan Reitman/David F..."	1 sheets		
	---"Captions for the Alas Poor Bugs Sequence" sheet & photos	1 sheet, 6 photos		
	------MJ & stand in actor	A		
	------Bugs & head, rough animation 2 dimensional version	B		
	------Bugs & head, assistant animation, clean-up animation	C		
	------Bugs & head, rough effects animation, 3 dimensional	D		
	------Bugs & head, effects animation, cleaned-up version	E		
	------MJ, Bugs & head, composite, live with MJ & 3D Bugs	F		
	---Production Information, "Ehhh, what's up Doc?"	22 pages		
	---"The House That Bugs Built," The Warner Bros. Cartoon and How It Grew, by Joe Adamson	10 pages		
	------"The Evolution of Bugs Bunny, 1940-1990," photo	SJ-A3		
	---"The Technical Background to Space Jam," by Bill Warren	10 pages		
	---Bugs pointing finger to MJ photo	SJ-8		
	---Monstars & MJ, center court	SJ-17		
	---Bugs hands folded & MJ hands on hips	SJ-18		
	---Bill Murry, Bugs & MJ	SJ-19		
	---Theresa Randle and MJ	SJ-26		
	---MJ & Bill Murry with umbrella on head	SJ-27		
	---Wayne Knight & MJ in baseball Barons uniform	SJ-23		
	---MJ, Tune Squad, & Wayne Knight on basketball court	SJ-30		
	---MJ & Bugs with thumb out	SJ-31		
	---MJ & Tweety/Blanko & MJ, double photo	SH-32		
96-97	Coupon, Decals/Poster & Hanes	HT-042	2.00	4.00
2-3/97	Pamphlet, Video Reporter, cover & inside (8.11)	1612	2.00	4.00
97	Coupon, Free Pack of '96 Cards		2.00	3.00
97	Calendar, Landmark Manufacturer	5110	12.00	20.00
2/97	Sticker, Free Trading Card Inside Cap, Mail-In Offer	1.5x1	2.00	4.00

Year	Special Fun Cards-Broader Baseball	cd #		
88-89	MJ holding bat, red shirt, white pants, blue hat, tan border, blue border back, 84-89 statistics		1.50	2.00
88-89	Rated Rookie, White Sox white uniform, holding bat on right shoulder, white back with 84-89 statistics, Fun City Cards Inc.		1.50	2.00
88-89	Rated Rookie, White Sox white uniform, holding bat on right shoulder, white back with 84-89 statistics		1.50	2.00
89-90	MJ White Sox, red shirt, white pants, black to white border, swinging bat, pink back with 84-86 Bulls stats, converted baseball statistics		1.50	2.00
89-90	MJ White Sox, red shirt, white pants, black to white border, swinging bat, white back with 84-90 Bulls stats, converted baseball statistics		1.50	2.00
89-90	MJ White Sox, red shirt, white pants, black to white border, swinging bat, tan back with 84-90 Bulls stats, converted baseball statistics		1.50	2.00
89-90	MJ White Sox, red shirt, white pants, black to white border, swinging bat, blue back with 84-90 Bulls stats, converted baseball statistics		1.50	2.00
89-90	MJ White Sox, red shirt, white pants, blue undershirt, swinging, blue with black dots border, blue back with 84-90 Bulls statistics, converted baseball statistics		1.50	2.00
89-90	MJ White Sox, red shirt, white pants, blue undershirt, swinging, blue with black dots border, blue back with 84-90 Bulls statistics, converted baseball statistics		1.50	2.00
89-90	MJ & Bo, Major League Prospect, WS uniform, red shirt, white pants, blue borders, MJ & Bo statistics on tan back		1.50	2.00
89-90	Chicago's Finest, MJ & Bo Jackson & Frank Thomas, tan back with statistics		1.50	2.00
90	Chicago's Finest, MJ & Bo, gold border, MJ red shirt, white pants, Bo & MJ stats on tan back		1.50	2.00
90	Chicago's Finest, MJ & Bo, gold border, MJ red shirt, white pants, Bo & MJ stats on white back, 10,000 produced	2673	1.50	2.00
90	Major League Prospect, MJ & F. Thomas, blue back with Career Highlights and stats		1.50	2.00
90	MJ swinging bat, black & red border, red WS shirt, blue cap, MJ, Chicago White Sox, 1990, STAR		1.50	2.00
91	American Sports Monthly, MJ batting in red WS shirt white pants, swinging, front gold border, yellow stripes, blue back & MJ picture	44	5.00	8.00
92	Sports Edition, WS red shirt, white pants, blue cap uniform, swinging, 84-91 stats, 10,000 produced		5.00	8.00
92	Sports Edition, White Sox Baseball Uniform, 10,000 produced		5.00	8.00
92-93	MJ throwing ball in WS uniform with Chicago skyline background, red signature, back has MJ in red 23 basketball uniform flying over skyline ball in right hand	NNO	1.50	2.00
92-93	MJ throwing ball in WS uniform with Chicago skyline background,			

Year	Description	#		
	gold signature, back has MJ Highlights from ROY 84-85 to 3 MVPs 91-93, white back	NNO	1.50	2.00
92-93	Pro Sports LTD., MJ in black WS hat, MJ in white #23, gold name, signature & "Sox," back has same front picture, red to light red fade, 86-93 stats		1.50	2.00
92-93	Sports 3000, "Jordan 3000," MJ swinging bat, WS black shirt, white pants, gold signature & stripes, back picture same as front, 90-93 stats, red to white to blue		1.50	2.00
93	Cartoons Card, "Just Air Jordan, Nothing But Air," batting, back "Just Air Jordan" (8.12)	95	10.00	15.00
93	Final Look, swinging bat, 12 background pictures, WS pinstripe uniform, gold signature, orange to red back, "Miscellaneous Notes"		1.50	2.00
93-94	Stadium Sports Baseball			
	-Rated Rookie, full swing, WS pinstripe, purple to blue back		1.50	2.00
	-Rated Rookie, WS pinstripe, pitching, yellow to orange back (8.13)		1.50	2.00
	-Rated Rookie, half swing, WS pinstripe, red to white to blue back		1.50	2.00
	-Jordan 3000, full swing, gold signature and right side stripes, yellow to orange back		1.50	2.00
	-Rookie of the Year, silver signature & border & "Jordan," swinging bat, white pinstripe uniform	69	5.00	8.00
	-1993 Rookie of Year, gold signature & "Jordan," swinging bat, gold border, yellow to blue back		1.50	2.00
	-full swing, gold border, "Jordan" & signature, red to white to blue back		1.50	2.00
	-half swing, gold border "Jordan" & signature, yellow to red back		1.50	2.00
94	Frontier Sports 1994, gold signature & lettering			
	-baseball, locker room glove, back same front picture, purple to blue		1.50	2.00
	-swinging bat, WS pinstripe uniform, back same front picture, yellow to blue fade		1.50	2.00
94-95	MJ running, red shirt, white pants, glove in left hand, MJ batting, MJ catching fly ball, gold signature, "Jordan" with stars in it, story, "Basketballs Best 94-95," 10,000 produced	205	1.50	2.00
94-95	Sports Stars USA			
	-MJ in WS hat closeup, MJ in red #23 flying, gold signature, name and "Special Out Of Retirement...," "Special Out of Retirement Card Feb. 9, 1994," black signature on back	87	1.50	2.00
	-MJ in WS black shirt and pinstripe pants holding bat, background closeup, gold signature & name, "Michael Jordan Chicago White Sox" + story," white back	96	1.50	2.00
	-MJ in WS black shirt and pinstripe pants holding bat, background baseball, gold signature & name, "Michael Jordan Chicago White Sox" + story, white back	98	1.50	2.00

8.12

8.13

NOTHIN' BUT AIR

JUST AIR JORDAN

RATED ROOKIE

MICHAEL JORDAN

Description	cd # / # of cds		
-MJ in white pinstripe swinging bat, & closeup, gold signature, gold printed name, white back with story	108	5.00	8.00
-MJ in red #23, black WS, pinstripe WS uniforms, gold signature and "?" on front, white back & story	109	4.00	6.00
-MJ batting in WS black shirt and white pants, gold signature & "Jordan," "Michael Jordan Chicago White Sox" + story, white back	132	1.50	2.00
-"Barons Official Minor League Card," gold signature & lettering, black shirt, white pants, holding bat, white back/story/date	135	1.50	2.00
-Barons uniform, 2 poses, white back, information, 10,000 produced	153	1.50	2.00
Air Knows, red "Air," holding bat right shoulder, back red, brown & black "Air," white back gray border		1.50	2.00
Air Knows, red "Air," swinging bat, color, back red, brown & black "air," white back gray border		5.00	10.00
MJ & Bo, Major League Prospect, WS uniform, red shirt, white pants, blue borders, MJ 84-85 & Bo 83-85 statistics on back		1.50	2.00
MJ Knows Baseball, kid picture, pink back, info		2.00	3.00
MJ with bat on right shoulder, WS white shirt, blue cap, red/yellow letters on bottom, "MJ Guard CB," college 7 pro NBA stats		1.50	2.00
MJ batting, purple border, red WS shirt, white back, MJ Chicago Bulls, STAR Rated Rookie, White Sox white uniform, holding bat on right shoulder, back MJ in red 23, "Rookie of the Year" vs. Lakers #4, gray white & red borders		1.50 1.50	2.00 2.00
Sports Edition double sided card-MJ in black WS shirt, green border, back MJ in black WS shirt, black & white border, "White Sox Michael Jordan"		2.00	3.00
"The Chicago Daily Scam, Sox Sign Jordan," white back, information		1.50	2.00
Toon, Inc., MJ swinging bat, crowd in background, WS black shirt pinstripe pants, gold signature, back picture same as front, blue to black side to bottom borders, "Toon Inc."		1.50	2.00

Year	Special Fun Cards-Broader Basketball	cd # # of cds		
84	"Air Jordan MJ Co-Captian & Guard," AAMER Sports, dunking, Olympic #9 blue uniform, gold border, white back with 82-84 stats, personal info, 10,000 produced		1.50	2.00
84	USA, "Michael Jordan" in red stripe bottom right, jump shot in front of basket, USA #9, black card white back 84 US Olympic Team Gold Medal Winner story		1.50	2.00
84	"1984 United States Basketball Team" top, "Michael Jordan Guard" bottom, layup, pink back with 82-84 UNC stats, Missing Link Productions		1.50	2.00
84	"1984 United States Basketball Team" top, "Michael Jordan Guard" bottom, dribbling, pink back with 82-84 UNC stats, Missing Link Productions	2	1.50	2.00
84	"1984 United States Basketball Team" top, "Michael Jordan Guard" bottom, white back with 82-84 UNC stats, blurred front		1.50	2.00
84	"1984 United States Basketball Team" top, "Michael Jordan Guard" bottom, Error Card, white back with 82-84 UNC stats, blurred front		4.00	8.00
84	"1984 United States Olympic Team" top, "Michael Jordan" bottom, red & white border, USA red #9, "MJ (Drafted by Chicago Bulls), 1984 USA Olympic Team Member" on back		1.50	2.00
84	"1984 USA Olympic Basketball" top, "MJ Co-Captain Gold Winning Team" bottom, MJ red #9 USA uniform, gold front with stars, white back with statistics		4.00	8.00
84	"Showtime! 84," "Gold Michael Jordan," MJ wearing blue #9, gold background, white back with 81-84 statistics, black border		1.50	2.00
85-86	Big Bang, hands on knees, red #23, gold swirls next to red and white lines, red back, same front picture, 84-86 stats, "Big Bang Cards"		1.50	2.00
85-86	Big Bang, MJ holding ball, red #23, gold swirls next to red and white lines, red back, same front picture, 84-86 stats, "Big Bang Cards"		1.50	2.00
85-86	Big Bang Cards, jumping with ball, gold swirls, red & white strips, back red white & black stripes, 84-86 stats, MJ picture		1.50	2.00
85-86	Sports Journal, Fleer Reprint Card, MJ shooting, red #23, red blue, white borders, stats 84-86, red to white to pink back, personal info		1.50	2.00
88-89	All Sports Superstars, Series 1, "Air Jordan" bottom, with Dumars #4, blue border/jump shot-front, gray border with 88-89 statistics		1.50	2.00
88-89	All Sports Superstars Series II, "Michael Jordan" bottom, white #23, blue border/layup shot-front, gray border with 88-89 statistics		1.50	2.00
88-89	MJ cartoon, holding ball above head with right hand and with tail, red uniform, blue border back, 84-89 statistics		1.50	2.00
88-89	MJ cartoon, slam dunk with fire tail, red shirt, blue shorts, blue border back, "Can't touch this!!!"		1.50	2.00
88-89	MJ cartoon slam dunk & holding trophy, red uniform, blue border back, 84-89 statistics		1.50	2.00
88-89	MJ red border, white #23 uniform, vs. Pistons running, tongue out, dribbling, white back 84-89 stats,		1.50	2.00
88-89	MJ red border, red #23 uniform, jump shot to dunk, white back with 84-89 statistics		1.50	2.00

88-89	Sports Stars, Elite 1 shooting foul shot, red #23 uniform, orange/silver front border, gray back with 88-89 stats		1.50	2.00
88-89	Sports Stars, Elite 1 dribbling, tongue out, red #23 uniform, orange/silver front border, gray back with 88-89 stats		1.50	2.00
88-89	Sports Stars, Elite 2 dribbling, tongue out, red #23 uniform, blue/purple front border, gray back with 88-89 stats		1.50	2.00
88-89	Sports Stars, Elite 2 close up face shot, red uniform, smiling, blue/purple front border, gray back with 88-89 stats		1.50	2.00
88-89	Sports Stars, Premier, Limited Edition, dribbling with right hand & cutting, red #23, orange/blue/white border, green/army green back with 88-89 stats		1.50	2.00
88-89	Sports Stars, Premier, Limited Edition, dribbling left hand, red #23, orange/blue/white border, gray/army green back with 88-89 stats		1.50	2.00
89-90	All Sports Superstars Series III, "Michael Jordan" bottom, red #23, blue border/jump shot-front, gray border with 89-90 statistics		1.50	2.00
89-90	All Sports Superstars Series IV, "Michael Jordan" bottom, red #23, blue border/catching ball-front, gray border with 89-90 statistics		1.50	2.00
89-90	"Michael Jordan," blue border, #23 red uniform, holding ball, white back, stats, All-Sports Superstars Series IV		1.50	2.00
89-90	"Air Jordan," jumping to dunk, red & black shirt & pants, background Chicago skyline, white back with 84-90 stats		1.50	2.00
89-90	"Diamond Sports February," "$.10" red & yellow card, white shirt, red shorts, blue back with 84-90 statistics		1.50	2.00
89-90	"Michael Jordan G," gold & blue border, #23 white, dribbling, tongue out, with Pistons player white back, 89-90 stats, "Michael Jordan-G (Chicago Bulls)"		1.50	2.00
89-90	"Michael Jordan," white to red border with red spots, dribbling ball left hand, looking to side, red #23, white back, 84-90 stats, "MJ Guard (Chicago Bulls)"		1.50	2.00
89-90	"Michael Jordan," white to red border with red spots, red #23 vs. Nets #52, white back, 84-90 stats, "MJ Guard (Chicago Bulls)"		1.50	2.00
90	Art Works, "Michael Jordan," MJ shooting ball, closeup, pink & white border, "Sky's No Limit," Limited Edition 10,000 sets, Art Work 1990		5.00	10.00
90	Art Works, "Michael Moon Jordan," MJ with moon in left hand above the world, pink & white border, "Sky's No Limit," Limited Edition 10,000 sets, Art Work 1990		5.00	10.00
90	Austin Cards, MJ two poses, closeup and shooting, drawing like, white back with 89-90 stats (8.14)	2	5.00	10.00
90	Daytona Graphics Inc., "MJ Four In One," 4 pictures of MJ in UNC, USA, CB & NBA AS uniforms, gold border, Bulls, College and All-Star Statistics, white back with red border, 7,000 produced		4.00	8.00
90	Daytona Graphics Inc., "MJ Four In One," 4 pictures of MJ in UNC, USA, CB & NBA AS uniforms, red border with black stars, Bulls, College and All-Star Statistics, white back with red border		1.50	2.00
90	"Michael Jordan," red & black border, with black diamonds, red #23 uniform, MJ with Nets, dribbling, tongue out, white back with "Career Highlights" from 82-89		1.50	2.00
90	"Michael Jordan," red & black border, with black diamonds, red #23 uniform, MJ dunking, tongue out, white back with "NBA Regular Season Record" from 84-89		1.50	2.00
90	"Michael Jordan," white to red border with red dots, MJ red #23 dribbling ball vs. Nets #10 white "MJ Career Information," 85-90 information		1.50	2.00
90	"Michael Jordan," white to red border with red dots, MJ white #23 fighting for ball vs. Nets #10 blue, "MJ Career Information," 85-90 information		1.50	2.00
90	"Michael Jordan," white to red border with red dots, MJ red #23 passing the ball, "MJ Career Information," 85-90 information		1.50	2.00
90	"Michael Jordan '90 Best of the Best 12 Card Set," "Jordan '90," red and black stripes on borders	13 cards	15.00	20.00
	---Title Card, back blank, black center outline	NNO	1.00	1.50
	---dribbling, tongue out, red #23, back "Personal Data"	1	1.00	1.50
	---jumping to shoot, red #23, mouth open, back "Collegiate Record" 81-84 stats	2	1.00	1.50
	---dribbling, mouth open, red #23, back "NBA Regular Season Record," 84-89 stats	3	1.00	1.50
	---dribbling, full body picture, old red #23, hair, back "NBA Regular Season Record-Rebounds," 84-89 stats	4	1.00	1.50
	---dunking with Jazz player, red #23, back "NBA Regular Season Record-3 Pt. F. G.," 84-89 stats	5	1.00	1.50
	---holding ball, red #23, #33 S. Pippen in background, back: "NBA Playoff Record," 84-89 stats	6	1.00	1.50
	---dunking, red #23, back: "NBA Playoff Record-Rebounds" 84-89 stats	7	1.00	1.50
	---dribbling, red #23, back: "NBA All-Star Game Record," 85-90 stats	8	1.00	1.50
	---holding ball, tongue out, red #23, back: "NBA All-Star Game Record-Rebounds, 85-90 stats	9	1.00	1.50

8.14

Michael Jordan   F

Year	Description	Card #	Low	High
	---dribbling with right hand, red #23, full pose, back: "Career Highlights," 85-88 information	10	1.00	1.50
	---closeup shot with hair, red uniform, back: "Career Highlights," 82-89 information	11	1.00	1.50
	---dribbling, tongue out, left hand on hip, red #23 back: "Career Highlights," 84-90 information	12	1.00	1.50
90	MJ Set, black & gold border with 3 gold triangles on sides	9 cards	15.00	20.00
	---holding ball overhead with two hands, NC #23 white & blue uniform, back: Collegiate Record, tan border, 81-84 stats		1.75	2.25
	---holding ball overhead with two hands, NC #23 white & blue uniform, back: Collegiate Record, tan border & writing, 81-84 stats		1.75	2.25
	---holding ball overhead with two hands, NC #23 white & blue uniform, back: Collegiate Record, black border & writing, 81-84 stats		1.75	2.25
	---holding ball with one hand, red #23, "Air Jordan" bottom, back: NBA Regular Season Record, 84-90 stats, tan border & writing		1.75	2.25
	---shooting ball over Rockets player, "Michael Jordan" bottom, back: NBA All-Star Game Record, 85-90 stats, tan border & writing		1.75	2.25
	---dunking ball, red #23, "Michael Jordan" back: NBA Playoff Record, 84-90 stats, tan border & writing bottom		1.75	2.25
	---cartoon like MJ in red #23, jumping with ball, #17 & #11 in picture, "Air Express" bottom, back: coins, $100 bill, MJ with arms extended to side, "They call him Money"		1.75	2.25
	---cartoon like MJ in red #23, jumping with ball, #17 & #11 in picture, "Air Express" bottom, back: "When it has to get there, send it air express," tan border & letters		1.75	2.25
	---cartoon like MJ in red #23, jumping with ball, #17 & #11 in picture, "Air Express" bottom, back: "When it has to get there, send it air express," tan border & letters		1.75	2.25
90	"Michael Jordan Chicago Bulls 1990," red uniform, tongue out, dribbling, white back with green statistics, "1990 NBA Superstars"		1.50	2.00
90	"Michael Jordan Chicago Bulls 1990," red uniform, tongue out, layup shot, side view, white back with green statistics, "1990 NBA Superstars"		1.50	2.00
90	"Michael Jordan Chicago Bulls 1990," white #23, reaching, mouth open, white back with green statistics, "1990 NBA Superstars"		1.50	2.00
90	"Michael Jordan Chicago Bulls 1990," red uniform, running, dribbling, jumping, Heat players, white back with blue statistics, "1990 NBA Superstars"		1.50	2.00
90	"Michael Jordan Chicago Bull 1990," red #23, dribbling, standing, mouth open, white back with blue statistics, "1990 NBA Superstars"		1.50	2.00
90	"Michael Jordan Chicago Bull 1990," red #23, grabbing ball, mouth open, white back with black statistics, "1990 NBA Superstars"		1.50	2.00
90	"Michael Jordan Chicago Bull 1990," red #23, under basket, dunking, mouth open, tongue out, white back with black statistics, "1990 NBA Superstars"		1.50	2.00
90	"Michael Jordan Chicago Bull 1990," red #23, layup shot, side view, vs. Thorpe, white back with black statistics, "1990 NBA Superstars"		1.50	2.00
90	"Michael Jordan Chicago Bull 1990," red #23, dribbling with left hand, vs. Blazers, white back with black statistics, "1989-1990 NBA Basketball Superstars," Wastach Cards	1 of 5	1.50	2.00
90	"Michael Jordan Chicago Bull 1990," red #23, dunk shot under basket, tongue out, white back with black statistics, "1989-1990 NBA Basketball Superstars," Wastach Cards	5 of 5	1.50	2.00
90	"Michael Jordan 1990," red #23, standing with ball at foul line, white back with black letters, "Basketball All-Stars 89-90," Wastach Cards	1 of 24	1.50	2.00
90	"Michael Jordan 1990," red #23, standing with hand on knees, side view, white back with black letters, "Basketball All-Stars 89-90," Wastach Cards	2 of 24	1.50	2.00
90	"Michael Jordan 1990," red #23, dunk shot from side of basket, white back with black letters, "Basketball All-Stars 89-90," Wastach Cards	3 of 24	1.50	2.00
90	"Michael Jordan 1990,"shooting layup front view, Wastach Card, white back, "Basketball All-Stars 89-90"	3 of 24	1.50	2.00
90	Sport Cards, Inc., close up picture, white uniform "MJ 1990 Superstar #1 Limited Edition 10,000"	1 of 20	1.50	2.00
90	Sport Cards, Inc., layup, white #23, "MJ 1990 Superstar #1 Limited Edition 10,000"	7 of 20	1.50	2.00
90	Sport Cards, Inc., jumping with ball, white #23 "MJ 1990 Superstar #1 Limited Edition 10,000"	13 of 20	1.50	2.00
90	Sport Cards, Inc., layup from side of basket, white #23 vs. Garland, "MJ 1990 Superstar #1 Limited Edition 10,000"	20 of 20	1.50	2.00
90	Sport Cards, Inc., defense vs. Thomas, white #23, "MJ 1990 Superstar #2 Limited Edition 10,000"	1 of 10	1.50	2.00
90	Sport Cards, Inc., 2 pictures-one closeup, one standing, red 23, "MJ 1990 Superstar #2 Limited Edition 10,000"	2	1.50	2.00
90-91	"Air Jordan," blue sky over the world, jumping to dunk, green #23 uniform, white back with 84-91 statistics		1.50	2.00
90-91	"Michael Jordan," gold border, dunking, white #23, white back with 84-91 stats		1.50	2.00
90-91	"Michael Jordan Chicago Bulls 1990-91," shooting & jumping with ball in right hand, red 23, "1990 Sports Superstars MJ CB," 88-89 stats, white back blue letters	8 of 14	1.50	2.00

219

Year	Description	Number	Price 1	Price 2
90-91	MVP "Michael Jordan Chicago Bulls 1990-1991," shooting, red 23, NBA BB Superstars MJ CB MVP	1 of 7	1.50	2.00
90-91	MVP "Michael Jordan Chicago Bulls 1990-1991," closeup, red 23, NBA BB Superstars MJ CB MVP	2 of 7	1.50	2.00
90-91	MVP "Michael Jordan Chicago Bulls 1990-1991," dribbling right hand, red 23, NBA BB Superstars MJ CB MVP	3 of 7	1.50	2.00
90-91	MVP "Michael Jordan Chicago Bulls 1990-1991," dribbling left hand, red 23, NBA BB Superstars MJ CB MVP	4 of 7	1.50	2.00
90-91	"League MVP, Championship MVP, MJ & Chicago Bulls, 90-91 World Champions," white back with 84-90 statistics, AAMER Sports, 10,000 produced		1.50	2.00
90-91	Slam Dunk, "Michael Jordan Best of the Best 1990-91, 12 Card Set," front gold borders with black, gold and red side strips, back orange border white center	15 cards	15.00	22.00
	---title card, back: "Personal Data"	NNO	1.00	1.50
	---golfing, blue shirt, white hat & pants, back: "Golf Data"	1	1.00	1.50
	---UNC #23 blue uniform, slam dunk shot, back: "Collegiate Record," 81-84 stats	2	1.00	1.50
	---USA #5, slam dunk shot, back has "1984 Olympic Stats," black border	3	1.00	1.50
	---red White Sox shirt, white pants, holding bat, blue hat, back: "NBA Regular Season Record," 84-90 stats	4	1.00	1.50
	---golfing, swinging club, white vest, shirt & pants, red hat, back: "NBA Regular Season Record-Rebounds," 84-90 stats	5	1.00	1.50
	---jumping holding ball overhead with right hand, side view, flames on ball, back: "NBA Regular Season Record-3 Pt. F. G.," 84-90 stats	6	1.00	1.50
	---USA black #5, jumping with ball, 4 other players, back: "NBA All-Star Game Record," 85-90 stats	7	1.00	1.50
	---jumping hold ball backwards shot to hoop, red #23, back: "NBA All-Star Game Record-Rebounds," 85-90 stats	8	1.00	1.50
	---hook shot over Lakers player, red #23, back: "NBA Playoff Record," 84-90 stats	9	1.00	1.50
	---dunk shot, back shirt, red shorts, back: "NBA Playoff Record," 84-90 stats	10	1.00	1.50
	---dribbling, red #23, tongue out, back: "Career Hightlights," 85-90 information	11	1.00	1.50
	---jump shot, red #23, with hair, back: "Career Hightlights," 85-90 information	12	1.00	1.50
90-91	Star, dribbling with left hand, tongue out, red #23, gold border, blue bottom, white back with "MJ, CB, 90-91, STAR"		1.00	1.50
90-91	Star, passing ball, tongue out, red #23, gold border, blue bottom, white back with "MJ, CB, 90-91, STAR"		1.00	1.50
90-91	Star, defending, white #23, bending over, gold border, blue bottom, white back with "MJ, CB, 90-91, STAR"		1.00	1.50
90-91	Star, dribbling, white #23, bending over, white back with "MJ, CB, 90-91, STAR"		1.00	1.50
90-91	Star, reaching, tongue out, red #23, white back with "MJ, CB, 90-91, STAR"		1.00	1.50
90-91	Star, holding the ball, white #23, mouth open, white back with "MJ, CB, 90-91, STAR"		1.00	1.50
90-91	Star, arm on head, purple border, white #23, yelling, white back with "MJ, CB, 90-91, STAR"		1.00	1.50
90-91	Star, jumping with ball, red #23, purple border, white back with "MJ, CB, 90-91, STAR"		1.00	1.50
91	America's Finest Card Company, 2 black & white poses of MJ, white back 84-90 stats		5.00	10.00
91	Artwork, "Michael Jordan -watercolor 1991," bending over with hands on knees, b&w, Gerald Jay Tysver, information about him, address of company	5	5.00	10.00
91	Cardboard Dreams, "Michael Jordan," 2 views, closeup in white shirt, dunking in red #23, white border, blue back, "MJ goes deep at WS batting practice" cartoon, "Michael says: "I think I'll make a couple more commercials"	8 of 16	5.00	10.00
91	Japanese Dream Team, hand on knees		1.50	2.00
91	Michael Jordan Jr. Set, red/gold borders	9 cards	15.00	20.00
	---front pose, dribbling, red #23, back: "On Tempo," Mike Powell/Allsport USA	1	1.50	2.00
	---side pose, tongue out, dribbling, red #23, back: "On Basketball," Mike Powell/Allsport USA	2	1.50	2.00
	---front pose, passing, red #23, back: "On Magic Johnson," Nathaniel Butler/NBA Photos	3	1.50	2.00
	---hands on knees, white #23, back: "On Perception," Nathaniel Butler/NBA Photos	4	1.50	2.00
	---walking, white #23, back: "On His Favorite Fans," Nathaniel Butler/NBA Photos	5	1.50	2.00
	---front pose, jumping, dribbling, red #23, back: "On The Future of The Game," Andrew D. Bernstein/NBA Photos	6	1.50	2.00
	---side pose, shooting, white #23, back "On His Success Formula," J. Daniel/Allsport USA	7	1.50	2.00
	---talking in to microphones, back "On Role Models," Andrew D. Berstein/NBA Photos	8	1.50	2.00
	---shooting to dunk, red #23, back-goal story, 1991 Final Record, Jerry Wachter	9	1.50	2.00
91	MJ, dunking, red #23, red & black border, black diamonds, white back with "NBA All-Star Game Record," 85-90 information		1.50	2.00
91	MJ, shooting the globe, red & black border, black diamonds, white back with "Career Highlights," 84-90 information		1.50	2.00
91	MJ, standing with hands on hips, red & black border, black diamonds, white back with "Career Highlights," 84-90 information		1.50	2.00

91	MJ, going after ball, white #23, pink/white border white back with "Career Highlights," 84-90 information,		1.50	2.00
91	"MVP Michael Jordan," holding trophy in suit, red borders, "Michael J. Jordan, NBA MVP 1990-1991 Season," white back		1.50	2.00
92	"Michael Jordan," holding flowers in Olympic uniform, smiling, "Michael Jordan USA 1992 Gold Medal Winner Barcelona, Spain," gray back with gold border & lettering		1.50	2.00
92	Sports Edition, USA #9 MJ & USA #15 Magic, 10,000 produced		4.00	8.00
92	Sports Edition, MJ & trophy, 10,000 produced		4.00	8.00
92-93	MJ shooting with Shaq behind, two gold signatures, white #23, MJ 86-93 stats, Shaq 89-92 stats, white back with black name bars		1.50	2.00
92-93	Pro Sports LTD, 2 poses, color and b&w, gold signature & "Jordan" & "Greatest Ever Retired 10/6/93," purple to blue back, 86-93 stats		1.50	2.00
92-93	Sports Journal, shooting, black card, gold signature, red back, MJ picture, 86-93 stats		1.50	2.00
93	American Holding Company Sets, gold signatures			
	---MJ grabbing ball, # of 10,000 sets	C of A	6.00	10.00
	---MJ jumping to shoot, # of 10,000 sets	1 of 5	6.00	10.00
	---MJ hands on knees, # of 10,000 sets	2 of 5	6.00	10.00
	---MJ kissing trophy, # of 10,000 sets	3 of 5	6.00	10.00
	---MJ swinging golf club, # of 10,000 sets	4 of 5	6.00	10.00
	---MJ dribbling in AS game, # of 10,000 sets	5 of 5	6.00	10.00
93	"American Sports 93 Monthly," white Olympic uniform & jacket, holding flowers, white back, same front picture & personal info, oval		1.50	2.00
93	"American Sports 93 Monthly," black Olympic #9, jumpshot, white back, same front picture & personal info, oval		1.50	2.00
93	"American Sports 93 Monthly," white USA #9 Olympic, holding ball standing, white back, same front picture & personal info, oval		1.50	2.00
93	"American Sports 93 Monthly," white USA #9 Olympic, dunking at rim, white back, same front picture, & person info, oval		1.50	2.00
93	Frontier Card, MJ flying in air over Chicago Skyline, ball in right hand, same front picture b&w on back, "Frontier Sports gives you the news before its news-we are a new frontier"		1.50	2.00
93	"Greatest Ever Retired Oct. 6, 1993," reaching for ball, white #23, "MJ Guard Chicago," stats 91-93, white back		1.50	2.00
93	"Greatest Ever Retired Oct. 6, 1993," dunking, red #23, "MJ Highlights," stats 84-93, black top, white bottom		1.50	2.00
93	"Greatest Ever Retired Oct. 6, 1993," dribbling, red #23, tongue out, "MJ Guard Chicago," stats 86-93, black top, white bottom on back		1.50	2.00
93	"Greatest Ever, Retired Oct. 6, 1993," dribbling in red #23, tongue out, gold signature, back-white back, black top, 86-93 stats	NNO	1.50	2.00
93	"Greatest Ever Retired Oct. 6, 1993," shooting, red #23, mouth open, "MJ Guard Chicago," stats 91-93, black middle stripe, white back		1.50	2.00
93	"Greatest Ever Retired Oct. 6, 1993," reaching mouth open, plane, closeup smiling, red uniform, "MJ Guard Chicago," stats 91-93, black middle stripe, white back		1.50	2.00
93	"Greatest Ever, Retired Oct. 6, 1993," flying with ball, 2nd picture closeup, red #23, blue background, white back with black stripe, 91-93 stats	NNO	1.50	2.00
93	"Michael Makes Retirement Official," gold letters & signature, MJ in suit & mics, "The Greatest Player that ever lived," Retirement announced October 6, 1993," white back		1.50	2.00
93	Skinny Retirement Cards			

(8.15)

scottie pippin   chicago
"THE CADDY"

	---#1, "High Flying Mike," red #23, holding ball with tongue out, 2-3/4 x 3-3/4	120	2.00	3.00
	---#2, "His Roller Coaster Year," gambling with dice, 2-3/4 x 3-3/4	119	2.00	3.00
	---#3, "Farewell," in suit with microphones, 2-3/4 x 3-3/4	118	2.00	3.00
	---#4, "Mr. Endorsement," Wheaties box, Gatorade shirt, 2-3/4 x 3-3/4	168	2.00	3.00
	---#5, "Field of Dreams," baseball uniform, 2-3/4 x 3-3/4	NNO	2.00	3.00
	---V. Maxwell, Houston Mad Max/MJ, 2-3/4 x 3-3/4	5	1.50	2.00
	---S. Pippen, Chicago The Caddy/MJ, 2-3/4 x 3-3/4 (8.15)	22	1.50	2.00
	---C. Ehlo, Atlanta Burn Victim/MJ, 2-3/4 x 3-3/4	40	1.50	2.00
	---H. Miner, Miami Can't Touch/MJ, 2-3/4 x 3-3/4	57	1.50	2.00
	---A. Johnson, San Antonio/MJ, 2-3/4 x 3-3/4	81	1.50	2.00
	---T. Kukoc, Chicago Bag Boy/MJ, 2-3/4 x 3-3/4	151	1.50	2.00

Year	Description	#		
93	Sports Edition, 10/6/93 Retirement Cards, Gold Signatures			
	---"American Dream," cartoon like card, dunking, "MJ The Greatest BB Player that has ever lived," yellow to blue fade		1.50	2.00
	---jumping with ball, white shirt, black shorts, gold "Jordan," border & signature, 10,000 produced		2.00	3.00
	---jumping with ball, purple & blue shirt & pants, gold "Michael," border, & signature, 10,000 produced		1.50	2.00
	---laughing, white shirt, gold "Greatest Ever Retired Oct. 6, 1993," gold "Michael," border & signature, 10,000 produced		2.00	3.00
	---shooting, white #23, gold "Special Retirement Card," gold "Jordan" & signature		1.50	2.00
	---drinking Gatorade, red uniform, holding cup, gold border, signature, "Greatest Ever Retired Oct. 6, 1993, back yellow and blue background, MJ picture, highlights from 84-93		1.50	2.00
	---shooting, 2 poses, red shirt & BW photo, gold "Jordan," signature & "Greatest Ever Retired Oct. 6, 1993," back yellow and blue background, MJ picture, 86-93 stats		1.50	2.00
	---pointing, repeats layup picture 16 times, red uniform		1.50	2.00
93	Sports Stars, arms folded, BB background, gold "Michael," "Special Retirement Card," gold signature & "Greatest Ever Retired Oct. 6, 1993," white back, 15,000 produced		2.00	3.00
93-94	Arena Sports, MJ dunking, white #23, view from above rim, gold signature, name & "Retired Oct 6, 1993, white back, "Michael Jordan Special Retirement Card," black signature		1.50	2.00
93-94	Arena Sports, MJ dunking, red #23, view from side, gold border, name & signature, "MJ #23 Chicago Bulls," "His gravity defying...," white back	72	1.50	2.00
93-94	Arena Sports, MJ drinking Gatorade, red #23, gold border, name, signature, & Greatest Ever Retired Oct 6, 1993, "MJ #23 Chicago Bulls," "His gravity defying...," white back	83	1.50	2.00
93-94	Sports Stars USA, gold signature			
	---"3 Peat" MJ with trophy, cigar and white hat, red uniform, "MJ, #23, CB," "His gravity defying...," 15,000 produced		1.50	2.00
	---"3 Peat" MJ with hands in air, holding ball in left, red #23, "MJ, #23, CB," "His gravity defying...," 15,000 produced		1.50	2.00
	---"Jordan" MJ going for a dunk, picture from above basket, white uniform, "MJ, #23, CB," "His gravity defying...," 15,000 produced		1.50	2.00
	---"Michael Jordan" MJ jumping in air with ball in right hand, background closeup head picture, "MJ, #23, CB," "His gravity defying...," 15,000 produced		1.50	2.00
	---MJ with hands on knees, gold signature, white back with blue sides, info in center, name on sides		1.50	2.00
94	Competitive Images	8 cards	15.00	24.00
	---holding ball	1	2.00	3.00
	---3 poses	2	2.00	3.00
	---jump shot	3	2.00	3.00
	---jumping with ball	4	2.00	3.00
	---Mike, 2 poses	5	2.00	3.00
	---3 poses	6	2.00	3.00
	---jumping with ball over Chicago skyline	7	2.00	3.00
	---3 poses, jumping	8	2.00	3.00
94	Frontier Sport Cards, Gold Signature			
	---basketball, shooting, t-shirt, back same front picture, red to white to blue		1.50	2.00
	---basketball, defense, red uniform, back same front picture, red to white to blue		1.50	2.00
	---basketball, underhand shot, "Greatest Ever Retired Oct. 6, 1993," back same front picture but b&w		1.50	2.00
	---basketball, right hand jump shot, "Greatest Ever Retired Oct. 6, 1993," back same front picture but b&w		1.50	2.00
94	Pantech, Inc, 3D Sheet, jump shot, side view, white 23, blue to green background on front, sheet size, white back, MJ CB 1984-1993 Now writing a new page in baseball, 1994, 8.5 x 11		15.00	20.00
94	Pantech, Inc, 3D Card, jump shot, side view, white 23, blue to green background on front, regular size, white to red back, MJ CB 1984-1993 Now writing a new page in baseball, 1994.		15.00	20.00
-	"Air Jordan" MJ, world in background, gold signature, Nitro Ltd., Inc., dunk shot, New York #21		1.50	2.00
-	"Air Knows," MJ jump shot right hand, red #23 & "Air," "Air Jordan" on back, red to black "Air"		4.00	8.00
-	"Air Jordan" on back, pencil like drawing, MJ shooting foul-like shot, "Bulls 23" upper left corner, white back, "Air Jordan" in black line outline		4.00	8.00
-	American Flag in background, side view, tongue out, standing, red #23, white back "Dream Team USA Michael Jordan"		1.50	2.00
-	Big Kids at the Bank, MJ $926 per point, 3 other players-Clemens, Montana, Hull, More Mega Salaries, Tyson, Sandberg, Stewart, & Johnson on white back		3.00	5.00

Bo spinning ball, MJ dribbling, red #23, white back "Bo Knows Jordan"	1.00	2.00
Cartoon Card, MJ holding ball, running, blocking with hand, back blue border, white middle, "Can't Touch This"	1.00	2.00
"Double Trouble" MJ & D. Robinson holding ball, blue background, white back with stats and info on both	1.00	2.00
"Double Double Trouble" on back, 4 poses of MJ on front, red border, UNC, USA, Bulls, NBA AS	1.00	2.00
"Hare Jordan," Bugs & MJ, white back	1.50	2.00
"Hare Jordan," Bugs in basket with carrot & MJ with ball, white back with "Hare Jordan"	1.50	2.00
"Hare Jordan," Bugs kissing MJ in center of orange circles, white back with "Hare Jordan"	1.50	2.00
"Hare Jordan," Bugs with carrot, MJ with ball standing, white back with "Hare Jordan"	1.50	2.00
"Jam & Slam," two MJ pictures on front, "Just Do It" on white back, BB court in background,	1.50	2.00
"Jordan/Shag," "Air to Throne," blue back, same front picture	1.50	2.00
"Legends Michael Jordan," dunk shot, red #23, gray border, white back, "Living Legend"	1.50	2.00
"Lord of the Rings," 5 Rings, 5 USA Team Members-MJ & Ewing & Magic & Malone & Barkley, standing, "Dream Team USA" plus 5 names	1.50	2.00
"Lord of the Rings," 5 Rings, 5 USA Team Members-Barkley & Magic & Ewing & MJ & Malone, closeup, "Dream Team USA" plus 5 names	1.50	2.00
MJ standing, hands on hips, red #23, orange border, white back, "Living Legend"	1.50	2.00
MJ standing, dribbling with left hand, red #23, orange border, white back, "Living Legend"	1.50	2.00
MJ closeup, red #23, blue border, white back, "Living Legend" Series 1 — 10	1.50	2.00
MJ running with #42 of Magic, gray top and bottom, red stars top, white back, "Living Legend"	1.50	2.00
MJ jumping with #25 Anderson of Magic, red #23, orange border, white back, "Living Legend"	1.50	2.00
MJ floorshot, warmup, orange border, white back, "Living Legend"	1.50	2.00
MJ flying in air on Chicago Skyline, reaching for ball in right hand, gold name & signature, "MJ #23 Chicago," "His gravity-defying..."white back	1.50	2.00
MJ holding trophy in brown suit, sky in background, blue back with "He's Out of This World"	1.50	2.00
MJ looking up at basket and ball, nothing on back	1.50	2.00
MJ 2 poses, closeup & dribbling, red #23, white back, 2 black line borders	1.50	2.00
MJ #9 USA & D. Robinson, USA, MJ dribbling, blue border, MJ & DR personal information on back, DR shooting, red to white to purple border	1.50	2.00
"Michael Knows," red #23, ball with fire hanging from hand, brown border, white back, "Michael Knows Offense"	1.50	2.00
"Michael Knows," MJ and Ewing, red #23, white back, "Michael Knows Defense"	1.50	2.00
"Michael Knows," white #23, dunking, white back, "Michael Knows Slam Dunk!!!"	1.50	2.00
"Michael Knows," holding trophy, red #23, white back, "Michael Knows Slam Dunk Competition"	1.50	2.00
MJ dunking, red & black shirt & pants, BB court in disco setting, blue back, Spectacular, Stupendous, Unbelievable!	1.50	2.00
MJ jumping in air and closeup, blue sky like background, black out bottom front edge, back has "Kodak Royal Paper," nothing else	4.00	6.00
MJ jumping to basket in three images, red, yellow & black stripes, black border, back has "Kodak Royal Paper," nothing else	4.00	6.00
Michael Jordan & Scottie Photo	1.50	2.00
"MVPs Michael Jordan," holding ball, red #23, silver and black border, red & white back, info & NBA record	3.00	5.00
Nitro Elite, white uniform, gold foil & same front picture, red corners upper left and lower right, "Nitro Elite" signature, close up shot,	4.00	6.00
Nitro Elite, white uniform, red foil & signature, close up shot, same front picture, red corners upper left and lower right, "Nitro Elite"	4.00	6.00
5 Olympic Rings, 5 USA Team Members-MJ & Ewing & Magic & Malone & Barkley, black borders, blue back "Going for the Gold" on back	1.50	2.00
5 Olympic Rings, 5 USA Team Members-MJ & Ewing & Magic & Malone & Barkley, gold border, blue back "Going for the Gold" on back	1.50	2.00
"Sports Edition Top Gun," USA white #9, gold signature & border, gray back, same front picture	3.00	5.00
"Sports Edition Top Gun," jumping, dunking, red #23, gold border & signature, gray back, same front picture	2.00	4.00
"Michael Jordan Sports Edition," silver border, dunking white uniform, blue back, same front picture	1.50	2.00
Sports Edition, MJ with trophy and 3!, gold signature, blue to purple back MJ picture, story	3.00	5.00
Sports Edition, MJ dunking with tongue out, insert catching baseball, gold signature, same front pictures on back, red to white to blue fade	3.00	5.00

-	Sports Edition II, MJ & Shaq pointing to each other, gold background, red signatures, "No, You Are the Man," red to pink fade, gray letters	3.00	5.00
-	Sports Journal, MJ rookie card, red #23, red blue white border, ed back, reprint of Fleer, 84-86 stats	3.00	5.00
-	"Sports Weekly Trivia Card Series," MJ dribbling with left hand, red #23, tongue out, trivia questions on back, red to white, MJ holding ball	15.00	20.00
-	"Top Picks," Magic & MJ, college uniforms, white back with blue border, info on each	1.50	2.00

Year — Special Fun Cards-Broader Football

-	Super Rookie MJ, MJ throwing a football in street clothes & tongue out, blue back, nickname Crazylegs, quote from Don McGuire, Ammer Sport (8.16)	2.00	3.00

Year — Special Fun Cards-Broader Golf

-	Air Knows II, green "Air II," golfing, back green & black "air," white back, gray border	1.50	2.00
-	MJ Knows, brown shirt, Maxfli hat, holding golf club, white back, "Michael Knows Golf" (8.17)	1.50	2.00
-	MJ Knows Golf, green border, swinging, pift helmet, green back, information	2.00	3.00
-	Sports Scoops, Jordan Eyes PGA Senior Tour, red signature white back MJ story, 10,000 set produced	1.50	2.00
-	Same picture as Sports Scoops Card, but larger, red signature, white back MJ story, 10,000 set produced	1.50	2.00

Year — Special Fun Cards-Broader Miscellaneous

Year		card #		
90-91	Gold border, cowboy outfit, white back with 84-91 stats		1.50	2.00
90-91	Gold border, yellow hair, black leather jacket, back with 84-91 stats		1.50	2.00
91	Legends Sports Memorabilia, red Nike shirt, hand folded, white, gray back, MJ story	11	3.00	5.00
93	Arena Sports			
	-MJ Christmas outfit, gold border & signature, closeup, white back, "Sincere Wishes for A Merry Christmas and a Happy New Year from MJ"		1.50	2.00
	-MJ Christmas outfit with ball under right arm, balls in front, gold border & signature, white back, MJ Special Christmas Card, Arena Sports 1993, 15,000 produced		1.50	2.00
93	High School Heroes II Set, 30 cards, red borders, 5,000 set produced	553	20.00	35.00
	---MJ in suit, close up (8.18)	12	5.00	10.00
	---MJ in warmup, hold BB (8.19)	13	5.00	10.00
	---MJ on checklist, head view (8.20)	30	5.00	10.00
-	MJ & Bart, "It's the Shoes Man!," white back, "Jordan Knows Bart"		1.50	2.00
-	MJ Knows Pool, yellow border, shooting, yellow back, information		1.50	2.00
-	Superman, white back		6.00	10.00
-	Superman, 3D		5.00	9.00

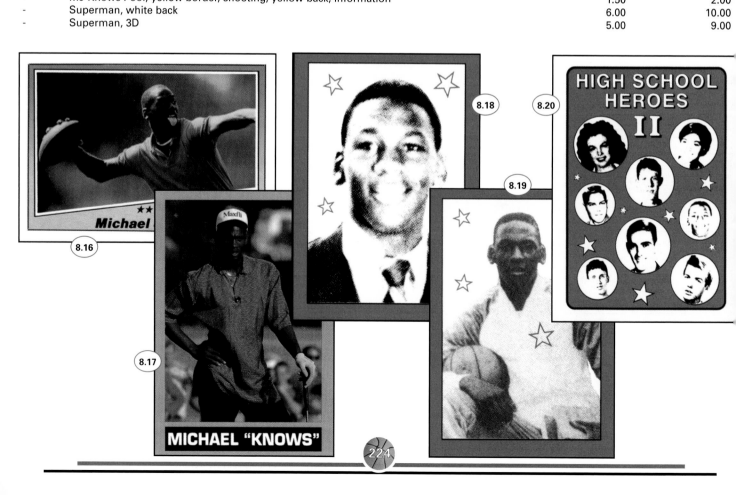

Year	Sport Educational Items	card #		
91-92	Magazine, Basketball Edition		30.00	45.00
	---MJ Card, dribbling right hand, tongue out, red 23, white back, blue statistics, 2 player picture	1		
92	Card, MJ dribbling, red 23, gold border, white & blue back with 86-91 stats	1	10.00	15.00

Year	Sport Strikes Metal Cards	card #		
2/96	Silver card, case, certificate (8.21)	88	250.00	350.00
2/96	Gold card, case, certificate (8.21a)	88	600.00	800.00

Year	Sported World Cards-England	card #		
95	Sported World Class Winners Set, pop up cards		45.00	60.00
	-Damon Hill, auto racing	1		
	-Michael Jordon, basketball, USA #9 white (8.22)	2	25.00	30.00
	-Maritin Offiah, soccer	3		
	-Prince Nassem, boxing	4		
	-Colin Jackson, track	5		
	-Steffi Graf, tennis	6		
	-Shaquille O' Neal, basketball	7		
	-Linford Christie, track	8		
	-Lennon Lewis, boxing	9		
	-Ryan Giggs, soccer	10		
	-Paul Gascoigne, soccer	11		
	-Dennis Bergkamp, soccer	12		
	-Jurgen Klinsmann, soccer	13		
	-Paolo Maldini, soccer	14		
	-Faustino Asprilla, soccer	15		

Year	Sports Channel TV Items	mag #		
91-92	Brochure, Blackhawks & Bulls Schedule		3.00	5.00

Year	Sports Heroes, Feats, & Facts	sheet #		
94	Binder and shipping box (8.23)		10.00	15.00
94	Ad flyer, "34 Free Gifts" MJ on binder featured on coupon	120710104	3.00	8.00
94	Ad flyer, "Now you can save $1.90 every month and complete your collection three times faster," MJ on binder featured on flyer, blank back	041055050 (9/94)	4.00	9.00
94	Ad flyer, "You Get All This Free!," MJ on binder featured on flyer, letter on back of flyer	120704104	3.00	8.00
94	Ad flyer, "Your Introductory package Includes All This:," MJ on binder featured on coupon, gift voucher on back of flyer	120505080	3.00	8.00
94	Poster page divider, MJ running with ball, blue back	041051010 (0994)	3.00	8.00
94	Poster page, "Just for Fun," MJ dribbling on front, MJ dunking inside, MJ cartoon on back, Poster Page 8	pkt04	5.00	10.00
94	Sheet, "MJ BB #1 Champions," #45 red, dribbling with left hand on front, folded, MJ Up Close on back side, shipped folded	120508752, pkt06b	5.00	10.00
94	Sheet, "MJ BB #1 Champions," #45 red, dribbling with left hand on front, unfolded, MJ Up Close on back side (8.24)	120508112, pkt06a	5.00	10.00
94	Sheet, "MJ BB #1 Champions," #23 red, holding ball with left hand on front, unfolded, MJ Up Close on back side	pkt06	5.00	10.00
94	Sheet, "The Shrug," MJ 2 pictures on front and 2 pictures on back, Greatest Moments 16	pkt30	5.00	10.00

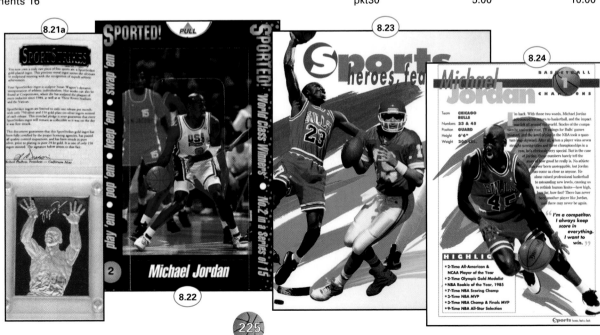

Year	Description			
94	Sheet, "Jordan vs. Celtics" MJ on front 2 pictures, MJ on back in 2 pictures, Greatest Moments 49	pkt25	5.00	10.00
94	Sheet, "NBA 3-Pointers," MJ on back jump shot, Record Book 5	pkt02	5.00	10.00
94	Sheet, "NBA All-Stars," MJ layup, red #23, Record 11 Book	pkt06	5.00	10.00
94	Sheet, "NBA All-Stars," MJ layup, red #23 (8.25)	120508109, pkt06a	5.00	10.00
94	Sheet, "NBA Scoring," MJ on back, hook shot, Record 25 Book	pkt18	5.00	10.00
94	Sheet, "NBA Finals," MJ on back layup, red 23, Record 40 Book	pkt26	5.00	10.00
94	Sheet, "Retiring On Top," MJ in cartoon like figure, Bloopers and Trivia 16	pkt07	5.00	10.00
94	Ad, Binder and Sheet Set, MJ on cover of foldout, holding ball, jumping, old red 23, "Get in on the Action!," MJ inside of foldout reverse dunk		5.00	10.00
94	Sheet, Dan Majerle/MJ, "Scorecard," MJ guarding Majerle	pkt22	5.00	10.00
94	Sheet, Chris Mullin/MJ, Basketball Champion 18, MJ back cover behind Mullin	pkt16	5.00	10.00
94	Sheet, Scottie Pippen/MJ, "Scorecard," MJ inside talking to Scottie,	pkt02	5.00	10.00
94	Sheet, John Starks/MJ, Basketball Champion 51, MJ defending against Starks	pkt21	5.00	10.00

Year	Sports Impression Plates & Mugs	plate # size		
91	MJ, gold rim with stars and basketballs, "Jordan" in 1-2 o'clock position, J. Catalano, four poses of MJ, gold signature, 1,991 issued	400204 10.25"	160.00	200.00
91	MJ, platinum rim, 4 MJ poses, M. Petronella, 1,991 issued,	400203 8.5"	70.00	85.00
91	MJ, gold rim, multi-colored background, J. Catalano, 4 MJ pictures	400202 4.25"	30.00	40.00
91	MJ, gold rim, multi-colored background, J. Catalano, date on plate 1991, gold lettering on back, number on box 4002X02, date on box 1990	NNO on plate 4.125"	35.00	45.00
92	MJ, gold rim & signature, 8 MJ pictures, R. Tanenbaum, gold signature, # of 1,992 issued	403204 10.25"	135.00	150.00
92	MJ, gold edition, gold rim, red partial rim, 3 MJ poses, Chicago Skyline, B. Vann	403203 8.5"	85.00	100.00
92	"MJ/Chicago Bull," bronze rim, "Jordan, # of 5,000 produced" top, 8 MJ poses, 1992 on plate, 1993 on boxed background, R. Tanenbaum	403202 4.25"	35.00	45.00
92	Dream USA Team BB 1992, gold rim with names, flag background, 12 pictured with gold background circles, R. Tanenbaun, MJ in 3:30 position toward middle, No Sports Impression Box, # of 1992 produced	550904 10.25"	85.00	100.00
92	Dream USA Team BB 1992, gold rim with names, flag background, 12 pictured with gold background circles, R. Tanenbaun, MJ in 3:30 position towards middle	550902 4.25"	25.00	35.00
92	1992 The Dream Team, gold rim, red & white stripes, purple background, "USA Basketball" right side, C. Hayes, MJ left side about 9 o'clock position, 12 players on plate, # out of 7,500 issued	550703 8.5"	70.00	85.00
92	1992 The Dream Team, gold rim, red & white stripes, purple background, "USA Basketball" right side, C. Hayes, MJ left side about 9 o'clock position, 12 players on plate	550702 4.25"	25.00	35.00
92	NBA 1st Ten Chosen, gold rim & signatures, blue background top, flag bottom, L. Salk, MJ in 6 o'clock position, 1,992 issued	550104 10.25"	160.00	200.00
92	NBA 1st Ten Chosen, gold rim, MJ at 3 o'clock, J. Catalano-blue plate background, red player background in circles/squares, # of 7,500 issued	550203 8.5"	70.00	85.00
92	NBA 1st Ten Chosen, gold rim, red background, "USA BB" center position, C. W. Mundy, MJ in 6 o'clock position, 7,500 issued,	550303 8.5"	70.00	85.00
92	"The First Ten Chosen" USA BB Players Ceramic Stein-16 oz, box included	550406 stein	25.00	35.00
92	NBA First 10 Chosen, names in gold rim, blue background, "USA Basketball" in middle, B. Vann, MJ in bottom center 6 o'clock position	550402 4.25"	25.00	35.00
92	NBA First 10 Chosen, gold rim, blue background with stars & red stripe, "USA Basketball" middle position, T. Fogarty, MJ upper left area about 11 o'clock position	550502 4.25"	25.00	35.00
92	NBA First 10 Chosen, gold rim, white background "USA Basketball" top position, R. Tanenbaum, MJ right side about 3 o'clock position	550602 4.25"	25.00	35.00
92	1992 USA Basketball Team Logo Plate, blue & red rim stripes, red, white & blue letters on white background, No MJ on plate	550802 4.25"	15.00	20.00
92	"1992 USA Basketball 1992," "First Ten Chosen" in blue rim, 10 pictures on orange basketball background, Collector's Club Presents "The First Ten Chosen USA BB Team Plate" on back	500830 6.5"	35.00	45.00
92	1992 Membership Kit Items-folder of literature, sports card, membership card, Sports Impression Catalog, 4 issues of the Line UP		25.00	40.00
93	1992 NBA World Champions Chicago Bulls, gold rim, red background, team members pictured, C. Hayes, with gold signatures, # of 1,992 issued	403304 10.25"	135.00	45.00
93	1992 NBA World Champions Chicago Bulls, platinum rim with stars, MJ in 6:30 position, players on perimeter, 7,500 issued	403303 8.5"	70.00	85.00
93	1992 NBA World Champions Chicago Bulls, gold rim, red background, team members pictured, C. Hayes	403302 4.25"	25.00	35.00
93	MJ Mug and Box, 12 oz., black background, white handle	400237 Mug	15.00	25.00

3	"1993 World Champions," Chicago Bulls + Logo, gold rim with stars, Paxson's shot with 3.9 seconds, B. Vann, No MJ on plate, 3 Points for 3 Peat, Bulls Logo left side 9 o'clock position, # of 7,500 issued	406203 8.5"	70.00	85.00
3	MJ, "Jordan" red letters, "Chicago Bulls + Logo" bottom center, 6 MJ pictures, black signature, 2,500 issued	404604 10.25	160.00	200.00
3	MJ, "Jordan" red letters, "Chicago Bulls + Logo" bottom center, 6 MJ pictures, black signature	404602 4.5	15.00	20.00
3	"1993 World Champions," Chicago Bulls + Logo, bronze rim, Paxson's shot with 3.9 3 Points for 3 Peat, Bulls Logo left side 9 o'clock position seconds, B. Vann, No MJ on plate	406202 4.25"	15.00	20.00

Year	Sports Pages Sheets	sheet#		
0	Ad Foldout Sheet, "Get in on the Action," MJ front, Field Publications (8.26)	CKP8-047	3.00	6.00
1	Ad Foldout Sheet, "Get in on the Action," MJ front, Field Publications	DDDC-047	2.50	5.00
4	Ad flyer, "It's A Hit," MJ sheet featured on flyer, red 23, slam dunk, "Free Gift Certificate Coupon" attached	GJJW0882	3.00	6.00
1	Champions and Record Holders, backward layup, red 23, Field Publication	SPT-03	2.50	5.00
3	Ad Foldout Sheet & Binder Sheet, MJ on binder sheet, sealed set, Newfield Publication	5252-04a	2.00	4.00
3	Champions and Record Holders, backward layup, red 23, Newfield Publication (8.27)	5241-01	2.00	4.00
4	Champions and Record Holders, slam dunk, red 23, New York #3, Newfield Publication (8.28)	5241-01	2.00	4.00
4	Champions and Record Holders, dunking, red 23, closeup	5241-01	2.00	4.00
4	Great Moments in Sports, MJ in blue #9 Olympic uniform, "The Original Dream Team"	5241-06		

Year	Sports Reading Series Kit	card #		
7	Pro Basketball Reading Kit Sheet, Educational Insights	34	45.00	60.00

Year	Stamps-Sheets & Singles	# of items		
2/15/92	St. Vincent "The Dream Team 1992 Olympics," Barcelona '92, Cachets, First Day Issue, gold medal winners	2 envelope 1st sheet	35.00	45.00

---M. Jordan (8.29)
---C. Barkley
---J. Stockton
---C. Mullin
---C. Drexler

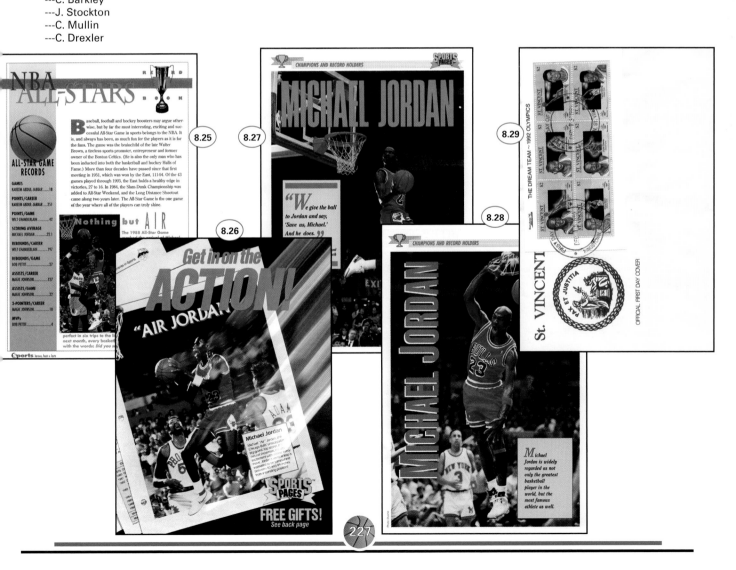

	---P. Ewing			
	---S. Pippen	2nd sheet		
	---E. Johnson			
	---L. Bird			
	---C. Laethner			
	---K. Malone			
	---D. Robinson			
92	St. Vincent "The Dream Team 1992 Olympics," Barcelona '92 gold medal winners	12 stamps	15.00	25.00
	---M. Jordan	1st sheet		
	---C. Barkley			
	---J. Stockton			
	---C. Mullin			
	---C. Drexler			
	---P. Ewing			
	---S. Pippen	2nd sheet		
	---E. Johnson			
	---L. Bird			
	---C. Laethner			
	---K. Malone			
	---D. Robinson			
1993	St. Vincent "1992 USA Olympic Basketball Dream Team, Barcelona, Spain," American Flag cover, plastic folder (8.30)	12 stamps	20.00	30.00
	---M. Jordan	1st sheet		
	---C. Barkley			
	---J. Stockton			
	---C. Mullin			
	---C. Drexler			
	---P. Ewing			
	---S. Pippen	2nd sheet		
	---E. Johnson			
	---L. Bird			
	---C. Laethner			
	---K. Malone			
	---D. Robinson			
7/15/93	Tanzania Famous Black Athletes Cachets, First Day Issue (8.31)	1 envelope	20.00	30.00
	---A. Ashe	20/-		
	---M. Jordan	40/-		
	---D. Thompson	50/-		
	---J. Robinson	70/-		
	---K. Abdul-Jabbar	100/-		
	---F. Joyner	150/-		
	---J. Owens	200/-		
	---J. Hohnson	400/-		
93	Tanzania Famous Black Athletes	9stamp	20.00	30.00
	---A. Ashe, 1st sheet	20/-		
	---M. Jordan	40/-		
	---D. Thompson	50/-		
	---J. Robinson	70/-		
	---K. Abdul-Jabbar	100/-		
	---F. Joyner	150/-		
	---J. Owens	200/-		
	---J. Hohnson	400/-		
	---Muhammad Ali, 2nd sheet, stamp in card frame	500/-		
95-96	SSCA First Day of Issue		45.00	55.00
	---Post Card, 4/17/96	1077		

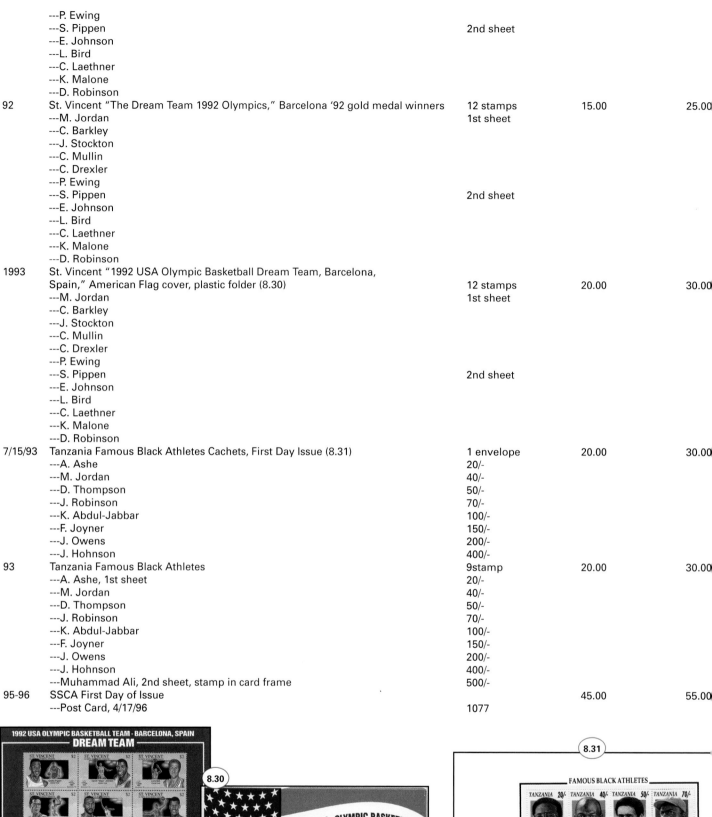

1992 USA OLYMPIC BASKETBALL TEAM · BARCELONA, SPAIN
DREAM TEAM
LIMITED EDITION COLLECTIBLE

8.30

1992 U.S.A. OLYMPIC BASKETBALL
DREAM TEAM
BARCELONA, SPAIN

8.31

FAMOUS BLACK ATHLETES

	---Gold Basketball Stamp			
	---Holder			
95-96	SSCA First Day of Issue			
	---Post Card, 4/17/96	2095	35.00	45.00
	---Gold Baseball Stamp			
	---Holder			
8/96	Palau Stamp Sheet-Olympic Athletes (8.32)	20 stamps	15.00	25.00
	---H. Olajuwon			
	---P. McCormick			
	---J. Thorpe			
	---J. Owens			
	---T. Gutsu			
	---M. Jordan			
	---F. Mingxu			
	---R. Zmeik			
	---H. Pedrosa			
	---N. Comanech			
	---J. Joyner-Kersey			
	---M. Johnson			
	---K. Otto			
	---V. Scherbo			
	---J. Weissmuller			
	---B. Dickson			
	---E. Tolan			
	---K. Egerszegi			
	---S. Kato			
	---A. Popov			
96	Stampers Collectibles Kit, US Postal Service Item		3.00	6.00
	---MJ Space Jam Poster			
	---Looney Tunes Comic Book with MJ ad on back (8.33)			

Year	Star Pins			
91-92	Series A, MJ sitting on his name, holding BB RH, red 23, back stats,			
	Salem Sportswear, sealed package, 1 x 1.5" (8.34)	41557 10001	15.00	20.00
92	Set, Barcelona Bound, sealed package	2 pins	20.00	25.00
	---Barcelona Bound 1992, Flag & Team Picture, 1-3/4" x 1-3/8"			
	---1992 Jordan Barcelona Bound, MJ holding flag & BB, 1"x1.5"			
92	"Barcelona Bound, Olympic Champions Dream, Gold Rush," team picture,			
	1-3/4" x 1-3/8," sealed package		15.00	20.00

Year	Starline			
88	Photo, MJ vs. Celtics #20	8x10	6.00	10.00
88	Puzzle with poster, "Jordan" mouth open, New York #8 dunking, white #23,		20.00	30.00
88	Puzzle with poster, "Michael Jordan" tongue out, red #23, dunking,			
	red border top/sides		20.00	30.00
88	Puzzle with poster, "Licensed to Jam Bucs #21," dunking, yellow strip m,			
	tongue out, red #23,		20.00	30.00

89	Book Cover, MJ front and back, red border, inside schedule for week and eight classroom periods, "Bulls" inside (8.35)		5.00	10.00
89	Greeting card, MJ dunking vs. #20 Clippers, view behind the basket, red border, scoreboard in background, red 23, inside "Happy Birthday Michael Jordan"	NBA-1	8.00	12.00
89	Greeting card, MJ layup vs. New York #33 Ewing, red border, red 23, inside "Michael Jordan"	NBA-1 NM	8.00	12.00
89	Greeting card, MJ waist up pose, red 23, red border, inside "Happy Birthday Michael Jordan"	NBA-5	8.00	12.00
89	Greeting card, MJ waist up pose, red 23, red border, inside "Michael Jordan"	NBA-5 NM	8.00	12.00
89	Greeting card, MJ dunking, side front view, red 23, 2 camera men on floor, black border, inside "Happy Birthday Michael Jordan"	NBA-23	8.00	12.00
89	Greeting card, MJ dunking side view, red 23, Gatorade sign in background, black border, inside "Michael Jordan"	NBA-23 NM	8.00	12.00
89	School folder, MJ front and back, red border, inside schedule for week and eight classroom periods, "Bulls" inside		3.00	6.00
89	Super Star Book Covers, sealed set		15.00	20.00
	---MJ reaching for ball vs. Celtics, red border			
	---MJ, red border			
	---NBA All-Stars, blue border			
90	Photo, MJ vs. Bucks, #21	8 x 10	6.00	10.00
95	Sticker, "Penny" passing ball behind MJ, "Orlando Magic" on front left, crowd in background (8.36)	5.5 x 8.5	10.00	15.00
-	Ad, reverse image window display, MJ white 23, "Poster Headquarters," W. Gretzky, J. Kelly, & D. Strawberry		20.00	35.00
-	"Soaring," ad card, gray border, jumping with ball right hand	3 x 5	10.00	15.00
-	Ad card, "Chicago Bulls," red border, 8 Bulls pictures + logo	3 x 5	10.00	15.00
-	Ad card, "Michael Jordan Bullseye," red border, MJ dunk, red 23 uniform, vs. the Nets	3 x 5	10.00	15.00
-	Ad card, "Michael Jordan," ad card, black border, MJ behind the back dunk, red 23	3 x 5	10.00	15.00
-	Ad card, "Licensed to Jam," ad card, black and yellow border MJ dunk shot, red 23, vs. Bucks,	3 x 5	10.00	15.00
-	Ad card, "Showtime at the NBA," black border, 10 pictures on card	3 x 5	10.00	15.00
-	Ad card, "Michael Jordan," red top border, no side borders, 8 MJ pictures, old red 23	3 x 5	10.00	15.00
-	Ad card, "Michael Jordan," black borders, MJ dunking vs. Lakers, hair, old red 23	3 x 5	10.00	15.00
-	Ad card, "Chicago Bulls," red black border, 6 pictures + logo	3 x 5	10.00	15.00
-	Ad card, "Michael Jordan," red border, MJ dunking front view from side of basket, old red #23	3 x 5	10.00	15.00
-	Ad card, "Michael Jordan Star Series," gray background, 2 MJ pictures, red and white #23, Bulls logo	3 x 5	10.00	15.00
-	Ad card, "Michael Jordan, Chicago Bulls," ad card, white 23, hook shot layup, SP & crowd in background	3 x 5	10.00	15.00
-	Ad card, "Jordan Chicago Bulls," MJ dunking from side of basket, MJ front view, red 23, both hands overhead	3 x 5	10.00	15.00

8.35

8.36

	Ad card, "Chicago Bulls," SP, DR & MJ, all jumping in air & shooting ball with right hand pictured in front of background United Center court & crowd, Bulls logo	3 x 5	10.00	15.00
	Ad card, "Jordan Out of this World," Bulls logo, MJ jumping with two hands on ball, world in background	3 x 5	10.00	15.00

Year	Starting Lineup			
88	Figure in box	88470	75.00	100.00
	---blue card		35.00	50.00
89	One on One	97570	150.00	250.00
89	White Box Slam Dunk Set, offered before Red Boxes, numbers and letters on mailing labels (8.37)	6 units		
	---Michael Jordan, #32 Bulls, #1327 615 0029 07 on box mailing label	A	200.00	300.00
90	Red Box Slam Dunk, labels attached with numbers for individual players, all boxes produced with same number #96500, left over White Boxes were then sold as Red Boxes (8.37)	96450	200.00	300.00
90	Figure in box, All-Star (8.38)	67826	80.00	110.00
	---2 cards			
91	Palming ball, jumping	67860	70.00	90.00
	---coin			
91	Shooting on floor	67879	70.00	90.00
	---coin			
92	Dribbling	67931	75.00	100.00
	poster, #6743314000	11" x 14		
92	Jump shot, in warm ups	67946	75.00	100.00
	---poster, New York player & SP in background, #6743301000	11" x 14		
92	USA	67990	90.00	125.00
92	Headliner	67970	70.00	90.00
93	Figure in box	68131	80.00	110.00
	---Topps Stadium Club Card			

Year	Statues and Figurines			
87	NBA Yalada from Spain, like SLU, white 23, feet flat, right hand out to side, holding basketball in left hand above head, red wrist band on left hand		125.00	150.00
87	MJ Horse Figure		25.00	40.00
92	USA #9 white, car window suction cup doll, suction cups on hands, cloth doll, plastic head with tongue out, black feet, 12" (8.39)		60.00	90.00
95	Bank, statue, MJ holding basketball in RH, red 23, Bugs in white #23, holding carrot in left hand, Made in Mexico (8.40)	14"	50.00	75.00
96	MJ by Renaissance Company, bronze		250.00	300.00

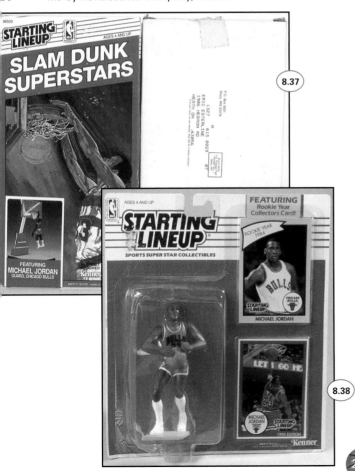

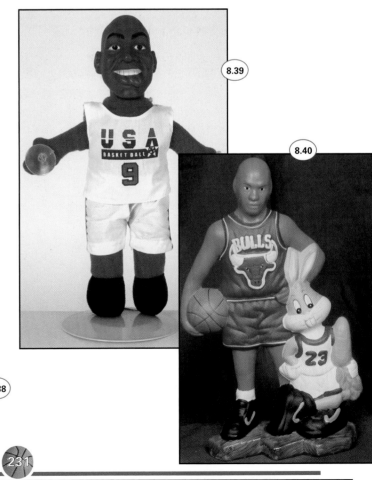

| 7/97 | MJ by Susan Wagner, bronze | | 23" | 11,000.00 | 15,000.00 |
| - | Celebrity Spoofs Dolls, 6," holding BB with right hand, cape, white #23, big brown eyes, tongue out, Christhomas Corp, Irvine CA (8.41) | | | 50.00 | 75.00 |

Year STICKERS: American Pro Basketball USA
95-96 Album and Stickers Service line, Modena italy (8.42) 190 stickers 100.00 150.00
—MJ 4 part sticker, layup, red 23, vs. Cavs. #22 (8.43) page 1

Year STS Telephone Card card #
96 NBA Commemorative Yearbook Sets 175.00 225.00
---MJ phone card, no minutes listed, plastic case, of 8,500 (8.44) 4,119
---Bulls Yearbook 95-96, 30 Years and Running (8.45)
---Ad folder, holds card, MJ front and back (8.46)
---Holder, clear plastic with white sticker "Chicago Bulls, Limited
Collectors Edition," #4119 of 8,500 (8.47)

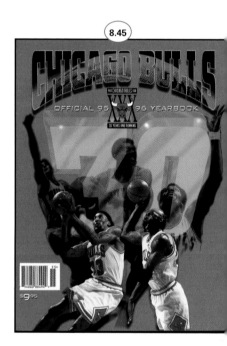

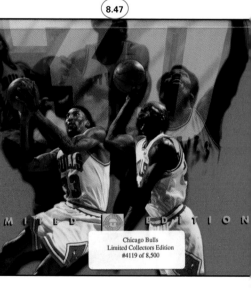

T

Year	Taco Bell			
93	Untouch-A-Bull in '91, WIN!, MJ behind trophy		6.00	12.00
93	Unbelieve-A-Bull in '92, MJ behind hand		6.00	12.00

Year	Team Schedules			
84-85	Team Schedule Pamphlet-cover, in USA #9 red, slam dunk		90.00	110.00
84-85	Bulls Schedule-inside		35.00	45.00
85-86	NBA Schedule Pamphlet with MJ & Jabbar cover		35.00	45.00
85-86	Team Schedule Pamphlet 20th Anniversary cover, white 23, slam dunk		30.00	40.00
85-86	Bulls Schedule-front (9.1)		30.00	40.00
86-87	Bulls Schedule-back		25.00	35.00
86-87	Individual/Group Ticket Order Form and Schedule, "Get Ready to Feel Chicago's Rolling Thunder"	back cover	25.00	35.00
87-88	Bulls Schedule-front		20.00	30.00
88-89	Bulls Schedule-front		15.00	25.00
88-89	Milwaukee Bucks Schedule-green, MJ & #43 Bucks on front	front	15.00	25.00
89-90	Bull Schedule-SP front, No MJ		5.00	8.00
89-90	Illinois Basketball-MJ on back with Chevy		10.00	20.00
89-90	TNT & NBA Schedule-front		10.00	20.00
90-91	Bulls Schedule-back		8.00	15.00
91-92	Bulls Schedule-Trophy front, No MJ		5.00	8.00
91-92	UD & NBA TV Schedule-front & inside, Catch All the Moves		6.00	12.00
91-92	Bulls Schedule, proof sheet, "Sky Man," MJ layup vs. Lakers, red 23, schedule on bottom, Roland & Miller Sheet-fed Press Systems	39x55"	75.00	125.00
91-92	Bulls Schedule-round disc, "World Champs," Cameo All-Stars		25.00	45.00
92-93	Bulls Schedule-front		5.00	8.00
92-93	Bulls Schedule-front, uncut double schedule, special insert in Chicago Sun Times Sports		15.00	25.00
92-93	NBA Schedule-inside, Includes, Broadcast & Cable...		5.00	8.00
92-93	Bulls Schedule-round disc, "3 Peat A Bull?	28"	25.00	45.00
93-94	Bulls Schedule-back		4.00	8.00
93-94	Bulls Schedule-round disc, "3 Time World Champ"	28"	25.00	35.00
94-95	Bulls Schedule-United front, No MJ		3.00	4.00
95	Birmingham Barons Schedule-front		5.00	8.0
95-96	Bulls Schedule-Logo front, MJ's shirt and shoes on back		2.00	3.00
96-97	Bulls Schedule Display with schedule, MJ on Display only, no MJ on schedule	2 items	15.00	20.00
96-97	NBA Schedule Book-MJ 3 pictures, NBA at 50		20.00	25.00

Year	Ticket Stubs and Pamphlets	game # size		
84-85	Season Ticket Pamphlet, red #9, '84 USA/Converse (9.2)	cover	100.00	125.00
84-85	Group/Individual Ticket Pamphlet, water damage, MJ in USA #9 & O. Woolridge #0 Bulls, b&w photos (9.3)	cover	75.00	100.00

85-86	Season/Group/Individual Ticket Brochure, "20th Season Chicago Bulls, A Whole New Breed," MJ reverse RH dunk under basket, white 23, 4 MJ photos in pamphlet (9.4)		60.00	75.00
86-87	Season Ticket Pamphlet, 4 MJ pictures	cover	50.00	65.00
87/88	Washington Bullets Ticket Pamphlet, MJ rebounding, Paxson (9.5)	cover	20.00	35.00
12/21/88	Milwaukee Bucks Ticket Stub, MJ waiting for rebound from #34 Bucks, red 23, aqua ticket, game 11 (9.6)	Game 11 / 4 x 2	20.00	
12/29/88	Bulls Ticket Stub, MJ back view & SP front view slapping one hand, New York Knicks, white 23, red ticket (9.7)	4.25 x 2	60.00	
4/4/89	Bulls Ticket Stub, MJ layup with left hand, 2 Cavs. Players, Charlotte Hornets, white 23, gray ticket, True Value banner background (9.8)	4.25 x 2	45.00	
4/21/89	Bulls Ticket Stub, MJ in background from #34 Bucks, aqua background, Milwaukee Bucks, see MJ number (9.9)	Game 4 1 / 2 x 4	25.00	
11/17/89	Portland Trail Blazers Ticket Stub, MJ on defense vs. #30 Terry, Chicago Bulls, red 23 with hair	Game 6 / 2 x 4.5	25.00	
11/21/89	Portland Trail Blazers Ticket Stub, MJ dribbling, Chicago Bulls, red 23 with hair, not used (9.10)	Game 7 / 2 x 5.75	30.00	
12/19/89	Bulls Ticket Stub, MJ back view slapping both hands with SP front view, Los Angeles Lakers, white 23, red ticket (9.11)	4.25 x 2	45.00	

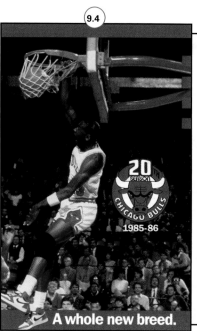

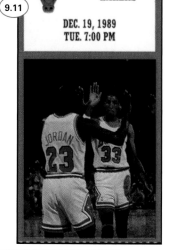

1/12/90	Charlotte Hornets Ticket Stub, MJ left hand layup from under basket, 3 players, white 23, aqua ticket, Milwaukee Bucks #22 in picture, game 18 (9.12)	Game18 4.25 x 2	25.00
2/27/90	Bulls Ticket Stub, MJ layup with right hand, 2 New York & 1 Bulls players, Milwaukee Bucks, white 23, red ticket (9.13)	4.25 x 2	40.00
4/9/91	Bulls Ticket Stub, MJ slam dunk with right hand in front of basket, New York Knicks, white 23, blue ticket (9.14)	4 x 2	35.00
4/19/91	Charlotte Hornets Ticket Stub, MJ blocking #3 Charlotte with right arm, aqua ticket, red 23 (9.15)	Game 41 4 x 2	25.00
11/5/91	Bulls Ticket Stub, MJ slam dunk with 2 players, Golden State Warriors, white 23, yellow ticket (9.16)	4.25 x 2	45.00
12/10/91	Bulls Ticket Stub, MJ dunking, white 23, gray background, Seattle Supersonics (9.17)	1.75 x 4	30.00
1/22/92	Bulls Ticket Stub, Bulls #23 jersey & Charlotte #50 jersey, vs. Charlotte Hornets, white background (9.18)	Game 19 4 x 2	10.00
12/12/92	Bulls Ticket Stub, MJ & Scottie right fists in air, MJ holding BB, gray background, New Jersey Nets, MJ in white hat, SP in black hat, 3rd guy holding trophy (9.19)	Game 9 6.25 x 3	25.00

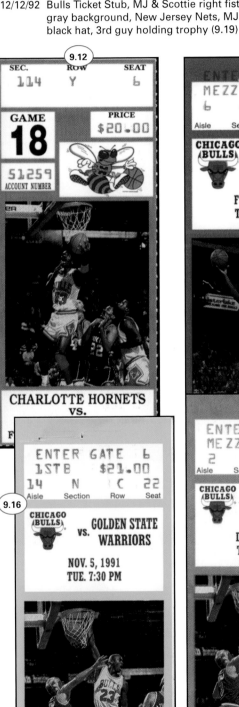

92	NBA Playoff Ticket-Chicago Stadium, Home Game "O," No MJ, Trophy & Logo, 91 NBA World Champions		5.5 x 2	25.00
12/9/92	Bulls Ticket Stub, MJ in huddle in warmups Cleveland Cavaliers, green ticket (9.20)	Game 7	7 x 3	20.00
1/22/93	Bulls Ticket Stub, MJ slam dunk with right hand, Charlotte Hornets, gold ticket, white 23 (9.21)	Game 21	6.25 x 3	65.00
2/17/93	Bulls Ticket Stub, MJ with hand in air and one with BB, Utah Jazz, green ticket, white 23 (9.22)	Game 25	7 x 3	40.00
3/5/93	Bulls Ticket Stub, MJ dunking, white 23, red background, San Antonio Spurs, MJ with defender in blue shirt (9.23)	Game 29	6.25 x 3	25.00
3/12/93	Bulls Ticket Stub, MJ & team in huddle, gray background, Charlotte Hornets, team in warm-ups (9.24)	Game 31	7 x 3	25.00
12/18/93	Bulls Ticket Stub, MJ in locker room getting champagne on head by SP, San Antonio Spurs, yellow ticket, red 23 (9.25)	Game 8	6.25 x 3	35.00
12/20/93	Bulls Ticket Stub, MJ in team huddle, Charlotte Hornets, yellow ticket, white 23 (9.26)	Game 9	6.25 x 3	25.00
2/16/94	Bulls Ticket Stub, MJ and Phil Jackson hugging, Miami Heat, black ticket, red 23 (9.27)	Game 21	6.25 x 3	30.00

2/23/94	Bulls Ticket Stub, SP pouring champagne over, Golden State Warriors, MJ & Team in locker room champagne over MJ, red 23, green background (9.28)	Game 24 6.25 x 3 25.00
2/26/94	Bulls Ticket Stub, team huddle in white uniform, blue background, Indiana Pacers, MJ front MJ, back of SP, BJA, HG (9.29)	Game 25 6.25x3 25.00
3/8/94	Bulls Ticket Stub, MJ and Phil Jackson hugging, red 23, yellow background, Atlanta Hawks, locker room, team in white hats (9.30)	5 x 3 25.00
3/25/94	Nets vs. Chicago, MJ layup RH, black background, gold "Michael," "Michael Jordan 3-Peat" (9.31)	Game 33 7.5 x 2 20.00
3/24/95	Bulls Ticket Stub, MJ layup shot, Orlando Magic	Game 1 20.00
11/2/96	Bulls Ticket Stub, Team Picture with Trophy, 76ers, yellow ticket (9.32)	5 x 3 25.00
12/5/96	Bulls Ticket Stub, Court Pictures from stands yellow & gold ticket (9.33)	Game 7 5 x 3 15.00
96	NBA Eastern Conference Finals Media Pass for all Games, postcard size with MJ & Scottie (9.34)	629 30.00
1/25/97	Bulls Ticket Stub, #23 blue NBA All-Star, MJ slam dunk, vs. Raptors (9.35)	Game 22 6.25 x 3 30.00

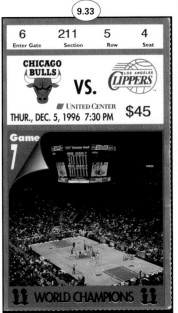

2/18/97	Bulls Ticket Stub, group picture in stands, vs. Denver Nuggets (9.36)	Game 25		
		5 x 3	20.00	
5/97	NBA Playoffs vs. Atlanta, Game C, MJ hand on trophy	Game 1	5.00	
5/97	NBA Playoff Game Ticket, SP & MJ pouring champagne, blue border, game not played, tickets not used (9.37)	Game 0 3 x 7	15.00	25.00
5/97	NBA Playoff Game Ticket, SP & MJ pouring champagne, gold border, game not played, tickets not used seat 1 (9.38)	Game 0 3 x 7	15.00	25.00
97	Media Pass NBA Playoffs, blank, Eastern Conference 1st Round		15.00	20.00
97	Media Pass NBA Playoffs, blank, Eastern Conference Semi Finals		20.00	25.00
97	Media Pass NBA Playoffs, blank, All Games, no clipped corners, Eastern Conference Finals (9.39)	1623	25.00	30.00
98	Playoff, Home Game C, Round 2, vs. Charlotte	No MJ	10.00	15.00

Year	**Ticketron**			
1/87	Brochure, Schedule for January (9.40)		20.00	

Year	**Tiger Electronic Computer Games**			
89	MJ vs. Bird One on One, IBM, hand held electronic, both tipping ball in basket, viewed from above basket		50.00	75.00
96	Instructions, Tiger Electronic LCD Game Space Jam		3.00	5.00
96	Tiger Space Jam Game, hand held		25.00	35.00

Year	**Time, MJ & Guy Laroche**			
85	Ad Piece, cardboard	8 x 10	50.00	75.00
85	Watch, white & black (9.41)	101122	175.00	225.00
	---box			
	---watch bag			
	---book			
85	Watch, red & black (9.41)	105115	175.00	225.00
	---box			
	---watch bag			
	---book			

Year	Time Jordan Watches	item #		
85-86	Time Jordan Slam Dunk Champion, Excelsior International Corp., Kids Watches, 8 different versions			
	-white band with white buckle and end loop, "Time Jordan" on buckle side above and through red lines, round white bezel, white face, blue number dots #6, 2 baskets/1 ball, red & white hands, "Time Jordan" on face (9.42)		50.00	75.00
	-black band with black buckle and end loop, "Time Jordan" on buckle side of band above and through white line, round black bezel, white face with black BB courts at 12, 3, 6 & 9, black and white hands, "Time Jordan" on face (9.42)		50.00	75.00
	-red & black band with red buckle and end loop, "Time Jordan" on buckle side of band below black line, round red bezel, 1/2 white 1/2 red face, BB & hoop, bouncing ball, black/white hands "Time Jordan" on face (9.42)		50.00	75.00
	-red & black band with red buckle and end loop, "Time Jordan" on buckle side of band above and through black line, round black bezel/white face with red-black circle, BB & hoop, black/white hands and "Time Jordan" on face (9.42)		50.00	75.00
	-red & black link band, round black bezel/red-black face, "Time Jordan" on face (9.42)		50.00	75.00
	-white band with red buckle & bezel band ends, white band end loop, rectangle orange BB court face with 2 red/white lines, white/black hands (9.42)		50.00	75.00
	-black band with red buckle & bezel band ends, black band end loop, rectangle black BB court face with 2 red/white lines, white/black hands (9.42)		50.00	75.00
	-black band with white buckle & bezel band ends, black band end loop, rectangle gray BB court face with 2 red/white lines, white/black hands (9.42)		50.00	75.00

Year	Topps & Rustoleum Sheets	card #	# cards		
92-93	Topps Ad Sheet for Deluxe Full Set			3.00	5.00
92-93	Topps Sheet, blank back		9 cards	15.00	25.00
	---D. Schrempf				
	---P. Ewing				
	---K. Malone				
	---R. Seikaly				
	---B. Williams				
	---M. Jordan Card				
	---C. Corchiani				
	---W. Burton				
	---M. Richmond				
92-93	Topps/Rustoleum Sheet, perforated sheet		12 cards	20.00	30.00
	---B.J. Armstrong	CB-1			
	---S. King	CB-5			
	---W. Perdue	CB-9			
	---B. Cartwright/MJ front	CB-2			
	---R. McCray	CB-6			
	---T. Tucker	CB-10			
	---H. Grant	CB-3			
	---J. Paxson	CB-7			
	---S. Williams	CB-11			
	---M. Jordan Card	CB-4			
	---S. Pippen	CB-8			
	---Rust-Oleum Card	NNO			
93	Beam Team, 7 cards on front, non perforated			10.00	15.00

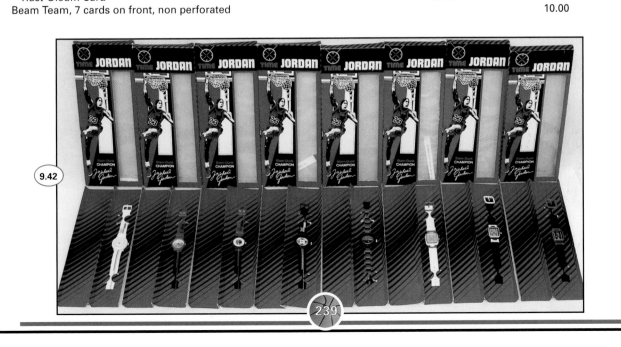

9.42

Year	True Value			
91-92	Coin & Package, MJ name on package, Back 2 Back wins Highlighting a Championship Year	bronze	15.00	25.00
92-93	Coin & Package, MJ name on package, Back to Back to Back	bronze	10.00	20.00

Year	TV Script			
93	Oprah Winfrey Show, MJ the guest (9.43)		25.00	30.00

Year	TV Sports Calendar Pamphlets	mag #		
11-15& 12-14/91	-NBA Action on TBS, Ads not completed	proto	10.00	15.00
11-15& 12-14/92	-NBA Action on TBS, Hass Pub at Dominick	cover	8.00	12.00
10-15& 11-14/93	-Slam into the New Season, Longs Pharmacy	cover	6.00	10.00
10-15& 11-14/93	-Slam into the New Season, Haas Pub. at Jewel	IS680	5.00	8.00

Year	Ultra Star Hair	card #		
87	Sheet, He's Got That Look.		10.00	15.00

Year	United Center	card #		
4/98	Schedule of events, April, layup, United Center-white 23	cover	2.00	4.00

Year	UD & UDA	item # size		
91-92	Ad Folder with 6 sides & 6 Sheets	low #s	20.00	30.00
	---Nobody Does Basketball Like UD, 7 MJ pictures on folder	folder		
	---We're Keeping the Best Players, in the NBA Under Wraps, MJ on sheet	sheet 1		
	---On the Courts & in the Locker Room, A New Way to Get ..., MJ on sheet	sheet 2		
	---All Pro. All Season., MJ on sheet	sheet 3		
	---Inaugural NBA BB 91-92 Season, b & w, MJ on sheet	sheet 4		
	---Low # Case Information, MJ on sheet	sheet 5		
	---Dear Hobby Customer Letter, MJ on sheet	sheet 6		
91-92	Ad Folder with 6 sides & 4 sheets	high #	25.00	35.00
	---Nobody Does Basketball Like UD, 7 MJ pictures on folder	folder		
	---"We're Keeping the Best Players in the NBA Under Wraps," MJ on sheet	sheet 1		
	---"On the Courts & in the Locker Room, A New Way to Get ...," MJ on sheet	sheet 2		
	---"Make a High Percentage Shot With the UD High Series," MJ on sheet	sheet 3		
	---All Pro All Season. MJ on sheet	sheet4		
92	Magazine, Upper Deck Direct Dealer Program, box, 15,000 produced		35.00	45.00
92-93	Ad Folder, 4 sided folder		20.00	30.00
91-92	Ad Sheet, magazine, Rise Above the Rest (9.44)	folded	1.00	2.00
91-92	Sheet, Orlando All-Star Weekend, 1 MJ picture Gatorade, blank back, 22,000 produced (9.45)		10.00	15.00
91-92	Sheet, Hologram Scoring Leader, uncut, non perforated		75.00	125.00
	---8 full MJ cards	AW-1		
	---4 top half MJ cards	AW-1		
	---4 bottom half MJ cards	AW-1		
92	Sheet, '92 USA BB Team, 1 MJ picture, Team Picture, blank back, 80,000 produced (9.46)		10.00	15.00

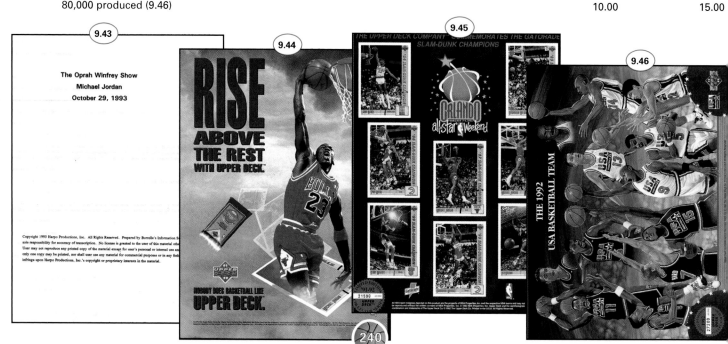

9.43

The Oprah Winfrey Show
Michael Jordan
October 29, 1993

Copyright 1993 Harpo Productions, Inc. All Rights Reserved. Prepared by Burrelle's Information S...

9.44

RISE ABOVE THE REST WITH UPPER DECK™

NOBODY DOES BASKETBALL LIKE UPPER DECK.

9.45

THE UPPER DECK COMPANY COMMEMORATES THE GATORADE SLAM-DUNK CHAMPIONS

ORLANDO all star weekend

9.46

THE 1992 USA BASKETBALL TEAM

92	Game, All-Stars, restickable items to cover walls, MJ & Mullin in USA Basketball Olympic Uniforms, #8082	20x20	10.00	20.00
92-93	Sheet, The Ultimate Hoop It Up 3 on 3 Matchup, 1 MJ picture, East vs. West, no perforations (9.47)	NNO	10.00	15.00
92-93	Sheet, 1992-93 Bulls, 4/20/93, 1 MJ picture, Jewel & Nabisco, blank back, 22,500 produced (9.48)		15.00	20.00
93	Ad Sheet, Pro View; MJ holding card, MJ on card and glasses (9.49)		5.00	8.00
93	Ad Sheet, Pro View; card, pack and box on sheet (9.50)		1.00	2.00
93	Sheet, Adventures in 'Toon World, 2 MJ pictures, movie ad sheet (9.51)		2.00	4.00
93	Sheet, 1993 National, Chicago July 20-25, 2 MJ pictures, UD Five Year Anniversary, blank back (9.52)	NNO	15.00	20.00
93	Sheet, NBA Jam Session, Sydney 8/31/93, Melbourne 9/3/93, 1 MJ picture, 48,500 issued (9.53)		10.00	15.00

9.47

9.48

9.49

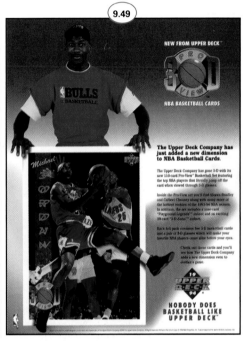

9.50

9.52

9.51

9.53

93	Standee, MJ waist up view, red 23, holding his own, 1993-94 UD Basketball card up with right hand (9.54)		50.00	75.00
93-94	Card, Soccer, World Cup Honorary Captain	HC-3	10.00	15.00
93-94	Card, Soccer, World Cup Honorary Captain, gold	HC-3	25.00	35.00
93-94	Card, Soccer, "World Soccer Cup USA Honorary Captain" blowup of '93 card HC-3, 8.5 x 11, 2,500 produced		25.00	35.00
93-94	Sheet, MJ Flight Team, uncut, MJ on backs	20 cards	100.00	150.00

---Pippen
---Weatherspoon
---Webb
---Wilkins
---Malone
---Miner
---Mourning
---O'Neal
---Ellis
---Gill
---Johnson
---Kemp
---Ceballos
---Coleman
---Drexler
---Elliott
---Augmon
---Barkley
---Benoit
---Brown

93-94	Sheet, 1993-94 Chicago Bulls, 11/13/93, blank back, 52,000 produced, no MJ on sheet (9.55)		4.00	
94	Ad Sheet, Pro View; card, pack and box on sheet		4.00	6.00
94	Golf balls, UDA CC, 3 pack, black picture & signature	80012	15.00	20.00
94	Magazine, Introducing MJ Memorabilia, UDA Catalog	Ed-8	8.00	12.00
94	Magazine, Amazing Michael, UDA Catalog	Ed-11	8.00	12.00
94	Magazine, Holiday Issue	Ed-12	8.00	12.00
94	Magazine, Holiday Issue	Ed-13	8.00	12.00
94	Magazine, UDA Catalog, "Can Mike Save Baseball"		8.00	12.00
94	Pins, Baseball Set, 2,500 sets issued	3 pins	30.00	45.00

---swinging, white #23
---running, black and white
---swinging, red and white

94	Pins, CC Collector Series Edition. Set	3 pins	15.00	25.00

---MJ Retirement
---Bull Logo
---Team MVP

94	Sheet, Father's Day, MJ, Montana, Gretzky, Williams, non perforated sheet, 7,500 issued (9.56)		15.00	20.00

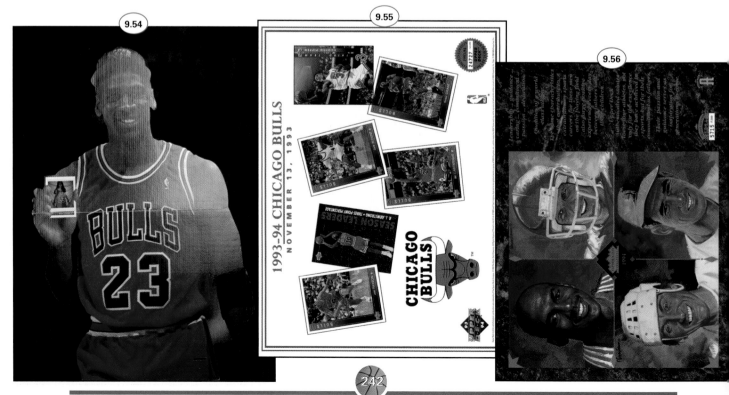

9.54   9.55   9.56

1993-94 CHICAGO BULLS
NOVEMBER 13, 1993

CHICAGO BULLS

94	Sheet, From Slam Dunk to Grand Slam Set, Salute to MJ Minor League Debut			
	---MJ Baseball Sheet, Salute to MJ, blank back, 50,000 produced (9.57)		12.00	15.00
	---8/1994 Minor League Packs	97 cards		
94	Sheet, Salutes MJ-9 Sensational NBA Seasons, sitting, 7 pictures,			
	blank back, 40,000 produced (9.58)		6.00	10.00
94	Sheet, Salutes MJ-9 Sensational NBA Seasons, flying, 7 pictures,			
	blank back, 40,000 produced (9.59)		6.00	10.00
94	Sheet, Salutes NBA Standouts During NBA All-Star Weekend,			
	MJ's name on Flight Team card, 30,000 produced		4.00	8.00
94	Sheet, USA Basketball High Lights, World Championship of Basketball,			
	MJ in USA #9, hands on knees, 8/4 to 14/94, Toronto Canada,			
	taken from magazine (9.60)	NNO	10.00	
94	Statue, Sam, Inc. Bobbing Head Doll & Box, Bulls Basketball,			
	10,000 produced, model #2300		75.00	100.00
94	Statue, Sam, Inc. Bobbing Head Doll & Box, Barons Baseball,			
	10,000 produced,		75.00	100.00
94-95	Ad Sheet, Collectors Choice Series 2 foil (9.61)		1.00	2.00
94-95	Card, Soccer, Spanish World Cup USA 94 Honorary Captain	C-6	35.00	50.00
94-95	Card, Soccer, Japanese World Cup USA 94 Honorary Captain	C-6	45.00	60.00
94-95	Foil Card, 24 K Gold Card & Pouch with "Chicago Bulls,"			
	Logo & #23, # of 2,500 produced (9.62)		275.00	350.00

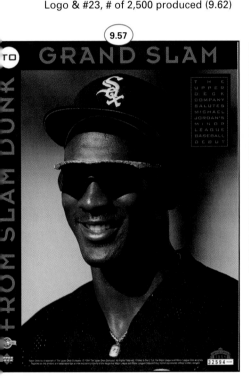

9.57

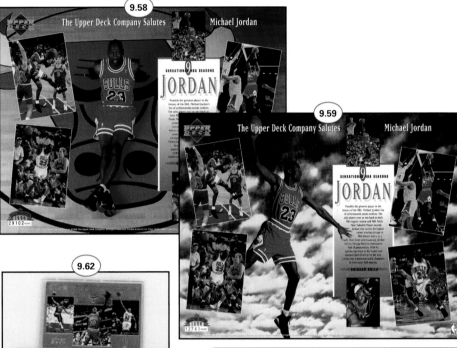

9.58

9.59

9.62

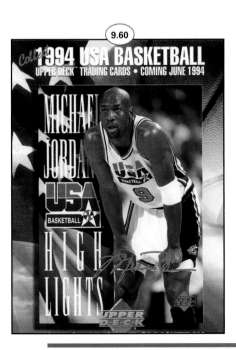

9.60

9.61

94-95	Metal Card, "Rare Air," double sided 24K gold, silver & nickel card, # of 1,994 produced		160.00	225.00
94-95	Sheet, Salutes MJ/Jewel, 3 MJ pictures, blank back, 50,000 produced (9.63)		10.00	20.00
95	Ad Sheet, CC NBA Series One (9.64)		1.00	2.00
95	Ad Sheet, MJ Bleacher Medal Card (9.65)		1.00	2.00
95	Ad Sheet, MJ Tribute Medal Card Set Baseball (9.66)		1.00	2.00
95	Foil Card, 23k Bleachers, gold box, red letters, basketball figure on front, on back baseball & basketball figures and basketball statistics (9.62)		30.00	45.00
95	Foil Card, 23k Bleachers, Triple Image, basketball figure on front, white box, red letters, on back basketball figure & basketball statistics (9.62)		30.00	45.00
95	Foil Card, 23k Bleachers, gold box, red letter, basketball figure front, on back baseball figure & statistics (9.62)		30.00	45.00
95	Pog Discs-7 different, red		15.00	20.00
	---23, Michael Jordan, 45, wood grain background	4"		
	---NBA Logo, Michael Jordan, UD logo, silver writing (9.67)	4"		
95	Pogs, Metal Slammers-20 different, Where to find them		40.00	60.00
	---45 with Signature, Foil Packs	1	2.00	3.00
	---45, Deluxe Starter Foil Packs	2	2.00	3.00

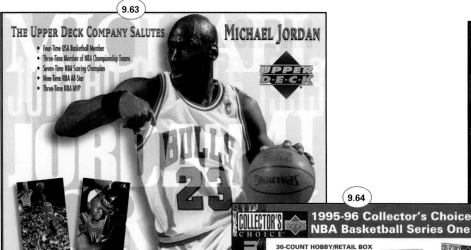

9.63

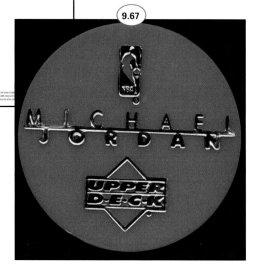

9.65

9.64

9.66

9.67

---He's Back, #45 Championship Box Exclusive	3	2.00	3.00
---23 with Signature, Rack Pack Exclusive	4	2.00	3.00
---MJ, Collector Pack Exclusive	5	2.00	3.00
---Basketball with Signature, Air Slammin' Exclusive	6	2.00	3.00
---Bulls, Deluxe Milk Cap Game Foil Packs	7	2.00	3.00
---23, Foil Packs	8	2.00	3.00
---MJ/23, Foil Pack Exclusive	9	2.00	3.00
---Bulls 23, Deluxe Starter Pack Exclusive	10	2.00	3.00
---Bulls 45, Foil Packs	11	2.00	3.00
---Michael Returns, Rack Pack Exclusive	12	2.00	3.00
---The Return, #45 Championship Box	13	2.00	3.00
---#23/Michael Jordan/45, Air Slammin' Exclusive	14	2.00	3.00
---Chicago Bulls, Foil Packs	15	2.00	3.00
---#45 Jump Shot, Foil Packs	16	2.00	3.00
---He's Back #45 Jump Shot, Deluxe Milk Cap Game Pack Exclusive	17	2.00	3.00
---MJ/#45, Collector Pack Exclusive	18	2.00	3.00
---MJ with Basketball, Foil Pack Exclusive	19	2.00	3.00
---23 front/45 back, Rack Pack Exclusive	20	2.00	3.00
5 Pogs, Foil Glossy-54 items		65.00	100.00
---holding ball in right hand, red 23, red left arm band	S-1	1.50	2.00
---close up of head, side view, red uniform	S-2	1.50	2.00
---dribbling with left hand, red 23, red left arm band	S-3	1.50	2.00
---jump shot over Laker, red 23, black left arm band	S-4	1.50	2.00
---holding ball overhead in right hand, red 23, mouth open	S-5	1.50	2.00
---looking to the right, red 23, mouth open, close up	S-6	1.50	2.00
---looking forward, white uniform, mouth open, close up	S-7	1.50	2.00
---holding ball both hands, red 23, referee in background	S-8	1.50	2.00
---dribbling right hand, white 23, black left arm band, smiling	S-9	1.50	2.00
---layup with right hand, white 23, black left arm band	S-10	1.50	2.00
---jump shot, red 23, view of back, black left arm band	S-11	1.50	2.00
---reaching, white 23, mouth open	S-12	1.50	2.00
---close up, white hat & uniform	S-13	1.50	2.00
---close up, looking forward, red uniform	S-14	1.50	2.00
---close up, shooting ball, red uniform	S-15	1.50	2.00
---hands in air overhead, white 23, black left arm band	S-16	1.50	2.00
---shooting, side view, red 23, black left arm band	S-17	1.50	2.00
---holding ball both hands, white 23, mouth open, looking down	S-18	1.50	2.00
---close up, looking, side view, red uniform	S-19	1.50	2.00
---close up, looking forward, red, 23, mouth open	S-20	1.50	2.00
---jump shot right hand, red 23, black left arm & right wrist	S-21	1.50	2.00
---close up, shooting right hand, red uniform	S-22	1.50	2.00
---dribbling left hand, red 45, black left arm band	S-23	1.50	2.00
---pointing & dribbling, white 23, black left arm band	S-24	1.50	2.00
---hands on knees, red 45, black left arm band	S-25	1.50	2.00
---dribbling right hand, red 23, black left arm & right wrist	S-26	1.50	2.00
---back view, red 23, black left arm band, waist high view	S-27	1.50	2.00
---dribbling right hand, white 23, black left arm band	S-28	1.50	2.00
---dribbling left hand, red 45, Pacer players	S-29	1.50	2.00
----holding ball both hands, blue NBA AS uniform, white left arm band	S-30	1.50	2.00
---close up, looking up, mouth open, red uniform	S-31	1.50	2.00
---dribbling left hand, red 23, black left arm band	S-32	1.50	2.00
---jump shot both hands, red 23, full side view	S-33	1.50	2.00
---jump shot both hands, white 23, front view	S-34	1.50	2.00
---pointing with right hand, white uniform, looking front	S-35	1.50	2.00
---	S-36	1.50	2.00
---looking up, white 45, uniform, looking front, black left arm band	S-37	1.50	2.00
---reaching both hands overhead, white 45, black left arm band	S-38	1.50	2.00
---looking up, side view, white 45, black left arm band	S-39	1.50	2.00
---	S-40	1.50	2.00
---walking, red 45, black left arm band	S-41	1.50	2.00
---hands on knees, red 45, side view, black left arm band	S-42	1.50	2.00
---holding ball both hands, red 45, black left arm band	S-43	1.50	2.00
---	S-44	1.50	2.00
---walking, closeup, red 45, black left arm band	S-45	1.50	2.00
---hands on knees, closeup, red 45, black left arm band	S-46	1.50	2.00
---shooting, back view, red 45, near backboard	S-47	1.50	2.00
---reaching right hand, red 45, 2 other players	S-48	1.50	2.00
---reaching left hand, closeup, white 45, black left arm band	S-49	1.50	2.00
---holding ball both hands, white 45, 2 other players	S-50	1.50	2.00
---hands on hips, red 45, waist view, Pacer player	S-51	1.50	2.00
---pointing right hand, white 45, front view, waist view	S-52	1.50	2.00

	---shooting both hands overhead, red 45, black left arm band	S-53	1.50	2.00
	---looking to right, red 45, right hand in fist (9.68)	S-54	1.50	2.00
95	Pogs, Regular-54 items		15.00	20.00
	---holding ball in right hand, red 23, red left arm band	1	.25	.35
	---close up of head, side view, red uniform	2	.25	.35
	---dribbling with left hand, red 23, red left arm band	3	.25	.35
	---jump shot over Laker, red 23, black left arm band	4	.25	.35
	---holding ball overhead in right hand, red 23, mouth open	5	.25	.35
	---looking to the right, red 23, mouth open, closeup	6	.25	.35
	---looking forward, white uniform, mouth open, closeup	7	.25	.35
	---holding ball both hands, red 23, referee in background	8	.25	.35
	---dribbling right hand, white 23, black left arm band, smiling	9	.25	.35
	---layup with right hand, white 23, black left arm band	10	.25	.35
	---jump shot, red 23, view of back black left arm band	11	.25	.35
	---reaching, white 23, mouth open	12	.25	.35
	---closeup, white hat & uniform	13	.25	.35
	---closeup, looking forward, red uniform	14	.25	.35
	---closeup, shooting ball, red uniform	15	.25	.35
	---hands in air overhead, white 23, black left arm band	16	.25	.35
	---shooting, side view, red 23, black left arm band	17	.25	.35
	---holding ball both hands, white 23, mouth open, looking down	18	.25	.35
	---closeup, looking, side view, red uniform	19	.25	.35
	---closeup, looking forward, red 23, mouth open	20	.25	.35
	---jump shot right hand, red 23, black left arm & right wrist	21	.25	.35
	---closeup, shooting right hand, red uniform	22	.25	.35
	---dribbling left hand, red 45, black left arm band	23	.25	.35
	---pointing & dribbling, white 23, black left arm band	24	.25	.35
	---hands on knees, red 45, black left arm band	25	.25	.35
	---dribbling right hand, red 23, black left arm & right wrist	26	.25	.35
	---back view, red 23, black left arm band, waist high view	27	.25	.35
	---dribbling right hand, white 23, black left arm band	28	.25	.35
	---dribbling left hand, red 45, NBA AS uniform, Pacer players	29	.25	.35
	----holding ball both hands, blue NBA AS uniform, white left arm	30	.25	.35
	---close up, looking up, mouth open, red uniform	31	.25	.35
	---dribbling left hand, red 23, black left arm band	32	.25	.35
	---jump shot both hands, red 23, full side view	33	.25	.35
	---jump shot both hands, white 23, front view	34	.25	.35
	---pointing with right hand, white uniform, looking front	35	.25	.35
	---	36	.25	.35
	---looking up, white 45, black left arm band	37	.25	.35
	---reaching both hands overhead, white 45, black left arm band	38	.25	.35
	---looking up, side view, white 45, black left arm band	39	.25	.35
	---	40	.25	.35
	---walking, red 45, black left arm view, black left arm band	41	.25	.35
	---hands on knees, red 45, side view, black left arm band	42	.25	.35
	---holding ball both hands, red 45, black left arm band	43	.25	.35
	---	44	.25	.35
	---walking, close up, red 45, black left arm band	45	.25	.35
	---hands on knees, close up, red, 45, black left arm band	46	.25	.35
	---shooting, back view, red 45, near backboard	47	.25	.35
	---reaching right hand, red 45, 2 other players	48	.25	.35
	---reaching left hand, close up, white 45, black left arm band	49	.25	.35
	---holding ball both hands, white , 45, 2 other players	50	.25	.35
	---hands on hips, red 45, waist, view, Pacer player	51	.25	.35
	---pointing right hand, white 45, front view, waist view	52	.25	.35
	---shooting both hands overhead, red 45, black left arm band	53	.25	.35
	---looking to right, red 45, right hand in fist	54	.25	.35
95	Pogs, MJ Alliance Box, 42 total caps, #20200127, bar code #2807404269, slammer #3, gold 'MJ & BB on plastic box cover	23 cap		
		2 slam		
		1board	15.00	25.00

95	Pogs, Jordans Back Milk CapStarter, Pack, Premier Edition, sealed pack		1.00	2.00
	---MJ caps	5 caps		
	---MJ metal slammer	#1		
95	Pogs, MJ Deluxe Milk Cap Game Set, Premier Edition, red, sealed set		5.00	10.00
	---MJ caps	10 caps		
	---MJ metal slammer	#10		
95	Pogs, MJ Deluxe Milk Cap Game Set, Premier Edition, black, sealed set		5.00	10.00
	---MJ caps	10 caps		
	---MJ metal slammer	#10		
95	Pogs, Air Slammin' Circles, sealed set		2.00	4.00
	---Rare Air Decade of Dominance Card, 3 x 5	1 of 5		
	---MJ caps	25 caps		
	---MJ metal slammer	#6		
	---MJ metal slammer	#14		
95	Pogs, Air Slammin' Circles		2.00	4.00
	---Rare Air Decade of Dominance Card, 3 x 5	2 of 5		
	---MJ caps	25 caps		
	---MJ metal slammer	#		
	---MJ metal slammer	#		
95	Pogs, Air Slammin Circles, sealed set		2.00	4.00
	---Rare Air Decade of Dominance Card, 3 x 5	3 of 5		
	---MJ caps	25caps		
	---MJ metal slammer	#6		
	---MJ metal slammer	#14		
95	Pogs, Air Slammin' Circles, sealed set		2.00	4.00
	---Rare Air Decade of Dominance Card, 3 x 5	4 of 5		
	---MJ caps	25 caps		
	---MJ metal slammer	#6		
	---MJ metal slammer	#14		
95	Pogs, Air Slammin' Circles		2.00	4.00
	---Rare Air Decade of Dominance Card, 3 x 5	5 of 5		
	---MJ caps	25 caps		
	---MJ metal slammer	#		
	---MJ metal slammer	#		
95	Pogs, Air Slammin' Circles		9.00	15.00
	---Rare Air Decade of Dominance Card, 3 x 5	1 of 5		
	---Cards	10 cards		
	---Card Magnifier			
	---MJ Metal Slammer	#		
	---MJ Metal Slammer	#		
95	Pogs, Air Slammin' Circles		9.00	15.00
	---Rare Air Decade of Dominance Card, 3 x 5	2 of 5		
	---Cards	10 cards		
	---Card Magnifier			
	---MJ Metal Slammer	#		
	---MJ Metal Slammer	#		
95	Pogs, Air Slammin Circles		9.00	15.00
	---Rare Air Decade of Dominance Card, 3 x 5	3 of 5		
	---Cards	10 cards		
	---Card Magnifier			
	---MJ Metal Slammer	#		
	---MJ Metal Slammer	#		
95	Pogs, Air Slammin' Circles		9.00	15.00
	---Rare Air Decade of Dominance Card, 3 x 5	4 of 5		
	---Cards	10 cards		
	---Card Magnifier			
	---MJ Metal Slammer	#		
	---MJ Metal Slammer	#		
95	Pogs, Air Slammin' Circles, sealed set		9.00	15.00
	---Rare Air Decade of Dominance Card, 3 x 5	5 of 5		
	---Cards	10 cards		
	---Card Magnifier			
	---MJ Metal Slammer	#4		
	---MJ Metal Slammer	#18		
95	Pogs, Air Slammin' Circle, Street Kaps, sealed set		9.00	15.00
	---#23 on front, #45 on back card, 3 x 5			
	---MJ caps	25caps		
	---MJ metal slammer	#6		
	---MJ metal slammer	#14		
95	Pogs, Air Slammin' Circle, Street Kaps, sealed set		9.00	15.00
	---#23 on front, #45 on back card, 3 x 5			
	---MJ caps	25 caps		
	---MJ metal slammer	#6		

	---MJ metal slammer	#14			
95	Pogs, Air Slammin' Circle, Street Kaps, sealed set			9.00	15.00
	---#45 on front, #23 on back card, 3 x 5				
	---MJ caps	25 caps			
	---MJ metal slammer	#6			
	---MJ metal slammer	#14			
95	Pogs, Street Kaps Set, tube set, red #45 shirt on lid			10.00	15.00
	---MJ caps	23 caps			
	---Regular caps	77 caps			
	---Double blue slammer	1 slam			
	---MJ metal slammer	#13			
	---MJ metal slammer	#13			
95	Pogs, Street Kaps Set, tube set, red #23 MJ on lid			10.00	15.00
	---MJ caps	23 caps			
	---Regular caps	77 caps			
	---Double green slammer	1 slam			
	---MJ metal slammer	#1			
	---MJ metal slammer	#1			
95-96	Metal Card, "The Shot," double side 24k gold, nickel & silver card, bag, 1,982 produced	NNO		125.00	150.00
95-96	Metal Card "He's Back," double sided 24k gold & nickel & silver card, bag, 2,345 produced			125.00	150.00
95-96	Metal Card, "The 1985 Rookie of the Year," double sided 24k gold & silver card, envelope, 1,985 produced			125.00	150.00
95-96	Metal Card, "1988 Slam Dunk Champion," double sided 24k gold, nickel, & silver card, bag & box, 1,988 produced			125.00	150.00
95-96	Metal Card, "4 Time Regular Season MVP," double sided 24kt gold, nickel, & silver card, bag, 1,996 produced			125.00	150.00
96	Ad Sheet, SPX Basketball (9.69)			1.00	2.00
96	Ad Sheet, UDA Catalog Products (9.70)			1.00	2.00
96	Ad Sheet, UDA Catalog Divider (9.71)			1.00	2.00
96	Display, Collector's Choice 3 card, 3 basketballs attached	NNO		12.00	15.00
	---MJ Bulls Victory Tour 95-96				
	---S. Kemp, Slam Dunks & Rebound				
	---A. Hardaway				
96	Foil & Photo Card, 22k, Bulls 72 Victories, white box, red letters, photos of DR, MJ, SP front, team on back (9.62)	3		30.00	40.00
96	Foil & Photo Card, Diamond Star, 23k Bleachers, 10th Time All-Star Selection, 2 view of MJ, black box, white letters, basketball figure & statistics on back (9.62)	4		30.00	40.00
96	Foil Card, Space Jam, 22kt., white box, blue letter, QVC-MJ/Bugs front, story back, 5000 produced (9.62)			35.00	45.00
96	Foil & Photo Card, Diamond Star, 23kt Bleachers, 91, 92, 93 in stars, 2 view of MJ, red box, white letters, 2 figures of basketball & basketball statistics on back (9.62)			25.00	35.00

Year	Description	Qty/ID		
96	Metal Card, Desk Top or Hanging Picture, MJ in white 23, 4 fingers up in right hand, walking, "Michael Jordan" around a BB with sun rays around, 8 x 10		10.00	15.00
96	Metal Cards, "Michael Jordan" on to, "4 All metal Cards" on bottom, MJ shoulder picture white shirt front, US Patent # 5363964, red & black metal can with yellow/orange stripes, back-card front & back shown, side-3 cards shown	4 cards	10.00	15.00
96	Metal Cards, "Michael Jordan" on top, "6 All Metal Collector Cards" on bottom, red & black can, QVC-3 views layup LH, 2 hand shot raised view, back view, red 23, US Patent #s 5363964 & 5538135	6 cards	20.00	30.00
96	Metal Card, "MJ 8 Time Scoring Champion Card," silver with 24kt, select, 1,996 mintage		35.00	45.00
96	Pogs, Refuse to Lose Pack, sealed pack		10.00	15.00
	---"Bulls Win 70 Games" card, red border, SP, MJ, DR front; SK, RH, TK-back, 3 x 5			
	---Upper Deck Collector Choice Cards	15 cards		
	---MJ metal slammer	#10		
	---Regular caps	18caps		
96	Sheet, Salutes The 1996 US Olympic Team at the Centennial Olympic Games, Atlanta, Georgia; blank back, MJ & AH-Passing the Torch card, 3 other cards pictured no MJ (9.72)	22407	15.00	20.00
96	Sheet, Salutes 1996 NBA All-Star Weekend, on MJ picture 96 All-Star Weekend at San Antonio, Texas, blank back (9.73)	NNO	12.00	15.00
96	Standee, MJ-Life Size Cardboard Display holding ball, white 23, "Jordan Standee"	14180	25.00	35.00
96-97	Binder, BB Card Kit, sheets, red/gray, black 23		2.00	4.00
97	Ad folder, 1997-1998 Diamond Vision Motion Cards, Premier		5.00	10.00
	---MJ in insert, Reel Time Card			
97	Foil & Photo Card, All-Star Power, 22kt, photos of Kemp, MJ & Hardaway, AS Weekend in Cleveland, 5,000 mintage (9.62)		20.00	25.00
97	Plates-MJ's Greatest Moments			
	---The 4th Title, holding trophy, jumping with BB, red 23, shooting ball with #23, June 16, 1996	3.5" 88181	8.00	15.00
	---97 Finals, Game 1 Win, dribbling RH white 23, holding fist white 23, shooting RH white 23, June 1, 1997	3.5" 88181	8.00	15.00
97	Standee, MJ Life Size Cardboard Display, shooting ball, red 23	40264	25.00	35.00

9.72

THE UPPER DECK COMPANY SALUTES
THE 1996 U.S. OLYMPIC TEAM
AT THE CENTENNIAL OLYMPIC GAMES
ATLANTA, GEORGIA

Highlights from the exclusive Upper Deck U.S. Olympic Champions Olympicard™ set featuring: Passing the Torch

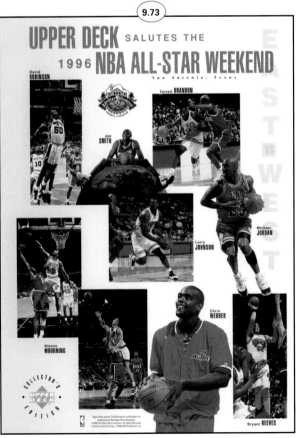

9.73

UPPER DECK SALUTES THE 1996 NBA ALL-STAR WEEKEND
San Antonio, Texas
EAST vs WEST

UDA Items

	Item	No.		
-	Baseball, Autographed		360.00	400.00
-	Basketball, MJ Autographed	14091	600.00	900.00
-	Basketball, MJ Autographed "I'm Back," laser, 1,995 issued	14154	650.00	950.00
-	Basketball, Wilson, "Jordan Portrait Basketball" Painting, autographed, 200 issues	13311	1600.00	2000.00
-	Basketball/Baseball, MJ Autographed, Nike, with Display, 1,000 issued	13609	350.00	450.00
-	Bat, Autographed, Baseball, 500 issued		800.00	1000.00
-	Book, "Rare Air," Linen Sleeve, autographed	12343	500.00	700.00
-	Book, "Rare Air," Linen Sleeve, 2,500 issued	12917	100.00	150.00
-	Book, "Rare Air," with black cover, slipcase, autographed, #12917, 2,500 issued	12343	500.00	600.00
-	Book, "Rare Air," with black cover, slipcase, unsigned, 2,500 issued	12343	100.00	150.00
-	Cap, Autographed, White Sox, 500 issued		200.00	250.00
-	Card, NC, "10 Time All-Star," die cut, commemorative, 3.5 x 5	14377	15.00	25.00
-	Cover, Sports Illustrated, 7/84, "USA," framed, 2,500 issued	13027	100.00	150.00
-	Cover, Sports Illustrated, '84 "A Star is Born," framed, 2,500 issued	12716	100.00	150.00
-	Floor, Autographed Chicago Stadium, with Gatorade 8 x 10,	14253	800.00	900.00
-	Jersey, Autographed, #23 Red, unframed	12701	950.00	1100.00
-	Jersey, Autographed, #23 White, unframed	12703	950.00	1100.00
-	Jersey, Autographed, #23 Black, unframed	14184	950.00	1100.00
-	Jersey, Autographed, #45 Red, N/A, unframed	14126	950.00	1100.00
-	Jersey, Autographed, #45 White, N/A, unframed	14127	950.00	1100.00
-	Jersey, Autographed Barons, white, unframed, 500 issued		700.00	1100.00
-	Newspaper, MJ Chicago Tribune Retirement, 2,500 issued, 10/13/93, framed	12736	100.00	200.00
-	Newspaper, MJ Chicago Tribune Cover, "Thanks for the Memories," 1000 issued	12736	100.00	200.00
-	Photo, Autographed "Returns," unframed Josten, 8 x 10	14136	300.00	400.00
-	Photo, Autographed "Gatorade Slam, Dunk," framed, 8 x 10	14087	300.00	400.00
-	Photo, Autographed "Crying Trophy," framed, 16 x 20	12705	600.00	700.00
-	Photo, Autographed "Crying Trophy," unframed, 16 x 20	12706	500.00	600.00
-	Photo, Autographed "Slam Dunk," unframed, 16 x 20	12711	500.00	600.00
-	Photo, Autographed "Slam Dunk," framed, 16 x 20	12712	600.00	700.00
-	Photo, Autographed "Jordan Flying," 16 x 20, framed	12712	600.00	700.00
-	Photo, Autographed "Jordan Flying," 16 x 20, unframed	12711	500.00	600.00
-	Photo, Autographed "Trophy," 16 x 20, framed	12705	600.00	700.00
-	Photo, Autographed "Trophy," 16 x 20, unframed	12706	500.00	600.00
-	Photo, Unsigned "Trophy," 16 x 20, frame	12708	150.00	250.00
-	Photo, MJ/Magic/Bird Autographs, 16 x 20, USA, framed	12888	1200.00	1300.00
-	Photo, MJ/Magic/Bird Autographs, 16 x 20, USA	12889	1200.00	1300.00
-	Photo, MJ/Magic Autographs, 91 Finals, 16 x 20, 1,991 issued	12879	900.00	1000.00
-	Photo, MJ/Magic Autographs, 91 Finals, 16 x 20, 1,991 issued	12880	800.00	900.00
-	Photo, MJ/Magic Autographs, At Net, 16 x 20 framed	12709	900.00	1000.00
-	Photo, MJ/Magic Autographs, At Net, 16 x 20 unframed	12710	800.00	900.00
-	Photo, NC, Autographed "17 Seconds," 8 x 10, unframed Josten	14260	300.00	400.00
-	Photo, NC, Autographed, "UNC Dunk," 16 x 20, framed	13258	600.00	700.00
-	Photo, NC, Autographed "UNC Dunk," 16 x 20, unframed	13259	500.00	600.00
-	Photo, NC, Autographed "17 Seconds," 16 x 20, unframed, 750 issued	14144	500.00	600.00
-	Photo & Spring Training Ticket, matted & framed	3312	100.00	200.00
-	Pins, MJ Individual, 12 Pack	14100	135.00	225.00

Year	USA Today Newspapers			
6/13/91	Bulls Capture 1st NBA Title	cover	12.00	20.00
6/15/91	Chicago Bulls to 2nd Title	cover	12.00	20.00
6/21/91	Bulls' Three-Peat Thriller	cover	12.00	20.00
6/4/93	Weekend Newspaper Insert-Is This the New National Past	cover	8.00	15.00
10/7/93	Goodbye To The Game	cover	8.00	15.00
4/19/94	Baseball Weekly, Michael Mania	cover	5.00	10.00
10/11/94	Baseball Weekly, Is Arizona Out of Jordan's League	cover	5.00	10.00
4/24/97	Who can beat the Bulls	cover	4.00	8.00
6/2/97	MJ Stops Jazz at Buzzer	cover	4.00	8.00
6/3/97	MJ Knows Malone's Agony	inside	4.00	8.00
6/4/97	Round 2 for Utah, Chica	inside	4.00	8.00
6/5/97	Bulls Silence Jazz	front	4.00	8.00
6/6-8/97	Can Jazz Stay Alive	front	4.00	8.00
6/9/97	Utah Ties Bulls 2-2	front	4.00	8.00
6/10/97	Jordan Hopes Tie	front	4.00	8.00
6/11/97	Sloan Has Jazz Rock	inside	4.00	8.00
6/12/97	Bulls Beat Jazz	front	4.00	8.00
6/13-15/97		front	4.00	8.00
6/16/97	Jazz & Bulls Look to Next Season	inside	3.00	5.00
4/28-26/98	Bulls Open Title Defense Tonight	front	3.00	5.00
6/8/98	Bulls Bash Jazz, 96-54	front	3.00	5.00
6/11/98	Bulls One Away, 86-82	front	3.00	5.00
6/12-14/98	The Final Show Down, Bulls vs. Jazz	front	3.00	5.00
6/15/98	Michael's Miracle Finish	front	3.00	5.00

Year	Videos & Related Items	product code number	
1996	America's Greatest Olympians, A Century of America's Best Athletes, highlights Barcelona's Games, MJ inside, Turner Original Productions #3293V (10.1)	53939 32933	20.00
1993	Best of Saturday Night Live, Hosted by MJ, Celebrity Sports, purple box with yellow circle around MJ, MJ front & back, 1991 NBC program, 1993 Starmaker Entertainment, Inc. #640001, Video by Technicolor (10.2)	92091 6401 3	20.00
1993	Blood Sweat & Glory, Hosted by NBC's Bob Costas, MJ front, name on back, Poly Gram Video, Trans World International (10.3)	440 086401 3	30.00
-	College Slam Basketball's Rams, Slams and Jams, MJ name on back, Aklaim Entertainment Inc., #51069, Best Buy Exclusive (10.4)	00027 13488	15.00
1989	Dazzling Dunks and Basketball Bloopers, cartoon like front with players, MJ picture on back, CBS fox Video Sports #2229, gray box, red letters front (10.5)	8616 22229 3	25.00
1993	Dazzling Dunks and Basketball Bloopers, cartoon like front with players, MJ picture on back, CBS fox Video Sports #2229, gray box, red letters front (10.6)	8616 22229 3	25.00
1988	Higher Ground, Chicago Bulls, 1987-88 Season, Official NBA Video Yearbook, MJ on front & back, red 23, back MJ with AS Trophy, NBA Entertainment Company, CBS Fox Video, #5213 (10.7)	8616 25213 3	40.00
1991	Learning to Fly, The World Champion Chicago Bulls' Rise to Glory, MJ front & back, CBS Fox Company #3272 (10.8)	8616 23272 3	25.00

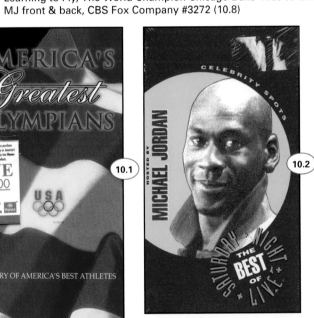

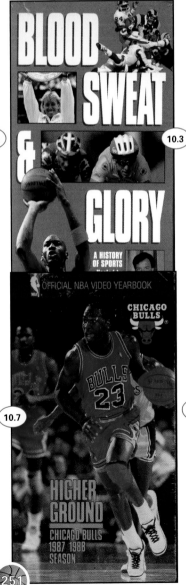

1992	Legendary Stars of Basketball, 50 All Time Greats, MJ front, name on back, Alpha Video Distributors, stock #39012 (10.9)	89218 39012 7	25.00	
1995	March Maddess, Greatest Games of the NCAA Championships, MJ front, name on back, CBS Sports Video, #4302 (10.10)	8616 243023	25.00	
1993	McDonald's Corporation Seizing The Global Marketplace, 1992 Annual Report Shareholder Audience Tape, MJ/Bird Nothing But Net Commercial Box, MJ on tape (10.11)		75.00	
1996	Michael Jordan: Above & Beyond, MJ front and back, CBS Fox Video Sports #8360, NBA Video (10.12)	8616 28360 3	20.00	
1993	Michael Jordan: Air Time, Hanes logo, MJ front and back, CBS Fox Video #5770 (10.13)	8616 25770 3	25.00	
1993	Michael Jordan: Air Time Video Ad Foldout Standie (10.14)	2 sheets	15.00	
1993	Michael Jordan: Air Time Video $5.00 rebate brochure & coupon, Hanes and Sara Lee promotion (10.15)		15.00	
1993	Michael Jordan 3 Video Set ---Learning to Fly Bulls ---UntouchaBulls Bulls ---Threepeat Bulls		40.00	50.00
1994	Michael Jordan 2 Video Set, MJ front & back, CBS Fox Sports Video #8186 (10.16) ---Air Time ---Come Fly with Me	8616 281863	35.00	

10.9

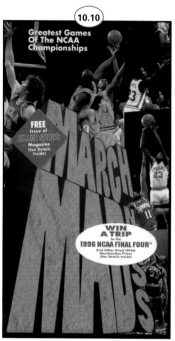

10.10

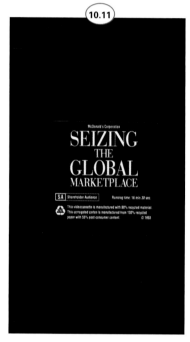

10.11

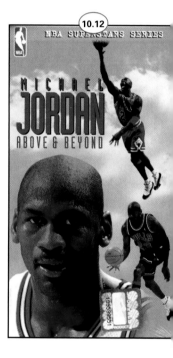

10.12

10.13

10.14

10.15

10.16

	---44 Page Booklet		
-	Michael Jordan 2 Video Set		40.00
	---Basketball Bloopers		
	---Amazing Slam, Rams & Jams		
1989	Michael Jordan: Come Fly With Me, MJ front & back, CBS Fox	8616	
	Video Sports #2173 (10.17)	22173	20.00
1989	Michael Jordan's Come Fly With Me free video ad with Coca-Cola (10.18)		20.00
16-18			
1989	Michael Jordan's Come Fly With Me insert card in video movie,		
	T shirt ad on back of card, 500 cards produced (10.19)		75.00
1991	Michael Jordan's Playground, Whole Grain Wheaties The Breakfast Of	8618	
	Champions, CBS Fox Video Sports #2858, MJ front & back (10.20)	22858 3	20.00
1996	Michael Jordan, The Ultimate Collection-3 video set,	8616	
	CBS Fox Video Sports #4101090 (10.21)	201090	35.00
	---Michael Jordan: Above & Beyond		
	---Michael Jordan: Air Time		
	---Michael Jordan: Come Fly With Me		
1987	MJ vs. The Sheens, War of the Stars, MJ front & back,	82554	
	Sports Legends Video (10.22)	15001	45.00
1994	NBA All Star Action The Greatest Players and Plays, Foot Locker,	8616	
	NBA Video, #8199, MJ name back (10.23)	281993	25.00
1996	NBA at 50, Golden Anniversary Collector's Edition, Bonus 50	8616	
	Greatest Players Feature, CBS Fox Video Sports #8450, MJ inside (10.24)	28450 3	20.00

(10.17)  (10.18)  (10.19) 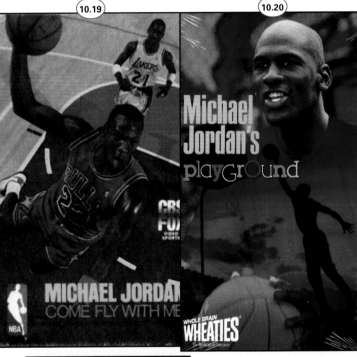 (10.20)

(10.21)  (10.22) 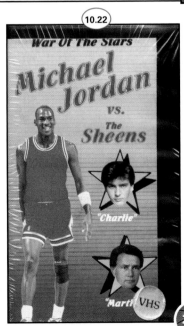 (10.23) 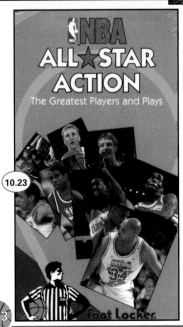 (10.24)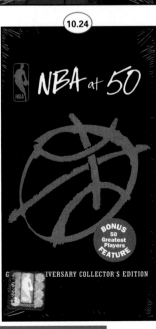

1990	NBA Awesome Endings, MJ picture front & name back,	8616			
	CBS Fox Video Sports #2288 (10.25)	222883	35.00		
1993	NBA Awesome Endings, MJ front & name on back,	8616			
	CBS Fox Video Sports #2288 (10.26)	222883	25.00		
1996	NBA Commemorative Set-3 video set, MJ listed on back and inside,	8616			
	CBS Fox Video Sports #5624 for all three (10.27)	256243	40.00		
	---UD NBA Commemorative Sheet				
	---Classic Confrontations	#2545			
	---Champions, The NBA's Greatest Teams	#2888			
	---Milestones, Record Breakers of the NBA	#2886			
1997	NBA Court Side Comedy-Action Series, CBS Fox Video, NBA Entertainment		15.00	20.00	
1992	NBA Dream Team, Highlights And Personalities of the Ultimate				
	Basketball Team, MJ name front & picture on back, CBS Fox	8616			
	Video Sports #5616 (10.28)	25616 3	30.00		
1997	NBA Finals 1997		15.00	20.00	
1996	NBA Furious Finishes, NBA Action Series, red & blue front,	8616			
	MJ white 23, MJ front, name on back CBS Fox Video Sports #8322 (10.29)	28322 3	20.00		
1994	NBA Guts and Glory, NBA Heroes in the Most Inspiring Performance,	8616			
	MJ in red 23, brown front CBS Fox Video Sports #5981, MJ front (10.30)	25981 3	25.00		
1996	NBA Guts and Glory, NBA Heroes in the Most Inspiring Performance,				
	NBA Action Series, MJ white 23, red blue front, CBS Fox Video	8616			
	Sports #5981, MJ front & back (10.31)	25981 3	20.00		
1993	NBA Jam Session, The Hottest NBA Players Jammin' to Today's	8616			
	Hottest Music, CBS Fox Company #5559, MJ name back (10.32)	255593	25.00		

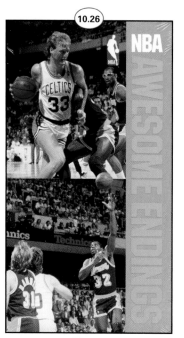

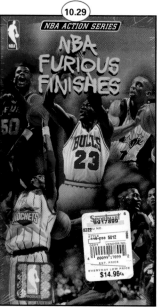

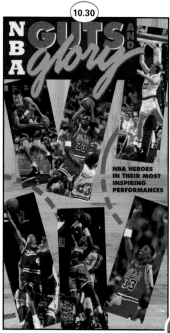

Year	Description	Code	Code2	Price
1995	NBA Legacy, Living Legends to Rising Stars, MJ picture & name on back, CBS Fox Video Sports #8328, NBA Video (10.33)	8616	283283	35.00
1993	NBA Showmen, The Spectacular Guards, MJ name front, picture back, CBS Fox Video Sports #2382 (10.34)	8616	223823	20.00
1995	NBA Super Slams-2, blue border front, SP in white 33, MJ picture and name on back, CBS Fox Video Sports #8198 (10.35)	8616	28198	15.00
1996	NBA Super Slams-2, NBA Action Series, red & blue border front, SP in red 33, MJ picture & name on back, CBS Fox Video Sports #8198	8616	28198 3	20.00
1990	NBA Superstars, Superstar Basketball Music Videos, MJ front & back, CBS Fox Video Sports #2422 (10.37)	8616	224223	20.00
1992	NBA Superstars 2, MJ front and name on back, CBS Fox Video Sports #5558 (10.38) ---Audio Cassette, Guy, The Outfield, Pattie Labelle	8616	255583	20.00
1992	One Shining Moment, Best of the NCAA Championships, MJ front & name on back, CBS Video, Inc., CBS Fox 5551, 92 NCAA Productions (10.39)	8616	255513	30.00
1988	OJ Simpson Sports Legend-Interview Hosted by MJ, MJ's first video, black banner "Interview Hosted by Michael Jordan," with MJ picture front Parade Video #563, Program Sports Legends INC, PPI Entertainment Group (10.40)	71083	00563	35.00

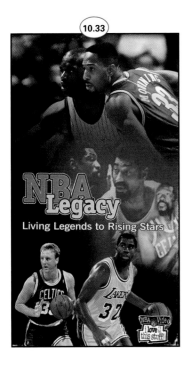

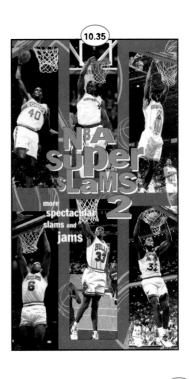

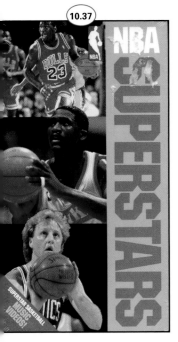

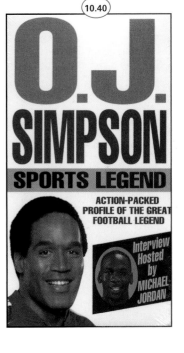

1988	OJ Simpson Sports Legend-Interview Hosted by MJ, MJ's first video, black banner "Revealing Interviews College & NFL Highlights," no MJ picture on front, Parade Video #563, Program Sports Legends INC, PPI Entertainment Group, back interview hosted by MJ (10.41)	71083 00563	15.00
1992	Ohio Sports "Play Like a Pro" video, free with purchase of MJ Pro Basketball Set, red box with blue edge, MJ on BB backboard, boy doing reverse layup (10.42)		65.00
-	Ohio Sports "Play Like a Pro" Video Ad, Error "Larry Jordan" (10.43)		15.00
-	Ohio Sports "Play Like a Pro" video, free with purchase of MJ Pro Basketball Set, instruction video with Larry Jordan, red box, MJ in red shirt, black vest like shirt, blue shorts, dunking backwards, view from above basket		50.00
1991	Pro Stars, Knightmare Riders, MJ front and back, DIC Video #2361 (10.44)	65362 3610 3	35.00
1991	Pro Stars, Short John's Revenge, MJ front and back, DIC Video #2362 (10.45)	65362 3630 3	35.00
1991	Pro Stars, The Slugger's Return, MJ front and back, DIC Video #2363 (10.46)	65362 3630 3	35.00
1994	Shooting Stars II of the NCAA Championships, MJ front, name on back, CBS Sports, #5972 (10.47)	8616 259723	25.00
1996	Space Jam Video, MJ front, Warner Brothers #16400 (10.48)	85391 64003	15.00

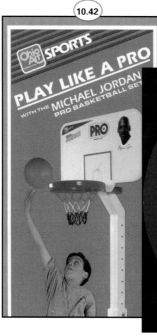

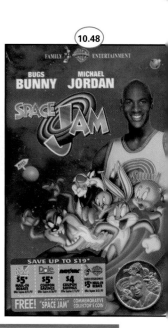

---Commemorative Collector's Coin				
---"The Monstars Go To Court," Courtside Action Sticker Book				
1996 Space Jam Video Holder Store Display with Basketball, "Take Your Best Shot..."			35.00	50.00
---Space Jam Basketball, green & black				
---Space Jam Video, Warner Brothers #16400	85391			
	64003			
---Commemorative Collector's Coin				
1992 Sports Pages: Basketball Funnies, Volume 2, MJ name on front, Combined	82551			
Artists, Similar Entertainment Inc., #2566 (10.49)	25663	15.00		
1922 Sport Illustrated 1992 The Year in Sports, Olympic Team & Washington				
Redskins on front, HBO Sports, Time Inc., MJ front cover (10.50)	NNO	20.00		
1991 Sports Illustrated Video Presents: MJ Come Fly with Me 1991,	8616			
MJ front and back, free with paid (10.51)	224593	45.00		
Sports Illustrated: Pro Basketball Hoops Bloops		20.00		
1991 Super Slams of the NBA, MJ, Kemp, Wilkens, Drexler, Dawkins, Erving on				
front cover, MJ front & name on back, CBS Fox Video #3244,	8616			
blue box cover front, Maximum DPM back (10.52)	23244 3	20.00		
1992 Super Stars of Sports-Basketball, Original Film Highlights,	8255			
MJ front & name on back, Entertainment #2520 (10.53)	425283	25.00		
1991 The Making of Michael Jordan's Playground, MJ front and back,	8616			
CBS Fox Video, #3378 (10.54)	233783	35.00		
1993 The Secret NBA, Players and Coaches Only, MJ front,	8616			
CBS Fox Video Sports #5789 (10.55)	25789 3	20.00		

Year	Description			
1993	The Story of A Game, The Official History of Basketball, Vol. 2, Hosted by Jim McKay, MJ name on front, TNT Express Worldwide, Molten, Wienerworld Sports, Strand Home Video #6502 (10.56)	95492 6502 3		15.00
1993	Threepeat: The Chicago Bulls' Historic Third Champion Season, Special Offer-Salem Sportwear NBA Championship T-Shirt, CBS Fox Video Sports #5809, MJ front and back (10.57)	8616 25809 3		20.00
1992	True Value, ACC Dream Team, Lever 2000, Raycom/JP Sports, MJ front & back, college superstars, wearing Converse (10.58)	NNO		20.00
1996	Unstop A Bulls, The Chicago Bulls 1995-96 Championship Season, NBA Video, CBS Fox Sports Video #8345 (10.59)	8616 28345 3		20.00
1992	UntouchaBulls The Chicago Bulls' Second Championship Season, Exclusive Bulls Music Video featuring M. Jackson's Jam, CBS Fox Sports Video #5560, MJ front & back (10.60)	8616 25560 3		20.00

Year	Wheaties Cereal Box	item # or size		
97	Basketball, Mail-In, MJ, General Mills Company		3.00	5.00
94/95	Card, Sports Stars USA, MJ in Sox Hat, silver signature, back "You Better Eat Your Wheaties," MJ signature	103	2.00	4.00
-	Card, Small Box Front-eating cereal from white bowl, bag on shoulder		2.00	4.00
-	Card, MJ jumping with ball in right hand, blue green shirt & shorts, back "You Better Eat Your Wheaties"		2.00	4.00
-	Card, MJ jumping with ball in right hand, blue green shirt & shorts, green triangle, back "You Better Eat Your Wheaties"		2.00	4.00
-	Card, MJ jumping with ball in right hand, blue green shirt & shorts, black signature, back "You Better Eat Your Wheaties," yellow to orange fade		2.00	4.00
97	Coupons, Honey Frosted Wheaties, Crispy Wheaties N'Raisins, sheet plus complete coupon folder	3 coupon	3.00	6.00
91-92	Puzzle, MJ Pouring Cereal in white Wheaties bowl, blue banner "Made with 100% Whole Grain, distributed at games, black signature and border Back-Whole Grain Wheaties Has It. 4 pictures, wheat stalk (10.61)	10.5 x 14	75.00	100.00

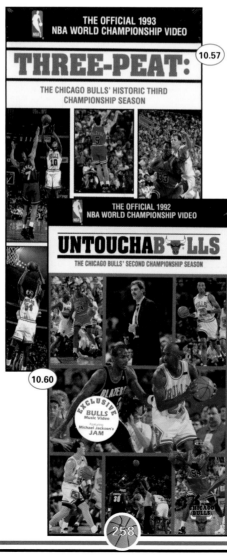

Year	Wichita Eagle Beacon Newspaper			
2/84	Wichita Eagle Beacon, pictures & article, with MJ, C.E. Lloyd, J. Colbert (10.62)	NNO	75.00	150.00

Year	Wilson			
'87	Magazine ad sheet, from Sports Illustrated, "Trask Jr. High, Wilmington, NC Site of MJ's Pick-Up Games," Wilson BB & logo on bottom right side of page, b&w school yard picture, BB hoop, fence and school buses in background, back has "From the Publisher" article Donald J. Barr on SI's Linda Verigan responses to letter (10.63)	8.5 x 11	20.00	25.00
'91-92	Action Watch, black band buckle end loop, 23 in red background & Wilson on end loop, Wilson BB "Michael Jordan" "Wilson" on hole side, round black face with silver bezel, red signature, MJ with BB and hoop, seal plastic holder		25.00	40.00
'91-92	Watch Set (10.64)	LMJ070 49353 06383	65.00	100.00
	---Watch			
	---Key Chain			
	---Wallet			
	---MJ ID Card			
'91-94	Action Watch, black band loop & buckle, red "23" on loop, red "W" on buckle end, MJ with BB in right hand & basket on hole end, This watch is in the FARLEY SECTION, square black face no bezel, red "Wilson" & "Michael Jordan," square digital opening, sealed plastic holder (10.65)	LMJ003 49353 05963	75.00	125.00
'91-94	Action Watch & Basketball shoe key chain, black band loop & buckle, four red stripes on each band end, red "W" on loop, Wilson BB on hole side, round black face no bezel, lift plastic cover, MJ with BB in right hand basket & white signature on cover, 5 function digital watch,	LMJ071 49353		

10.62

10.63

10.64

10.65

259

	sealed plastic holder (10.65)	06788	45.00	65.00
91-95	Watch, black band & loop, silver buckle, orange Wilson BB on hole side, blue "Water Resist" on face bottom, white "30m" on face bottom, square digital opening with second square opening with days of week, roung black face, silver bezel with "Alarm Chrono Water Resist," MJ dribbling & white signature on face top, orange lines on face sides (10.65)	LMJ075	25.00	45.00
91-96	Action Watch, black band loop and buckle, four red stripes on each band end, red "W" on loop, Wilson BB on hole side, round black face no bezel, lift plastic cover, MJ with BB in right hand basket & white signature on cover, 5 function digital watch, sealed plastic holder (10.65)	LMJ002 49353 05962	15.00	25.00
91-96	Watch-black band & loop, silver buckle, orange Wilson BB on hole side, round black face, lines in black bezel, MJ with BB in right hand on face top, leg & red signature on face bottom, square digital opening, 3 silver side buttons, with cardboard box (10.65)	LMJ053	30.00	40.00
91-97	Watch, black band, white face, BB net/ball on face, MJ shooting on face, black signature, second hand with BB, gray plastic box case (10.65)	LMJ056	60.00	75.00
92-96	Action Watch, black band & end loop, silver buckle, "W" on end loop side, white "Michael Jordan" signature on hole side, round gold bezel with 60 second marks, black digital face, gold signature, MJ with BB in right hand, "Wilson" on top, "Sports" on bottom, sealed plastic holder (10.65)	LMJ073 49353 07645	20.00	30.00
93	Calculator & Watch Set, black band & loop, silver buckle, red "W" & "Wilson" on loop side, calculator with protractor & ruler on outside, square like face no bezel, MJ with BB in hand no back, square digital face, gold white red blue lines on face, sealed plastic holder (10.64)	LMJ2005 49363 08995	30.00	45.00
94	Ad sheet, MJ Makes Wilson a Big Hit, Tennessee Sports Offers 11 models, in MJ Signature Series, wooden bat in Adult, LL, & T-ball, 2 anodized & 2 painted aluminum in both Little League & Dixie Youth (10.66) ---Wilson, MJ white signature, Official Model#13MJBB ---Gray/red signature ---Gray signature over red "Jordan" next to batter swinging ---Gray signature over red "Jordan" ---Red signature over gray "Jordan" that fades light to dark		15.00	25.00
94	Bat Set, Kid (10.67) ---Black bat ---Ball on end of bat ---MJ cutout card on ball, card top MJ #45, back Wilson information, bottom Birmingham Barons, all black borders, red signature, # of 2,000		60.00	100.00
94	"MJ Action Watch," black band buckle end loop, red 23 on end loop, white/red "W" on band buckle side, MJ figure & basket on band end, square face with black bezel, red "Wilson" top face, red "Michael Jordan" bottom face, 2 silver buttons/bottom sides (10.65)		20.00	25.00
95	Pocket Calendar, white t-shirt & black shorts, 4 MJ pictures/3 negative-like pictures (10.68)		35.00	45.00
95	"Wilson MJ Action Stop Watch," 3 red buttons, gray face, white sign, red cord (10.65)		15.00	20.00

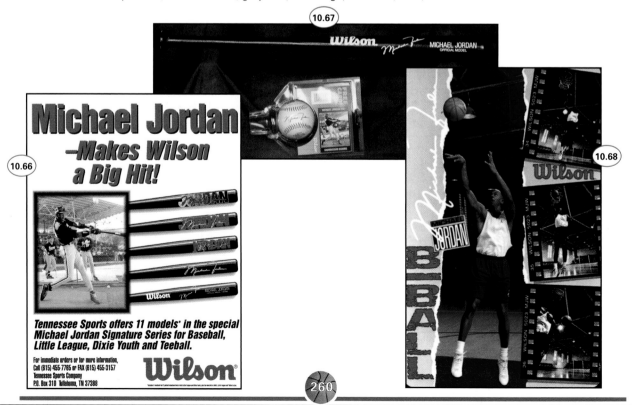

95-96	He's Back/Glo Watch, black band and loop, silver buckle, red "Glowatch" & "45" on loop end, red "Wilson & Michael Jordan" on hole end, "Wilson BB on hole end, inside lid MJ picture in red 45 tongue out, round black face with black bezel/red triangles, MJ red 45 BB in right hand on face top, red "He's Back" on face bottom, square digital opening, tan leather case with red/black "45," black signature & Wilson BB on top, red/black "Michael Jordan" on front lid (10.65)	LMJ206 X CR2016	45.00	60.00
95-97	Glo Watch, black band & loop, silver plastic buckle, red "Wilson" & "23" on loop side, red "Wilson" & "Michael Jordan" & Wilson BB on hole side, round black face with silver bezel, MJ with BB in right hand and basket, square digital opening, red signature, gray plastic box (10.65)	LMJ210	25.00	35.00
95-97	Glo Watch, black band, loop, & black plastic buckle, red "Wilson" & "23" on loop side, red "Wilson" & "Michael Jordan" & Wilson BB on hole side, round black face with silver bezel, MJ with BB in right hand and basket, square digital opening, red signature, sealed holder (10.65)	LMJ210	20.00	30.00
95-97	Watch, black band, multi-color face, shooting BB on face, gold & silver bezel, white signature, red & black basketball case (10.65)	LMJ208 X	60.00	80.00
96	Watch, black flex like bands & loop, gold buckle & holes, large face, plastic case no lid, round face, gold bezel with number, MJ dribbling with left hand, tongue out, red 23, gold hands (10.65)	WLS104 3MJ	15.00	20.00
96	Watch, black leather band & loop, gold buckle, white autograph on hole side, small face, plastic case no lid, round face, gold bezel with number, MJ dribbling with left hand, tongue out, red 23, gold hands (10.65)	WLS104 3MJ	15.00	20.00
96	Watch, black flex like bands & loop, gold buckle & holes, small face, plastic case no lid, round face, gold bezel with number, MJ hands on hips, tongue out, white 23, gold hands (10.65)	WLS104 3MJ	15.00	20.00
96	Watch, black leather bands & loop, gold buckle, white signature on hole side, large face, plastic case no lid, round face, silver bezel with number, MJ hands on hips, tongue out, white 23, silver hands (10.65)	WLS104 3MJ	15.00	20.00
96	Watch, black flex like band & loop, gold buckle & holes, large face, plastic case no lid, round face, gold bezel with number, MJ closeup, towel on shoulders, mouth open, red 23, gold hands (10.65)	WLS104 3MJ	15.00	20.00
96	Watch, black leather band & loop, silver buckle, white signature on hole side, large face, plastic case no lid, round face, silver bezel with number, MJ closeup, towel on shoulders, mouth open, red 23, silver hands (10.65)	WLS104 3MJ	15.00	20.00
96	Watch, black flex like band & loop, gold buckle & holes, large face, plastic case no lid, round face, gold bezel with number, MJ dribbling with right hand, mouth open, white 23, gold hands (10.65)	WLS104 3MJ	15.00	20.00
96	Watch, black leather band & loop, silver buckle, white signature on hole side, small face, plastic case no lid, round face, silver bezel with number, MJ dribbling with right hand, mouth open, white 23, silver hands (10.65)	WLS104 3MJ	15.00	20.00
96	Watch, black flex like band & loop, silver buckle & holes, large face, plastic case no lid, round face, silver bezel with number, MJ hands on knees, mouth open smiling, red 23, gold hands (10.65)	WLS104 3MJ	15.00	20.00
96	Watch, black leather band & loop, gold buckle, white signature on hole side, large face, plastic case no lid, round face, gold bezel with number, MJ hands on knees, mouth open smiling, red 23, gold hands	WLS104 3MJ	15.00	20.00
96	Watch, black flex like band & loop, gold buckle & holes, small face, plastic case no lid, round face, gold bezel with number, MJ close up, mouth open smiling, white 23, gold hands	WLS104 3MJ	15.00	20.00
96	Watch, black leather band & loop, gold buckle, white signature on hole side, large face, plastic case no lid, round face, gold bezel with number, MJ closeup, mouth open smiling, white 23, gold hands	WLS104 3MJ	15.00	20.00
96	Watch, black flex like band & loop, silver buckle & holes, large face, plastic case no lid, round face, silver bezel with number, MJ hands overhead shooting, white 23, silver hands	WLS104 3MJ	15.00	20.00
96	Watch, black leather band & loop, gold buckle, white signature on hole side, small face, plastic case no lid, round face, gold bezel with number, MJ hands overhead shooting, white 23, gold hands	WLS104 3MJ	15.00	20.00
96	Watch, black flex like band & loop, silver buckle & holes, small face, plastic case no lid, round face, silver bezel with number, "Jordan 23" & white autograph on face, silver hands	WLS104 3MJ	15.00	20.00
96	Watch, black leather band & loop, gold buckle, white signature on hole side, large face, plastic case no lid, round face, gold bezel with number, "Jordan 23" & white autograph on face, gold hands	WLS104 3MJ	15.00	20.00
96-97	Watch, "MVP," blue band, black buckle and end loop, red "Michael" BB on loop side, red "Michael," blue "Jordan" on hole side of band, blue to black face, no bezel, MJ red 23 with BB & Wilson on face, bald MJ, digital, sealed plastic holder		45.00	65.00
96-97	Watch, black band with 2-#23 patches, MJ dribbling on face, numbers on bezel, silver bezel white #23 & signature on red & black basketball case	LMJ214 X	45.00	65.00
96-97	Watch, black band with engraved autograph, numbers on gold bezel, white signature on inside and outside of BB red and black case, MJ shooting ball on face, gold hands, black signature on face	LMJ215	55.00	75.00

96-97	Watch, black band and loop, gold buckle, white signature on hole side on band, round face, gold bezel with numbers, MJ with towel on face, gold hands, black plastic case	LMJ224	65.00	85.00
-	Action Watch, black band end loop & buckle, "W" on loop end, red "23" on loop, MJ with bb in right hand & basket on hole side, square red face no bezel, square digital opening, black "Wilson" & "Michael Jordan" on face, sealed plastic holder	CD125 49353 06149	20.00	30.00
-	Action Watch, black band end loop & buckle, "W" on band and loop, 2 red stripes on loop side, red "23" & MJ with BB in right hand & basket & 2 red stripes on hole side, round black face, not bezel, digital square opening, "Wilson" gold BB in hoop on face, sealed plastic holder	CD125 49353 06149	20.00	30.00
-	Backboard, MJ Limited Edition 10 year warranty, MJ dribbling LH on right side, fiberglass, red to black border	08461-LTF	50.00	100.00
-	Backboard, MJ Limited Edition 20 year warranty, MJ dribbling LH on right side, graphite, black to red border	08461-LTG	100.00	200.00
-	Basketball, hand painted, 2 MJ views, holding BB, red 23 & background: white 23, Indoor/Outdoor "Pro Staff" ball, Last Built, inflate to 7-9 lbs. (10.68)	C32312	110.00	150.00
-	Slam Dunk Watch, black band & loop, silver buckle, red "W" & "Wilson" on loop side, square like face no bezel, MJ with BB in hand no back, square digital face, gold white red blue lines on face, sealed plastic holder		25.00	35.00

Year	Wincraft Salem Company Pins	pin # & size		
92	"USA America's Team, Made in the USA," team picture with flag in the background	2"x 2"	5.00	10.00
92	"World Champions USA BB Dream Team," blue top, gold stars, red & white stripe bottom	3.5"	10.00	15.00
-	"Michael Jordan," dunking behind back, black border & signature, red background, white #23 (10.69)	07209 2"x 2"	5.00	10.00
-	"Michael Jordan," holding ball in right hand, cartoon like, red 23, Bulls Logo bottom right, red boarder, blue background	07209 2"x 2"	5.00	10.00

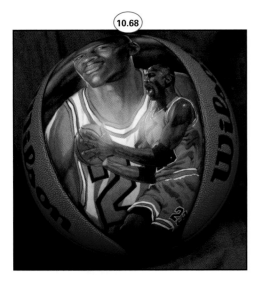

10.68

10.69

WinCraft INCORPORATED

OFFICIALLY LICENSED PLAYER BUTTON

10.70

VITAMIN D MILK

GROW LIKE A PRO

Year	Wisconsin Dairy Council			
89-90	Wisconsin Dairy Council			
	---Grow Like A Pro School Folder (10.70)		35.00	45.00
	---Card, 4 x 8 (10.71)		100.00	135.00

Year	Yugoslavian			
89	MJ Sticker, slam dunk layup, old uniform & shoes, "#72 C'AO & Muflon" on card back (10.72)	72	550.00	850.00
89	Player #30 Sticker/MJ front, "#15 C'AO & Muflon" on card back	15	5.00	10.00
96	Kent All Sport		125.00	200.00
	-MJ Sticker, white 45, ball right hand over head, 1 MJ in 300 pieces of gum, blank back (10.73)	USA 14		
	-Basketball Card Wrapper and Gum, blank back (10.74)			

The Collector's Dream

The information provided in this section is meant to serve as a basic guide to collecting Jordan jerseys should you ever have the good fortune (and resources) to find and purchase one. With the value and scarcity of jerseys, it's important to be certain that what you come across is not a counterfeit or a forgery. What follows is some basic sizing and tagging information that will be helpful when you first encounter a Jordan jersey. Still, this section should not be mistaken for a guide to authentication. It is advised that you contact a professional in this area should you have any doubt about an item.

Michael Jordan's game-worn equipment commands higher prices than nearly any other current sports figure's. This is apparent when you consider what the jerseys have sold for in recent years. Each year the Chicago Bulls hold a charity fund-raiser, the Fest-a-Bulls dinner, where jerseys are auctioned off. Here is what some game-worn items have been sold for:

- 1996: Home jersey with shorts sold for $16,500
  This outfit later sold at the 1996 National Sports Card Convention auction for $33,500
- 1997: Home jersey with shorts sold for $40,000
- 1998: Home jersey with shorts sold for $40,000
- 1995-98: Game-worn shoes sold for an average of $6,000 a pair

Generally, these extremely high prices are not the norm. Charity auctions tend to realize higher prices than the normal retail market. These prices do, however, reflect the value associated with purchasing your game jersey directly from the team, where authenticity is guaranteed. Jordan jerseys sold through other auction houses and retail sales typically range from $15,000 to $25,000.

These high prices open the door for forgeries. There are so few authentic game-worn Jordan jerseys on the market that collectors must be extremely careful before they purchase one. Make sure the party selling the jersey is reputable, has some knowledge in this field and will guarantee their product. Jerseys should also come with a letter of authenticity. For instance, the letter could come from the Chicago Bulls or another professional team that received the jersey as part of a charity event. Without a team letter, the jersey should have a letter from a qualified expert.

You may someday have the opportunity to purchase a Jordan game jersey with no letter of authenticity. How would you know if it was a store model or an actual game jersey? This chapter attempts to familiarize you with what to look for on a game jersey. There are certain unique characteristics of game jerseys, which we will attempt to explain. There are also inconsistencies in the making of jerseys, but the focus will be on the common characteristics including manufacturer, size, extra length, etc. The information in this book is not intended to be used to authenticate jerseys. It is merely a factual overview of some of the characteristics real jerseys possess.

Basic Characteristics of Jordan Jerseys

Michael Jordan put on his first Chicago Bulls uniform in 1984. There were two types of jerseys the Bulls wore then–white or red. The white jerseys have red lettering and numbers and are worn at the Chicago Stadium (now the United Center) and are called "home jerseys." The red jerseys have black lettering and numbers and are worn at opponents' stadiums. The red jersey is called the "road jersey." In 1995, the Bulls introduced a new jersey color–black with a red pinstripe. This jersey has red lettering and numbers and is worn as their alternate road jersey. The lettering and numbers were ironed on the jersey through the 1991 season. Beginning in 1992, the letters and numbers are made of cloth and are sewn to the jerseys.

The players' names are placed approximately 5-1/4 inches down from the top of the collar, on the back of the jersey. Non-game jerseys do not have this feature–the name is only 3-1/2 inches from the top of the collar. On the front in the bottom left corner, tags are sewn to the jersey. These vary according to manufacturer and year. One tag states the name of the manufacturer and size, while the others tell the year and extra length. Different companies have produced the jerseys for the Chicago Bulls over the years. In 1984, Rawlings® made Jordan's jersey. Right after that, Sand-Knit® (MacGregor) made the jerseys. Jordan's jerseys were made by Sand-Knit® through 1990 when Champion® began making them, and continued until 1996. From 1997 to present, Nike® makes the jerseys.

The biggest difficulty with authenticating jerseys yourself is the irregularities you will encounter. Sand-Knit had two forms of manufacturing tags, one with a gold crown and one without (see illustration). Some jerseys did not have a year tag sewn onto the jersey. Others were not the proper size, or fell between size changes with Jordan. For example, Jordan wore a Size 44+2 in 1989. During the first half of 1990 he continued to wear that size, but his 1990 All-Star jersey is a 44+3. At some point he went to a larger size, and some experts still argue which is correct.

Another distinguishing characteristic of the 1991 and 1993 jerseys is a black, iron-on band on the top front, left collar strip, in memory of Sheri Berto in '91 and Michael's father in '93.

Variations in Sand-Knit tagging:

Regular Tagging:

Crown Tagging:

The following are some examples of game-worn jerseys I have come across over the years. This is just a sampling of what's out there, but it will give you an idea of what to look for and what's authentic. An example of game-worn Jordan jerseys and shorts are given, showing manufacturer and size for the jersey for that given year.

1989-90 Home Jersey, Sand-Knit, Size 44 + 2

1995-96 Home Jersey, Champion, Size 46 + 3

1989-90 Shooting Shirt, Sand-Knit, Size 46 + 3

1994-95 Home Shorts, Champion, Size 38 + 2" rise + 3" inseam

1996 All-Star Jersey, Champion, Size 46 + 3

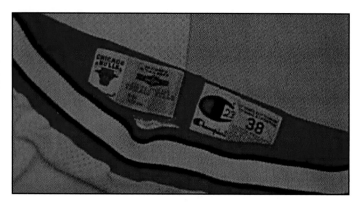

1994-95 Home Shorts, Closeup of Tagging

1996 All-Star Jersey, Closeup of Tagging

1990-91 Home Jersey, Champion, Size 44 + 2

'89-90, Example of Tagging, Sand-Knit, (Horace Grant, Bulls)

'88-89, Example of Tagging, Sand-Knit, (Will Perdue, Bulls)

Collar Drop of 1990-91 Home Jersey

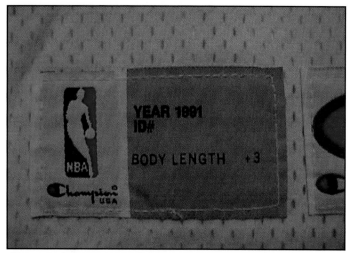

'91-92, Example of Tagging, Champion, (Scottie Pippen, Bulls)

Example of Stitched Collar Drop, (Cartwright, game-worn)

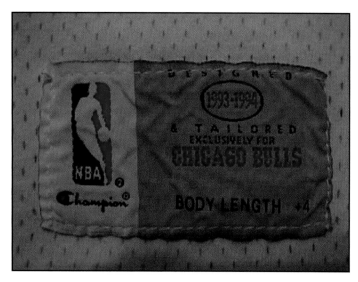

'93-94, Example of Tagging, Champion, (Bill Cartwright, Bulls)

Closeup of Collar Drop, (Cartwright, game-worn, Jordan not)

'96-97, Example of Tagging, Champion, (MJ, Bulls)

Example of Iron-On Collar Drop, (game-worn: Pippen, Grant, Perdue, MJ)

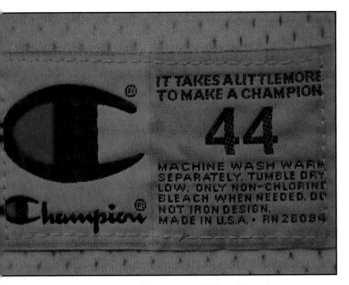

1990-91 Home Jersey, Closeup of Size Tagging

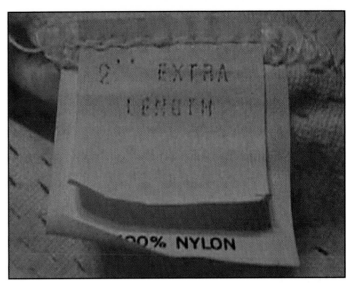

1990-91 Home Jersey, Closeup of Inside Extra Length Tag

1990-91 Home Jersey, Closeup of Iron-On Numbers

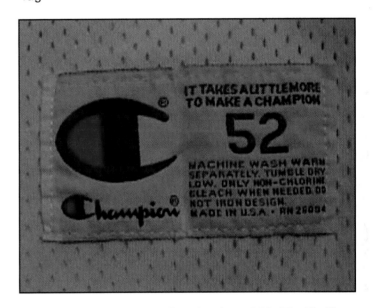

Example of Size Tag (Single) for 1996-97, (Caffey, Bulls)

1990-91 Home Jersey, Closeup of Iron-On Name

Example of Inside Extra Length Tag for 1996-97, (Caffey, Bulls)

1996-97 Home Shorts, Closeup of Size Tag

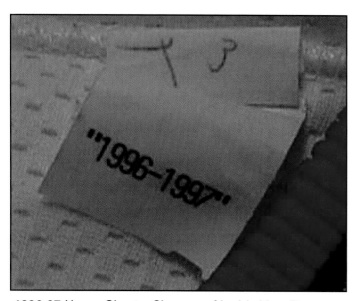

1996-97 Home Shorts, Closeup of Inside Year Tag

1996-97 Example of Size Tag in Shorts, Player Number Written on Tag, (Caffey, Bulls)

Tagging Styles

Below is a list of various Michael Jordan game-worn jerseys, including year, manufacturer, size, etc., which illustrates how the styles have changed over the years.

1984-85 White home, Rawlings, Size 42

1986-87 White home, Sand-Knit, Size 44+3 (normal extra length for this time period was +2)

1988-89 White home, Sand-Knit, Size 44+2, regular tagging

1988-89 Red away, Sand-Knit, Size 44+2, crown on Sand-Knit tagging

1989-90 White home, Sand-Knit, Size 44+2, crown tagging

1989-90 Red away, Sand-Knit, Size 44+2

1990-91 White home, Champion, Size 44+2. First year of Champion Jerseys. No outside year/extra length tag, extra length +2 tag on left inside inseam.

1990-91 Red away shorts, Champion, Size 36, 2" rise

1991 All-Star, Champion, Size 44+3

1991 All-Star, shorts, Size 36, 1" rise, 2" inseam

1994 All-Star, Champion, Size 46+3

1994 All-Star, shorts, Size 38, 1" rise, 2" inseam

1995-96 White home, Champion, Size 46+3, No outside year/extra length tag, extra length +3 tag on inside inseam. This jersey was auctioned off by the Charit-a-Bulls at the Fest-a-Bulls dinner, March 19, 1996. The shorts that went with this jersey were year marked 1994-95

1995-96 White Shorts (also auctioned 3/19/96), Champion, Size 38, 2" rise, 3" inseam.

1996-97 White home, Champion, Size 46+3, Both tags on outside as normal. Auctioned off by the Charit-a-Bulls at the Fest-a-Bulls dinner, March 26, 1997.

1996-97 White Shorts (also auctioned 3/26/97), Champion, Size 38, 2" rise, 3" inseam.

1997-98 White home, First year for Nike jerseys. Included the game-worn shorts. Auctioned off by the Charit-a-Bulls at the Fest-a-Bulls dinner, April 1, 1998.

These jerseys have actually been worn in a game by Michael Jordan. Buying a game jersey does not necessarily mean that the jersey was worn. The Bulls have given game jerseys to charity events that haven't been worn. The letter that accompanies these jerseys states only that they are game jerseys and makes no mention of whether they were worn or not. They may have been made for him to use and he never did. It's arguable how many are actually worn each season.

–William Huffman

A sports card collector since 1974, William Huffman is the owner of Player's Hand–a Chicago-based store that deals strictly with Michael Jordan cards and memorabilia. The knowledge he's shared in this section comes from years of dealing, seeing and owning game-worn jerseys and apparel.

"Pre-1995"

As stated in the Introduction, collecting Michael Jordan Cards be quite an endeavor—especially since in recent years, card companies have flooded the market with numerous offerings. So many have been produced in recent years in fact, that we've divided the cards into two sections. Cards that cover the years 1995, 1996 and 1997 are grouped together and are located at the end of the card section. Cards produced before 1995 start on this page. Again, what we've attempted to provide is a nice sampling of the cards available. To find more information on the many cards not included, refer to one of Krause Publications' other sports card price guides.

Baseball Major League Cards

91	Upper Deck Special Player (11.1)	SP1	5.00	10.00
94-95	Collector's Choice (11.2)			
	-Regular card	23	2.00	4.00
	-Regular card, silver	23	8.00	16.00
	-Regular card, gold	23	75.00	100.00
	-Up Close and Personal	635	2.00	4.00
	-Up Close and Personal, silver	635	6.00	12.00
	-Up Close and Personal, gold	635	75.00	100.00
	-Rookie Class	661	4.00	8.00
	-Rookie Class, silver	661	15.00	25.00
	-Rookie Class, gold	661	120.00	150.00
94	Fun Pack (11.3)	170	10.00	15.00
94	SP			
	-Central Region (11.4)	CR-2	20.00	30.00
	-Holoview FX blue	16/38	25.00	35.00
	-Holoview FX red, die-cut	16/38	275.00	350.00
94-95	Upper Deck			
	-Next Generation	8 of 18	20.00	35.00
	-Next Generation Electric Diamond	8 of 18	35.00	50.00
	-Star Rookies	19	8.00	12.00
	-Star Rookies Electric Diamond	19	20.00	30.00
	-Then and Now, basketball and baseball	359	1.00	2.00
	-Baseball The American Epic Set	81 cards	12.00	15.00
	---MJ Card	BC-2	5.00	8.00
	-Diamond Collection Central Region (11.5)	C-2	25.00	45.00

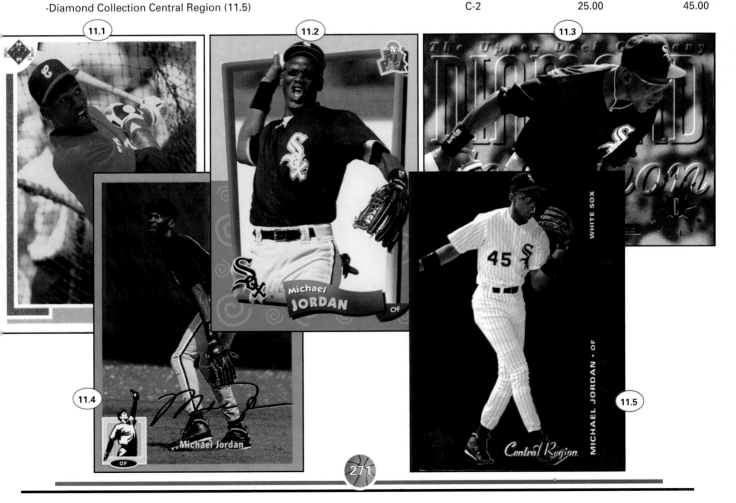

95-96	Collector's Choice			
	-Special Edition	238	2.00	4.00
	-Special Edition, silver (11.6)	238	4.00	8.00
	-Special Edition, gold	238	100.00	125.00
	-Regular	500	1.00	2.00
	-Regular, silver	500	4.00	10.00
	-Regular, gold	500	35.00	60.00
95	Upper Deck			
	-Electric Diamond	200	2.00	4.00
	-Electric Diamond, silver	200	8.00	16.00
	-Electric Diamond, gold (11.7)	200	75.00	125.00
	-Steal of a Deal	SD-15	20.00	35.00
	Baseball Minor League Cards			
94	Action Packed Scouting Report (11.8)	23	4.00	8.00
94	Classic Barons, with glasses on cap (11.9)	1	12.00	20.00
94	Classic Best Set	30 cards	12.00	20.00
	---MJ Card, with bat (11.10)	23	5.00	10.00
94	Fleer Pro, Birmingham Barons Set	28 cards	15.00	20.00
	---MJ Card (11.11)	663	5.00	10.00

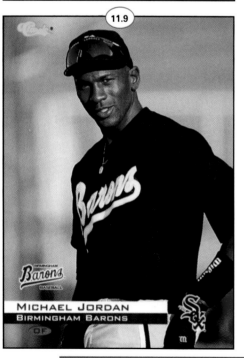

94	Ted Williams Gardiner Set	9 cards	30.00	40.00
	---MJ Card	DG-1	15.00	20.00
	---MJ Card	DG-9	5.00	10.00
94-95	Upper Deck Minor League			
	-White Sox Prospects, silver	MJ23	10.00	20.00
	-White Sox Prospects, gold, 1 of 15,000	MJ23	50.00	75.00
95	SP Top Prospect Minor League			
	-Time Capsule	TC-1	8.00	12.00
	-Time Capsule	TC-2	8.00	12.00
	-Time Capsule	TC-3	8.00	12.00
	-Time Capsule	TC-4	8.00	12.00
	-Autograph Card, 100 made, 30 issued	14		
95	Upper Deck			
	-Future Stock	45	15.00	25.00
	-White Sox Top Prospect	45	4.00	6.00
	-Baseball Scrapbook	MJ1	15.00	25.00
	-Baseball Scrapbook	MJ2	15.00	5.00
	-Baseball Scrapbook	MJ3	15.00	5.00
	-Baseball Scrapbook	MJ4	15.00	5.00
	-Baseball Scrapbook	MJ5	15.00	5.00
	-Baseball Scrapbook	MJ6	15.00	5.00
	-Baseball Scrapbook	MJ7	15.00	5.00
	-Baseball Scrapbook	MJ8	15.00	5.00
	-Baseball Scrapbook	MJ9	15.00	5.00
	-Baseball Scrapbook	MJ10	15.00	5.00
	-Organizational Sox Pro File Birmingham Barons	OP-6	20.00	30.00

11.12

-One on One Card Set	10 cards	10.00	15.00
---One on One Card (11.12)	1	1.00	1.50
---One on One Card	2	1.00	1.50
---One on One Card	3	1.00	1.50
---One on One Card	4	1.00	1.50
---One on One Card	5	1.00	1.50
---One on One Card	6	1.00	1.50
---One on One Card	7	1.00	1.50
---One on One Card	8	1.00	1.50
---One on One Card	9	1.00	1.50
---One on One Card	10	1.00	1.50

ERROR CARDS

Year	Error-NBA Cards			
87-88	Fleer			
	-Error Regular Card, MJ back & Gene Banks front	59	150.00	250.00
88-89	Fleer			
	-Error Super Star Sticker, MJ on front, P. Ewing on back	5 of 11	150.00	200.00
	-Error Super Star Sticker, MJ on back, P Ewing front	7 of 11	150.00	200.00
89-90	Hoops			
	-Error Card, Regular Card, blank back	200	50.00	75.00
90-91	Fleer			
	-Error Regular Card, blank back	26	50.00	75.00
	-Error Regular Card, double print back with stats & card front	26	60.00	90.00
	-Error Card, Stacy King/MJ, blank back, with card backs	NNO	15.00	30.00
90-91	Hoops			
	-Error Card, Regular Card #65, Pro Set, football back, R. White	423	350.00	450.00
90-91	Skybox			
	-Error Card, Regular Card, two different cards on front	41	60.00	90.00
	-Error Card, Checklist, MJ's name, no names on back	295	60.00	90.00
91-92	Fleer			
	-Error Regular Card, bad cut, only 3/4 MJ front back	29	60.00	90.00
	-Error Card League Leader, blank back	220	50.00	75.00
	-Error Card, All-Star Team, blank back	221	50.00	75.00
	-Error Card, All-Star Game/MJ front, blank back	233	50.00	75.00
	-Error Card, All-Star Game/MJ front, blank back	238	50.00	75.00
	-Error Card, Team Leader, blank back	375	50.00	75.00
	-Error Card, Pro Vision, blank back	NNO	20.00	30.00
	-Error Card, Pro Vision, MJ front, Karl Malone back	5 of 6	25.00	35.00
91-92	Hoops			
	-Error Card, USA BB Team/MJ front, #62, back C Daly, MJ USA #9	61	100.00	150.00
91-92	Upper Deck			
	-Error Card, Stay in School/MJ on back, blank back	22	50.00	75.00

-Error Card, Magic vs. Jordan, blank back	34	50.00	75.00
-Error Card, Regular Card, blank back	44	50.00	75.00
-Error Card, MJ East All-Stars, blank back	69	50.00	75.00
-Error Card, Bulls Checklist/MJ front, blank back	75	50.00	75.00
-Error Card, Hologram Award Winner/MVP, David Robinson front	AW-4	100.00	150.00

92-93 Fleer

-Error Card, MJ Regular Card, A.J. English on back	27	150.00	200.00
-Error Card, A.J. English front	187	150.00	200.00

92-93 Stadium Club

-Error Card, Beam Team, no foil on top half	1 of 21	75.00	125.00
-Error Card, Members Choice, blank back	210	50.00	75.00

92-93 Ultra

-Error Card, Grant Long/MJ front, Lionel Simmons on back	159	100.00	150.00

93-94 Finest

-Error Card, Tribute, 2 half card on front put together to make one complete MJ, back has complete card of #220 & #217	1	150.00	200.00

93-94 Sky Box

-Error Card, Showdown Series, MJ vs. Drexler, b&w test print front, back-8 cards overlaid with each other	SS-11	35.00	60.00

93-94 Stadium Club

-Error Proof Card, Triple Double, no "Michael," blue "Jordan," no gold on card, larger card-2-5/8 x 3-5/8	1	60.00	90.00
-Error Card, Beam Team, no print or foil on front, proof card	4	60.00	90.00
-Error Card, Frequent Flyers #181, wrong back	242	75.00	125.00
-Members Only Set, Series 1, Error Set, 180 cards, 13 Beam Teams, 27 Super Teams	220 cards	400.00	600.00
---Beam Team, has incorrect "Members Only," logo on front	4	300.00	400.00

93-94 Ultra

-Error Card, NBA All Defense First Team, front has David Robinson, with MJ name printed, no gold print on back, MJ on back	2 of 10	150.00	250.00
-Error Card, NBA All Defense First Team, no gold print front/back	2 of 10	50.00	75.00
-Error Card, NBA All Defense First Team, gold print front only	2 of 10	60.00	90.00
-Error Card, Inside Outside, front has no print	4 of 10	60.00	90.00
-Error Card, Regular Card, front has no print	30	60.00	90.00

93-94 Upper Deck

-Playoff Error Card, 2 halves of 2 cards on fronts/MJ back, film strip on back with 4 MJ pictures	180	100.00	150.00
-Error Card, 93 NBA Playoff Highlight: First Round: Bulls 3, wrong front, has 2 halves from other cards	180	100.00	150.00
-Error Card, bad cut, 3/4 MJ front, back is #220	220	100.00	150.00
-Error Card, Special Edition Retirement, back top 1/4 of card, has white space, looks like it's for an autograph	MJR-1	200.00	300.00

94-95 Finest

-Error Card, Regular Card, back cut, 2 MJ cards front & back	331	100.00	150.00

94-95 Upper Deck

-Error Card, Basketball Heroes, no print on front	39	60.00	90.00
-Error Card, Basketball Heroes, no print on front	44	60.00	90.00
-UDA "Salutes These Heroes of the NBA," Bird & MJ, error card, blank space of 2,500, 3 x 5 (11.13)	NNO	100.00	150.00

95-96	Finest			
	-Error Card, Mystery, front .5 MJ & .5 Grant Hill, back all MJ	M-1	35.00	60.00
95-96	SPX			
	-Error Card, Regular Card, blank back	8	20.00	30.00
	-Error Card, Regular Card, MJ not in hologram, its a Sixer Rookie	8	150.00	200.00
95-96	Topps			
	-Error Card, Top Flight, no print on front	TF-1	75.00	100.00
95-96	Ultra			
	-Error Card, Regular Card, front no print on bottom (11.14)	25	60.00	90.00
	Error-NBA UD Foreign Issued Card			
92-93	Upper Deck Spanish			
	-Error Card, Shaqulle O'Neal/No MJ, Utah AS	4	25.00	40.00

Year	**Error-Ball Street Card**			
93	Error Card, Ball Street News, Alexandre Daigle's Name with MJ's Picture, jump shot to dunk, white 23, silver foil on right front (11.15)			
	For Promo Use Only on back, purple and orange back (11.16)		5.00	15.00
Year	**Error-Star Company Cards**			
86	Error Jordan Set, no ring around Bulls Logo	10 cards	300.00	500.00
	---NBA Cards			
86-87	Fleer			
	-Regular Card	57	525.00	800.00
	-Sticker	8 of 11	60.00	75.00
87-88	Fleer			
	-Regular Card (11.17)	59 of 132	75.00	135.00
	-Sticker	2 of 11	15.00	30.00
88-89	Fleer			
	-Regular Card (11.18)	17of 132	20.00	40.00
	-All-Star Team	120	6.00	12.00
	-Super Star Sticker	7 of 11	6.00	12.00
89-90	Fleer			
	-Scoring Average Leader (11.19)	21	3.00	8.00
	-All-Star Sticker	3	2.00	4.00

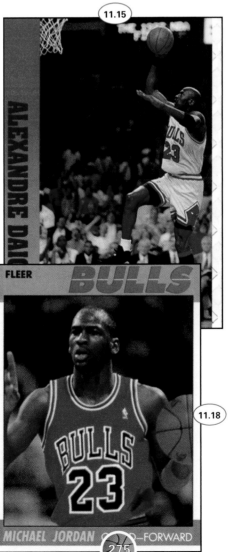

89-90	Hoops				
	-'89 NBA All-Star Game, All-Star Weekend in Houston (11.20)	21	.50	1.00
	-Regular Card	200	1.00	2.00
90-91	Fleer			
	-Regular Card (11.21)	26	.50	1.00
	-'90 All-Stars	5 of 12	2.00	4.00
90-91	Hoops			
	-AS East Weekend, Miami, February 9-11, 1990	5	.50	1.00
	-Regular Card	65	.50	1.00
	-MJ Playground	382	.35	.75
	-Super Streak, MJ & Magic	385	.35	.75
90-91	Skybox			
	-Regular Card (11.23)	41	1.00	2.00
91-92	Fleer			
	-Regular Card	29	.50	1.00
	-All-Star Team, Michael Jordan (11.24)	211	.35	.75
	-League Leader	220	.35	.75
	-Team Leader	375	.35	.75
91-92	Hoops			
	-MVP (11.25)	30	1.00	2.00
	-1992 USA Basketball Team, team picture front, blue front, flag like top	62	.75	1.00
	-All-Star Weekend Charlotte, February 8-10, 1991	253	.50	1.00
	-League Leaders Scoring '91, MJ & K. Malone	306	.35	.75
	-Milestones Points 1991	317	.50	1.00
	-Supreme Court '91-92	455	.50	1.00
	-All Time Active Leader in Scoring Average	536	.50	1.00

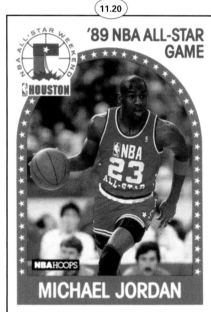

11.20

11.21

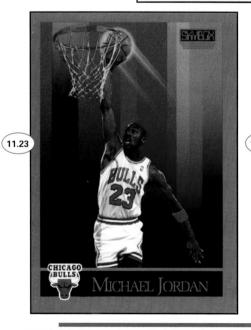

11.23

11.24

11.25

-Tribune Set		6 cards		
---Tribune, Game 1, MJ name on back with others, Perkins' 3 Pointer Gives...		538	.50	1.00
---Tribune, Game 2, MJ name on back with others, Bulls Rout Lakers to Even..		539	.50	1.00
---Tribune, Game 3, MJ name on back with others, Bulls Win OT Thriller...		540	.50	1.00
---Tribune, Game 4, MJ name on back with others, Bulls One Game Away From...		541	.50	1.00
---Tribune, Game 5, MJ & Lakers, Jordan & Bulls, Bulls Win First...		542	.50	1.00
---Tribune, Game 5, MJ Kissing Trophy front, 1991 NBA Champions, 90-91 Team Picture with MJ		543	.50	1.00
-1992 USA Basketball Team		579	2.00	4.00
-1992 USA Basketball Team, gold, MJ name on back		NNO	4.00	8.00
-Slam Dunk Set		6 cards		
---MJ, Slam Dunk, 87 & 88 Champion		IV	6.00	12.00
-All-Star East '88 MVP All-Star		IX	6.00	12.00
91-92	Sky Box			
	-Regular Card	39	1.50	3.75
	-Stats, Per 48 Minutes: Point Leader (11.26)	307	1.00	2.00
	-MJ vs. Magic, Great Moments from the NBA	333	.50	1.50
	-MJ, Great Moments from the NBA	334	1.00	2.00
	-MJ & Scottie Pippen	462	.50	1.00
	-Barcelona USA'92	534	4.00	8.00
	-Salutes MJ	572	1.00	2.00
	-Sky Master	583	1.00	2.00
91-92	Upper Deck			
	-Magic vs. Jordan	34	.50	1.00
	-Regular Card	44	1.00	2.00
	-MJ, East All-Stars, Charlotte, February 8-10, 91 (11.27)	69	.50	1.00
	-MJ, East All-Star Orlando, February 7-9, 1992	452	1.00	2.00
	-Hologram Award Winner Scoring	AW-1	5.00	10.00
	-Hologram Award Winner MVP	AW-4	5.00	10.00
92-93	Fleer			
	-Regular Card	32	1.00	2.00
	-League Leader Scoring	238	.50	1.00
	-Award Winner NBA MVP & Finals MVP (11.28)	246	.50	1.00
	-Slam Dunk, NBA Jam Session	273	.50	1.00
	-All Slam Dunk Team/MJ front, Mail in, NBA Jam Session	NNO	5.00	10.00
	-Team Leader	4	.50	1.00
	-Total D	5 of 15	30.00	50.00
	-MJ, Orlando All-Star Weekend	6 of 24	25.00	45.00
92-93	Hoops			
	-Regular Card (11.29)	30	1.00	2.00
	-MJ, Orlando All-Star Weekend East	298	.50	1.00

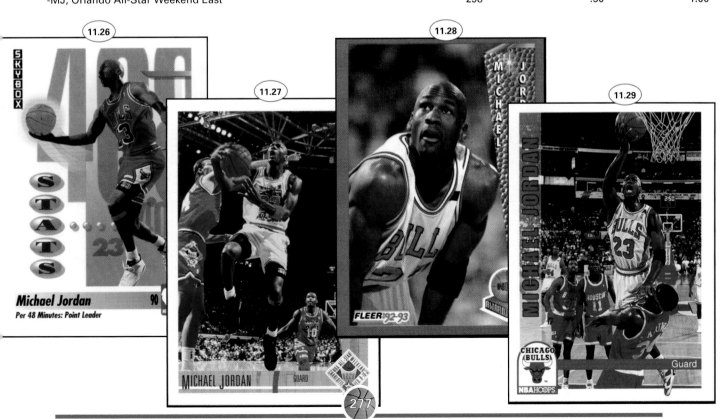

	-MJ & K. Malone, League Leader '92, Scoring	320	.50	1.00
	-D. Barros & D. Petrovic & MJ, League Leader 92 in 3 point percentage	321	1.00	2.00
	-MJ, BB Tournament of Americas, Portland, 6/27-7/5/92	341	.50	1.00
	-MJ, Supreme Court 1992-93, Fans Choice	SC-1	8.00	16.00
92-93	Skybox			
	-Regular Card (11.30)	31	2.00	5.00
	-MJ, NBA Update, USA BB	37	.50	1.00
	-MJ, NBA Rookie, USA BB	38	.50	1.00
	-MJ, Game Strategy, USA BB	39	.50	1.00
	-MJ, NBA Best Game, USA BB	40	.50	1.00
	-MJ, Off the Court, USA BB	41	.50	1.00
	-MJ, NBA Playoffs, USA BB	42	.50	1.00
	-MJ, NBA All-Star Record, USA BB	43	.50	1.00
	-MJ, NBA Shooting, USA BB	44	.50	1.00
	-MJ, NBA All Time Record, USA BB	45	.50	1.00
	-Magic on Jordan, USA BB	105	.50	1.00
	-'92 NBA Finals, MJ NBA Finals MVP	314	1.00	2.00
	-MJ, The Road to Gold USA, Gold Medal Game vs. Croatia	USA-11	2.00	3.00
	-Worthy & MJ & Perkins, School Ties	ST-16	2.00	3.00
92-93	Stadium Club			
	-Regular Card	1	3.00	6.00
	-Beam Team (11.31)	1 of 21	40.00	60.00
	-Members Choice	210	1.00	3.00
	-Members Only Set, # of 12,000	421cds		
	---Regular Card, Member Only Logo	1	10.00	15.00
	---Beam Team, Member Only Logo	1 BT	50.00	80.00
	---Members Choice, Member Only Logo	210	8.00	12.00
92-93	Topps			
	-Archives MJ Card	52	4.00	7.00
	-Archives Gold MJ Card	52	7.00	12.00
	-Beam Team, K. Johnson, MJ, Rodman	3 of 7	2.00	4.00
	-Beam Team Gold Card, MJ	3 of 7	12.00	20.00
	-Highlight	3	.50	1.00
	-Highlight gold (11.32)	3	1.00	3.00
	-NBA All-Star	115	.50	1.00
	-NBA All-Star gold	115	1.00	3.00
	-Regular Card	141	.50	1.00
	-Regular Card gold	141	3.00	6.00
	-50 Point Club	205	.50	1.00
	-50 Point Club gold	205	1.00	3.00
92-93	Ultra			
	-Award Winners 92 MVP	1 of 5	12.00	20.00
	-NBA Jam Session Team Card/MJ back, mail-in card offer	2	5.00	9.00
	-All NBA First Team	4 of 15	15.00	25.00
	-Regular Card (11.33)	27	2.00	5.00
	-Slam Dunk 16, NBA Jam Session, Top 20 Jammer	216	.50	1.00

92-93	Upper Deck			
	-MJ, Team MVP Holograms	4	8.00	10.00
	-NBA All-Star Collector Set, Utah, February 19-21, 1993	40 cards		
	---NBA All-Star Heroes Card	15	2.00	4.00
	-NBA All-Star Collector Set, gold, Utah, February 19-21, 1993	40 cards		
	---NBA All-Star Heroes Card gold	15	35.00	60.00
	-Regular Card (11.34)	23	1.00	3.00
	-Scoring Threats, MJ & S. Pippen	62	.50	1.00
	-Back to Back MVP, Regular Season & NBA Finals	67	.50	1.00
	-MJ, Utah All-Star Weekend, February 19-21, 1993	425	.50	1.00
	-Two Time Slam Dunk Champion, 1985-1990, error in date	453a	12.00	20.00
	-Two Time Slam Dunk Champion, 1987-1988, correct date	453b	.50	1.00
	-MJ, Game Faces	488	.50	1.00
	-Agent 23, FaniMation	506	.50	1.00
	-Birdman & Agent 23, FaniMation	510	.50	1.00
	-MJ, All Division Team, Central	AD-9	4.00	8.00
	-MJ, All NBA First Team	AN-1	15.00	25.00
	-Award Winner Hologram, Scoring	AW-1	6.00	12.00
	-Award Winner Hologram, MVP	AW-9	6.00	12.00
	-Jerry West Selects Best Shooter	JW-1	8.00	15.00
	-Jerry West Selects Best Defender	JW-4	8.00	15.00
	-Jerry West Selects Best All Around Player	JW-8	8.00	15.00
	-Jerry West Selects Best Clutch Player	JW-9	8.00	15.00
	-MJ, 15,000 points	PC-4	20.00	35.00
	-MJ & Wilkins 20,000 points	SP-2	4.00	6.00
	-MJ, Team MVP	TM-5	12.00	25.00
93-94	Finest			
	-Tribute	1	10.00	15.00
	-Refractor Tribute, dull finish (11.35)	1	150.00	250.00
93-94	Fleer			
	-Sharpshooters (11.36)	3 of 10	10.00	20.00
	-Living Legend	4 of 6	8.00	15.00
	-MJ, Utah All-Star Weekend, February 19-21, 1993	5 of 24	12.00	25.00
	-NBA Superstars	7 of 20	4.00	8.00
	-Regular Card	28	1.00	2.00
	-League Leader Scoring & Steals	224	.50	1.00
93-94	Fleer NBA Jam Session, 4-5/8" x 2.5" (11.37)	33	2.00	4.00
93-94	Hoops			
	-Regular Card	28	1.00	2.00
	-5th Anniversary Gold Bulls Team Set	15 cards		
	---MJ Card (11.38)	28	10.00	15.00

11.34

11.35

11.36

11.37

11.38

		-MJ, Utah All-Star Weekend East	257	.50	1.00
		-MJ, Utah All-Star Weekend, gold	257	1.00	2.00
		-League Leaders, Scoring, MJ & Wilkins & Malone	283	.50	1.00
		-League Leaders, Scoring, gold, MJ & Wilkins & Malone	283	.50	1.00
		-League Leaders, Steals, MJ & Blaylock & Stockton	289	.50	1.00
		-League Leaders, Steals, gold, MJ & Blaylock & Stockton	289	.50	1.00
		-Face to Face, MJ front, H. Miner on back	FTF-10	6.00	12.00
		-MJ, Supreme Court 1993-94	SC-1	15.00	30.00
93-94	Sky Box				
		-MJ, NBA on NBC Game 4	14	.50	1.00
		-Regular Card (11.39)	45	1.00	3.00
		-MJ, The Center Stage	CS-1	12.00	20.00
		-Dynamic Dunks	D-4	8.00	15.00
		-Showdown Series, MJ vs. Drexler	SS-11	.50	1.00
93-94	Stadium Club				
		-Triple Double	1	1.00	2.00
		-Triple Double, 1st Day Issue, 1st Day Issue Logo	1	100.00	125.00
		-Triple Double, Members Only, Members Only Logo	1	25.00	35.00
		-Beam Team	4	8.00	15.00
		-Beam Team, Members Only, Members Only Logo	4	65.00	85.00
		-Regular Card	169	2.00	4.00
		-Regular Card, 1st Day Issue, 1st Day Issue Logo (11.40)	169	90.00	120.00
		-Regular Card, Members Only, Members Only Logo	169	12.00	18.0
		-Frequent Flyers	181	1.00	2.00
		-Frequent Flyers, 1st Day Issue, 1st Day Issue Logo	181	80.00	110.00
		-Frequent Flyers, Members Only, Members Only Logo	181	12.00	20.00
		-MJ Members Only, #6 of a 59 card Set, MJ with 1993 NBA Finals trophy, MJ in blue suit and tie, back multi-colored, Jordan Wins 3rd Straight Playoff MVP (11.41)	NNO	60.00	90.00
		-1994 NBA Western Finals Set	360 cards		
		---Triple Double, The NBA Finals Logo	1		
		---Regular Card, The NBA Finals Logo	169		
		---Frequent Flyer, The NBA Finals Logo	181		
93-94	Topps				
		-Regular Card	23	1.00	2.00
		-Regular Card, gold	23	5.00	10.00
		-50 Point Club	64	.50	1.00
		-50 Point Club, gold	64	2.00	4.00
		-All-Star First Team	101	.50	1.00
		-All-Star First Team, gold	101	2.00	4.00
		-Top Reigning Playoff MVP	199	.50	1.00
		-Top Reigning Playoff MVP, gold (11.42)	199	2.00	4.00
		-Reigning Scoring Leader	384	.50	1.00
		-Reigning Scoring Leader, gold	384	2.00	4.00

93-94	Ultra			
	-All NBA First Team	2 of 14	15.00	25.00
	-NBA All Defense First Team (11.43)	2 of 10	50.00	75.00
	-Power in the Key	2 of 9	20.00	30.00
	-Inside Outside	4 of 10	3.00	6.00
	-Famous Nicknames "Air"	7 of 15	10.00	20.00
	-Regular Card	30	1.00	3.00
	-Scoring King	5 of 10	50.00	75.00
93-94	Upper Deck			
	-Regular Card, MJ name in red stripe on back goes whole length of card, Born: February 17, 1963 on back	23	1.00	3.00
	-Season Leaders, Scoring	166	.50	1.00
	-Season Leaders, Steals	171	.50	1.00
	-93 NBA Playoffs Highlights: Jordan Scores 54 points	193	.50	1.00
	-93 NBA Finals Highlights Game 4: Jordan's 55 Points Gives Chicago...	201	.50	1.00
	-93 NBA Finals Highlights: Jordan Earns 3rd Straight NBA Finals MVP	204	.50	1.00
	-Hang Time	237	.50	1.00
	-Breakaway Threats	438	.50	1.00
	-Skylights	466	.50	1.00
	-First Team All NBA	AN-4	3.00	6.00
	-Behind the Glass MJ Card	G-11	12.00	20.00
	-Holojam Regular, logo right front	H-4	8.00	12.00
	-Special Edition Cards, Kilroy	JK-1	2.00	4.00
	-Locker Talk (11.44)	LT-1	15.00	30.00
	-Mr. June	MJ-1	10.00	15.00
	-Mr. June	MJ-2	10.00	15.00
	-Mr. June	MJ-3	10.00	15.00
	-Mr. June	MJ-4	10.00	15.00
	-Mr. June	MJ-5	10.00	15.00
	-Mr. June	MJ-6	10.00	15.00
	-Mr. June	MJ-7	10.00	15.00
	-Mr. June	MJ-8	10.00	15.00
	-Mr. June	MJ-9	10.00	15.00
	-Mr. June	MJ-10	10.00	15.00
	-Special Edition Cards, Retirement	MJR-1	4.00	8.00
	-Seven Straight Scoring Titles	SP-3	3.00	6.00
	-Three Straight Championships	SP-4	3.00	6.00
	-Triple Double 3D Standouts	TD-2	6.00	12.00
	-USA Exchange Set MJ Card	USA-5	10.00	15.00
	-Pro View			
	---Regular Card	23	2.00	4.00
	---3D Jams	91	2.00	4.00
	-Looney Tune Set, MJ on 51 cards	100 cards	15.00	20.00
	---Holograms	2 cards	2.00	4.00
	---BBH	3	2.00	4.00
	---BBH	5	2.00	4.00

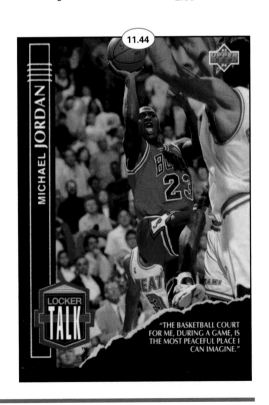

	---Act 1, Scene 2, 3, 4, 5, 8, 16, 17, 18	1.00	2.00
	---Act 2, Scene 6, 7, 13, 14, 15, 18	1.00	2.00
	---Act 3, Scene 8, 12	1.00	2.00
	---Act 5, Scene 8, 9	1.00	2.00
	---Act 6, Scene 2, 3, 4, 5, 11	1.00	2.00
	---Act 7, Scene 2, 5, 6, 7, 9, 14, 17, 18, 19	1.00	2.00
	---Act 8, Scene 4, 5, 9, 10, 12, 13, 14	1.00	2.00
	---Act 9, Scene 2, 8, 10	1.00	2.00
	---Act 10, Scene 6, 8, 9, 10, 11	1.00	2.00

94-95	Collector's Choice			
	-Pro Files, golfing (11.45)	204	.50	1.00
	-Pro Files, silver, golfing	204	1.00	3.00
	-Pro Files, gold, golfing	204	25.00	50.00
	-Commemorative	240	.50	1.00
	-Commemorative, silver	240	1.00	3.00
	-Commemorative, gold	240	25.00	50.00
	-Dr. Basketball	402	.50	1.00
	-Dr. Basketball, silver	402	1.00	3.00
	-Dr. Basketball, gold	402	25.00	50.00
94-95	Finest			
	-Refractor (11.46)	331	200.00	300.00
	-Regular Card with covering	331	15.00	20.00
94-95	Flair Regular Card (11.47)	326	6.00	12.00
94-95	Sky Box			
	-Emotion Air Jordan (11.48)	100	5.00	10.00
	-Emotion Ntense	N-3	20.00	40.00
94-95	SP			
	-He's Back March 19, 1995, red	MJ-1	2.00	4.00
	-He's Back March 19, 1995, silver	MJ-1	12.00	20.00
	-Championship E	4	1.00	3.00
	-Championship E, die-cut	4	6.00	12.00
	-Championship He's Back	41	3.00	6.00
	-Championship He's Back, die-cut	41	10.00	15.00
	-Championship Playoff Hero	P-2	15.00	25.00
	-Championship Playoff Hero, die-cut (11.49)	P-2	70.00	125.00

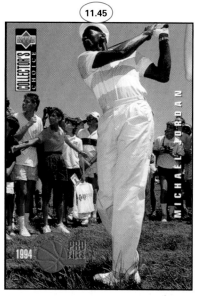

11.45

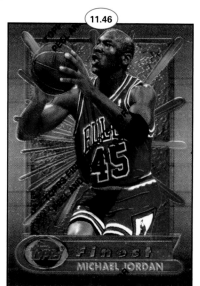

11.46

11.47

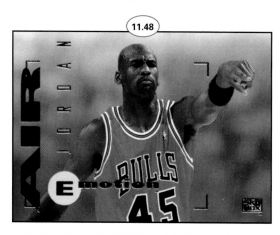

11.48

11.49

04-95	Topps			
	-Embossed (11.50)	121	4.00	8.00
	-Embossed Gold Idols	121	12.00	20.00
04-95	Upper Deck			
	-Basketball Heroes	37	4.00	8.00
	-Basketball Heroes	38	4.00	8.00
	-Basketball Heroes	39	4.00	8.00
	-Basketball Heroes	40	4.00	8.00
	-Basketball Heroes	41	4.00	8.00
	-Basketball Heroes	42	4.00	8.00
	-Basketball Heroes	43	4.00	8.00
	-Basketball Heroes	44	4.00	8.00
	-Basketball Heroes Checklist Card	45	4.00	8.00
	-Basketball Heroes Header Card	JH	4.00	8.00
	-USA Basketball All Time Greats	85	2.50	5.00
	-USA Basketball All Time Greats, Gold	85	6.00	12.00
	-Then and Now	359	1.00	2.00
	-USA Jordan Highlights	JH-1	10.00	15.00
	-USA Jordan Highlights	JH-2	10.00	15.00
	-USA Jordan Highlights	JH-3	10.00	15.00
	-USA Jordan Highlights (11.51)	JH-4	10.00	15.00
	-USA Jordan Highlights	JH-5	10.00	15.00
	-He's Back Set	9 cards		
	---91 92 UD	44	.50	1.00
	---92 93 UD	23	.50	1.00
	---92 93 UD	425	.50	1.00
	---92 93 UD	453	.50	1.00
	---93 94 UD	23	.50	1.00
	---93 94 UD	204	.50	1.00
	---93 94 UD	237	.50	1.00
	---94 95 CC	240	.50	1.00
	---94 95 CC	402	.50	1.00
	-MJ Decade of Dominance, Rare Air	10 cards	20.00	30.00
	---	J-1	2.00	3.00
	---	J-2	2.00	3.00
	---	J-3	2.00	3.00
	---	J-4	2.00	3.00
	---	J-5	2.00	3.00
	---	J-6	2.00	3.00
	---	J-7	2.00	3.00
	---	J-8	2.00	3.00
	---	J-9	2.00	3.00
	---	J-10	2.00	3.00
	-Rare Air Card Set & Box	91 cards	35.00	60.00
	-Rare Air Card Set & Box, gold	91 cards	100.00	150.00
95-96	Collector's Choice			
	-MJ Commemorative Card from Factory Set	NNO	2.00	4.00
	-Regular Card (11.52)	45	1.00	2.00

(11.50)

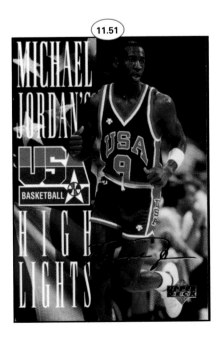

(11.51)

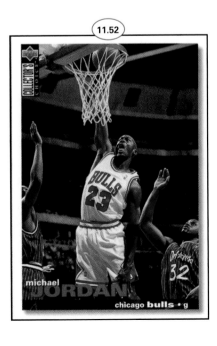

(11.52)

-Players Club	45	3.00	6.00
-Players Club Platinum	45	30.00	60.00
-Fun Club	169	.50	1.00
-Fun Club Players Club	169	1.00	3.00
-Fun Club Players Club Platinum	169	15.00	30.00
-Professor of Dunk	195	.50	1.00
-Professor of Dunk Players Club	195	1.00	3.00
-Professor of Dunk Players Club Platinum	195	15.00	30.00
-Scouting Report	324	.50	1.00
-Scouting Report Players Club	324	1.00	3.00
-Scouting Report Players Club Platinum	324	15.00	30.00
-Jordan Collection	JC-1	5.00	8.00
-Jordan Collection	JC-2	5.00	8.00
-Jordan Collection	JC-2	5.00	8.00
-Jordan Collection	JC-3	5.00	8.00
-Jordan Collection	JC-4	5.00	8.00
-Jordan Collection	JC-9	5.00	8.00
-Jordan Collection	JC-10	5.00	8.00
-Jordan Collection	JC-11	5.00	8.00
-Jordan Collection	JC-12	5.00	8.00
-Crash the Game Houston Rockets, silver	C1-A	5.00	10.00
-Crash the Game New York Knicks, silver	C1-B	5.00	10.00
-Crash the Game Orlando Magic, silver	C1-C	5.00	10.00
-Crash the Game Barkley & SA, send in	silver	4.00	8.00
-Crash the Game Silver Set, UD Redemption-Series I	30 cards	5.00	10.00
---MJ Card	C-1	2.00	4.00
---MJ Card	C-30	2.00	4.00
-Crash the Game Houston Rockets, gold	C1-A	30.00	50.00
-Crash the Game New York Knicks, gold	C1-B	30.00	50.00
-Crash the Game Orlando Magic, gold	C1-C	30.00	50.00
-Crash the Game Rice & Washington, send in	gold	10.00	15.00
-Crash the Game Gold Set, UD Redemption-Series I	30 cards	10.00	15.00
---MJ Card	C-1	3.00	5.00
---MJ Card	C-30	3.00	5.00
-Crash the Game January 30th	C1-A	10.00	15.00
-Crash the Game February 22nd	C1-B	10.00	15.00
-Crash the Game March 19th	C1-C	10.00	15.00
-Crash the Game January 30th, gold	C1-A	40.00	60.00
-Crash the Game February 22nd, gold	C1-B	40.00	60.00
-Crash the Game March 19th, gold	C1-C	40.00	60.00
-Crash the Game, Anderson, 2/29, send in	C-17	5.00	10.00
-Crash the Game Silver Set, Series 2, UD Redemption-Assists & Rebounds	30 cards	5.00	10.00
---MJ Card	C-1	3.00	5.00
-Crash the Game Gold Set, Series 2, UD Redemption-Assists & Rebounds	30 cards	15.00	20.00
---MJ Card	C-1	10.00	15.00
-#45 He's Back MJ Champion	M-1	.50	1.00
-#45 He's Back MJ Champion	M-2	.50	1.00
-#45 He's Back MJ Champion	M-3	.50	1.00
-#45 He's Back MJ Champion	M-4	.50	1.00
-#45 He's Back MJ Champion	M-5	.50	1.00

95-96 Finest

-Veteran & Rookie	RV-20	50.00	75.00
-Regular, with cover (11.53)	229	6.00	12.00
-Refractor, with cover	229	200.00	300.00

11.53

-Dish and Swish, MJ & SP, with cover	DS-4	75.00	100.00
-Hot Stuff, with cover	HS-1	12.00	20.00
-Mystery Bordered	M-1	5.00	10.00
-Mystery Bordered with black cover	M-1	5.00	10.00
-Mystery Borderless	M-1	75.00	125.00
-Mystery Borderless Refractor	M-1	150.00	250.00
95-96 Fleer-Flair			
-Anticipation (11.54)	2 of 10	30.00	50.00
-Hardwood	4 of 27	3.00	6.00
-Hot Number	4 of 15	50.00	75.00
-New Heights	4 of 10	20.00	400.00
-Regular	15	5.00	10.00
-Style	235	1.00	3.00
95-96 Fleer			
-Total O	2 of 10	12.00	20.00
-Total O Hot Pack MJ Card	2	5.00	10.00
-Total D	3 of 12	3.00	6.00
-Metal Slick Silver	3 of 10	12.00	20.00
-Maximum Metal, die-cut	4 of 10	15.00	30.00
-Metal Scoring Magnet	4 of 8	25.00	50.00
-End to End	9 of 20	4.00	8.00
-Metal	13	2.00	4.00
-Metal Silver Spotlight	13	6.00	12.00
-Regular Card (11.55)	22	1.00	2.00
-Metal Nuts and Bolts	212	1.00	2.00
-Firm Foundation	323	.50	1.00
95-96 Fleer NBA Jam Session			
-Connection Collection, 4-5/8 x 2.5	13	2.00	4.00
-Connection Collection, die- cut, 4-5/8 x 2.5 (11.56)	D-13	5.00	10.00
-Show Stoppers, 4-5/8 x 2.5	S-3	90.00	135.00
95-96 Hoops			
-Power Pallet	1 of 10	12.00	20.00
-Hot List	1 of 10	12.00	20.00
-Number Crunchers (11.57)	1	2.00	4.00
-Regular Card	21	1.00	2.00
-Earth Shakers	358	.50	1.00
-Top Ten	AR-7	10.00	15.00
-Skyview Pallet	SV-1	30.00	50.00

95-96	Sky Box			
	-Regular (11.58)	15	1.00	2.00
	-Electrified	278	.50	1.00
	-Larger than Life	L-1	.50	1.00
	-Standout Hobby	SH-1	.50	1.00
	-Meltdown	M-1	25.00	50.00
	-EXL Regular Card, black border	10	4.00	8.00
	-EXL Regular Card, blue border	10	10.00	15.00
	-EXL Natural Born Thriller	1 of 10	60.00	90.00
	-EXL No Boundary	1 of 10	25.00	45.00
95-96	SP			
	-Regular Card, silver left back (11.59)	23	2.00	3.00
	-NBA All-Star die-cut silver	AS-2	10.00	15.00
	-NBA All-Star die-cut gold	AS-2	75.00	150.00
	-Holoview	5 of 40	15.00	25.00
	-Holoview, die-cut	5 of 40	90.00	140.00
	-Jordan Collection	JC-17	5.00	10.00
	-Jordan Collection	JC-18	5.00	10.00
	-Jordan Collection	JC-19	5.00	10.00
	-Jordan Collection	JC-20	5.00	10.00
95-96	SP Championship			
	-Regular Card	17	2.00	4.00
	-Race for the Playoff	121	1.00	2.00
	-Champions of the Court	C-30	15.00	25.00
	-Champions of the Court, die-cut	C-30	150.00	200.00
	-Shots silver (11.60)	S-16	5.00	8.00
	-Shots gold	S-16	50.00	90.00
	-Jordan Collection	JC-21	5.00	10.00
	-Jordan Collection	JC-22	5.00	10.00
	-Jordan Collection	JC-23	5.00	10.00
	-Jordan Collection	JC-24	5.00	10.00
95-96	SPX			
	-Regular Card	8	10.00	15.00
	-Regular Card, gold (11.61)	8	25.00	35.00
	-Holoview Heroes	H-1	15.00	25.00
	-Record Breaker	R-1	10.00	15.00
	-Autograph Trade Card, 100 issued	NNO	2500.00	3500.00

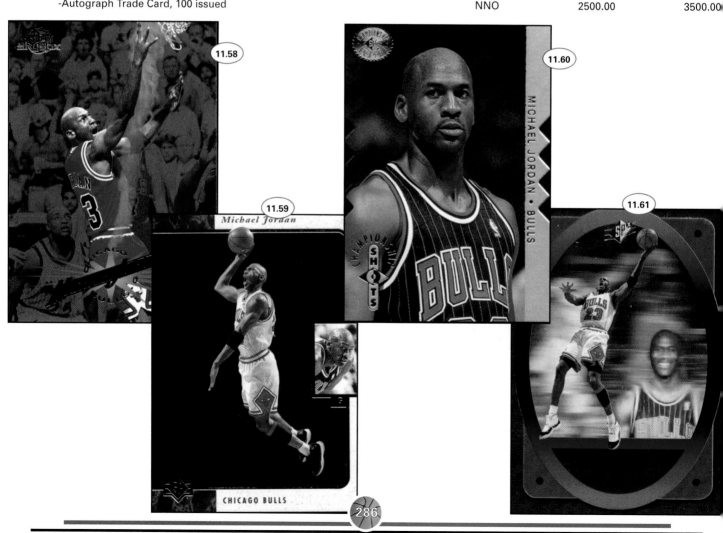

11.58

11.59

11.60

11.61

5-96	Stadium Club		
-Regular Card	1	2.00	4.00
-Beam Team (11.62)	BT-14	25.00	45.00
-Nemeses, MJ vs. Dumars	N-10	15.00	25.00
-Reign Man	RM-2	25.00	45.00
-Spike Says	SS-1	6.00	12.00
-Warp Speed	WS-1	30.00	50.00
-Members Only Set, Members Only Club-# of 1000			
---Regular Card, Members Only Logo	1	10.00	20.00
---Beam Team, Members Only Logo	BT-14	125.00	250.00
---Nemeses, MJ vs. Dumars, Members Only Logo	N-10	75.00	150.00
---Reign Man, Members Only Logo	RM-2	125.00	250.00
---Spike Says, Members Only Logo	SS-1	40.00	75.00
---Warp Speed, Members Only Logo	WS-1	150.00	300.00
-Members Only Set, Members Only Logo	50 cards		
---MJ Card	20	5.00	10.00
-Members Only "Break the Rules Set," Topps NBA at 50, Members Only Club-Topps Stars Set, # of 750 produced	225 cards		
---Imagine MJ & Robertson, Topps Stars Logo	I-6	35.00	5.00
---MJ Card, Topps Stars Logo	24	10.00	20.00
---Golden Season 90-91, Topps Stars Logo	74	25.00	40.00
---Star Reprint	101	45.00	60.00
---MJ Card, Topps Stars Logo	124	25.00	35.00
5-96	Topps		
-Active Leader Scoring	1	.50	1.00
-Active Leader Steals	4	.50	1.00
-Active Leader Scoring Power Boosters	1	.50	1.00
-Active Leader Steals Power Boosters	4	.50	1.00
-Gallery The Masters	10	2.00	4.00
-Regular Card	277	1.00	2.00
-Regular Card Power Boosters	277	25.00	45.00
-Gallery Expressionist (11.63)	EX-2	25.00	45.00
-Mystery Finest	M-1	30.00	55.00
-Mystery Finest Refractor	M-1	150.00	250.00
-Spark Plugs	SP-2	7.00	12.00
-Show Stoppers	SS-1	20.00	35.00
-Top Flight	TF-1	12.00	25.00
5-96	Ultra		
-Double Trouble	3 of 10	2.00	4.00
-Double Trouble, gold (11.64)	3 of 10	10.00	20.00
-Jam City	3 of 12	12.00	20.00
-Jam City Hot Pack MJ Card	3 of 12	4.00	8.00
-Scoring Kings	4 of 12	25.00	45.00
-Scoring Kings Hot Packs MJ Card	4 of 12	6.00	12.00
-Fabulous 50's	5 of 7	6.00	12.00
-Fabulous 50's, Gold Medallion Edition	5 of 7	25.00	40.00
-Regular Card	25	2.00	4.00
-Gold Medallion Edition	25	12.00	25.00

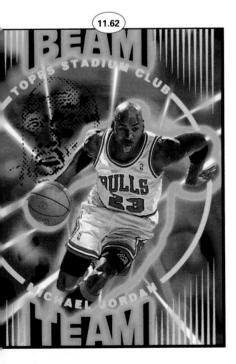

11.62

11.63

11.64

95-96	Upper Deck			
-Regular, Bulls-G, front; back has 2/17/63 birth, date & statistics in brown area	23	2.00	4.00
-Regular Card Electric Court	23	5.00	10.00
-Regular Card Electric Court, gold	23	75.00	150.00
-Rookie Years 84-85	137	1.00	2.00
-Rookie Years 84-85 Electric Court	137	3.00	6.00
-Rookie Years 84-85 Electric Court, gold	137	40.00	75.00
-Images of 95	335	1.00	2.00
-Images of 95 Electric Court	335	3.00	6.00
-Images of 95 Electric Court, gold (11.65)	335	40.00	75.00
-Major Attractions	337	1.00	2.00
-Major Attractions Electric Court	337	2.00	3.00
-Major Attractions Electric Court, gold	337	30.00	60.00
-Major Attractions	339	1.00	2.00
-Major Attractions Electric Court	339	2.00	3.00
-Major Attractions Electric Court, gold	339	30.00	60.00
-Major Attractions	341	1.00	2.00
-Major Attractions Electric Court	341	2.00	3.00
-Major Attractions Electric Court, gold	341	30.00	60.00
-Slams and Jams	352	1.00	2.00
-Slam and Jams Electric Court	352	2.00	3.00
-Slam and Jams Electric Court, gold	352	40.00	75.00
-Predictor NBA Player of the Week, 11/95, gold lettering front, game rules on back	H-1	10.00	12.00
-Predictor NBA Player of the Week, 1/96, gold lettering front, game rules on back	H-2	10.00	12.00
-Predictor NBA Player of the Week, 2/96, gold lettering front, game rules on back	H-3	10.00	12.00
-Predictor NBA Player of the Week, 3/96, gold lettering front, game rules on back	H-4	10.00	12.00
-Predictor NBA Player of the Week, 4/96, gold lettering front, game rules on back	H-5	10.00	12.00
-Predictor NBA Player of the Week Set, UD Redemption Set	10 cards	10.00	20.00
---MJ 11/95, silver lettering front, story on back	H-1	1.00	2.00
---MJ 1/96, silver lettering front, story on back	H-2	1.00	2.00
---MJ 2/96, silver lettering front, story on back	H-3	1.00	2.00
---MJ 3/96, silver lettering front, story on back	H-4	1.00	2.00
---MJ 4/96, silver lettering front, story on back	H-5	1.00	2.00
-Predictor Scoring Leader, gold lettering front, game rules on back	H-1	6.00	12.00
-Predictor Assists Leader, gold lettering front, game rules on back	H-2	6.00	12.00
-Predictor Steals Leader, gold lettering front, game rules on back	H-3	6.00	12.00
-Predictor 3 Point Shooting Percent Leader, gold lettering front, game rules on back	H-4	6.00	12.00
-Predictor Playoff Scoring Leader, gold lettering front, game rules on back	H-5	6.00	12.00
-Predictor Scoring Set, UD Redemption Set	10 cards	10.00	20.00
---MJ Scoring Leader, silver lettering front, story on back	H-1	1.00	2.00
---MJ Assists Leader, silver lettering front, story on back	H-2	1.00	2.00
---MJ Steals Leader, silver lettering front, story on back	H-3	1.00	2.00
---MJ 3 Point Shooting % Leader, silver lettering front, story on back	H-4	1.00	2.00
---MJ NBA Playoff Scoring Leader, silver lettering front, story on back	H-5	1.00	2.00
-Jordan Collection	JC-5	6.00	12.00
-Jordan Collection	JC-6	6.00	12.00
-Jordan Collection	JC-7	6.00	12.00
-Jordan Collection	JC-8	6.00	12.00
-Jordan Collection	JC-13	6.00	12.00
-Jordan Collection	JC-14	6.00	12.00
-Jordan Collection	JC-15	6.00	12.00
-Jordan Collection	JC-16	6.00	12.00
-Predictor NBA Player of the Month, 11/95, gold lettering front, game rules on back	R-1	5.00	10.00
-Predictor NBA Player of the Month, 1/96, gold lettering front, game rules on back	R-2	5.00	10.00

11.65

-Predictor NBA Player of the Month, 2/96, gold lettering front, game rules on back	R-3	5.00	10.00
-Predictor NBA Player of the Month, 3/96, gold lettering front, game rules on back	R-4	5.00	10.00
-Predictor NBA Player of the Month, 4/96, gold lettering front, game rules on back	R-5	5.00	10.00
-Predictor NBA Player of the Month, UD Redemption Set	10 cards	10.00	20.00
---MJ 11/95, silver lettering front, story on back	R-1	1.00	2.00
---MJ 1/96, silver lettering front, story on back	R-2	1.00	2.00
---MJ 2/96, silver lettering front, story on back	R-3	1.00	2.00
---MJ 3/96, silver lettering front, story on back	R-4	1.00	2.00
---MJ 4/96, silver lettering front, story on back	R-5	1.00	2.00
-Predictor 1996 NBA MVP, gold lettering front, game rules on back	R-1	5.00	10.00
-Predictor 1996 All NBA Team, gold lettering front, game rules on back	R-2	5.00	10.00
-Predictor 1996 Defensive Player of Year, gold lettering front, game rules on back	R-3	5.00	10.00
-Predictor 1996 NBA All Defensive Team, gold lettering front, game rules on back	R-4	5.00	10.00
-Predictor 1996 NBA Finals MVP, gold lettering front, game rules on back	R-5	5.00	10.00
-Predictor MVP Set, UD Redemption Set	10 cards	10.00	20.00
---MJ 1996 NBA MVP, silver lettering front, story on back	R-1	1.00	2.00
---MJ 1996 All NBA Team, silver lettering front, story on back	R-2	1.00	2.00
---MJ 1996 Defensive Player of the Year, silver lettering front, story on back	R-3	1.00	2.00
---MJ NBA All Defensive Team, silver lettering front, story on back	R-4	1.00	2.00
---MJ 1996 NBA Finals MVP, silver lettering front, story on back	R-5	1.00	2.00
-Special Edition	SE-100	5.00	10.00
-Special Edition, gold	SE-100	50.00	90.00
-USA Olympicard Moment	11	5.00	10.00
-USA Olympicard MJ & Hardaway	134	5.00	10.00
-USA Olympicard Reflections	RG-1	12.00	20.00
-USA Olympicard Reflections of Gold, Autograph Redemption Card	RG-1	2000	3000
-USA Olympicard Reign of Gold	RN-1	20.00	25.00
-USA Deluxe Gold Edition American Made, Scoring	M-1	20.00	25.00
-USA Deluxe Gold Edition American Made, Defense	M-2	20.00	25.00
-USA Deluxe Gold Edition American Made, Desire	M-3	20.00	25.00
-USA Deluxe Gold Edition American Made, Leaders	M-4	20.00	25.00
-UDA The Jordan Experience, 23 Nights, Fenton Hill Manufacturer		35.00	50.00
---MJ cards	23 cards		
---MJ CD	1 item	4.00	8.00

NBA UD Foreign Issued NBA Cards

91-92	Upper Deck Italian			
	-MJ, MVP, Hologram, blank backs	NNO	4.00	8.00
	-MJ, Scoring, Hologram, blank backs	NNO	4.00	8.00
	-Orlando AS Weekend, MJ card	4	2.00	4.00
	-MJ, vs. Lakers, layup	38	2.00	4.00
	-MJ, Back to Back MVP (back) (11.66)	107	2.00	4.00
	-92 Playoffs, Chicago vs. Miami, 1st round	158	1.00	2.00
	-92 Playoffs, Chicago vs. New York, semifinals	166	1.00	2.00
	-92 Playoffs, Chicago vs. Portland, game 1	172	1.00	2.00
	-92 Playoffs, Chicago vs. Portland, game 3	174	1.00	2.00
	-92 Playoffs, Chicago vs. Portland, game 5	176	1.00	2.00
	-92 Playoffs, Chicago vs. Portland, game 6	177	1.00	2.00
	-MJ, Cards on Collecting	178	2.00	4.00
	-MJ, Cards on Collecting	181	2.00	4.00

91-92	Upper Deck Spanish			
	-MJ, MVP, Hologram, blank backs	NNO	4.00	8.00
	-MJ, Scoring, Hologram, blank backs	NNO	4.00	8.00
	-Orlando AS Weekend, MJ card	4	2.00	4.00
	-MJ, vs. Lakers, layup	38	2.00	4.00
	-MJ, Back to Back MVP	107	2.00	4.00
	-92 Playoffs, Chicago vs. Miami, 1st round	158	1.00	2.00
	-92 Playoffs, Chicago vs. New York, semifinals	166	1.00	2.00
	-92 Playoffs, Chicago vs. Portland, game 1	172	1.00	2.00
	-92 Playoffs, Chicago vs. Portland, game 3	174	1.00	2.00
	-92 Playoffs, Chicago vs. Portland, game 5	176	1.00	2.00
	-92 Playoffs, Chicago vs. Portland, game 6	177	1.00	2.00
	-MJ, Cards on Collecting	178	2.00	4.00
	-MJ, Cards on Collecting (back) (11.67)	181	2.00	4.00
92-93	Upper Deck French			
	-Utah All-Star Weekend, East	5	5.00	10.00
	-In Your Face Slam Dunk, 87088	33	5.00	10.00
	-All Division Team, Central (back) (11.68)	43	5.00	10.00
	-Fanimation, Agent 23	86	5.00	10.00
	-Fanimation, Birdman & Agent 23	90	10.00	15.00
	-Regular Card	118	5.00	10.00
	-Scoring, hologram	EB-1	10.00	15.00
	-MVP, hologram	EB-9	10.00	15.00
92-93	Upper Deck Italian			
	-Utah All-Star Weekend, East	5	2.00	4.00
	-In Your Face Slam Dunk, 87088	33	2.00	4.00
	-All Division Team, Central	43	2.00	4.00
	-Fanimation, Agent 23	86	2.00	4.00
	-Fanimation, Birdman & Agent 23	90	4.00	8.00
	-Regular Card	118	2.00	4.00
	-Scoring, hologram	EB-1	4.00	8.00
	-MVP, hologram	EB-9	4.00	8.00
92-93	Upper Deck Spanish			
	-Utah All-Star Weekend, East	5	4.00	8.00
	-In Your Face Slam Dunk, 87088	33	4.00	8.00
	-All Division Team, Central	43	4.00	8.00
	-Fanimation, Agent 23	86	4.00	8.00
	-Fanimation, Birdman & Agent 23	90	8.00	12.00
	-Regular Card	118	4.00	8.00
	-Scoring, hologram	EB-1	8.00	12.00
	-MVP, hologram	EB-9	8.00	12.00
93-94	Upper Deck-French			
	-MJ regular card	23	5.00	10.00
	-Mr. June	166	10.00	15.00
	-Mr. June	167	10.00	15.00
	-Mr. June	168	10.00	15.00
	-Mr. June	169	10.00	15.00
	-Mr. June	170	10.00	15.00
	-Mr. June	171	10.00	15.00

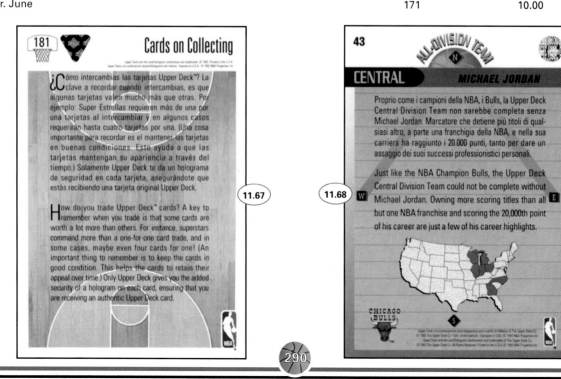

-Mr. June	172	10.00	15.00
-Mr. June	173	10.00	15.00
-Mr. June	174	10.00	15.00
-Mr. June	175	10.00	15.00
-Signature Move	176	45.00	60.00
-Triple Double (back) (11.69)	TD-2	10.00	15.00
-MJ Flight Team Regular Set, MJ name on front, picture on back	12 cards		
---Charles Barkley	181	6.00	12.00
---Cedric Ceballos	182	6.00	12.00
---Derrick Coleman	183	6.00	12.00
---Clyde Drexler	184	6.00	12.00
---Larry Johnson	185	6.00	12.00
---Shawn Kemp	186	6.00	12.00
---Harold Miner	187	6.00	12.00
---Alonzo Mourning	188	6.00	12.00
---Shaquille O'Neal	189	6.00	12.00
---Scottie Pippen	190	6.00	12.00
---Clarence Weatherspoon	191	6.00	12.00
---Dominique Wilkins	192	6.00	12.00
3-94 Upper Deck-German			
-Regular Card	23	5.00	10.00
-Mr. June	166	10.00	15.00
-Mr. June	167	10.00	15.00
-Mr. June	168	10.00	15.00
-Mr. June	169	10.00	15.00
-Mr. June	170	10.00	15.00
-Mr. June	171	10.00	15.00
-Mr. June	172	10.00	15.00
-Mr. June	173	10.00	15.00
-Mr. June	174	10.00	15.00
-Mr. June	175	10.00	15.00
-Signature Move, Hang Time (back) (11.70)	176	45.00	60.00
-Triple Double, 3D Standout	TD-2	10.00	15.00
-MJ Flight Team Regular Set, MJ name on front, picture on back	12 cards		
---Charles Barkley	181	6.00	12.00
---Cedric Ceballos	182	6.00	12.00
---Derrick Coleman	183	6.00	12.00
---Clyde Drexler	184	6.00	12.00
---Larry Johnson	185	6.00	12.00
---Shawn Kemp	186	6.00	12.00
---Harold Miner	187	6.00	12.00
---Alonzo Mourning	188	6.00	12.00
---Shaquille O'Neal	189	6.00	12.00
---Scottie Pippen	190	6.00	12.00
---Clarence Weatherspoon	191	6.00	12.00
---Dominique Wilkins	192	6.00	12.00
3-94 Upper Deck Italian			
-Regular Card	23	4.00	8.00
-Mr. June	166	8.00	12.00

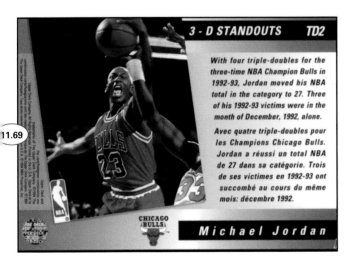

	-Mr. June		167	8.00	12.00
	-Mr. June		168	8.00	12.00
	-Mr. June		169	8.00	12.00
	-Mr. June		170	8.00	12.00
	-Mr. June		171	8.00	12.00
	-Mr. June		172	8.00	12.00
	-Mr. June		173	8.00	12.00
	-Mr. June		174	8.00	12.00
	-Mr. June		175	8.00	12.00
	-Signature Move		176	20.00	30.00
	-Triple Double, 3D (back) (11.71)		TD-2	8.00	12.00
	-MJ Flight Team Regular Set, MJ name on front, picture on back		12 cards		
	---Charles Barkley		181	5.00	10.00
	---Cedric Ceballos		182	5.00	10.00
	---Derrick Coleman		183	5.00	10.00
	---Clyde Drexler		184	5.00	10.00
	---Larry Johnson		185	5.00	10.00
	---Shawn Kemp		186	5.00	10.00
	---Harold Miner		187	5.00	10.00
	---Alonzo Mourning		188	5.00	10.00
	---Shaquille O'Neal		189	5.00	10.00
	---Scottie Pippen		190	5.00	10.00
	---Clarence Weatherspoon		191	5.00	10.00
	---Dominique Wilkins		192	5.00	10.00
93-94	Upper Deck Spanish				
	-Regular Card (back) (11.72)		23	4.00	8.00
	-Mr. June		166	8.00	12.00
	-Mr. June		167	8.00	12.00
	-Mr. June		168	8.00	12.00
	-Mr. June		169	8.00	12.00
	-Mr. June		170	8.00	12.00
	-Mr. June		171	8.00	12.00
	-Mr. June		172	8.00	12.00
	-Mr. June		173	8.00	12.00
	-Mr. June		174	8.00	12.00
	-Mr. June		175	8.00	12.00
	-Signature Move, Hang Time		176	20.00	30.00
	-Triple Double, 3D Standout		TD-2	8.00	12.00
	-MJ Flight Team Regular Set, MJ name on front, picture on back		12 cards		
	---Charles Barkley		181	5.00	10.00
	---Cedric Ceballos		182	5.00	10.00
	---Derrick Coleman		183	5.00	10.00
	---Clyde Drexler		184	5.00	10.00
	---Larry Johnson		185	5.00	10.00
	---Shawn Kemp		186	5.00	10.00
	---Harold Miner		187	5.00	10.00
	---Alonzo Mourning		188	5.00	10.00
	---Shaquille O'Neal		189	5.00	10.00
	---Scottie Pippen		190	5.00	10.00

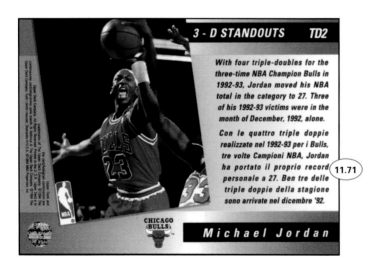

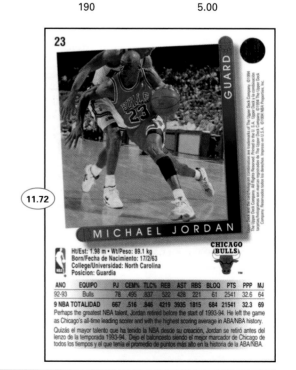

---Clarence Weatherspoon	191	5.00	10.00
---Dominique Wilkins	192	5.00	10.00
94-95 UD Collectors Choice-French			
-Regular Card, baseball, Series 1	23	5.00	8.00
-Pro Files, golfing	204	3.00	6.00
-Heroes, 1985 NBA ROY	211	8.00	15.00
-Heroes, 1986 63 Point Game (back) (11.73)	212	8.00	15.00
-Heroes, 1987-88 NBA Slam Dunk Champions	213	8.00	15.00
-Heroes, Unstoppa-Bull 3 Time NBA MVP	214	8.00	15.00
-Heroes, 1985-93 Nine Time NBA AS	215	8.00	15.00
-Heroes,1986-87 3,000 Point Season	216	8.00	15.00
-Heroes, 1991-92 3 NBA Championship	217	8.00	15.00
-Heroes, 1985-94 MJ Decade of Dominance	218	8.00	15.00
-Regular Card, Series 2	240	4.00	6.00
-Dr. Basketball's World of Trivia	402	3.00	5.00
-Dr. Basketball's World of Trivia, gold	402	45.00	60.00
-Decade of Dominance	J-1	6.00	12.00
-Decade of Dominance	J-2	6.00	12.00
-Decade of Dominance	J-3	6.00	12.00
-Decade of Dominance	J-4	6.00	12.00
-Decade of Dominance	J-5	6.00	12.00
-Decade of Dominance	J-6	6.00	12.00
-Decade of Dominance	J-7	6.00	12.00
-Decade of Dominance	J-8	6.00	12.00
-Decade of Dominance	J-9	6.00	12.00
-Decade of Dominance	J-10	6.00	12.00
94-95 UD Collectors Choice-German			
-Regular Card, baseball, Series 1	23	5.00	8.00
-Pro Files, golfing	204	3.00	6.00
-Heroes	211	8.00	15.00
-Heroes	212	8.00	15.00
-Heroes	213	8.00	15.00
-Heroes	214	8.00	15.00
-Heroes	215	8.00	15.00
-Heroes	216	8.00	15.00
-Heroes	217	8.00	15.00
-Heroes	218	8.00	15.00
-Regular Card, Series 2	240	4.00	6.00
-Dr. Basketball's World of Trivia (back) (11.74)	402	3.00	5.00
-Dr. Basketball's World of Trivia, gold	402	45.00	60.00
-Decade of Dominance	J-1	6.00	12.00
-Decade of Dominance	J-2	6.00	12.00
-Decade of Dominance	J-3	6.00	12.00
-Decade of Dominance	J-4	6.00	12.00
-Decade of Dominance	J-5	6.00	12.00
-Decade of Dominance	J-6	6.00	12.00
-Decade of Dominance	J-7	6.00	12.00
-Decade of Dominance	J-8	6.00	12.00
-Decade of Dominance	J-9	6.00	12.00
-Decade of Dominance	J-10	6.00	12.00
94-95 UD Collectors Choice-Italian			
-Regular Card, baseball, Series 1	23	3.00	6.00
-Pro Files, golfing (back) (11.75)	204	2.00	4.00

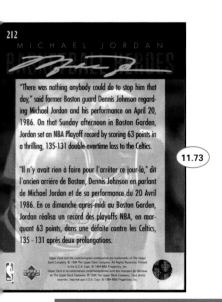

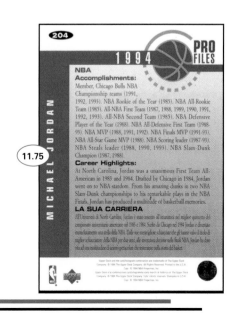

-Heroes, 1985 NBA ROY		211	4.00	8.00
-Heroes, 1986 63 Point Game		212	4.00	8.00
-Heroes, 1987-88 NBA Slam Dunk Champions		213	4.00	8.00
-Heroes, Unstoppa-Bull 3 Time NBA MVP		214	4.00	8.00
-Heroes, 1985-93 Nine Time NBA AS		215	4.00	8.00
-Heroes,1986-87 3,000 Point Season		216	4.00	8.00
-Heroes, 1991-92 3 NBA Championship		217	4.00	8.00
-Heroes, 1985-94 MJ Decade of Dominance		218	4.00	8.00
-Regular Card, Series 2		240	2.00	4.00
-Dr. Basketball's World of Trivia		402	1.00	2.00
-Dr. Basketball's World of Trivia, gold		402	20.00	30.00
-Decade of Dominance		J-1	3.00	6.00
-Decade of Dominance		J-2	3.00	6.00
-Decade of Dominance		J-3	3.00	6.00
-Decade of Dominance		J-4	3.00	6.00
-Decade of Dominance		J-5	3.00	6.00
-Decade of Dominance		J-6	3.00	6.00
-Decade of Dominance		J-7	3.00	6.00
-Decade of Dominance		J-8	3.00	6.00
-Decade of Dominance		J-9	3.00	6.00
-Decade of Dominance		J-10	3.00	6.00
94-95	UD Collectors Choice-Japanese			
-Regular Card, baseball, Series 1		23	10.00	15.00
-Pro Files, golfing		204	8.00	12.00
-Heroes		211	10.00	15.00
-Heroes		212	10.00	15.00
-Heroes		213	10.00	15.00
-Heroes		214	10.00	15.00
-Heroes		215	10.00	15.00
-Heroes		216	10.00	15.00
-Heroes		217	10.00	15.00
-Heroes		218	10.00	15.00
-Regular Card, Series 2		240	8.00	12.00
-Dr. Basketball's World of Trivia		402	6.00	10.00
-Dr. Basketball's World of Trivia, gold		402	60.00	80.00
-Decade of Dominance		J-1	8.00	15.00
-Decade of Dominance		J-2	8.00	15.00
-Decade of Dominance		J-3	8.00	15.00
-Decade of Dominance		J-4	8.00	15.00
-Decade of Dominance		J-5	8.00	15.00
-Decade of Dominance		J-6	8.00	15.00
-Decade of Dominance		J-7	8.00	15.00
-Decade of Dominance		J-8	8.00	15.00
-Decade of Dominance		J-9	8.00	15.00
-Decade of Dominance (back) (11.76)		J-10	8.00	15.00

11.76

J10

rare AIR

decade of DOMINANCE

If Michael Jordan were asked to get over 30 points a night, Jordan believes he could easily accommodate the request. "No problem," Jordan says. "I can do that anytime. That's not being cocky. That's confidence." In his nine-year NBA career, Jordan accumulated 21,541 points, an average of 32.3 ppg.

もし、マイケル・ジョーダンが"一晩に30点以上点をとってくれ"と頼まれたら、彼はそんなリクエストには簡単に応えられると思うだろう。「簡単だよ」とジョーダンは言うにちがいない。「僕は毎晩やっているからね。これはうぬぼれじゃない。自信なのさ」と。彼の9年間のNBA現役プレイヤー中、667試合に出場し、総得点は21541点、アベレージ32.3得点の記録が、その自信を証明しているのである。

mj

michael JORDAN

Upper Deck and the cardshologram combination are trademarks of The Upper Deck Company. ©1994 The Upper Deck Company. All Rights Reserved. Printed in the U.S.A. Copr. ©1994 NBA Properties, Inc. ©1994 Rare Air Ltd./Walter Iooss, Jr.

4-95	**UD Collectors Choice-Spanish**			
	-Regular Card, baseball, Series 1	23	3.00	6.00
	-Pro Files, golfing	204	2.00	4.00
	-Heroes	211	4.00	8.00
	-Heroes	212	4.00	8.00
	-Heroes	213	4.00	8.00
	-Heroes	214	4.00	8.00
	-Heroes	215	4.00	8.00
	-Heroes	216	4.00	8.00
	-Heroes	217	4.00	8.00
	-Heroes	218	4.00	8.00
	-Regular Card, Series 2 (back) (11.77)	21	2.00	4.00
	-Dr. Basketball World of Trivia	183	1.00	2.00
	-Dr. Basketball World of Trivia, gold	183	20.00	30.00
	-Decade of Dominance	J-1	3.00	6.00
	-Decade of Dominance	J-2	3.00	6.00
	-Decade of Dominance	J-3	3.00	6.00
	-Decade of Dominance	J-4	3.00	6.00
	-Decade of Dominance	J-5	3.00	6.00
	-Decade of Dominance	J-6	3.00	6.00
	-Decade of Dominance	J-7	3.00	6.00
	-Decade of Dominance	J-8	3.00	6.00
	-Decade of Dominance	J-9	3.00	6.00
	-Decade of Dominance	J-10	3.00	6.00
5-96	**UD Collector's Choice-England**			
	-MJ Regular Card, Series 1	20	4.00	8.00
	-MJ Fun Fact Card	169	4.00	8.00
	-MJ Professor Dunk Card	195	4.00	8.00
	-Jordan Collection, Series 2	JC-1	5.00	10.00
	-Jordan Collection	JC-2	5.00	10.00
	-Jordan Collection	JC-3	5.00	10.00
	-Jordan Collection	JC-4	5.00	10.00
	-Crash the Game Silver	C-1		
5-96	**UD Collectors Choice-French**			
	-MJ Regular Card, Series 1	20	4.00	8.00
	-MJ Fun Fact Card	169	4.00	8.00
	-MJ Professor Dunk Card	195	4.00	8.00
	-MJ Scouting Report, Series 2 (back) (11.78)	114	4.00	8.00
	-Jordan Collection	JC-1	6.00	12.00
	-Jordan Collection	JC-2	6.00	12.00
	-Jordan Collection	JC-3	6.00	12.00
	-Jordan Collection	JC-4	6.00	12.00
	-Crash the Game Silver, Knicks	C-1	35.00	50.00
5-96	**UD Collectors Choice-German**			
	-MJ Regular Card, Series 1	20	4.00	8.00
	-MJ Fun Fact Card (back) (11.79)	169	4.00	8.00

	-MJ Professor Dunk Card	195	4.00	8.00
	-MJ Scouting Report, Series 2	114	4.00	8.00
	-Jordan Collection	JC-1	6.00	12.00
	-Jordan Collection	JC-2	6.00	12.00
	-Jordan Collection	JC-3	6.00	12.00
	-Jordan Collection	JC-4	6.00	12.00
	-Crash the Game Silver	C-1	35.00	50.00
95-96	UD Collectors Choice-Italian			
	-MJ Regular Card, Series 1	20	4.00	8.00
	-MJ Fun Fact Card	169	4.00	8.00
	-MJ Professor Dunk Card (back) (11.80)	195	4.00	8.00
	-MJ Scouting Report, Series 2	114	4.00	8.00
	-Jordan Collection	JC-1	6.00	12.00
	-Jordan Collection	JC-2	6.00	12.00
	-Jordan Collection	JC-3	6.00	12.00
	-Jordan Collection	JC-4	6.00	12.00
	-Crash the Game Silver	C-1	35.00	50.00
95-96	UD Collectors Choice-Japanese			
	-MJ Regular Card, Series 1	20	5.00	10.00
	-MJ Fun Fact Card	169	5.00	10.00
	-MJ Professor Dunk Card (back) (11.81)	195	5.00	10.00
	-MJ Scouting Report, Series 2	324	5.00	10.00
	-Jordan Collection	JC-1	4.00	8.00
	-Jordan Collection	JC-2	4.00	8.00
	-Jordan Collection	JC-3	4.00	8.00
	-Jordan Collection	JC-4	4.00	8.00
	-Crash the Game Silver	C-1	35.00	50.00
95-96	UD Collectors Choice-Portuguese			
	-Scouting Report (back) (11.82)	114	5.00	10.00
	-Jordan Collection	JC-1	8.00	12.00
	-Jordan Collection	JC-2	8.00	12.00
	-Jordan Collection	JC-3	8.00	12.00
	-Jordan Collection	JC-4	8.00	12.00
95-96	UD Collectors Choice-Spanish			
	-MJ Regular Card, Series 1	20	4.00	8.00
	-MJ Fun Fact Card	169	4.00	8.00
	-MJ Professor Dunk Card	195	4.00	8.00
	-MJ Scouting Report, Series 2	114	4.00	8.00
	-Jordan Collection	JC-1	6.00	12.00
	-Jordan Collection	JC-2	6.00	12.00

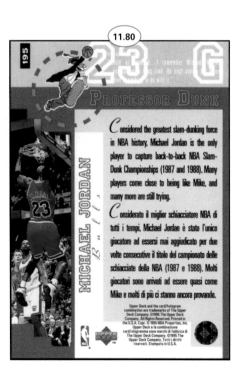

	-Jordan Collection (back) (11.83)	JC-3	6.00	12.00
	-Jordan Collection	JC-4	6.00	12.00
	-Crash the Game Silver	C-1	35.00	50.00

Year	Star Company Cards	card #	# cards	
84-85	NBA	101	2000.00	2600.00
84-85	NBA Olympic	195	250.00	350.00
84-85	NBA Special	288	250.00	350.00
84-85	Court Kings Set	50 cards		
	---MJ Card, 5 x 7	26	150.00	200.00
85	Crunch'n Munch All-Star	4	200.00	250.00
85	Gatorade Slam Dunk Championship, 2nd Annual	7	125.00	175.00
85	Lite Beer All-Stars	4	125.00	175.00
85	Last 11 ROY Set	11 cards	125.00	175.00
	---MJ Card	4		
85	Slam Dunk Supers Set	10 cards		
	---MJ Card, 5 x 7	5	125.00	175.00
85	Team Supers Set, 5 x 7	5 cards		
	---MJ Card	CB-1	125.00	175.00
85	NBA	117	600.00	900.00
85	All Rookie Team	2	175.00	200.00
86	Best of the Best (11.84)	9	125.00	200.00
86	Best of New & Old	2	125.00	200.00
86	Court Kings	18	125.00	200.00
86	Jordan Set	10 cards	500.00	750.00

11.83

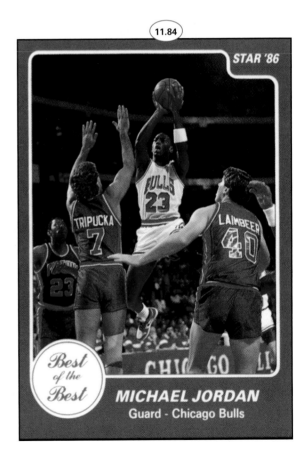

11.84

A Sampling of Michael Jordan Cards from 1995, 1996, 1997 and 1998

1995-96 Bulls Jewel/Nabisco	1	3.00	1995-96 Finest Dish and Swish	DS4	150.00
1995 Cardtoons	95	3.75	1995-96 Finest Hot Stuff	HS1	25.00
1995-96 Collector's Choice	45	2.25	1995-96 Finest Mystery	M1	15.00
1995-96 Collector's Choice	169	1.25	1995-96 Finest Mystery Borderless Refractors/Gold	M1	400.00
1995-96 Collector's Choice	195	1.25	1995-96 Finest Refractors	229	425.00
1995-96 Collector's Choice	324	1.00	1995-96 Finest Veteran/Rookie	RV20	120.00
1995-96 Collector's Choice	410	.50	1995-96 Flair	15	12.00
1995 Collector's Choice	500	2.50	1995-96 Flair	235	5.00
1995-96 Collector's Choice Crash The Game	C1A	12.00	1995-96 Flair Anticipation	2	80.00
1995-96 Collector's Choice Crash The Game II	C1A	8.00	1995-96 Flair Hardwood Leaders	4	8.00
1995-96 Collector's Choice Crash The Game	C1B	12.00	1995-96 Flair Hot Numbers	4	80.00
1995-96 Collector's Choice Crash The Game II	C1B	8.00	1995-96 Flair New Heights	4	50.00
1995-96 Collector's Choice Crash The Game	C1C	12.00	1995-96 Fleer	22	2.00
1995-96 Collector's Choice Crash The Game II	C1C	8.00	1995-96 Fleer	323	1.00
1995-96 CC European Sticker M. Jordan	MJ1-MJ9	4.00	1995-96 Fleer End 2 End	9	10.00
1995-96 Collector's Choice European Stickers	120	12.00	1995-96 Fleer Total D	3	10.00
1995 Collector's Choice Gold Signature	500	80.00	1995-96 Fleer Total O	2	20.00
1995 Collector's Choice Int. Decade of Dominance	J1-J10	15.00	1995-96 Highland Mint Medallions	2	10.00
1995 Collector's Choice Int. Spanish II	21	2.50	1995 Highland Mint Mint-Cards	38b	55.00
1995 Collector's Choice Int. Japanese I	23	10.00	1995 Highland Mint Mint-Cards	38s	225.00
1995 Collector's Choice Int. Spanish I	23	5.00	1995 Highland Mint Mint-Cards	38g	600.00
1995 Collector's Choice Int. Japanese Gold Signature II	402	50.00	1995-96 Hoop Magazine/Mother's Cookies	4	25.00
1995 Collector's Choice Int. Japanese II	240	5.00	1995-96 Hoops	21	2.00
1995 Collector's Choice Int. European Gold Signature	402	50.00	1995-96 Hoops	358	1.00
			1995-96 Hoops Hot List	1	30.00
1995 Collector's Choice Int. Spanish II	183	2.50	1995-96 Hoops Number Crunchers	1	5.00
1995 Collector's Choice Int. Japanese II	402	5.00	1995-96 Hoops Power Palette	1	30.00
1995 Collector's Choice Int. Spanish II	201	1.25	1995-96 Hoops Skyview	SV1	70.00
1995 Collector's Choice Int. Japanese II	420	2.00	1995-96 Hoops Top Ten	AR7	20.00
1995 Collector's Choice Int. European	204	5.00	1995-96 Jam Session	13	3.00
1995 Collector's Choice Int. Japanese I	204	5.00	1995-96 Jam Session Show Stoppers	S3	120.00
1995 Collector's Choice Int. Spanish I	204	2.50	1995-96 Metal	13	6.00
1995 Collector's Choice Int. European	211-219	15.00	1995-96 Metal	212	3.00
1995 Collector's Choice Int. Japanese I	211-219	15.00	1995-96 Metal Maximum Metal	4	40.00
1995 Collector's Choice Int. Spanish I	211-219	10.00	1995-96 Metal Scoring Magnets (11.85)	4	70.00
1995 Collector's Choice Int. Japanese II	T1	20.00	1995-96 Metal Slick Silver	3	28.00
1995 Collector's Choice Int. European	240	5.00	1995-96 Panini Stickers	83	5.00
1995 Collector's Choice Int. European	402	5.00	1995-96 SkyBox	15	2.00
1995 Collector's Choice Int. European	420	2.00	1995-96 SkyBox	278	1.50
1995-96 Collector's Choice Jordan He's Back	M1-M5	1.50	1995-96 SkyBox E-XL	10	10.00
1995 Collector's Choice Michael Jordan Jumbo	661	25.00	1995-96 SkyBox E-XL Natural Born Thrillers	1	100.00
1995 Collector's Choice Silver Signature	500	10.00	1995-96 SkyBox E-XL No Boundaries	1	60.00
1995 Collector's Choice/SE Gold	238	140.00	1995-96 SkyBox Larger Than Life	L1	65.00
1995 Collector's Choice/SE Silver	238	20.00	1995-96 SkyBox Meltdown	M1	50.00
1995 Collector's Choice/SE	238	3.50	1995-96 SkyBox Standouts Hobby	SH1	40.00
1995-96 Finest	229	14.00	1995-96 Stadium Club	1	3.00
			1995-96 Stadium Club Beam Team	14	60.00

11.85

1995-96 Stadium Club Members Only I	1	12.00
1995 Stadium Club Members Only 50	20	5.00
1995-96 Stadium Club Members Only II	B14	50.00
1995-96 Stadium Club Members Only II	RM2	50.00
1995-96 Stadium Club Members Only II	SS1	12.00
1995-96 Stadium Club Members Only I	WS1	25.00
1995-96 Stadium Club Nemeses	N10	25.00
1995-96 Stadium Club Reign Men	RM2	65.00
1995-96 Stadium Club Spike Says	SS1	25.00
1995-96 Stadium Club Warp Speed (11.86)	1	50.00
1995-96 SP	23	6.00
1995-96 SP All-Stars	AS2	25.00
1995-96 SP Championship	17	5.00
1995-96 SP Championship	121	2.00
1995-96 SP Championship Champions of the Court	C30	30.00
1995-96 SP Championship Champions of the Court Die-Cut	C30	250.00
1995-96 SP Championship Jordan Collection	JC17-JC20	10.00
1995-96 SP Championship Shots	S16	12.00
1995-96 SP Holoviews	PC5	40.00
1995-96 SP Holoviews Die-Cuts	PC5	225.00
1995-96 SP The Jordan Collection	JC17-JC24	15.00
1995-96 Topps	1	1.25
1995-96 Topps	4	1.25
1995-96 Topps	277	1.50
1995-96 Topps Gallery (11.87)	10	5.00
1995-96 Topps Gallery Expressionists	EX2	50.00
1995-96 Topps Mystery Finest	M1	60.00
1995-96 Topps Power Boosters	1	70.00
1995-96 Topps Power Boosters	4	70.00
1995-96 Topps Power Boosters	277	70.00
1995-96 Topps Show Stoppers	1	30.00
1995-96 Topps Spark Plugs	SP2	12.00

1995-96 Topps Top Flight	1	30.00
1995-96 Topps World Class	WC1	25.00
1995-96 Ultra	25	4.00
1995-96 Ultra Double Trouble	3	7.00
1995-96 Ultra Fabulous Fifties	5	13.00
1995-96 Ultra Jam City	3	30.00
1995-96 Ultra Scoring Kings	4	50.00
1995-96 Upper Deck	23	3.00
1995 Upper Deck	133	3.00
1995-96 Upper Deck	137	1.50
1995 Upper Deck	200	4.00
1995-96 Upper Deck	335	1.50
1995-96 Upper Deck	337	.75
1995-96 Upper Deck	339	.75
1995-96 Upper Deck	341	.75
1995-96 Upper Deck	352	1.50
1995-96 Upper Deck Ball Park Jordan	BP1	10.00
1995-96 Upper Deck Ball Park Jordan	BP2	10.00
1995-96 Upper Deck Ball Park Jordan	BP3	10.00
1995-96 Upper Deck Ball Park Jordan	BP4	10.00
1995-96 Upper Deck Ball Park Jordan	BP5	10.00
1995 UD Minor League M. Jordan Highlights	MJ-1-MJ-5	5.00
1995 UD Minor League Michael Jordan One-On-One	1-10	.50
1995 UD Minor League Michael Jordan's Scrapbook	1-10	15.00
1995 UD Minor League Organizational Pro-Files	OP6	25.00
1995 Upper Deck Minor League	45	6.00
1995-96 UD Predictor Hobby Player of the Week	H1-H5	10.00
1995-96 UD Predictor Retail Player of the Month	R1-R5	10.00
1995-96 UD Predictor Hobby Scoring	H1-H5	10.00
1995-96 Upper Deck Predictor Retail MVP	R1-R5	10.00
1995-96 Upper Deck Special Edition	SE100	12.00
1995 Upper Deck Steal of a Deal	SD15	40.00
1995 Upper Deck/Metallic Impressions Michael Jordan	JT1-JT5	4.00
1995 UD/SP Top Prospects Jordan Time Capsule	TC1-TC4	10.00

11.86

11.87

1995 Upper Deck/SP Top Prospects Autographs	(15)	4750.00
1996-97 Bowman's Best (11.88)	80	10.00
1996-97 Bowman's Best Cuts	BC2	45.00
1996-97 Bowman's Best Honor Roll	HR2	60.00
1996-97 Bowman's Best Shots	BS6	20.00
1996-97 Collector's Choice	23	3.00
1996-97 Collector's Choice	25	1.00
1996-97 Collector's Choice	26	1.00
1996-97 Collector's Choice	195	1.00
1996-97 Collector's Choice	362-366	.50
1996-97 Collector's Choice Chicago Bulls Team Set	B1	2.00
1996-97 Collector's Choice Chicago Bulls Team Set	CH3	3.00
1996-97 Collector's Choice Crash the Game	C30	10.00
1996-97 Collector's Choice Crash the Game II	C30	10.00
1996-97 Collector's Choice Factory Blow-Ups	1	4.00
1996-97 Collector's Choice Factory Blow-Ups	4	4.00
1996-97 Collector's Choice Game Face	GF2	7.00
1996 Collector's Choice Int. Jordan Collection	JC1-JC4	10.00
1996 Collector's Choice International I	45	6.00

1996 Collector's Choice International Japanese	45	6.00
1996 Collector's Choice International II	114	3.00
1996 Collector's Choice International II	143	3.00
1996 Collector's Choice International I	169	3.00
1996 Collector's Choice International Japanese	169	3.00
1996 Collector's Choice International I	195	3.00
1996 Collector's Choice International Japanese	195	3.00
1996 Collector's Choice International II	200	1.50
1996 Collector's Choice International I	210	1.50
1996 Collector's Choice International Japanese	210	1.50
1996 Collector's Choice International Japanese	324	3.00
1996 Collector's Choice International Japanese	353	3.00
1996 Collector's Choice International Japanese	410	1.50
1996-97 Collector's Choice Jordan A Cut Above	CA1-CA10	2.50
1996-97 Collector's Choice Mini-Cards	1	5.00
1996-97 Collector's Choice Memorable Moments	1	10.00
1996-97 Collector's Choice Stick-Ums	S30	6.00
1996-97 Collector's Choice Stick-Ums II	S30	6.00
1996-97 Finest (11.89)	50	12.00

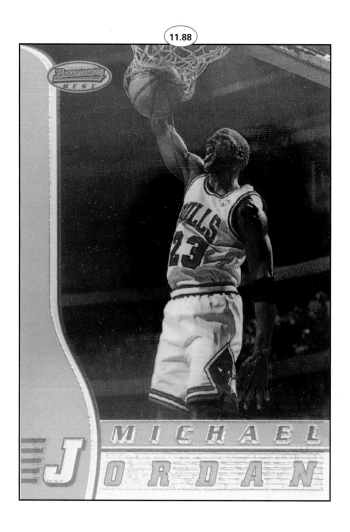

1996-97 Finest (11.90)	127	30.00	
1996-97 Finest (11.91)	291	125.00	
1996-97 Finest Refractors	50	150.00	
1996-97 Finest Refractors	127	200.00	
1996-97 Finest Refractors	291	900.00	
1996-97 Flair Showcase Hot Shots (11.92)	1	175.00	
1996-97 Flair Showcase Legacy	23	550.00	

1996-97 Flair Showcase Row 0	23	125.00
1996-97 Flair Showcase Row 1	23	15.00
1996-97 Flair Showcase Row 2	23	10.00
1996-97 Fleer	13	2.50
1996-97 Fleer	123	1.25
1996-97 Fleer	282	1.50
1996-97 Fleer Decade of Excellence	4	130.00

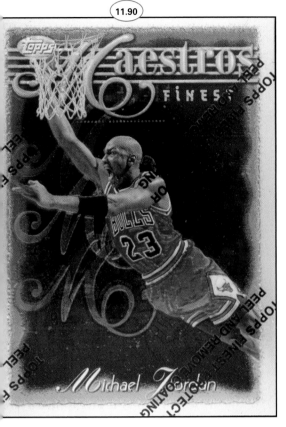

11.90

11.91

11.92

1996-97 Fleer Game Breakers	1	100.00
1996-97 Fleer Stackhouse's All-Fleer	4	14.00
1996-97 Fleer Thrill Seekers	6	175.00
1996-97 Fleer Total "O"	4	50.00
1996-97 Hoops	20	3.00
1996-97 Hoops	176	1.25
1996-97 Hoops	335	1.25
1996-97 Hoops Head to Head	HH2	25.00
1996-97 Hoops Hot List (11.93)	8	60.00
1996-97 Hoops Starting Five	4	15.00
1996-97 Hoops Superfeats	1	60.00
1996-97 Metal	11	5.00
1996-97 Metal	128	2.50
1996-97 Metal	241	2.50
1996-97 Metal Decade of Excellence	4	50.00
1996-97 Metal Maximum Metal	4	150.00
1996-97 Metal Molten Metal	18	120.00
1996-97 Metal Net-Rageous	NR5	200.00
1996-97 Metal Platinum Portraits	PP5	80.00
1996-97 Metal Steel Slammin	6	90.00
1996-97 SkyBox	16	4.00
1996-97 SkyBox	247	2.00
1996-97 SkyBox Bulls Triple Threat	TT11	75.00
1996-97 SkyBox E-X2000	9	15.00
1996-97 SkyBox E-X2000 A Cut Above	8	225.00
1996-97 SkyBox E-X2000 Net Assets	8	50.00
1996-97 SkyBox Golden Touch	5	160.00
1996-97 SkyBox Larger Than Life	L7	175.00
1996-97 SkyBox Net Set	8	80.00
1996-97 SkyBox Rubies	16	200.00
1996-97 SkyBox Rubies	247	100.00
1996-97 SkyBox Thunder and Lightning	1	100.00
1996-97 SkyBox Z-Force	11	5.00

1996-97 SkyBox Z-Force	179	2.00
1996-97 SkyBox Z-Force Big Men On The Court	4	200.00
1996-97 SkyBox Z-Force BMOC Z-Peat	4	600.00
1996-97 SkyBox Z-Force Slam Cam	SC5	200.00
1996-97 SkyBox Z-Force Vortex	V5	60.00
1996-97 Stadium Club	101	4.00
1996-97 Stadium Club Class Acts	CA1	20.00
1996-97 Stadium Club Finest Reprints	24	45.00
1996-97 Stadium Club Fusion	F1	60.00
1996-97 Stadium Club High Risers	HR14	60.00
1996-97 Stadium Club Members Only II	101	25.00
1996-97 Stadium Club Members Only 55	41	6.00
1996 Stadium Club Members Only I	F1	25.00
1996-97 Stadium Club Members Only II	CA1	15.00
1996 Stadium Club Members Only I	GM3	2.00
1996 Stadium Club Members Only I	SF4	15.00
1996 Stadium Club Members Only I	SM2	2.50
1996-97 Stadium Club Members Only II	HR14	25.00
1996 Stadium Club Members Only I	TC9	12.00
1996-97 Stadium Club Moments	GM3	3.50
1996-97 Stadium Club Moments	SM2	4.00
1996-97 Stadium Club Player's Private Issue	10	300.00
1996-97 Stadium Club Special Forces	SF4	40.00
1996-97 Stadium Club Top Crop (11.94)	TC9	40.00
1996-97 SP	16	5.00
1996-97 SP Game Film	GF1	120.00
1996-97 SP Holoviews	PC5	35.00
1996-97 SP Inside Info	25K	60.00
1996-97 SP SPx Force	F1	200.00
1996-97 SP SPx Force	F5	200.00
1996-97 SP SPx Force	F5A	2000.00
1996 SPx (11.95)	8	20.00
1996 SPx Holoview Heroes	H1	60.00

11.93

11.94

11.95

1996 SPx Record Breaker Card	R1	25.00		1996 Upper Deck USA Michael Jordan	M1-M4	25.00
1996-97 Topps	139	2.50		1996 Upper Deck 23 Nights Jordan Experience	1-23	1.50
1996-97 Topps Chrome	139	40.00		1996 Upper Deck 23 Nights Jordan Experience	NNO	1.50
1996-97 Topps Chrome Pro Files	PF3	20.00		1997-98 Bowman's Best (11.96)	60	6.00
1996-97 Topps Chrome Refractors	139	425.00		1997-98 Bowman's Best	96	3.00
1996-97 Topps Chrome Season's Best	SB1	20.00		1997-98 Bowman's Best Mirror Image	M1	50.00
1996-97 Topps Chrome Season's Best	SB18	20.00		1997-98 Bowman's Best Techniques	T2	20.00
1996-97 Topps Holding Court	HC2	50.00		1997 Coll. Choice Int'l Italian Crash the		
1996-97 Topps Mystery Finest Bordered	M14	50.00		Game Scoring	C30A	30.00
1996 Topps NBA Stars	24	4.00		1997 Coll. Choice Int'l Italian Crash the		
1996 Topps NBA Stars	74	4.00		Game Scoring	C30B	30.00
1996 Topps NBA Stars	124	4.00		1997-98 Collector's Choice	23	2.50
1996 Topps NBA Stars Imagine	I6	40.00		1997-98 Collector's Choice	186-395	.75
1996 Topps NBA Stars Reprints	24	60.00		1997 Collector's Choice Int'l Italian Jordan's Journal	J1-J6	10.00
1996-97 Topps Pro Files	PF3	15.00		1997 Collector's Choice Int'l Italian 1	23	8.00
1996-97 Topps Season's Best	SB1	25.00		1997 Collector's Choice Int'l Italian 1	25	4.00
1996-97 Topps Season's Best	SB18	25.00		1997 Collector's Choice Int'l Italian Mini-Cards	M78	10.00
1996-97 Ultra	16	4.00		1997 Collector's Choice Int'l Italian 1	26	4.00
1996-97 Ultra	143	2.00		1997 Collector's Choice Int'l Italian Stick Ums	S30	10.00
1996-97 Ultra	280	2.00		1997 Collector's Choice Int'l Italian 1	195	4.00
1996-97 Ultra Board Game	7	30.00		1997-98 Collector's Choice MJ Bullseye	B1-B30	2.00
1996-97 Ultra Court Masters	2	140.00		1997-98 Collector's Choice NBA Miniatures	M30	3.00
1996-97 Ultra Decade of Excellence	U4	75.00		1997-98 Collector's Choice Stick-Ums	S30	3.00
1996-97 Ultra Full Court Trap	1	20.00		1997-98 Collector's Choice StarQuest	SQ83	75.00
1996-97 Ultra Give and Take	5	30.00		1997-98 Collector's Choice StarQuest	SQ171	75.00
1996-97 Ultra Platinum	16	500.00		1997-98 Collector's Choice You Crash the Game	C30	10.00
1996-97 Ultra Platinum	143	250.00		1997-98 Finest	39	8.00
1996-97 Ultra Platinum	280	200.00		1997-98 Finest	154	90.00
1996-97 Ultra Scoring Kings	4	50.00		1997-98 Finest	271	6.00
1996-97 Ultra Starring Role	4	160.00		1997-98 Finest	287	25.00
1996-97 Upper Deck	16	4.00		1997-98 Finest Refractors	39	90.00
1996-97 Upper Deck	165	2.00		1997-98 Finest Refractors	154	700.00
1996-97 Upper Deck Ball Park Jordan	1-5	10.00		1997-98 Finest Refractors	271	90.00
1996-97 Upper Deck Fast Break	FB23	30.00		1997-98 Finest Refractors	287	100.00
1996-97 Upper Deck Italian Stickers	88-91	2.50		1997-98 Flair Showcase Legacy	1	500.00
1996-97 Upper Deck Italian Stickers	114	5.00		1997-98 Flair Showcase Row 1	1	80.00
1996-97 Upper Deck M. Jordan-Greater Heights	GH1-			1997-98 Flair Showcase Row 2	1	15.00
	GH10	20.00		1997-98 Flair Showcase Row 3	1	10.00
1996-97 Upper Deck Michael's Viewpoints	VP1-VP10	16.00		1997-98 Fleer	23	3.00
1996-97 Upper Deck Predictor II	P2	30.00		1997-98 Fleer Decade of Excellence	5	50.00
1996-97 Upper Deck Predictor	P3	30.00		1997-98 Fleer Flair Hardwood Leaders	4	15.00
1996-97 Upper Deck Rookie of the Year	RC13	120.00		1997-98 Fleer Game Breakers	1	150.00
1996-97 Upper Deck Smooth Grooves	SG8	90.00		1997-98 Fleer Soaring Stars	9	4.00
1996-97 Upper Deck UD3	23	8.00		1997-98 Fleer Thrill Seekers	7	120.00
1996-97 UD UD3 Court Commemorative Autographs	C1	2500.00		1997-98 Fleer Total "O" (11.97)	5	30.00
1996-97 Upper Deck UD3 SuperStar Spotlight	S5	150.00		1997-98 Fleer Zone (11.98)	10	30.00
1996-97 Upper Deck UD3 Winning Edge	W1	40.00		1997-98 Hoops	1	1.50

11.96

11.97

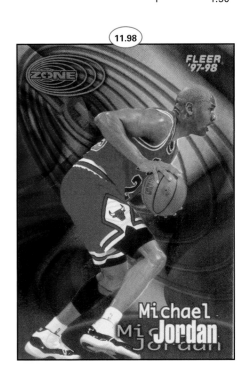

11.98

1997-98 Hoops	220	3.00
1997-98 Hoops Dish N Swish	DS5	20.00
1997-98 Hoops Frequent Flyer Club	FF4	40.00
1997-98 Hoops High Voltage	HV14	30.00
1997-98 Hoops HOOPerstars	H1	100.00
1997-98 Hoops Rock the House	RH6	30.00
1997-98 Hoops 911	N1	125.00
1997-98 Metal	23	4.00
1997-98 Metal Planet Metal (11.99)	1	30.00
1997-98 Metal Platinum Portraits	1	180.00
1997-98 Metal Titanium	1	100.00
1997-98 Metal Universe (11.100)	23	4.00
1997-98 Metal Universe All-Millenium Team	5	12.00
1997-98 Metal Universe Championship Galaxy	1	120.00
1997-98 Metal Universe Hardware	5	180.00
1997-98 SkyBox	29	4.00
1997-98 SkyBox	235	8.00
1997-98 SkyBox and One	10	70.00

1997-98 SkyBox Competitive Advantage	CA3	70.00
1997-98 SkyBox E-X 2001	9	15.00
1997-98 SkyBox E-X 2001 Gravity Denied	9	70.00
1997-98 SkyBox E-X 2001 Jam-Balaya	6	400.00
1997-98 SkyBox Golden Touch	GT1	250.00
1997-98 SkyBox Premium Players	1	120.00
1997-98 SkyBox Silky Smooth	1	175.00
1997-98 SkyBox Thunder & Lightning	TL5	100.00
1997-98 SkyBox Z-Force	23	3.50
1997-98 SkyBox Z-Force	190	1.50
1997-98 SkyBox Z-Force B.M.O.C.	B9	140.00
1997-98 SkyBox Z-Force Boss (11.101)	10	12.00
1997-98 SkyBox Z-Force Limited Access	6	20.00
1997-98 SkyBox Z-Force Quick Strike	QS5	70.00
1997-98 SkyBox Z-Force Rave Reviews (11.102)	6	150.00
1997-98 SkyBox Z-Force Slam Cam	SC5	25.00
1997-98 Stadium Club (11.103)	118	5.00
1997-98 Stadium Club Hardcourt Heroics (11.104)	H1	20.00

11.99

11.100

11.101

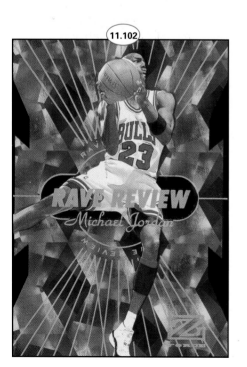

11.102

11.103

11.104

1997-98 Stadium Club Hoop Screams (11.105)	HS10	20.00	
1997-98 Stadium Club Never Compromise	NC1	40.00	
1997-98 Stadium Club Royal Court (11.106)	RC6	20.00	
1997-98 Stadium Club Triumvirate	T1B	60.00	
1997-98 SP Authentic	23	6.00	
1997-98 SP Authentic Profiles	P1	16.00	
1997 SPx	5	16.00	
1997 SPx Holoview Heroes	H1	120.00	
1997 SPx NBA Pro-Motion	1	150.00	

1997 SPx PROmotion Autographs	1	2500.00	
1997-98 Topps	123	3.00	
1997-98 Topps Bound for Glory	BG10	40.00	
1997-98 Topps Chrome	123	25.00	
1997-98 Topps Chrome Season's Best	SB6	25.00	
1997-98 Topps Chrome Topps 40 (11.107)	T40-5	25.00	
1997-98 Topps Clutch Time	CT1	40.00	
1997-98 Topps Generations	G2	50.00	
1997-98 Topps Inside Stuff (11.108)	IS1	25.00	

(11.105)

(11.106)

(11.108)

(11.107)

1997-98 Topps Rock Stars	RS1	50.00
1997-98 Topps Season's Best (11.109)	SB6	30.00
1997-98 Topps 40	5	15.00
1997-98 Ultra (11.110)	23	5.00
1997-98 Ultra	259	10.00
1997-98 Ultra Big Shots	1	10.00
1997-98 Ultra Court Masters	CM1	100.00
1997-98 Ultra Platinum	23	625.00
1997-98 Ultra Platinum	259	300.00
1997-98 Ultra Star Power	SP1	8.00
1997-98 Ultra Stars	1	120.00
1997-98 Ultra Ultrabilities (11.111)	1	10.00
1997-98 Ultra View to a Thrill	ST1	20.00
1997-98 Upper Deck (11.112)	18	4.00
1997-98 Upper Deck	139	2.00
1997-98 Upper Deck	165	2.00

1997-98 Upper Deck	316	2.50
1997-98 Upper Deck	NNO	25.00
1997-98 Upper Deck	NNO	12.00
1997-98 Upper Deck AIRLines	AL1-A12	100.00
1997-98 Upper Deck Diamond Dimensions	D23	700.00
1997-98 Upper Deck Diamond Vision Dunk Vision	D1	175.00
1997-98 Upper Deck Diamond Vision Reel Time	R1	400.00
1997-98 Upper Deck Diamond Vision	4	40.00
1997-98 Upper Deck Game Dated Memorable Moments	18	1000.00
1997-98 Upper Deck Game Jersey	GJ13	2600.00
1997-98 Upper Deck Game Jersey	GJ13S	8500.00
1997-98 Upper Deck Great Eight	G5	180.00
1997-98 Upper Deck High Dimensions	D23	110.00
1997 Upper Deck Holojam	1	30.00
1997-98 Upper Deck Records Collection	RC30	40.00

(11.109)

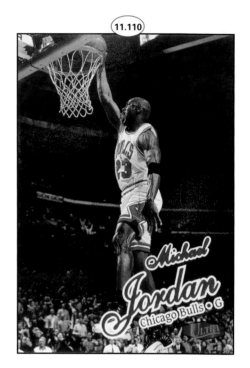

(11.110)

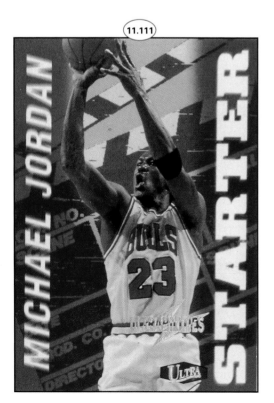

(11.111)

(11.112)

6-1-97 With the game in his hands. M.J. nails the game-winning shot vs. Utah in Game 1 of the 1997 NBA Finals.

23-G

1997-98 Upper Deck Teammates (11.113)	T7	12.00
1997-98 Upper Deck Teammates (11.114)	T59	12.00
1997-98 Upper Deck Ultimates	U1	45.00
1997-98 Upper Deck UD3 (11.115)	15	6.00
1997-98 Upper Deck UD3	23	6.00

1997-98 Upper Deck UD3	45	8.00
1997-98 Upper Deck UD3 Awesome Action (11.116)	A1	30.00
1997-98 Upper Deck UD3 Michael Jordan		
MJ3	I	30.00
1997-98 Upper Deck UD3 Michael Jordan MJ3	II	60.00

1997-98 Upper Deck UD3 Michael Jordan MJ3 (11.117)	III	100.00	
1997-98 Upper Deck UD3 Season Ticket Autographs	MJ	2600.00	
1997-98 SPx	6	12.00	
1997-98 SPx Grand Finale	6	500.00	
1997-98 SPx Hardcourt Holoview	HH1	60.00	
1997-98 SPx Pro-Motion	PM1	120.00	
1998-99 Topps (11.118)	77	3.00	
1998-99 Topps Roundball Royalty	R1	40.00	
1998-99 Topps Season's Best	SB6	20.00	
1998 Upper Deck Hardcourt Jordan-Holding Court	J1	5.00	
1998 Upper Deck Hardcourt Jordan-Holding Court	J2	40.00	
1998 Upper Deck Hardcourt Jordan-Holding Court	J3	10.00	
1998 Upper Deck Hardcourt Jordan-Holding Court	J4	30.00	
1998 Upper Deck Hardcourt Jordan-Holding Court	J5	25.00	
1998 Upper Deck Hardcourt Jordan-Holding Court	J6	10.00	
1998 Upper Deck Hardcourt Jordan-Holding Court	J7	10.00	
1998 Upper Deck Hardcourt Jordan-Holding Court	J8	50.00	
1998 Upper Deck Hardcourt Jordan-Holding Court	J9	5.00	
1998 Upper Deck Hardcourt Jordan-Holding Court	J10	15.00	
1998 Upper Deck Hardcourt Jordan-Holding Court	J11	10.00	
1998 Upper Deck Hardcourt Jordan-Holding Court	J12	5.00	
1998 Upper Deck Hardcourt Jordan-Holding Court	J13	70.00	
1998 Upper Deck Hardcourt Jordan-Holding Court	J14	10.00	
1998 Upper Deck Hardcourt Jordan-Holding Court	J15	10.00	
1998 Upper Deck Hardcourt Jordan-Holding Court	J16	50.00	
1998 Upper Deck Hardcourt Jordan-Holding Court	J17	30.00	
1998 Upper Deck Hardcourt Jordan-Holding Court	J18	10.00	
1998 Upper Deck Hardcourt Jordan-Holding Court	J19	35.00	
1998 Upper Deck Hardcourt Jordan-Holding Court	J20	40.00	
1998 Upper Deck Hardcourt Jordan-Holding Court	J21	15.00	
1998 Upper Deck Hardcourt Jordan-Holding Court	J22	10.00	
1998 Upper Deck Hardcourt (11.119)	23	10.00	
1998 Upper Deck Hardcourt Jordan-Holding Court	J23	10.00	
1998 Upper Deck Hardcourt	23a	20.00	
1998 Upper Deck Hardcourt Jordan-Holding Court	J24	60.00	
1998 Upper Deck Hardcourt Jordan-Holding Court	J25	15.00	
1998 Upper Deck Hardcourt Jordan-Holding Court	J26	20.00	
1998 Upper Deck Hardcourt Jordan-Holding Court	J27	15.00	
1998 Upper Deck Hardcourt Jordan-Holding Court	J28	25.00	
1998 Upper Deck Hardcourt Jordan-Holding Court	J29	15.00	
1998 Upper Deck Hardcourt High Court	H30	150.00	
1998 Upper Deck Hardcourt Jordan-Holding Court	J30	100.00